CANADIAN POLITICS

CONCISE FIFTH EDITION

CANADIAN POLITICS

CONCISE FIFTH EDITION

RAND DYCK

Carleton University

NELSON / EDUCATION

NELSON / EDUCATION

Canadian Politics, Concise Fifth Edition
by Rand Dyck

**Vice President,
Editorial Director:**
Evelyn Veitch

**Editor-in-Chief,
Higher Education:**
Anne Williams

Acquisitions Editor:
Anne-Marie Taylor

Marketing Manager:
Ann Byford

Senior Developmental Editor:
Linda Sparks

Photo Researcher:
Daniela Glass

Permissions Coordinator:
Daniela Glass

Content Production Manager:
Christine Gilbert

Production Service:
MPS Limited, a Macmillan Company

Copy Editor:
Jessie Coffey

Proofreader:
Jennifer McIntyre

Indexer:
David Luljak

Production Coordinator:
Ferial Suleman

Design Director:
Ken Phipps

Managing Designer:
Franca Amore

Interior Design:
Peter Papyanakis

Cover Design:
Jennifer Leung

Cover Image:
First Light/Alamy

Compositor:
MPS Limited, a Macmillan Company

Printer:
Edwards Brothers

**Library and Archives Canada
Cataloguing in Publication**

Dyck, Rand, 1943-
    Canadian politics / Rand Dyck. --
Concise 5th ed.

Includes bibliographical references
and index.
ISBN 978-0-17-650343-7

    1. Canada--Politics and
government--Textbooks. I. Title.

JL75.D93 2011   320.971
C2010-906249-3

ISBN-13: 978-0-17-650343-7
ISBN-10: 0-17-650343-9

To Kiera,
the sweetest granddaughter in the world

Contents in Brief

Contents

Part 2   Linking People to Government   131

6   Political Culture, Socialization, and Participation   133

7   The Mass Media and Public Opinion Polls   155

8   Elections and the Electoral System   177

9   Political Parties   205

10 Advocacy Groups, Social Movements, and Lobbying   231

Part 3   The Constitutional Context   255

11   The Canadian Constitution and the Charter of Rights and Freedoms   257

12   The Provinces and the Federal System   287

Preface

It is very gratifying to be writing a fifth edition of the concise version of *Canadian Politics* for those who want a briefer and less detailed version of *Canadian Politics: Critical Approaches*. As in previous editions, this book is most appropriate for first-year university courses and community college use.

Canadian Politics: Concise Fifth Edition addresses Canadian government and politics in two separate but equal parts, either of which can be studied first. Chapters 2 through 10 might be called "politics," and Chapters 11 to 16 might be called "government." In this way, the book remains a comprehensive treatment of the whole subject, although it is more factual and less analytical than *Critical Approaches*.

In Part 1, this edition continues to emphasize the societal setting in which most political activity originates, including cleavages and identities related to region, class, French Canada and Quebec, Aboriginality, minority ethnocultural groups, gender, and the ever-increasing importance of external forces. Part 2 turns to linking people to government, including political culture, socialization, and participation; the mass media and public opinion polls; elections and the electoral system; political parties; and advocacy groups, social movements, and lobbying. Part 3 deals with the constitutional context, including the Constitution, the Charter of Rights and Freedoms, and federalism. Part 4, "Governing," contains chapters on the executive, the bureaucracy, Parliament, and the courts.

The chapter structure of the book remains the same as in the previous edition, but all the statistics, graphs, and tables have been updated with the most recent data available. New photos and cartoons have been added, and all significant recent political developments have been addressed. These include

- the Great Recession and its widespread effects on the economy and government policy;
- the increasing concern in Quebec about the threat that immigrants are seen to pose to the predominance of the French language and the province's traditional way of life;
- changes in mass media ownership and mass communications technologies;
- recent Federal and Supreme Court Charter decisions, especially on "terrorism" cases;
- recent developments on the relationship between the Governor General and the Prime Minister, especially regarding prorogation of parliament; and
- the malfunctioning of Parliament, including the conflict over the disclosure of documents.

The book is accompanied by its own website at http://www.concise5e.nelson.com and the two are intended to be used as an integral unit. On the website you will find

- regular updates of material in the book that has changed since publication;
- constitutional documents, such as parts of the Constitution Act, 1867; the Constitution Act, 1982 (including the Charter of Rights and Freedoms); and the 1987 Meech Lake Accord;
- relevant weblinks for each chapter;
- additional discussion questions;
- detailed citations for important Supreme Court decisions; and
- chapter-by-chapter test-yourself questions.

In addition, Nelson has prepared instructor resources, including an Instructor's Manual, which are also available on the companion website.

Introducing the *Nelson Education Teaching Advantage* (NETA). In most college and university courses, a large percentage of student assessment is based on multiple choice testing. Many instructors use multiple choice reluctantly, believing that it is a methodology best used for teaching what a student remembers rather than what she or he has learned. Furthermore, the quality of publisher-supplied test banks can vary.

Nelson Education Ltd. believes that a good-quality multiple choice test bank can test not just what students remember, but higher-level thinking skills as well. Recognizing the importance of multiple choice testing in today's classroom, Nelson has created the Nelson Education Teaching Advantage (NETA) program to ensure the high quality of our test banks.

The test bank for *Canadian Politics, Concise Fifth Edition* was developed using the guidelines of the Nelson Education Teaching Advantage. NETA was created in partnership with David DiBattista, a 3M National Teaching Fellow and professor of psychology at Brock University. NETA ensures that test bank authors have had training in two areas: developing clear multiple choice test questions while avoiding common errors in construction, and creating multiple choice test questions that "get beyond remembering" to assess higher-level thinking.

The outcome of NETA development is that as you select multiple choice questions from your Nelson test bank for inclusion in tests, you can easily identify whether items are memory-based or require your students to engage in higher-level thinking. By making your selections appropriately, you can construct tests that contain the proportion of recall and higher-level questions that reflects your personal instructional goals.

All NETA test banks are accompanied by David DiBattista's guide for instructors, "Multiple Choice Tests: Getting Beyond Remembering." This guide has been designed to assist you in using Nelson test banks to achieve your desired outcomes in the classroom.

The NETA test materials are provided in Rich Text Format for easy editing and printing with all common word-processing formats.

Once again, I extend my thanks to everyone who helped in the preparation of this book, including those who contributed to previous editions. Many individuals and organizations were generous in providing information, and I have a particular affection for the cartoonists and photographers who permitted their work to be used. I am also grateful for the many constructive suggestions made by reviewers of previous editions.

As usual, it was a delight to work with the staff of Nelson Education Ltd. I primarily interacted with Linda Sparks and Anne-Marie Taylor, but there were many others behind the scenes who also contributed their magical talents to this production. The original manuscript bears little resemblance to the final product, and I thank them all most warmly.

Rand Dyck

Chapter 1

Introduction

If you are reading this book, you are probably already open to the excitement and importance of the subject of politics and government in Canada. How a whole society makes collective, public decisions is a fascinating question. Political personalities can be as interesting as movie stars, and the conflicts between them and their respective teams are as hard-fought as any hockey game. Politics often brings out the worst in human nature—ambition, selfishness, greed, and the will to control—but it is sometimes characterized by the best—an altruistic desire to serve the public interest and to improve the lives of the less fortunate. Politics and government are the only way to solve many societal problems, and may well be the best way to solve some of your own!

Chapter Objectives

After you have completed this chapter, you should be able to:

Identify the many ways in which government action affects your life

Draw a model of the Canadian political system

Explain the main function of each of the major institutions of Canadian government, including the prime minister and Cabinet, House of Commons, Senate, bureaucracy, and judiciary

Appreciate the concentration of power in the executive branch of the government

Outline the basic differences between the Canadian and American systems of government regarding the separation or fusion of powers, party discipline, and the framework of federalism

The Political System

Perhaps it is best to begin with the 34 million residents of Canada. All these individuals have an array of needs that they attempt to satisfy, ranging from water, food, and shelter through security and friendship to self-esteem and self-fulfillment. Some of these needs are felt personally and individually, while others are concerns shared with people of similar position, in small or large groups. Most of us spend much of our time trying to satisfy such needs.

In the first instance, we do so by our own efforts, in pairs, in families, in organizations of all kinds, at work, and at play. By not automatically calling for government help, we are essentially operating in the private or voluntary sectors. At some point, however, we may begin to feel that the satisfaction of our needs is beyond personal, interpersonal, family, or group capacity, and we come to the conclusion that the government should step in to help us. When we express the opinion that the government should take some action, we are converting a "need" into a "demand" and crossing the threshold between the private or voluntary sectors and the public sector. We can say that a demand is the expression of opinion that government take some action (or desist from an action that it is already taking).

The first fundamental question that arises in politics and government is therefore whether people should solve their own problems or whether they should ask the government or the state to intervene. Almost everyone agrees that the government should provide certain security measures, such as police services and armed forces. Most people also support public highways and a public education system. The population may be more divided, however, on the extent to which the government should provide such programs as social assistance, social housing, public pensions, and universal health care. One of the main reasons for such divisions of opinion is that government intervention normally costs money and usually relies on taxes of one kind or another. People also disagree on which areas of life the state should regulate and on how much regulation is appropriate. There is currently much controversy in Canada over the role of government in the protection of the environment. What combination of taxation, regulation, and incentives would be most effective?

The largest group of people reading this book will be young students. If you think about the role of government in your life, many interesting questions come to mind. To what extent should you be expected to pay for your postsecondary education, and to what extent should it be financed by the state? Why do tuition fees keep increasing, and what form and level of student assistance is most appropriate?

The Canadian Federation of Students demonstrates against rising tuition fees. (CP *Photo/Toronto Star/Steve Russell*)

Should the state (provincial or municipal) provide a transit system and/or subsidize bus or subway fares for students travelling to school or work? Should the state (federal or provincial) intervene to regulate the price of gasoline? For the housing needs of students living away from home, should the province regulate the private rental market, or should the municipality, university, or college provide public housing? For those who work, should there be a minimum wage, and if so, what is an appropriate rate? Should all colleges and universities be public institutions, or is private postsecondary education a good idea?

Many of these and other questions go beyond one's status as a student. For example, should affluent people be able to get quicker medical attention because they can pay for such health care, or should Canada maintain a universal system in which no one can jump the queue? Should the public health care system be extended to pharmaceutical drugs and dental care, or should physiotherapy and chiropractic treatment be removed?

Should the state put more restrictions on carbon production, gasoline exhaust, and other environmental hazards, or should companies be minimally constrained in their pollution emissions in the interest of providing jobs? How far should the state go in prohibiting discrimination in the workplace? Should it engage in employment equity programs to enhance the employment prospects of those who were discriminated against in the past? Should the federal government enact a national daycare program, or should it give cash to families and let them find their own childcare solutions? Should people be able to enjoy pornographic materials, or should these be censored by the state? Such a list barely scratches the surface of issues involving potential government action, but it serves to demonstrate the relevance of government to our daily lives.

Many demands arise from deep, persistent divisions within society that political science calls "cleavages." The cleavages in Canadian society that generally have the greatest political significance are those between the geographic regions; between English, French, Aboriginal, and other ethnocultural and linguistic groups; and between various socioeconomic classes. Other common cleavages are related to gender, religion, and age. The relative importance and nature of these cleavages changes over time, and they are the subject of Chapters 2, 3, and 4.

Another way to look at these characteristics of Canadian society is in terms of identities. Each of us has many identities—male or female, Newfoundlander or Albertan, Roman Catholic or Muslim, francophone or Aboriginal, young or old. Indeed, issues relating to ethnicity, gender, and sexual orientation are commonly referred to today as the "politics of identity." But only if people are conscious of a particular characteristic—if it is part of their identity—are they likely to act on it politically. In any case, many of the demands with which the authorities have to contend originate from such cleavages and identities.

Linking People to Government

Both those who seek state intervention and those who prefer that the authorities leave them alone must transmit their demands to the government. In either case, such action requires knowledge and other resources that may well exclude a large proportion of people on the margins of society. On the other hand, those in authority may seek out such demands, asking what different groups in the electorate really want.

Figure 1.1 shows that individuals can communicate their needs directly to the government. This can be done on a personal basis, such as by means of a letter, fax, telephone call, e-mail, or face-to-face encounter. Sometimes such directly transmitted demands achieve their desired result, but very often they do not. When they fail, it may be time to consider some kind of group action.

Canadian society contains many groups, and quite likely a group already exists to articulate the demand that any individual decides to transmit to the government. If such a group is not already in existence, it may be worthwhile to create

· ·

Figure 1.1 A Model of the Political System

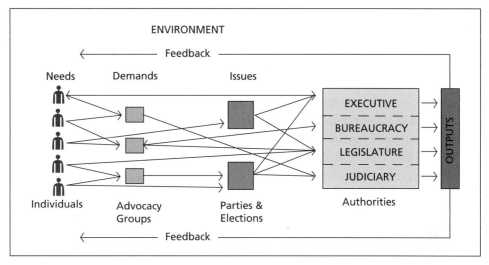

Source: Rand Dyck

one, since, as a general rule, the authorities are more likely to respond to a demand coming from a group than from a single individual. Such groups are usually called **advocacy groups**, **interest groups**, **pressure groups**, or social movements, and they constitute an important part of Canadian political activity. The Canadian Chamber of Commerce, the Canadian Labour Congress, and the Canadian Federation of Students are prominent examples. Corporations and other institutions also make demands, either individually or in groups.

A special kind of group that is even more overtly political is the **political party**, and it can also be used to transmit demands to the government. People join a political party or support it financially and try to get it to recognize their concerns in its platform or policies. If the party comes to power, it can incorporate the demand into government policy; if the party is in opposition, it may be able to press the government to address it or use the mass media to bring the problem to national attention. Parties are particularly responsive to people's demands during an election campaign, as they appeal for the support of large numbers of individuals and groups by promising to take the action they seek. Those dissatisfied with how existing parties are responding to their demands can create new parties, such as occurred with the appearance of the Green Party, the Reform Party, and the Bloc Québécois.

Another means of transmitting the demand to the government is, as suggested earlier, via the **mass media**—principally television, newspapers, and radio. The media are usually eager to publicize controversial issues and often delight in pointing out problems that the government has failed to resolve. They pay attention to individual and advocacy group concerns on a regular basis, cover political party activities, and are especially active in election campaigns, all of which help to bring demands to the attention of the government. More than that, the media also provide the electorate with most of its information about politics, and in so doing serve to shape the whole nature of political discourse in Canada. All of these aspects of linking people to government are discussed in Chapters 6 to 10.

Despite the various avenues that can be used to transmit demands to the government, relatively few demands have any impact. The authorities are likely to ignore demands that do not concern very many people or that are contrary to their own values. Since the number of demands under serious consideration at any given time constitutes such a small proportion of the total number being made, it is sometimes useful to distinguish between demands and "issues," the latter including only those demands that the government has taken under serious consideration. It should be added that those in authority usually have their own concerns, which sometimes carry more weight than demands arising from the wider society.

Government authorities are thus bombarded by demands from all directions, but even more striking than the vast quantity of demands is the usually intense conflict among them. The essence of politics and government, therefore, is choosing among competing demands, trying to resolve conflict, or making social choices in the midst of social conflict. Politics can be defined as that activity in which conflicting interests struggle for advantage or dominance in the making and execution of public policies. Politics is closely linked to the concept of **power**, which is often defined as the ability of one actor to impose its will on another, to get its own way, or to do or get what it wants.

Government

Having repeatedly mentioned **government**, we may now define it as the set of institutions that make and enforce collective, public decisions for a society. In Canada, those institutions primarily consist of the prime minister and Cabinet, the House of Commons and Senate, the bureaucracy or public service, and the courts. Backed up by armed forces, police, and punishments, if necessary, government possesses a particular kind of power called **coercion**. That is, it has the ability to impose its will upon us by means of sanctions or penalties. Indeed, as a general rule, only the government, as an agent of the state, is allowed to use force or coercive power in society. But if we (or our ancestors) had a hand in the creation of such a government apparatus, as well as in the selection of the current governors, then we have in a sense agreed to be bound by its decisions. In other words, we have cloaked the government's power with legitimacy, a term defined as "being accepted as morally binding." Such legitimate power is often called "authority," and a synonym for government is "the authorities." To some extent, we obey the government because of the threat or expectation of penalties if we do not, but we also obey because we accept government decisions as binding upon us and necessary for the general good. Think of stopping at a red light or paying income taxes.

Individuals and groups raise conflicting demands, but because there is a widespread consensus on the legitimacy of the government, people generally abide by its authoritative decisions, even when they disagree with them. It is sometimes said, therefore, that politics and government are characterized by both conflict and consensus. The daily conflict normally operates within an underlying consensus about the decision-making apparatus and about remaining together as part of a united political community. Moreover, the authorities usually seek to develop some kind of consensus out of the conflicting demands.

A couple prepare for another federal election. (Graham Harrop/Artizans.com)

Who are these government authorities? As can be seen in the diagram in Figure 1.1, political scientists usually divide them into four branches: the **legislature**, the **executive**, the **bureaucracy**, and the **judiciary**. The authoritative decision that a demand seeks can sometimes be made by a single branch of government. The legislature or Parliament passes laws, so if the demand requires the passage of a law, action by the legislative branch will be necessary. The executive, consisting of the prime minister and Cabinet, has a wide variety of powers. These include deciding where the government will spend money and appointing people to public positions. Thus, if the demand can be satisfied by an appointment or large monetary grant, it should be addressed to the executive. The bureaucracy is made up of public servants who work for the government, providing services, advising the politicians, and issuing regulations. If the demand is for the provision of routine government services or for changes in regulations, bureaucratic action will probably suffice. Finally, the judiciary comprises the courts, which interpret the laws and make other decisions in case of dispute, and if the demand can be settled only by a judicial ruling, it should be transmitted in that direction.

In many instances, however, the demand will require the combined actions of any two of the executive, legislative, and bureaucratic branches, or even all three working together, such as in the formulation, passage, and implementation of a new law. The courts normally stand somewhat apart, and judicial decisions usually follow authoritative actions in other branches of government. For example, the Supreme Court invalidated the abortion provisions of the Criminal Code as being a violation of the Charter of Rights and Freedoms. But judicial decisions may also lead to subsequent legislative action. For example, after the Supreme Court ruled that a total ban on tobacco advertising was unconstitutional, the government introduced a revised law with fewer restrictions.

Government decisions take many forms—laws, regulations, appointments, grants, contracts, services, and judgments—that are sometimes called "outputs." Authoritative decisions are also made in the provinces and territories and in an assortment of regional and local councils and boards, and they often require the agreement of two or more levels of government.

Completing the Picture

Whatever the type of authoritative decision, it usually sparks a reaction in the rest of the system. This leads us to the concept of "feedback"—that is, a communication of the outputs back into the system. If a decision satisfies a particular demand, that demand will no longer have to be articulated. For example, many

French-speaking Canadians demanded that their language be designated as equal to English in federal government operations. The Pearson and Trudeau governments, which grasped at the opportunity to counter nationalism in Quebec, enacted the Official Languages Act as a result. But that was not the end of it: there was feedback or reaction to this decision. On the one hand, some francophones then demanded French-language services at the provincial as well as the federal level. On the other, many anglophones protested that the Act (as well as Quebec language legislation favouring French) went too far. Thus, the reaction to one demand created a new pattern of demands, and the language issue is still very much alive. The political system is thus characterized as a dynamic, circular process in which the authorities react to demands, convert some of them into decisions, and then respond in turn to whatever changes in the pattern of demands have resulted from the feedback from such decisions.

The modern world is composed of some 200 states such as Canada, and each has a government that makes its public decisions. Each state claims its own sovereignty, that is, its right to be self-governing; it has the final say over its own territory and people. But today's world is characterized by a tremendous amount of interplay among such states, as well as cross-border interaction and movement in terms of individuals, corporations, other organizations, and information. States often join international organizations and sign international agreements, and transnational corporations operate around the world. These developments constitute the phenomenon of globalization. Beyond the internal demands discussed above, such external actions increasingly serve as the source of demands on national political systems, such as the 1997 Kyoto Protocol which Canada ratified but failed to implement. Other external influences such as the North American Free Trade Agreement act as constraints upon domestic policymaking. As noted in Chapter 5, external pressures of these kinds often lead a government into actions that it otherwise would not take, and no state is as sovereign as it would like to be. Especially since the terrorist attacks on the United States in September 2001, governments have had to give additional attention to the adequacy of their security measures.

What Do You Think?

Is it fair to owners of apartment buildings, hotels, bars, and restaurants to prohibit smoking by means of provincial laws or municipal bylaws? Is it fair to smokers? Whose interests should prevail: those of smokers, non-smokers, owners, employers, customers, tenants, or employees?

Foundations of Canadian Government Institutions

The state called Canada was created in 1867, but remained a British colony until the Statute of Westminster provided for complete autonomy in 1931. At its origins, Canada was a federation composed of four provinces, but it eventually grew to encompass ten provinces and three territories.

The Parliamentary System

Before going any farther, let us outline more specifically the basic institutions of government in Canada, which are dealt with in detail in Chapters 11 to 16. Within the central or national government in Ottawa (often called the "federal government"), the British parliamentary system provides the foundations of these governmental institutions. This system is based on the popular election of the members of the House of Commons. Parliament also has a second or "upper" chamber, the Senate, whose members are appointed by the prime minister. Such a two-chamber legislature is labelled "bicameral." The third part of Parliament is the monarch or the Crown. Because it was a British colony at the time the Constitution was adopted in 1867, Canada automatically shared the British monarch. The current monarch, Queen Elizabeth II, still resides in Britain, so on a practical basis, her representative, the governor general, exercises the functions of the Crown.

The British system is sometimes called the **Westminster model** or **parliamentary government**, but the latter label is somewhat misleading. The core of the parliamentary system, even in 1867, was the executive branch—the prime minister and the Cabinet ministers. Although they must be members of Parliament (MPs), they are such an important part of Parliament that they often relegate both the monarch and other members of the House of Commons and Senate to a position of insignificance. Like the executive of any organization, the prime minister and Cabinet are given the powers to lead and make the most important decisions. But the principle of **responsible government** holds that they retain their position and powers only as long as they are supported by a majority in the House of Commons. If the House of Commons declares a lack of confidence in the prime minister and Cabinet, they must either resign and make way for another group to take their place or call an election. Because the prime minister and Cabinet ministers have seats in the legislative branch, mostly the House of Commons, the system is often described as involving a "fusion of powers"—that is, a combination of legislative and executive powers.

The executive dominance of the parliamentary system can be seen in the power of the prime minister and Cabinet ministers to control most of the agenda of the legislature and to introduce most legislation. They have the exclusive power to introduce legislation of a financial nature—laws either to raise or to spend money. They have other wide powers as well: to make appointments, to draft subordinate legislation under the authority of laws, and to make decisions relating to international affairs—essentially all powers necessary to provide effective political leadership for the country. Other members of Parliament may criticize, delay, and propose amendments, but the prime minister and Cabinet almost always get their way. This is because a majority of the members of Parliament normally belong to the same political party as the prime minister and Cabinet; together they constitute a **majority government**. In this situation prime ministers usually impose rigid party discipline on their MPs to support their every move. On the other hand, Canada is increasingly characterized by **minority governments**, in which the opposition members outnumber those on the government side. In such a situation, the PM may be somewhat less dominant.

The significance of the Senate has declined since Confederation because being appointed rather than elected diminishes its members' legitimacy in a democratic age. The powers of the Senate have remained virtually equal to those of the House of Commons, but senators have rarely felt it proper to exercise them. Moreover, independent behaviour has been discouraged by the fact that the same party has usually held a majority both in the Senate and in the Commons. If for any reason the Senate should ultimately defeat a government bill, such an action does not affect the constitutional standing of the prime minister and Cabinet. The model outlined here is also operational in each of the provinces, except that they all possess one-chamber ("unicameral") legislatures.

Government was small and simple at the time of Confederation, but it has gradually developed another important branch, the bureaucracy or public service. The bureaucracy essentially advises the prime minister and Cabinet ministers on their decisions and then carries out whatever government programs have been authorized. The current Canadian bureaucracy consists of about 400 000 public servants who make a vast array of government decisions.

Figure 1.2   An Outline of Canadian Political Institutions

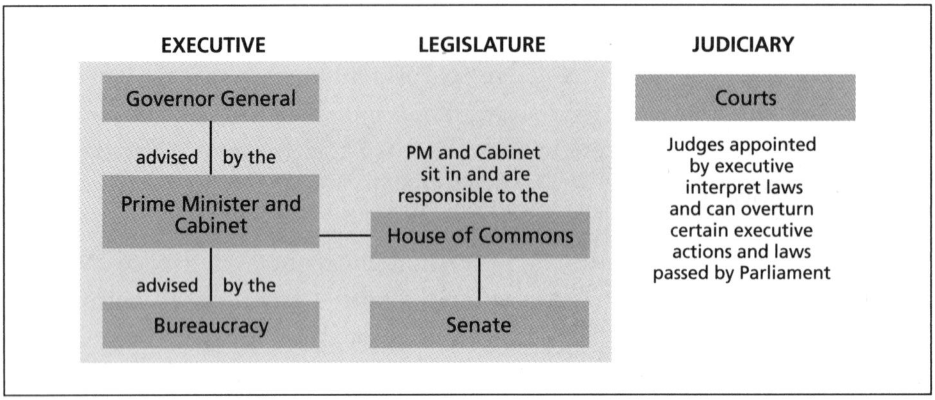

Source: Rand Dyck

The British parliamentary system also incorporates the principle of judicial independence. Although courts are established by acts of Parliament, and judges are appointed by the prime minister and Cabinet, the whole judicial system is expected to operate independently of the executive and legislative branches of government, as can be seen in Figure 1.2. In the case of Britain itself, judges have considerable discretion in interpreting laws but lack the power of judicial review, that is, the power to declare them invalid. The Canadian judiciary soon appropriated to itself the power to invalidate laws that violated the federal–provincial division of powers but was otherwise quite restrained.

Since the Canadian institutional structure was established in 1867, the only major change has been the adoption of the Charter of Rights and Freedoms in 1982. That addition had the effect of expanding the scope of judicial review to include the new task of protecting individual rights and freedoms. Henceforth, the courts could disallow federal or provincial legislation or other government actions that violated the Constitution in terms of either the division of powers or the Charter of Rights and Freedoms.

The British parliamentary system is distinct in many ways from the presidential–congressional system of the United States. There, the president and the two houses of the legislature (Congress) are independently elected, and no one is permitted to sit in more than one branch of government. The "separation of powers" means that executive, legislative, and judicial powers are distributed to three separate branches of government: president, Congress, and the courts respectively. Moreover, as indicated in Figure 1.3, the U.S. system is also

Figure 1.3   U.S. System of Separation of Powers and Checks and Balances

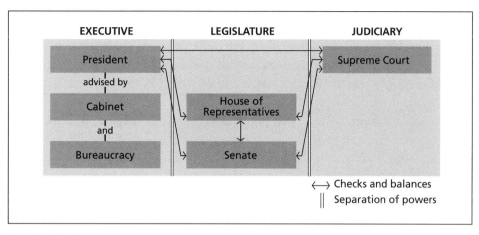

Source: Rand Dyck

characterized by a maze of "checks and balances" designed to ensure that the actions of any one branch of government are subject to veto by another. Members of the House of Representatives and the Senate have much more legislative power than their counterparts in the parliamentary system, in terms of both initiating bills themselves and amending or vetoing those bills emanating from the executive. Party discipline is also much looser. Even if a majority of the members of Congress belong to the same party as the president, there is no guarantee that the legislature will pass the president's initiatives. The Supreme Court also has the power of judicial review and can overturn any legislation that it feels is in violation of the Constitution. Thus, even though it often appears that the U.S. president has enormous power, largely because of the manner in which that country often tries to enforce its will across the globe, the fact is that, at least in domestic policy areas, the president actually has less control than the prime minister does in Canada.

Federalism

The Fathers of Confederation were dealing with a large piece of territory and were contending with colonies that had separate identities and a previous semi-autonomous existence. In this respect, the new country had to be a **federation** of some kind. **Federalism** is characterized by two levels of government—central and provincial—and a division of powers between them.

Confederation was, to a large extent, the work of Sir John A. Macdonald, who went on to become the first Canadian prime minister. Macdonald preferred a unitary state or legislative union, in which the new central government would have almost all the powers, and the provinces would be little more than municipalities. But Quebec and the Maritimes were not prepared to join such a system. Quebec demanded an autonomous provincial government so that its cultural concerns, such as education and civil law, would be placed in the hands of a French-speaking majority. Hence, the logical compromise was a system that contained a central government to deal with purposes common to the whole country and provincial governments to look after local concerns.

Macdonald accepted a federal form of government, allowing the former colonies to retain some of their political and economic independence, but he intended the new country to be highly centralized. He felt that its economic and defensive objectives required a strong central government. This conviction was reinforced by the predominant view that the American Civil War (which was ending just as they began their deliberations) had been the result of leaving too much power at the state level. Thus, at their creation, the Canadian and American federations were quite different. The United States deliberately established a weak central government and strong states, while Canada preferred a strong central government and weak provinces.

Besides dividing powers between the two levels of government, constitutional architects in both the United States and Canada had to decide how the provinces or states would be represented at the national level. In both cases, the lower house of the legislature would be based on the principle of representation by population, so that the most populous provinces or states would have the largest number of members in that chamber. To protect the interests of the smaller states, however, the U.S. decided that each state, regardless of population, would have two senators at the national level. Some Fathers of Confederation also preferred this idea, but others wanted representation by population in both houses of Parliament. The Canadian compromise was to base the Senate on the principle of equal *regional* representation rather than equal provincial representation.

Fusing the Parliamentary System with Federalism

The basic governmental institutions established in 1867 thus combined the parliamentary system from Britain with a more centralized form of federalism than that found in the United States. But the whole ethos underlying the Canadian and U.S. systems was different. In the parliamentary system, everything is designed to *facilitate* government action by concentrating power in the hands of the executive, in terms of its relationship both with other institutions of government, such as Parliament and the courts, and with territorial units, such as provincial and local governments. In the American system, everything is designed to *inhibit* government action by preventing the concentration of power in the hands of any government. In the United States, the individual institutions of the national government are able to veto each other and are collectively kept in line by a division of powers that was intended to give most authority to the states. It is largely because the British system is designed to facilitate government action, whereas the American system is designed to inhibit it, that the fusion of the two systems in Canadian Confederation was such a distinctive creation. Macdonald saw the contradiction and therefore tried to establish a federal system that was much more centralized than that next door. He would turn over in his grave if he saw how powerful Canadian provinces have become and how much of a constraint they impose on the actions of the national government!

As well, all provinces in Canada have found it convenient to delegate certain powers to local municipal governments. These are often headed by a mayor and council, usually include an autonomous school board, and sometimes incorporate other local elected or appointed authorities. Their responsibilities vary from province to province, and sometimes within a province, but municipal authorities are a significant part of the government structure in Canada. Unlike the federal and provincial governments, which are not subordinate to each other and whose specific powers are laid out in the Constitution, municipal governments are subordinate to provincial governments, and their responsibilities and taxing powers can be expanded or contracted at the province's whim. Municipalities typically have more responsibilities than their taxation powers can support, leading them to plead for increased provincial (or federal) funding.

This book concentrates on the federal or national system of government in Canada but does not deny the significance of the provinces and municipalities. Indeed, Chapter 12 deals with the relationship between the provinces and the national government. It also notes that municipalities have succeeded in recent years in getting the federal government to pay them more attention.

SUMMARY

This chapter illustrates the many ways in which government action affects our everyday lives. It provides a model of the Canadian political system, showing how demands are transmitted from individuals and groups to, or solicited by, the main institutions of government and are sometimes transformed into public decisions. It outlines the main function of each organ of the Canadian government, emphasizing the concentration of power in the executive branch. The chapter contrasts this concentration with the separation of powers in the U.S. system of government, and it also shows the differences between Canada and the United States as federations.

DISCUSSION QUESTIONS

1. Which actions of the federal government or your own provincial or municipal governments do you disagree with? Should a different approach be used, or should these actions not be taken at all? Which additional actions should one or more of these governments undertake?
2. What are the relative advantages and disadvantages of the structures of the Canadian and U.S. systems of government?
3. Do you feel that you are part of the political process? What would prompt you to be more involved?

KEY TERMS

Advocacy group/interest group/pressure group Any group seeking to influence government policy without contesting elections; an organization whose members promote their common interest by acting together to influence public policy.

Bureaucracy The permanent officials employed by the government, also known as the public service.

Charter of Rights and Freedoms Part of the Constitution Act, 1982, that guaranteed fundamental freedoms and legal, democratic, linguistic, mobility, and equality rights.

Coercion Power based on authorized physical force, including police, armed forces, and jails, on which government has a near-monopoly.

Executive That branch of government which provides leadership and makes the major decisions.

Federalism (federation) A system of government characterized by two levels of authority (federal and provincial) and a division of powers between them such that neither is subordinate to the other.

Globalization The pattern of deepening supraterritorial interaction around the world, characterized by comprehensive free trade agreements, massive diffusion of technological change, and worldwide corporate competition or megamergers that challenge the sovereignty of the state.

Government The set of institutions that make and enforce collective, public decisions for a society.

Judicial independence The constitutional principle that the courts should function independently of the rest of the government apparatus, especially of the politicians.

Judicial review The power of the courts to overturn legislation or actions of the executive branch of government.

Judiciary The court system.

Legislature That branch of government whose function is to represent the people and make laws.

Majority government A situation in which the party in power has over 50 percent of the seats in the House of Commons.

Mass media Sources of information for the mass public—principally radio, television, and newspapers.

Minority government A situation in which the government party has fewer than 50 percent of the seats in the House of Commons.

Parliamentary government A form of government, distinct from the U.S. congressional system, characterized by the dominance of the political executive whose members also sit in parliament.

Political party An organized group that makes nominations and contests elections in the hope of influencing the policy and personnel of government.

Politics The activity in which conflicting interests struggle for advantage or dominance in the making and execution of public policies.

Power The ability of one actor to impose its will on another, to get its own way, or to do or get what it wants, usually considered to be the essence of politics and government.

Private sector That part of the economy operated by individuals and corporations, based on the profit motive.

Public sector That part of the economy operated or financed by government.

Responsible government A form of government in which the political executive must retain the confidence of the elected legislature and resign or call an election if and when it is defeated on a vote of non-confidence.

Sovereignty Ultimate control or independence, such as Canadian national sovereignty vis-à-vis that of other countries.

Voluntary Sector That part of the economy operated on a not-for-profit basis by non-governmental groups.

Westminster model The model of government developed in Britain in which the political executive is given extensive power to provide effective leadership.

PART 1

The Societal Context

The next four chapters deal with the main elements of the societal context of the Canadian political system. The aspects of Canadian society most relevant to politics are its regional, ethnocultural, and class features. Gender issues have also become a prominent feature of Canadian politics, age will probably be of increasing significance in the future, and new dimensions of religious questions are arising.

Political science has traditionally regarded these features as deep, persistent divisions in society called cleavages—West versus Centre; French versus English; Rich versus Poor. Of course, if people are not conscious of such cleavages, they will not be politically significant. Thus, another way to look at the political aspects of Canadian society is in terms of identities. Such divisions are related to the fact that people identify with one or more of these characteristics because of their regional, ethnic, economic, and gendered experiences. Cleavages and identities are the source of many of the demands with which the authorities have to contend.

Beyond the factors mentioned are the external forces that also affect the Canadian political system. The world has become a "global village," and international, multinational, transnational, and supranational factors are important elements of any national political system. This is especially true of Canada, which has always been open to such external influences.

Chapter 2

Geography,
Economy,
and Class

Canada's deep-seated geographic and economic divisions are some of its most obvious characteristics. Regional economic cleavages and regional identities are a daily fact of Canadian political life and many government decisions are direct responses to them. These cleavages and identities can be most usefully discussed in terms of distance and division, regional economic differences, regional economic conflicts, regional economic disparities, and regional identities. But economic divisions exist as well in non-geographic terms, usually referred to as class—that is, disparities and conflicts among people with different levels of income and wealth and varied degrees of economic power. Even though class-consciousness or class identities are not as prominent in Canada as might be expected, governments must also deal with such class conflicts on a regular basis.

Chapter Objectives

After you have completed this chapter, you should be able to:

Discuss how distance, division, and the distribution of population affect the operation of the Canadian political system

Identify the principal regions in Canada and the relationship between regions and provinces

Identify the key economic factors that distinguish one region from another

Enumerate the principal regional economic conflicts in Canada

Discuss different means of measuring regional economic disparities and programs that have been adopted to reduce them

Discuss regional identities in economic and non-economic terms

Define the concept of class

Identify the traditional demands made by the upper class, middle class, and working class

Discuss the causes, extent, and implications of poverty in Canada

Geography

Distance and Division

Canada's tremendous distances have always had a crucial influence on its political system. But such distances are immensely complicated by divisions caused by natural physical barriers running essentially in a north–south direction. Distance and division are constant factors in Canada in inducing regional identities and generating regional economic demands. Canada is usually divided into seven geographic regions, as shown in Figure 2.1.

Figure 2.1   Canada's Geographic Regions

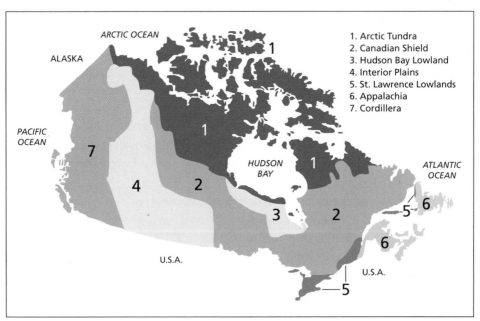

1. Arctic Tundra
2. Canadian Shield
3. Hudson Bay Lowland
4. Interior Plains
5. St. Lawrence Lowlands
6. Appalachia
7. Cordillera

Source: Rand Dyck.

Demands to overcome distances and divisions have featured prominently in Canadian politics, and the establishment of great transportation and communications projects for this purpose dominated whole eras of Canadian history. Governments responded to these demands primarily by giving assistance to private corporations, establishing their own Crown corporations, and creating regulatory agencies in these fields.[1] The major transportation and communications links and agencies with which the federal government has been associated are as follows:

- Canadian Pacific Railway (CPR)
- Canadian National Railway (CNR)
- VIA Rail
- Trans-Canada Highway
- Trans-Canada Airlines/Air Canada
- Trans-Canada PipeLines
- Canadian Broadcasting Corporation (CBC)
- Canadian Radio-television and Telecommunications Commission (CRTC)

In short, in order to create and hold together a nation, Canadians built east–west institutions that ran counter to the natural north–south geographic features of the continent and the perpetual pull of the United States. The list ultimately included satellite services linking Canadians domestically and to the rest of the world. After 1985, however, successive federal governments deregulated, privatized, or reduced financial support for a number of these government operations.

Since people are not spread uniformly throughout Canada's gigantic territory, the distribution of population also complicates the distances involved. The overall density of the Canadian population is one of the lowest in the world, but what is really more significant is that there is no permanent settlement in nearly 90 percent of the country and that two-thirds of the population is huddled together within 100 kilometres of the U.S. border. The population of the various provinces in January 2010 can be seen in Table 2.1. Provincial population disparities affect the allocation of seats in the House of Commons—indeed, the whole power structure in Ottawa—and the calculation of federal transfer payments. Quebec is sensitive to the fact that in recent years its proportion of the total Canadian population has fallen below a symbolic 25 percent.

Ontario and Quebec combined contain about 62 percent of the population, and the Toronto–Ottawa–Montreal triangle obviously constitutes the "core" or "heartland" of Canada. While central Canada forms the political core of the country, it is also the economic heartland, with more large corporate head offices, especially in the Toronto area, than anywhere else. Moreover, it is the communications

TABLE 2.1 ESTIMATED POPULATION OF PROVINCES AND TERRITORIES, JANUARY 2010

	Number	Percentage
Ontario	13 134 455	38.7
Quebec	7 870 026	23.2
British Columbia	4 494 232	13.2
Alberta	3 711 845	10.9
Manitoba	1 228 984	3.6
Saskatchewan	1 038 018	3.1
Nova Scotia	940 744	2.8
New Brunswick	750 658	2.2
Newfoundland and Labrador	510 805	1.5
Prince Edward Island	141 232	0.4
Northwest Territories	43 281	0.1
Yukon	33 992	0.1
Nunavut	32 558	0.1
Canada	33 930 830	

Source: Adapted from Statistics Canada, *The Daily*, 11-001-XWE Thursday, March 25, 2010, http://www.statcan.gc.ca/daily-quotidien/100325/t100325a2-eng.htm (retrieved April 2, 2010).

and cultural core, containing the headquarters of CBC, CTV, Radio-Canada and private French-language television, the national newspapers, many Canadian cultural institutions, and much of the Canadian high-tech industry. Given such a concentration of population at the centre, the rest of the country, the "periphery" or "hinterland," regularly complains that it is overlooked by both public and private decision-makers.

Regions, Provinces, and Territories

In speaking of regionalism in Canada, then, we begin with great distances complicated by geographic barriers and concentrations of population that cause variations in political and economic power. In addition, it is partly because of such distances and divisions that the provinces and territories were created. The constitutional basis of such units is somewhat different from the natural, geo-graphic basis of regions, however, and the fit between regionalism and provincial-ism is not perfect. Feelings of regionalism can exist within a province, such as in the northern parts of many provinces; regional sentiment can cut across provinces, as in the case of people in northwestern Ontario feeling psychologically closer to Manitoba than to southern Ontario; and provinces can be lumped into regions, such as the Maritimes or the Prairies. Nevertheless, as the 1979 Task Force on Canadian Unity pointed out, "the provinces … are the basic building blocks of Canadian society and the logical units on which to focus a discussion of Canadian regionalism, even though they may not be the most 'natural' regions from an eco-nomic point of view."[2] It could be added that the creation of such provinces has served to enhance regional sentiment, as provincial politicians became exponents of regional problems and protectors of provincial interests.

In the 1990s, Quebec came closer than ever before to separating from the rest of Canada. If it were to leave with its existing borders intact (a somewhat debatable issue), Quebec would take with it almost one-quarter of the Canadian population, about 16 percent of the territory, and 20 percent of Canada's gross domestic product. From a strictly geographic point of view, the separation of Quebec would raise the question of continuing transportation links between Atlantic Canada and Ontario, border-crossing impediments, and jurisdiction over the St. Lawrence Seaway.

Regional Economic Cleavages

A discussion of the economies of the Canadian regions and provinces reveals striking regional economic differences that serve to reinforce their geographic distinctive-ness and create another pattern of demands facing the Canadian political system.

Regional Economic Differences

Regional economic differences begin with primary industries or the natural resource base of the various provinces. The importance of natural resources to the national economy has been a central tenet of Canadian politics and economics for generations, usually termed the **staples theory** and identified with economic historian Harold Innis.[3] It postulates that Canadian economic development has relied on a succes-sion of resource exports—furs, fish, timber, wheat, minerals, and energy—rather than manufacturing; Canadians are mere "hewers of wood and drawers of water."

Secondary industry consists of manufacturing, construction, and utilities, including electricity. Manufacturing includes the initial processing and refining of primary products as well as the making of finished goods. Generally speaking, the secondary sector produces more revenue and jobs than primary industry, is less seasonal, and commands higher wages. Primary and secondary industries are often combined as "goods-producing" industries.

Economists put transportation and communications, trade, finance, insurance and real estate, private services, and public administration into the "tertiary" or "services-producing" category. Manufacturing was never an important factor in the Canadian economy, and much political attention in this post-industrial era is focused on the services sector. The tertiary sector now furnishes about three-quarters of the employment in the country. With this background, let us highlight the economic differences among the various regions.

THE ATLANTIC PROVINCES

Historically, the Atlantic provinces had a distinctive and heavy reliance on fishing, especially in Newfoundland and Labrador. This industry fell into deep trouble in the 1990s, primarily due to a dramatic reduction in cod stocks; however, the abundance of shellfish has led to a partial recovery. The three Maritime provinces (New Brunswick, Nova Scotia, and Prince Edward Island) have a substantial agricultural base, while New Brunswick, Nova Scotia, and Newfoundland and Labrador also engage in forestry and mining, and there are great quantities of hydroelectric power in Labrador. Some processing and refining of natural resources takes place in the region, but the small local market and the distance from major population centres have left the region in a state of underdevelopment. Nevertheless, led by New Brunswick, a new emphasis on communications technology has revitalized the Atlantic provinces' economies to some extent, for in the modern technological world, physical distance is not the hindrance it was in the past. The Hibernia and other offshore oil projects have had a profound economic impact on Newfoundland and Labrador, as has the natural gas Sable Island Offshore Energy Project on Nova Scotia. The nickel mine at Voisey's Bay in Labrador should also provide badly needed income and employment.

QUEBEC

The Quebec economy is more diversified than that of the Atlantic region and it is somewhat more prosperous. Quebec's outstanding primary industries include farming in the St. Lawrence Lowlands and mining and forestry in the Canadian Shield.

The Shield is also traversed by numerous powerful rivers, making hydroelectricity Quebec's most valuable resource. Huge dams have been built on many of its rivers, including the controversial James Bay hydroelectric project. Electricity is the basis of Quebec's aluminum industry, as well as many other secondary industries. Quebec also stands out in the production of pulp and paper, especially newsprint, and is much stronger than the Atlantic region in the more sophisticated aspects of manufacturing, including aeronautics and pharmaceuticals. It also houses a large financial sector. The fact that economic power in Quebec used to rest largely in Anglo-Canadian and foreign hands fuelled the nationalist debate in that province. But since 1960 a major transformation has occurred, and both the public and francophone private sectors in Quebec have repatriated a great deal of economic power.

ONTARIO

Ontario historically had the most diversified and strongest economy of any region. The province has a great expanse of prime agricultural land in the south, as well as vast stretches of trees and almost every conceivable mineral in the Canadian Shield. Ontario's early development of hydroelectricity and of a steel industry gave it a head start over other regions. A skilled labour force, a large domestic market, proximity to the automobile industry in the United States, and the advantage of federal tariff and banking policies also helped to make it the manufacturing heartland of the country. This sector has weakened in recent years, however, and Ontario's dominance has also declined because it lacks the petroleum resources that are of increasing economic importance. But it continues to lead the country in the tertiary sector, especially finance.

THE PRAIRIE PROVINCES

The Prairie provinces are historically associated with agriculture, especially wheat, other grain, and livestock. Alberta doubles as Canada's petroleum province, now heavily dependent on the northern oil sands, and has become the richest part of the country by almost any measure. Petroleum is also of increasing significance in Saskatchewan, in concert with that province's other mineral resources, potash and uranium. Forestry is of some importance in Manitoba and Alberta, while Manitoba's hydroelectricity complements the petroleum of the other two Prairie provinces. The Prairies are also engaged in an increasing amount of manufacturing, as well as in finance, trade, and other service industries.

Supportive Alberta in abusive relationship with Ontario and Quebec
(Vance Rodewalt/Artizans.com)

BRITISH COLUMBIA

Mountainous British Columbia is the leading forestry province and also specializes in mining, especially of natural gas, copper, and coal. Several fertile river and lake valleys provide for farming, and B.C. also possesses a significant fishing industry. The mountains are the source of several large rivers that have been dammed for the production of hydroelectricity. Manufacturing is primarily related to the forestry, mining, and agricultural bases of the B.C. economy, and finance stands out among the services sector.

THE NORTH

The inhospitable climate, isolation, small and transient labour force, and poor transportation facilities conspire to retard economic development in the three northern territories. It is primarily mining that has inspired many southerners to venture north over the years. Northern Aboriginal peoples used to be self-sufficient in hunting, fishing, and trapping, activities that continue to occupy them to some extent, but their lives have been disrupted by the arrival of newcomers. Settlement of many Aboriginal land claims and increased autonomy from Ottawa should allow the Northern territories to better respond to local needs in the future. Tourism is on the increase, a Mackenzie Valley natural gas pipeline may be developed, and diamond mines are already making a difference.

Regional Economic Conflicts

As a result of such regional economic differences, the national government regularly faces demands to assist the economy of a single province, region, or industry. Such demands do not necessarily involve conflict between one region and another, and sometimes government responses to them are of general benefit. More often than not, however, demands from one region do conflict with those from another. Leaving aside Quebec, which will be examined in Chapter 3, the most common expression of such regional economic conflict has undoubtedly been between the Prairie and central regions. Since central Canada's regional interests have historically been persuasive with the federal government, the analysis is usually put in terms of the economic complaints of the West against the central core of the country.[4]

TRADITIONAL WESTERN ECONOMIC COMPLAINTS

The traditional complaints of Western Canada relate to natural resources, tariffs, and banking. For example, while the other provinces always had jurisdiction over their own natural resources, Ottawa decided to retain such control when Manitoba was created in 1870, as well as with Saskatchewan and Alberta in 1905. The logic of this discrimination was that the federal government (i.e., central Canada) should control such resources in the national interest, allowing Ottawa to guide the development of the West. The Prairie provinces fought vehemently against this discrimination and were finally successful in gaining control of their natural resources in 1930.

The West complained for generations that Canadian tariff policy was designed in the interests of Ontario at the expense of the Prairies. In the 1879 **National Policy**, John A. Macdonald saw the tariff as a means of promoting and protecting the industrial heartland of central Canada. Adding a tariff (an import tax) to the price of imported manufactured goods would raise their price above that of goods manufactured in Canada, allowing domestic goods to be sold more cheaply than imports. Ontario thus gained employment in producing tractors, for example, but Western Canadians felt that this was contrary to their interests. In the absence of such a tariff, they would have been able to buy cheaper tractors from the United States. The West demanded lower tariffs at every opportunity, and in the 1920s sent its own farmer representatives—the Progressive Party—to the House of Commons to fight on this front.

Canada deliberately developed a centralized branch banking system in an attempt to construct a sound, stable banking community that would avoid frequent local collapses. The result was a handful of large national banks with headquarters in Toronto or Montreal and local branches spread across the country. From a hinterland perspective, money deposited in the local branch of a national bank did not remain in the community to be lent out for local purposes but was sent to headquarters in central Canada to be used in the economic development of Ontario or Quebec. This was another reason for the farmers' revolt of the 1920s, and displeasure with the Canadian banking system had much to do with the rise of the Social Credit party in Alberta in the 1930s.

These policy areas can be put in a broader context called the metropolitan–hinterland thesis. It suggests that the West was created as a colony of central Canada and was intended to be held in a subordinate and dependent relationship.[5]

MODERN WESTERN ECONOMIC COMPLAINTS

Some of these traditional issues continue to rankle the West in different forms, and additional concerns have emerged in recent times. The conflict over natural resources re-emerged in the 1970s and 1980s, for example, especially with respect to petroleum pricing. After the OPEC (Organization of Petroleum Exporting Countries) cartel agreed on an artificial rise in the international price of oil in 1973, federal policy began to favour the consumer/manufacturing interest of central Canada at the expense of the producer interest of the West. The height of the regional economic conflict occurred in 1980 with the Trudeau government's **National Energy Program** (NEP), which imposed new federal taxes, kept the national price below the world level, encouraged frontier development, and promoted Canadianization of the industry, all objectives opposed by most Westerners. Eventually, a partial compromise between central and Western interests was reached in 1981, and the Mulroney government later scrapped the NEP entirely, but not before the program had had a profoundly isolating effect on the Western Canadian psyche.

Tariffs among all countries have gradually come down since 1945, but this issue took on a new life in the 1980s with the Western demand for a free trade agreement between Canada and the United States. By this time, business interests in central Canada also supported such a measure, and it was adopted to their mutual satisfaction.

Perhaps the most sensitive Western economic demand in the 21st century, at least from the Alberta perspective, is not to touch its petroleum industry, especially the development of the oil sands. This includes the threat of the imposition of federal environmental controls. Alberta was the leading opponent of the Kyoto Protocol and even though the oil sands are among the leading emitters of greenhouse gases, that province continues to resist restrictions that would hinder the incredible expansion of that industry.

OTHER ASPECTS OF REGIONAL ECONOMIC CONFLICTS

Many of the Western economic conflicts with central Canada have been echoed by the Atlantic provinces. Nova Scotia and New Brunswick entered Confederation in 1867 as proud and prosperous colonies, but their economies quickly declined. While changes in marine technology (from wooden sailing ships to steel steamships) were probably the principal factor responsible, Maritimers blamed federal economic policy for much of their difficulty. Post-Confederation tariff policy appeared to do the Maritimes more harm than good, and the Atlantic provinces fought for provincial ownership of offshore petroleum in the 1990s. They also complained that the federal government was not sufficiently aggressive when it came to protecting Atlantic fish stocks from foreign overfishing.

Smaller-scale regional economic disputes are also a routine occurrence in Canadian politics. Awarding the CF-18 maintenance contract to a company in Montreal infuriated supporters of a superior bid from a competitor in Winnipeg; extending drug patent protection for multinational pharmaceutical firms in Quebec offended Canadian generic drug producers in Ontario; and promoting frontier petroleum exploration (including federal assistance to Newfoundland's Hibernia project) upset conventional oil and gas producers in Alberta. Former Ontario premier Mike Harris complained that employment insurance premiums were too high, especially when Ontarians paid a large part of the premiums and residents of the five Eastern provinces collected a disproportionate amount of the payments.

Regional Economic Disparities

Conflicts between regions are exacerbated in Canada because of regional economic inequalities or disparities. Whatever the fault of federal policies, Canada's primary resources are not evenly distributed, the regions have different sizes and populations, they are located at variable distances from key export markets, and such markets affect them in particular ways.

Among the available ways to measure regional economic disparity is provincial gross domestic product (GDP), that is, the total value of all goods and services produced in a province. Because of great discrepancies in the size of provincial populations, it is more useful to divide each province's GDP by its population, giving the GDP per capita. A second measure of provincial disparities is per capita income, and a third is provincial unemployment rates. These measures are provided in Table 2.2, but have become quite divergent in recent years.

TABLE 2.2 Provincial Gross Domestic Product Per Capita (2008), Per Capita Income (2008), and Unemployment Rate (2009)

	GDP Per Capita ($)	Per Capita Income ($)	Unemployment Rate (Percent)
Newfoundland/Labrador	38 748	30 504	15.5
Prince Edward Island	29 950	28 963	12.0
Nova Scotia	31 312	31 938	9.2
New Brunswick	31 667	31 080	8.9
Quebec	34 657	33 406	8.5
Ontario	41 305	37 309	9.0
Manitoba	35 310	33 329	5.2
Saskatchewan	40 923	35 400	4.8
Alberta	52 168	48 110	6.6
British Columbia	37 466	36 457	7.6

Source: Adapted by author from Statistics Canada. Data, "Gross Domestic Product, Expenditure-Based, by Province and Territory," http://www40.statcan.ca/101/cst01/econ15-eng.htm, divided by 2008 provincial population; CANSIM, "Personal Income per Person," Table 384-0013; and "Labour Force, Employed and Unemployed, Numbers and Rates, by Province," http://www40.statcan.ca/101/cst01/labor07a-eng.htm, retrieved April 2, 2010.

In addition to developing national social programs and assisting various industries in a general way, successive federal governments have focused on two principal means to deal with the specific question of regional economic disparities. One is to give federal funding to have-not provincial governments, and the other is to provide grants to individual firms in designated have-not regions of the country.

EQUALIZATION PAYMENTS

In 1957, Ottawa finally responded to repeated demands to make **equalization payments** to have-not provinces. These payments are funded by various federal taxes levied in all provinces, but the revenue comes disproportionately from Ontario and Alberta. These annual cash grants to the have-not provinces are designed to allow them to raise their services to an acceptable national level but can be spent for any purpose. In other words, they are unconditional grants with no strings attached. The sums involved are quite impressive, as Table 2.3 reveals. For

TABLE 2.3 EQUALIZATION PAYMENTS, 2010–11

Quebec	$8 552 000 000
Manitoba	$1 826 000 000
New Brunswick	$1 581 000 000
Nova Scotia	$1 110 000 000
Ontario	$972 000 000
Prince Edward Island	$330 000 000
Total	$14 372 000 000

Source: Adapted from Department of Finance Canada, "Major transfers to provinces and territories, 2010–11" http://www.fin.gc.ca/fedprov/mtpt-ptfp10-eng.asp. Reproduced with the permission of the Minister of Public Works and Government Services, 2010.

several years, Newfoundland and Labrador and Nova Scotia complained, however, that when they took in additional natural resource revenues, they experienced a proportional decrease in their equalization payments. This issue caused a major conflict with the federal government, and the Martin and Harper governments responded with adjustments to the Equalization program. In fact, the 2007 budget was supposed to end the "fiscal imbalance" between the federal and provincial governments for all time. Two startling but contrary developments occurred as of 2009: Newfoundland and Labrador no longer qualified for equalization payments, while Ontario began to qualify. British Columbia and Saskatchewan joined Alberta as the other three have-provinces.

REGIONAL ECONOMIC DEVELOPMENT PROGRAMS

The second means of trying to reduce regional economic disparities is to establish federal regional economic development programs. The basic thrust of these programs is to designate those parts of the country that are in need of economic assistance, and then to provide grants to firms that would locate or expand existing operations in such areas. Some grants also go to provinces or municipalities in order to provide the basic infrastructure that might attract industry, such as highways, water and sewage systems, and industrial parks. Several separate regional economic development agencies now exist, principally the Atlantic Canada Opportunities Agency (ACOA), Federal Economic Development Initiative for Northern Ontario (FedNor), the new Southern Ontario Development Agency, Western Economic Diversification Canada (WD), and Canada Economic Development for Quebec Regions (CED).

> ## What Do You Think?
>
> To what extent should richer provinces share their wealth with poorer provinces, especially through the mechanism of federal equalization payments? To what extent do Quebec's superior social programs depend on contributions from other provinces?

Regional Identities

Many of the economic factors discussed above, reinforced by geography, have given rise to regional or provincial identities, a subject that was touched upon earlier. But there are also non-economic factors involved in such identities. In 1980, for example, **Western alienation** was defined as follows:

> *A regionally distinct political culture through and within which are expressed economic discontent, the rejection of a semi-colonial status within the Canadian state, antipathy towards Quebec and French-Canadian influence within the national government, the irritation of the West's partisan weakness within a succession of Liberal national governments, and the demand from provincial political elites for greater jurisdictional autonomy.*[6]

After it defeated the Liberals in 1984, the Mulroney Conservative government also gave priority to Quebec, leading to the formation of the Reform Party, whose initial slogan was "The West Wants In." The Reform Party won the majority of seats west of Ontario in the 1993 and 1997 elections, including almost all of the seats in British Columbia and Alberta. In 2000, the party changed its leader and name (to the Canadian Alliance) in an effort to become more appealing to the rest of the country. In 2003, it reabsorbed the Progressive Conservative Party and adopted another new name, but it retained its Alberta-based leader, Stephen Harper. Table 2.4 illustrates the regional support of the various political parties in the 2008 federal election and shows that the new Conservative Party of Canada continued to have a predominant Western base. On the other hand, the Harper government was at least as concerned as any party in power in the past 50 years to increase its representation in Quebec, risking the emergence of a new round of western alienation.

TABLE 2.4 REGIONAL DISTRIBUTION OF POPULAR VOTE BY PARTY, 2008 ELECTION (PERCENTAGES)

	Atlantic	Quebec	Ontario	West	North
Conservatives	29.6	21.7	39.2	52.4	35.1
Liberals	35.0	23.7	33.8	16.3	29.7
NDP	26.1	12.1	18.2	21.5	25.4
Bloc Québécois	—	38.1	—	—	—

Source: Elections Canada. Calculations by author.

What are other distinctive, non-economic elements of the Western regional identity? Given their relative prosperity, many Western Canadians tend to prefer individual self-reliance over collective, public solutions to demands being made. Since the principle of representation by population gives central Canada a majority of votes in the House of Commons, Westerners often propose to decentralize the federal system or to give the Senate more power to protect regional interests. Albertans generally take the most extreme positions on such issues as opposition to liberal interpretations of the Charter of Rights and Freedoms and to the requirement in the Canada Health Act that publicly funded health services be provided in the public sector. The Alberta government also wants a scaled-down gun registry and a role for provinces in international agreements that affect provincial jurisdiction. Other outlying regions in Canada feel isolated and discriminated against, too, sentiments that lead to regional identities in the Atlantic provinces and the North. Given the federal obsession with Quebec and a deteriorating economy, a distinctive Ontario identity may also be developing.

Class Cleavages

Let us turn from economic disparities based on geography to inequalities in individual incomes, wealth, and power, that is, to class cleavages. The concept of class is not as clear-cut as that of region, and Canadians are generally more aware of their regional and ethnic identities. In fact, because of such other divisions, class may not be as important a generator of political activity in Canada as it is in most countries. We do have significant class divisions but lack a strong consciousness of class and class conflict. This part of the chapter will begin by discussing various definitions and measurements of class, and will then examine the political role of the different classes.

Defining and Measuring Class

When dealing with the concept of class, it is customary to start with Karl Marx, who predicted that every capitalist economy would produce a class system consisting primarily of the bourgeoisie, the owners of the means of production, and the proletariat, the workers. Owners of the "means of production" are those who own mines, factories, banks, and other businesses. The proletariat would sell their labour for a price; the bourgeoisie would pay them as little as possible (and less than they were worth), thereby accumulating profit or surplus value. While religion and the prospect of a pleasant afterlife might keep them content for a while, the workers would come to resent their low wages and state of exploitation and eventually engage in a violent revolt.

Some social scientists continue to provide a neo-Marxist analysis of class cleavages in society, making provision for a new middle class as well. But others divide individuals and families into the upper, middle, and working classes primarily based on income. When such a measure is used, the divisions between the classes are less clear-cut than in Marxist analysis.

One means of measuring income inequality is to divide the population into five equal groups, or quintiles, from highest to lowest income, and to indicate the share of total income received by each group. Figure 2.2 presents such proportions for the year 2006. It also shows that the income shares before social program transfers (such as employment insurance and social assistance) were dramatically inequitable, and that the tax system takes only a little away from the rich to redistribute to the poor. Thus, even after taxes and transfers, the highest-earning 20 percent of the population still receive 44 percent of the total income, while the lowest 20 percent receive just five percent.

One of the problems in using the concept of class is the distinction between "objective" and "subjective" class. Objective class refers to the class into which analysts place a person, according to criteria such as type of work or level of income, while subjective class means the class to which people think or feel they belong, even if it contradicts objective standards. Many people who consider themselves to be middle-class would be categorized as working class by social scientists. Behaving as if they belonged to a different class than they really do, such people could be said to be lacking in **class-consciousness**, something that Marx also foresaw and called

Figure 2.2   Income Shares of Quintiles: Market Income, Total Income (Income after Transfers and before Tax), and Income after Tax, 2006

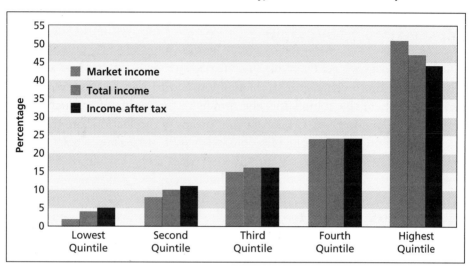

Source: Adapted from Statistics Canada, "Income in Canada, 2006," Catalogue 75-202-XTE 20060000 2006. Released May 5, 2008. http://www.statcan.gc.ca/pub/75-202-x200600-eng.htm

"false consciousness." This factor reduces the significance of class in motivating political activity.

The Upper Class and Corporate Elite

Canada is home to many fabulously rich entrepreneurs and some of the wealthiest families on earth. At the top of the 2009 edition of the *Canadian Business* "Rich 100" list, which included 55 Canadian billionaires, were the Thomson family, at $22 billion; the Irving family, at $7.3 billion; Galen Weston, at $6.5 billion; Jimmy Pattison, at $5 billion; the Rogers family, at $4.7 billion; and Paul Desmarais, at $4.3 billion.[7] The Thomson family now specializes in electronic databases and media companies; the Irving family owns most of New Brunswick, including large tracts of woodlands, pulp mills, oil refineries, gas stations, trucking firms, bus lines, railways, potato operations, and all the English-language daily newspapers in the province; and Galen Weston is the proprietor of Loblaws, Holt Renfrew, and Weston Bakeries. Jimmy Pattison owns a wide variety of companies centred in British Columbia; the Rogers family owns the vast Rogers Communications empire; and Paul Desmarais' holdings include Power Corp., Investors Group, and Great-West Life.

Another category of wealthy Canadians comprises the corporate chief executive officers who do not necessarily own their firms. According to the Canadian Centre for Policy Alternatives, the total average compensation of the top 100 CEOs in Canada in 2007—for one year alone—was over $10 million, which includes the value of salary, bonus, incentives, shares, stock options, and other benefits. This figure compared to $17 739 for the full year earnings of a person working at the average minimum wage, and $40 237 for the full year earnings at the average wage and salary in Canada.[8]

The general lines of the public policy demands of the upper class and corporate elite are easily drawn. Essentially, they want to be left alone; they prefer to minimize the role of government and have society rely more extensively on private market forces. They want to cut government spending on social programs so that their taxes can be minimized, balance the annual government budget, and reduce the accumulated national debt. If taxes are necessary, they want governments to avoid corporate and progressive individual taxes as much as possible and to provide generous loopholes, write-offs, and tax shelters. Their goal is to minimize government regulation, including labour standards and environmental protection.

Governments have normally been only too happy to respond to such demands. The Canadian state gives priority to big-business demands in the first place because it depends on the private sector to create jobs. Politicians are especially sensitive to a corporate threat to move to a country with more favourable policies. Second, corporate executives and politicians often come from the same ranks, including prime ministers and ministers of finance. Brian Mulroney and Paul Martin provide perfect examples. Third, companies have many avenues of influence available: making a direct, personal pitch for favourable decisions, using professional lobby firms to help them contact public decision-makers for a fee, and taking advantage of their membership in pressure groups. Among the hundreds of business groups in existence, the **Canadian Council of Chief Executives** is probably most powerful, representing the chief executive officers of the 150 largest firms in the country. Fourth, the corporate elite also control the mass media to a large extent and can use them to foster self-serving attitudes among authorities and the public. Finally, throughout their history, both the Conservative and Liberal parties were financed primarily by large corporate contributions. Such donations guaranteed access to decision-makers, if not specific favours, and it was not difficult to establish a link between corporate contributions and general public policy. As a result of actions taken by the Chrétien and Harper governments, however, corporations can no longer donate money to political parties and candidates.

The progressive nature of the personal income tax was reduced when the Mulroney government reduced ten tax brackets to three, and capital gains continue to be taxed at a lower rate than other forms of income. In her book *Behind Closed Doors*, Linda McQuaig shows how the rich use their political influence to obtain tax breaks that are paid for by those with lesser incomes.[9] Personal and corporate income taxes are riddled with loopholes, and Canada is one of the few countries in the world without a tax on wealth or inheritance, but the Harper government slashed corporate taxes. Beyond the recent moves toward deregulation, the various free trade agreements represent a commitment on the part of governments not to restrict the operations of corporations. Moreover, for a fee of $500 000, a corporation could send its CEO to address the national leaders at the Summit of the Americas in Quebec City in April 2001, while anti-globalization protesters were kept outside by a high fence and tear gas. And the reluctance of governments to enact effective measures to deal with climate change can be primarily explained by the opposition of large corporations, making the environment an issue related to class.

What Do You Think?

Do the economic elite—corporate owners and CEOs—owe their wealth and power to their own effort, creativity, and intelligence? Or have they largely inherited their wealth or gained it through exploiting their workers, deceiving consumers, and manipulating the political system—the tax laws, the labour laws, the environmental laws, etc.? Why don't more people see the political system in class terms?

Three principal exceptions to this corporate pressure to minimize the role of government must be noted. First, while the economic elite demands that government minimize spending on others, it often expects sizable chunks of public funds for itself, such as in government contracts and grants. Even after 25 years of primary reliance on free market forces, the Canadian government continues to give generous financial assistance to some of the largest companies in the country. A second exception is the rare occasion on which the economic elite actually favours new social programs. Such programs tend to increase the purchasing power of lower-income people, reduce the amounts that companies themselves have to pay in employee benefits, and ensure the basic stability of society so that upper classes do not have to worry about violent protests from the poor or unemployed. Third, business leaders expect government to provide such basics as roads, railways, and electricity that decrease their costs or increase their profits. Despite the overwhelming tendency of governments to respond to demands from the corporate elite, however, it should not be forgotten that politicians ultimately get elected by voters, the great majority of whom belong to other classes. Thus, other classes can influence events to some extent, but only if they act as a class.[10]

The Middle Class

On a subjective basis, a majority of Canadians probably think that they belong to the middle class. Academic analysts challenge this view, although they do agree that there is a large middle class in a modern society. They often divide the middle class between the upper middle class and the new middle class, the former being made up of small-business people, self-employed professionals (e.g., lawyers and doctors), and affluent farmers. The new middle class incorporates middle managers (who take orders from the corporate elite and give them to the working class), civil servants, teachers, nurses, and other salaried professionals. While the middle class is far from being a unified force, its members are normally well educated and receive above-average levels of income. Their main assets are their homes, their cars, and assorted other material possessions. While members enjoy such tax shelters as RRSPs, the middle class often claims that it pays a disproportionate amount of the taxes to finance government programs of all kinds. On the other hand, such groups as teachers and nurses increasingly feel that they are being treated by governments as if they belonged to the working class, and the proportion of the new middle class that belongs to public sector unions is constantly increasing.

The Working Class

The working class is generally identified as doing manual or routine work. Members of the working class are typically engaged in resource exploitation, assembly line production, secretarial and clerical work, sales, and a variety of crafts and trades.

Less affluent farmers might also be included. Some academic analysts put the bulk of the population into this category, even though many who are so labelled identify subjectively with the middle class. Normally lacking postsecondary education, members of the working class usually receive less income than those in the middle class.

Karl Marx's predictions of a violent proletarian revolt were dealt a blow when governments unexpectedly legalized trade unions and extended the franchise to the working class. Nevertheless, most governments and companies have been hostile toward the formation of labour unions, and Canada has experienced a large number of violent strikes, either over the formation of a union or over its subsequent demands. Among the key labour struggles in Canadian history were the 1919 Winnipeg General Strike, the 1937 General Motors Strike in Oshawa, the 1945 Ford Strike in Windsor, the 1949 Asbestos Strike in Quebec, and the woodworkers' strike in Newfoundland in 1959.[11] While legislation dealing with conciliation, mediation, arbitration, picketing, labour standards, occupational health and safety, and compensation for injury on the job is ostensibly passed to protect the working class, governments usually avoid offending their own corporate supporters in the design or implementation of labour laws.

Others things being equal, it is in the interests of members of the working class to belong to a trade union. Unionized employees usually have higher wages, more adequate benefits, better working conditions, and more protection against arbitrary dismissal than those who do not engage in collective bargaining. For example, unionized workers are much more likely to have private medical, dental, life, and disability insurance, as well as pension coverage. In spite of these advantages, the rate of unionization in Canada is very low (except in comparison to the United States) and is in decline. Total union membership in 2009 was 4.2 million, or about 30 percent of the paid workers in the country.[12]

Moreover, the number of blue-collar jobs is falling in such areas as resource industries, construction, and manufacturing, where unionization used to be most common. New jobs in the post-industrial society are found largely in sales and services, especially in the private sector, where workers are traditionally part-time, poorly paid, and hard to organize. Lacking a union, and given the nature of their job, those in sales and service occupations are not as likely to be class-conscious or to develop social democratic values as those who produce goods.

The composition of the unionized workforce is also changing in other ways. Once comprising primarily private sector, male, manual workers, it is increasingly composed of public sector unions, and over 50 percent of union members in Canada are now women. While only about 16 percent of private sector employees are unionized, the rate rises to 71 percent in the public sector. Indeed, public sector unions make up three of the seven largest unions in the country: the Canadian Union of Public Employees, the National Union of Public and General Employees, and the Public Service Alliance, along with the Canadian Auto Workers, the United Steelworkers of America, the United Food and Commercial Workers, and the Communications, Energy and Paperworkers Union.[13]

Given that most labour legislation is passed at the provincial level, the principal federal measure is the Employment Insurance (EI) Act. This program, originally called Unemployment Insurance, was introduced in 1941 to tide workers over between jobs. Given the high national unemployment rates in many years since, and the even higher rates in certain regions in every year, it is relied upon much more heavily than was originally anticipated. With such large numbers of workers drawing on the fund, it became a vital source of both individual and regional income, although governments repeatedly restricted its coverage in the 1980s and 1990s. The Chrétien and Martin governments siphoned off the significant surplus in the EI account to pay down the national debt and then loosened up the program, especially for Atlantic Canada, just prior to the 2000 and 2004 elections. Not surprisingly, the deficiencies in the EI program raised much controversy in the Great Recession of 2008–09.

Health care has become a serious problem on both federal and provincial political agendas. The rich can afford to take care of themselves, but public health care is a priority for many in the middle and working classes, to say nothing of the poor. The Canada Health Act requires that public institutions provide all basic medical care, so that public funds do not end up in profit-oriented firms. The Act also purports to prohibit two-tier health care in which those who can afford it can obtain faster care than those without such resources. The extent to which for-profit and two-tier health services are allowed has become a major class-based issue in modern times.

The **Canadian Labour Congress** (CLC) is the main lobbying body for over three million workers. The CLC is thus one of the largest pressure groups in the country and represents a significant number of voters. Its influence is diminished, however, by its outsider status in Ottawa, as well as by the fact that not all unions belong to it. The historic factionalism within the Canadian union movement has also hindered the cause of the working class.[14] Governments are often justified in assuming that a gap exists between labour leaders and rank-and-file members with respect to policy positions and party support. Union leaders often support the NDP, while large numbers of rank-and-file members vote for each of the other major parties.

Couple living in car hope to use home renovation tax credit
(Sue Dewar/Artizans.com)

The Poor

The poor can be defined as those living below the **poverty line**. The most widely accepted definition of poverty in Canada is the low-income cut-off provided annually by Statistics Canada. According to this measure, any individual or family that spends more than 64 percent of its income on food, clothing, and shelter is living in poverty (given that the average family spends 44 percent of its income on these three necessities). By this definition, Canada has over four million residents living in poverty, or about 15 percent of the population. Although these figures represent a decline since 1969, a large proportion of these people live far below the poverty line, and these figures do not include the large group of near-poor that exists just above it. Moreover, the gap between those with the lowest and highest incomes widened significantly between 1984 and 2005.[15]

Probably the most heartbreaking and most intractable aspect of poverty is that it includes about a million children. The high-school dropout rate among children from poor families is much higher than that of others, and the tie between low income and low education is self-perpetuating. *The Canadian Fact Book on Poverty* documents how children from low-income families stand out from their better-off peers:

> They are less healthy, have less access to skill-building activities, have more destructive habits and behaviours, live more stressful lives, and are subject to more humiliation. In short, they have less stable and less secure existences and as a result they are likely to be less secure as adults.[16]

Many poor people work full-time, and others part-time; in fact, the poor can be about equally divided between those who work and those who are unemployed or unemployable. The working poor try to scrape by on the minimum wage or on more than one low-paying job, but they are sometimes better off if they go on social assistance. Rather than raising the minimum wage, however, some provincial governments actually reduced welfare benefits in the last half of the 1990s, and only Quebec provided an adequate daycare program. From about 1995 to 2004, the most common government action was to cut taxes, even at the expense of social programs. The Centre for Social Justice points out that people living in poverty have no taxable income and so tax cuts are of no benefit to them; tax cuts merely create larger income disparities.[17]

As indicated earlier, improvement in the economy after 1995 resulted in a decline in the proportion of people living below the poverty line. Unfortunately, that decline came to an abrupt end with the worldwide economic meltdown at the end of 2008. Among the ideas for improving the lot of the poor are

- raising the federal minimum wage (partly as a model for the provinces and territories);
- restoring eligibility for Employment Insurance to earlier periods;
- creating an effective child benefit system that provides enough income support to keep parents out of poverty;
- building a universally accessible system of early child education and child care;
- expanding affordable housing to end homelessness; and
- renewing the national social safety net through the new Canada Social Transfer, with increased federal funding.[18]

One of the great weaknesses of the poor in the political system is that they are generally unorganized and collectively inarticulate. They lack the skills to organize effectively as advocacy groups, primarily because they are without the education, money, and time to develop such skills. Because of their low voter turnout rate, they tend to be ignored by both federal and provincial governments. Nevertheless, several groups and think tanks exist to research the poverty problem and to speak for the poor in the cacophony of the political process: the Canadian Council on Social Development, the National Council of Welfare, the National Anti-Poverty Organization, the Centre for Social Justice, the Caledon Institute of Social Policy, the Canadian Centre for Policy Alternatives, and Campaign 2000. Still, no one should expect any degree of equality in the struggle among interest groups representing different classes.

SUMMARY

The first part of the chapter deals with the political significance of geography and the economy. It begins by showing how distance, division, and the distribution of population have given rise to demands on the political system and influenced the nature of its responses, and notes the imperfect relationship between regions and provinces. The next section provides an overview of the economic differences among the various regions, especially between the West and the centre, both historically and in contemporary times. It presented statistics on measures of regional economic disparities, identified policies adopted to reduce them, and raised the question of regional identities such as Western alienation in economic and non-economic terms. The second part of the chapter discusses class cleavages, beginning with various definitions of class and the general lack of class-consciousness in Canada. It then lists the typical demands made by each of the main classes, along with the typical government responses. The chapter concludes with a discussion of poverty in Canada—who and how many are poor and what policies have been or could be adopted to improve the lot of poor Canadians.

DISCUSSION QUESTIONS

1. What should be the role of the federal government in overcoming Canada's great distances and divisions? To what extent can the private sector fulfill this function?
2. Are you conscious of living in a particular region, and if so, what regional and provincial complaints do you have about federal policies?
3. What, if anything, can be done to lessen the problem of regional economic disparities?
4. Why is union membership among the working class not higher? Why is class-consciousness in Canada relatively low?
5. Should Canada make a more concerted effort to reduce poverty? If so, how?

KEY TERMS

Canadian Council of Chief Executives The most powerful peak business pressure group in Canada, representing the 150 largest firms in the country.

Canadian Labour Congress The largest labour pressure group in Canada; the political voice of over three million members.

Class-consciousness An awareness of the social class to which one belongs.

Equalization payments Large annual cash payments made by the federal government to have-not provinces to help them provide a satisfactory level of public services.

National Energy Program The 1980 policy associated with Pierre Trudeau designed to skim off petroleum tax revenue for Ottawa, keep the price of petroleum below world levels, encourage conservation, and Canadianize the industry, which met with great opposition in Western Canada.

National Policy The broad nation-building 1879 policy of John A. Macdonald that included tariff protection for central Canadian manufacturing, massive immigration, and the construction of a national transportation system.

New middle class A term from class analysis describing salaried professionals such as teachers, public servants, and nurses.

Poverty line An amount of income such that anyone who received less would be living in poverty.

Regionalism Strong feelings of attachment to the region or province where one lives that often generate political activity.

Staples theory The notion that Canadian economic development has gone through a series of stages based on the exploitation of one natural resource or another and the export of such resources, without the development of a secondary or manufacturing sector.

Western alienation The feeling shared by many Western Canadians that their interests are not taken seriously in the national policymaking process.

FURTHER READING

Abella, Irving, ed. *On Strike*. Toronto: James Lewis & Samuel, 1974.

Braid, Don, and Sydney Sharpe. *Breakup: Why the West Feels Left Out of Canada*. Toronto: Key Porter Books, 1990.

Brownlee, Jamie. *Ruling Canada: Corporate Cohesion and Democracy*. Black Point, N.S.: Fernwood Publishing, 2005.

Gibbins, Roger, and Loleen Berdahl. *Western Visions, Western Futures*. Peterborough: Broadview Press, 2003.

Hale, Geoffrey. *The Uneasy Partnership: Politics of Business and Government in Canada*. Peterborough: Broadview Press, 2006.

Kerstetter, Steven. *Rags and Riches: Wealth Inequality in Canada*. Ottawa: Canadian Centre for Policy Alternatives, 2002.

McQuaig, Linda. *Shooting the Hippo: Death by Deficit and Other Canadian Myths.* Toronto: Viking, 1995.

Osberg, Lars. *A Quarter Century of Economic Inequality in Canada: 1981–2006.* Ottawa: Canadian Centre for Policy Alternatives, April 2008.

Savoie, Donald J. *Visiting Grandchildren: Economic Development in the Maritimes.* Toronto: University of Toronto Press, 2006.

Young, Lisa, and Keith Archer, eds. *Regionalism and Party Politics in Canada.* Toronto: Oxford University Press, 2002.

Chapter 3

French Canada and
the Quebec
Question

The French–English cleavage has been of great significance from the very beginning of Canadian politics. The prominence given to concerns of French Canadians primarily reflects the large number of people involved, their historical rights, the territorial base of Canada's francophones in Quebec, and their strong ethnic, cultural, and linguistic identity. The French–English cleavage is at least as problematic as the regional economic cleavages in Canadian politics, and the two reinforce each other in the question of Quebec's place in Confederation.

Chapter Objectives

After you have completed this chapter, you should be able to:

Outline the historical evolution of French–English interaction in Canada

Enumerate the French–English crisis points in our history

Explain and appreciate the concept of Quebec nationalism and different francophone identities

Contrast the values, attitudes, and demands of the Québécois before and after the Quiet Revolution

Distinguish between contrasting approaches to protect and promote the French language and culture in Canada

Comment on the responses of federal, Quebec, and other provincial governments to francophone demands

Outline the attempts at constitutional change since 1980

Discuss optional mechanisms for dealing with the Quebec question in the future

Historical Overview of French–English Relations

Pre-Confederation Developments

Almost every Canadian political decision for over 200 years has reflected the French–English division to some extent, and the tensions that threaten the continued existence of the country are best understood in historical context. The French first colonized what is now the province of Quebec, and populated it with farmers, clergy, and seigneurs. But when the British defeated the French on the Plains of Abraham in 1759, the conquerors took control of the non-agricultural economy and the government.

Time Line
Constitutional Developments, 1759–1867

1759   British conquest of Quebec
1774   Quebec Act
1791   Constitutional Act
1840   Act of Union
1867   British North America Act (Constitution Act, 1867)

The Quebec people, however, continued to speak French and attend the Roman Catholic Church, which became a highly influential and autonomous organization. It would probably have been impossible to make Quebec into an Anglo-Protestant colony; in any case, after a brief attempt at assimilation, the British exhibited a policy of tolerance and accommodation. In the 1774 Quebec Act they guaranteed the French their religious rights and their own system of civil law.

A large component of "English" immigrants—especially the United Empire Loyalists from the new United States—moved into what is now Ontario in the 1780s. The colony was soon divided into two by the Constitutional Act of 1791: Lower Canada (Quebec) would be essentially French-Catholic, and Upper Canada (Ontario) would be Anglo-Protestant. In the 1830s, conflict erupted in both colonies between the elected assembly and the appointed executive, which in the case of Lower Canada translated into discord between the French (assembly) and the English (executive).

The colonies were reunited by the 1840 **Act of Union** on the recommendation of Lord Durham, who believed that the ethnic problem in Canada could be solved only by another attempt to assimilate the French. But this objective was quickly abandoned as unrealistic, and the French language came to be used alongside English in the government of the colony of Canada in the pre-Confederation period. The governments of the day were usually alliances between English and French leaders, and the legislature operated on the informal principle of the double majority—legislation had to have the approval of a majority of members from both sections of the colony.

Given this historical evolution, the federal union incorporated in the British North America Act (BNA Act)—now called the **Constitution Act, 1867**—is perfectly understandable. As a separate province, Quebec would have considerable autonomy, as provided by the division of powers between the federal and provincial governments. Not all Quebec participants were satisfied, however, with the degree of autonomy it was accorded. Most adhered to the "compact theory of Confederation," according to which Confederation was a compact between two equal founding nations, and any change in the Constitution would require unanimous provincial consent, or at least the consent of Quebec.

As for cultural guarantees, both French and English were given official status in the operations of the federal Parliament, and laws were to be passed in both languages. English and French could also be used in whatever federal courts were later established, as well as in the legislature and courts of Quebec.

Post-Confederation Conflicts

Although the two language groups have been regularly accommodated in government circles since 1867, a number of serious linguistic/ethnic conflicts erupted from the time of Confederation to the Second World War. The first consisted of two Riel Rebellions, led by French Catholic Métis Louis Riel, one of which precipitated the creation of the province of Manitoba in 1870. In 1884–85, Riel re-emerged in what is now Saskatchewan to lead another rebellion on behalf of Western Aboriginals, who had been treated shamefully by the government. After quelling the rebellion, federal authorities charged Riel with treason. This raised ethnic and religious tensions across the country to a fever pitch. While Anglo-Protestants regarded Riel as a murderer, traitor, and madman, French Catholics believed he was a patriot and a saint. The hanging of Riel heightened the level of French-Catholic outrage, especially in Quebec, and seriously damaged the close attachment of the people of that province to the Conservative Party.

What really happened on the Plains of Abraham (Dale Cummings/Artizans.com)

The second linguistic conflict occurred in Manitoba in 1890. At its origin, the small settlement had been about equally divided between French and English, and (at Riel's insistence) the 1870 Manitoba Act followed the Quebec precedent of giving the two languages official status in the new province's legislature and courts. Afterwards, however, Manitoba attracted thousands of English-speaking immigrants and others who chose to identify with the anglophone community. Hence, 20 years after its creation, the anglophone majority passed the Official Language Act, removing the official status of French.

Time Line
Major French–English Conflicts, 1867 to 1945

1870	First Riel Rebellion
1885	Second Riel Rebellion
1890	Manitoba's Official Language Act
1913	Ontario's Regulation 17
1917	First conscription crisis
1944	Second conscription crisis

The third linguistic conflict concerned minority French-language education rights in Ontario. In 1913, the government's Regulation 17 virtually abolished the use of French in the Ontario school system; English was to become the sole language of instruction after the third year, and the study of French as a subject was limited to one hour a day.

The **conscription crisis** of the First World War was the fourth major French–English confrontation. Having little in the way of standing armed forces, the Canadian military effort rested heavily on appeals for volunteers. These appeals initially had promising results, but as reinforcements were needed later in the war, few recruits came forward. The government therefore decided to resort to conscription—compulsory military service—in 1917. Isolated from Europe for centuries, French Canadians felt that the war was of no concern to them, and certainly did not justify risking their lives. Prime Minister Robert Borden knew that French Canada generally felt indifferent to the conflict and that conscription would divide the country along ethnic lines. He therefore appealed to Liberal leader Wilfrid Laurier to join him in a coalition government. Laurier refused the offer, although most English-speaking Liberal MPs did join in the Union government. The subsequent enforcement of conscription entailed considerable violence, including a riot in Quebec City in the spring of 1918 that left four people dead and many others injured. This confrontation destroyed what little French-Canadian support for the Conservative Party was left after the execution of Louis Riel.

Ontario repealed Regulation 17 in 1927, and French–English tensions returned to their normal, controllable level until they were inflamed by the fifth conflict, another conscription crisis during the Second World War. But in 1939 Canada was led by Liberal Prime Minister Mackenzie King, with a strong contingent of ministers and MPs from Quebec. King knew that French Canada would resist conscription, so on the basis of the slogan "conscription if necessary, but not necessarily conscription," he held a national referendum in 1942 to release his government from an earlier pledge not to conscript. Happily, King then managed to postpone the adoption of compulsory military service until almost the end of the war.

Quebec Nationalism

Central to the question of French–English relations and the position of Quebec in Canada is the phenomenon of Quebec nationalism. It is a feeling, shared by most francophones in that province, of primary loyalty to Quebec, and emanates from the widely held notion that it is home to a distinctive French-Canadian nation, centred on language, ethnicity, culture, and territory, and—prior to 1960—religion. Over the centuries, Quebec nationalism has taken many twists and turns, but it remains a driving force in both provincial and federal politics, where it has always stood for a substantial degree of political autonomy or self-determination. Quebeckers valued autonomy because Quebec was different and because they felt that such autonomy had been guaranteed in 1867. Quebec sometimes also considered itself to be morally superior to the rest of the country and often believed that it was fighting for its life. Before 1960, Quebec nationalism was largely inward-looking and defensive, primarily concerned with ensuring that the federal government kept out of that province's affairs. After 1960, it was activist and self-confident, as the province wanted to take over many federal responsibilities. Post-1960 Quebec nationalism also sought to reverse the dominance of Anglo and external economic power in the province.

While most francophone Quebeckers are nationalists, there are variants of this feeling. Some nationalists merely advocate the protection and promotion of the French language and culture, increased powers for the province, and more French-Canadian control of the economy. Other nationalists fight for provincial sovereignty with a loose connection to Canada or outright separation. In other words, while almost all francophone Quebeckers are nationalists, only about half support Quebec sovereignty, and among those, not all favour complete independence from Canada. Somewhat complicating the picture, however, is the declining French-Canadian birthrate in Quebec and the presence in the province of about one million residents (including Aboriginal peoples, anglophones, and those of other origins, called "allophones") who do not usually embrace the same ethnic/linguistic/cultural objectives. As noted in Chapter 2, Quebec's population has recently fallen below a symbolic 25 percent of the total Canadian population, and any future increase will be based on immigration.

The French–English Cleavage, 1960–82

The Quiet Revolution: Quebec in the 1960s

Until 1960, Quebec was a traditional, conservative, rural, poorly educated, patronage-oriented society, heavily influenced by the Roman Catholic Church. Dominated by the authoritarian Premier Maurice Duplessis from 1935 onward, the population was taught that only he could protect them from evil external influences, such as Ottawa. The Quebec of the past 50 years, however, is quite a different province and society. In the 1960s, Quebec francophones experienced a **Quiet Revolution**, consisting of a dramatic change of values and attitudes, especially toward the state, a new collective self-confidence, and a new brand of nationalism. These features of the new Quebec had many implications for French–English relations in both the Quebec and the Canadian political systems.

QUEBEC'S CHANGES AND DEMANDS

The government of Jean Lesage (1960–66) took over many functions previously administered by the Church.[1] The most important of these, education, was radically modernized, and health and welfare programs were also made public rather than charitable responsibilities. With the nationalization of private power companies, Hydro-Québec became a huge Crown corporation supplying most of the electricity in the province and serving as an engine of economic development. Lesage also reformed almost every piece of legislation on the books, especially labour and electoral laws, added reams of new ones, and created many government agencies. All these new and expanded public responsibilities required substantial additional revenues, and Lesage put immense pressure on Ottawa to increase federal–provincial grants, to allow Quebec to opt out of the conditions attached to them, and to give the province a greater share of joint taxation. In areas of provincial jurisdiction, Quebec began to move toward distinctive programs; it designed its own pension plan, for example, which was then used as a model for the Canada Pension Plan. As time went on, the province began to demand ever-larger jurisdiction, leading to perpetual federal–provincial discord.

Time Line
French–English Relations, 1945–70

1949–59	Opposition to Maurice Duplessis grows
1960–66	Quiet Revolution
1963–68	B&B Commission
1968	Pierre Trudeau becomes PM
1968–69	Official Languages Act
1970	FLQ crisis

Federally oriented Quebec francophones, such as future prime minister Pierre Trudeau, had a different vision of French Canada, one that did not focus on Quebec. This group of French Canadians began to demand that French be used as a language equal to English in the corridors of power in Ottawa. They were also concerned about the fate of francophone minorities in the other provinces, helped by the fact that the new self-confidence of the Québécois inspired these dwindling minorities to greater self-assertiveness.

FEDERAL RESPONSES

During the 1960s, the federal government grappled somewhat haphazardly with these demands. The Diefenbaker government (1957–63) introduced simultaneous interpretation into Parliament, began printing federal government cheques in a bilingual format, and appointed a French-Canadian governor general. Immediately upon taking office, the Pearson government (1963–68) established the Royal Commission on Bilingualism and Biculturalism (the B&B Commission). Pearson also gave Quebec and the other provinces more federal funds and taxation powers, removed conditions from many shared-cost programs, and permitted Quebec to make international arrangements with France and other francophone countries.

Since the federal Parliament and courts were already theoretically bilingual, the main gap in official bilingualism at the national level was in the executive branch, where English was essentially the working language at the policymaking levels of the public service. Pearson therefore introduced the **Official Languages Act** to make the Canadian public service bilingual. Since its passage under Trudeau in 1969 Canada has become officially and effectively bilingual in its federal institutions. Ottawa also began to assist francophone minorities in other provinces in order to try to stem their increasing assimilation into the anglophone majorities, as well as to promote bilingualism through support of French immersion educational programs.

The question of French–English relations, or "national unity," was the principal political issue throughout the Trudeau era (1968–79, 1980–84). It eventually became clear that two basic models existed to deal with the problem. The first was to recognize Quebec as the homeland of French Canada and to give that province the necessary powers and resources to protect and promote its linguistic and cultural distinctiveness. Quebec would be essentially "French" and the rest of Canada primarily "English." The second option was to treat Quebec as *une province comme les autres* and to promote bilingualism at the federal level and in the other provinces so that any Canadian could use either language anywhere in the country and Quebec could not claim to be linguistically distinctive.

English Canadians had difficulty accepting these demands, which seemed excessive and contradictory: making Quebec more French and more autonomous at the same time as promoting the French language in Ottawa and the other provinces. Most people did not understand that the two demands came largely from two different groups of francophones, the vast majority concentrating on Quebec and a minority that wanted to expand French Canada beyond that province. Trudeau was not representative of mainstream thought in Quebec in his fight against the recognition of Quebec as the homeland of French Canada and in his opposition to giving that province any special status or power, which he thought would be the first step toward separation. Part of Trudeau's popularity in English Canada stemmed from the perception that he was "anti-Quebec," but he was passionately "pro-French" in promoting French power and bilingualism in Ottawa and across the country.[2]

THE SEPARATIST OPTION

During the 1960s, advocates of a third option—Quebec separatism—began to emerge. Most people supporting this option were committed to democratic processes, but one wing of the separatist movement, the **Front de libération du Québec (FLQ)**, resorted to violence. It believed that the normal political process was not responding quickly enough to the demands of the Quiet Revolution, and its periodic bombings killed two people and injured many others. In October 1970, two small cells of the FLQ kidnapped a British diplomat, James Cross, and abducted and murdered Quebec Cabinet minister Pierre Laporte. Trudeau invoked the **War Measures Act**, giving the police and armed forces special powers to quell the violence. In the process, over 400 innocent, democratic supporters of separatism were arrested. By crushing the FLQ, by giving French Canadians more clout in Ottawa, and by guaranteeing pan-Canadian bilingualism in the Constitution Act, 1982, Trudeau hoped to undercut any Quebec demand for special status or separatism in the defence of French Canada.

The invocation of the War Measures Act in 1970 in connection with the FLQ crisis included the visible presence of armed soldiers on the streets of Montreal and Ottawa. (CP PHOTO/CP)

Quebec–Canada Relations, 1970–82

The first Robert Bourassa government in Quebec (1970–76) passed Bill 22 to give primacy to the French language in many spheres in the province, such as in the operations and documents of public authorities. As far as education was concerned, immigrant children were generally forced to attend French-language schools. This was an attempt to have such children join the majority French linguistic group in the province rather than become "English," as so many previous immigrants had done. In fact, relying on immigration to bolster the francophone segment of the population became essential after the French-Canadian birthrate plummeted in the 1960s. Bill 22 also aimed at the francization of the private sector by pressuring companies to use French as the language of internal corporate operations. The more Quebec moved in the direction of French unilingualism, of course, the greater the number of anglophones who left Quebec and the greater the resistance in English Canada to Trudeau's policy of national bilingualism.

Time Line

Quebec–Canada Relations, 1970–82

1974	Quebec Bill 22
1976	Election of Parti Québécois
1977	Quebec Bill 101
1980	First Quebec Referendum
1982	Constitution Act, 1982

The Parti Québécois (PQ) was elected to office in 1976 under René Lévesque with an even more nationalistic program than that of Bourassa.[3] Faced with a hostile Trudeau government in Ottawa, the PQ made few gains in provincial autonomy. But in 1977 it passed Bill 101, the Charter of the French Language, which considerably extended Bill 22 in making French the predominant language in the province. The bill generally turned the persuasive and optional aspects of Bill 22 into coercive and mandatory ones. It made French the only official language of the legislature (although laws continued to be translated unofficially into English); only individuals (not corporations) could use English in Quebec courts; essentially the only children who could go to English-language schools in the province were those who had at least one parent who had done so; and all commercial signs had to be in French only. Over the next decade or so, all four of these clauses were ruled unconstitutional by the courts, but they were subsequently modified to comply with the court decisions. Thus, most of Bill 101 still stands, and French continues to be the official language of the province.

In 1980, the PQ government held a **referendum** on the question of pursuing a more independent relationship with Canada called **sovereignty-association**. Many prominent politicians, including Trudeau, Justice Minister Jean Chrétien, and several provincial premiers, encouraged Quebeckers to defeat the PQ proposal, promising them "constitutional renewal" if they did so. When sovereignty-association was turned down by a vote of 60 percent to 40 percent, new federal–provincial constitutional negotiations began, culminating in the **Constitution Act, 1982**.[4] Ironically, even though the whole effort was supposed to appeal to the residents of Quebec, that province alone objected to the act as reflecting the Trudeau vision of a centralized, bilingual, symmetrical Canada rather than recognizing the distinctive francophone character of Quebec and giving it additional powers. Nevertheless, the Act became law in all parts of the country. As far as language was concerned, it reinforced official bilingualism at the federal level and in New Brunswick, and guaranteed **minority language education rights** in all provinces wherever numbers warranted. Many Quebeckers never forgave Trudeau and Chrétien for adopting such a significant constitutional document without Quebec's consent.

French–English Relations in the Other Provinces

The distribution of French- and English-language communities in the various provinces in 2006 is shown in Table 3.1. Defined by mother tongue, the largest francophone minorities are located in Ontario (508 000) and New Brunswick (235 000), where they respectively constitute 4.2 and 32.7 percent of the provincial population.

The Quebec government and most Quebeckers have been more concerned about internal linguistic matters than about what happened to French-language minorities in other provinces. Nevertheless, the Quiet Revolution led francophones outside Quebec to make a last-ditch attempt to preserve their language and culture. Often under pressure from Prime Minister Trudeau, some provincial premiers hoped that by extending rights or services to their francophone minority they would help to forestall separatism in Quebec. Thus, many provinces made considerable improvement in minority francophone rights after 1965. As mentioned, all were also bound by the Constitution Act, 1982, to provide education in the minority official language where numbers warranted. Under an amendment to

TABLE 3.1 MOTHER TONGUE BY PROVINCE, 2006 CENSUS (PERCENTAGES)

	English	French	Other
Newfoundland and Labrador	97.6	0.4	2.0
Prince Edward Island	93.6	4.2	2.3
Nova Scotia	92.3	3.7	3.9
New Brunswick	64.7	32.7	2.6
Quebec	8.2	79.6	12.3
Ontario	69.1	4.2	26.6
Manitoba	74.6	4.0	21.4
Saskatchewan	85.5	1.8	12.8
Alberta	79.6	2.0	18.4
British Columbia	71.2	1.4	27.4
Nunavut	27.0	1.3	71.7
Northwest Territories	77.3	2.4	20.3
Yukon	84.5	3.9	10.8
Total	57.8	22.1	20.1
Canada outside Quebec	73.3	4.1	22.6

Source: Adapted from Statistics Canada, 2006 Census: The Evolving Linguistic Portrait 2006 Census 9, -555-XWE2006001 http://www12.statcan.ca/english/census06/analysis/language/tables/annexA1.htm

the Official Languages Act in 1988, all provinces were also committed to provide for criminal trials in French if demanded by the accused.

New Brunswick went farthest with its own Official Languages Act of 1969, which was constitutionalized at provincial request in 1982. New Brunswick also improved the Acadian educational system at all levels and provided provincial government services in both languages. The province strengthened the act further in 2002, and it can now be said to be effectively bilingual.

Even before Trudeau, Ontario provided for French-language secondary schools, and later recognized the right of every Franco-Ontarian to go to a French-language school. Ontario then guaranteed French trials in the provincial courts and gradually extended French-language provincial services. Bill 8, coming into effect in 1989, guaranteed provincial government services in French in designated regions of the province and required that laws be drafted in both languages. Meanwhile, simultaneous interpretation in the legislature began in 1987, and French-language schools were to be run by trustees elected by the francophone population.

Manitoba moved very slowly in this direction on its own but was pushed by a series of Supreme Court of Canada decisions beginning in 1979. The result was that the 1890 Official Language Act was declared unconstitutional, all laws had to be passed in both languages, trials had to be available in French, and most government documents had to be bilingual.

Quebec–Canada Relations Since 1982

Three years after the controversial adoption of the Constitution Act, 1982, Quebeckers defeated the Parti Québécois and put Robert Bourassa's Liberals back in power. The second Bourassa government found the federal Mulroney government to be more receptive to its demands than Trudeau had been, and Quebec was allowed to play a fuller part in the international French-speaking community, the Francophonie. Then, in 1988, the Supreme Court of Canada declared the sign provision of Bill 101 to be unconstitutional as a violation of freedom of expression, that Charter right including "commercial expression." Bourassa responded by using the "notwithstanding clause" in the federal and Quebec charters of rights to pass Bill 178, providing for French-only outdoor signs but allowing some bilingual signs indoors. Such violation of a constitutional right of anglophones produced a vehement reaction among Anglo-Quebeckers and an anti-Quebec and anti-French response in the rest of the country. On the other hand, some aspects of Bill 101 had been voluntarily relaxed in 1983, and in 1986 Quebec had ensured the provision of social and health services in English to its anglophone minority. Moreover, when the five-year limit on Bill 178 ran out in 1993, Bourassa replaced it with Bill 86, which allowed bilingual signs outside as well as inside stores, as long as the French letters were larger than the English.

Time Line
Quebec–Canada Relations Since 1982

1987–90	Meech Lake Accord
1992	Charlottetown Accord and national referendum
1995	Second Quebec referendum
1998	Supreme Court decision on Quebec secession from Canada
2000	Clarity Act

The Meech Lake Accord

The Constitution Act, 1982, including the Charter of Rights and Freedoms, was operative in Quebec even though the government of that province refused to endorse it. When Brian Mulroney became prime minister, however, he was determined that Quebec should symbolically rejoin the Canadian constitutional family "with honour and enthusiasm." He included several Quebec nationalists in his cabinet and, in 1985, asked Bourassa to outline his conditions for such a reunion. The Quebec government proceeded to make five demands:

1. Constitutional recognition of Quebec as a "distinct society" within Canada
2. Increased jurisdiction over immigration
3. Participation in Supreme Court appointments
4. Power to veto constitutional amendments related to Quebec
5. Right to opt out, with compensation, of national programs within provincial jurisdiction

Mulroney called the premiers together at Meech Lake in April 1987, where they agreed to a document that addressed Quebec's demands and became known as the **Meech Lake Accord**.[5] The prime minister secured unanimous provincial consent by extending to the other provinces the same rights that were demanded by Quebec, except for the **distinct society clause**. The document also would have constitutionalized the Supreme Court of Canada, guaranteed annual first ministers' conferences on the Constitution and the economy, and—at the behest of the Alberta delegation—provided for provincial participation in appointments to the Senate.

Despite the relative ease with which it was drafted, the Meech Lake Accord generated much controversy. Its critics, led by ex-prime minister Trudeau, did not approve of Quebec's designation as a distinct society within Canada, and they objected to the phrase that it was the role of the government and legislature of Quebec to "preserve and promote" that distinctiveness. No one was sure of the implications of the **distinct society clause** for the federal–provincial division of powers, leaving the interpretation of it to the courts on an issue-by-issue basis. Some argued that, armed with that constitutional support, Quebec would immediately begin to challenge federal powers in a variety of fields; others worried about the status of the English and Aboriginal minorities within Quebec, as well as of the francophone minorities in other provinces.

A second objection to the accord was that it enlarged the list of subjects that required unanimous provincial consent in the constitutional amending formula.

Many critics felt that Senate reform and the transformation of the Northern territories into provinces would be virtually impossible if such changes required the agreement of all ten provinces instead of only seven.

Much concern was expressed about the provision that allowed provinces to opt out of national programs within provincial jurisdiction and be compensated by Ottawa. Fears were expressed that satisfactory new national social programs (such as daycare) would never materialize because provinces would be compensated for programs that merely met national *objectives*, not national *standards*.

Others condemned the process through which the accord had emerged—a behind-the-scenes gathering of (male) first ministers. In the post-Charter era, individual Canadians in all parts of the country insisted on being part of the constitutional amendment process; moreover, the primacy of Quebec's concerns was rejected by those given constitutional standing by the Charter—women, Aboriginal peoples, and cultural and other minorities.[6]

Supporters of Meech Lake argued that it would symbolically bring Quebec back into the constitutional fold and overcome the isolation and betrayal that many residents of that province felt after 1982. Indeed, it responded to the most modest list of demands ever to come out of Quebec. Defenders called this the "Quebec round" and argued that Aboriginal, Northern, Western, and other concerns would be the next items on the constitutional agenda. They felt that rather than promote incremental separatism, the accord would give Quebec the flexibility to remain satisfied within Confederation. Its proponents contended that in demographic, linguistic, and cultural terms, the distinctiveness of the Quebec society could not be denied.

Many political scientists and others had long argued that the provinces should have a say in the appointment of senators and Supreme Court judges. In the former case, this was because the Senate was intended to represent the provinces within Ottawa's decision-making structure; in the latter, because the Supreme Court rules on federal–provincial disputes and hence its judges should not be unilaterally appointed by one side. Many true federalists also contended that Ottawa should not be able to invade provincial jurisdiction with its spending power and set up national programs without provincial consent, as had often happened in the past.

According to the constitutional amending formula adopted in 1982, the Meech Lake Accord then had to be approved by Parliament and all provincial legislatures within three years, that is, before June 1990. In most cases, such legislative approval came rather easily, but new governments in Newfoundland and Manitoba had reservations about the accord. In the end, it was not approved by the legislatures in either of those provinces, in Manitoba because Aboriginal MLA

Prime Minister Brian Mulroney makes a pitch for the Meech Lake Accord in the House of Commons in June 1990. (The Canadian Press/ Chuck Mitchell)

Elijah Harper delayed passage beyond the deadline in the absence of any advance for Native peoples.

The Charlottetown Accord

With the death of the Meech Lake Accord, many Quebeckers felt betrayed again, and nationalist and separatist sentiment in Quebec mushroomed. Both the Quebec Liberals and Parti Québécois issued more nationalistic constitutional positions, and demands arose for a referendum on sovereignty to be held in 1992. Meanwhile, several Quebec members of Parliament quit the Conservative and Liberal parties to sit as Quebec *indépendantistes* in the Bloc Québécois (BQ) led by Lucien Bouchard, a former minister in the Mulroney cabinet.

Prime Minister Mulroney appointed Joe Clark as the minister responsible for constitutional affairs, and Clark tried to develop a collective federal–provincial–territorial–Aboriginal response to offer to Quebec before its constitutional referendum. After several rounds of negotiations, Clark, the nine premiers, and territorial and Aboriginal leaders all agreed on a comprehensive constitutional proposal in July 1992. Quebec then entered the bargaining process, and the participants unanimously signed a new constitutional accord in Charlottetown in August.[7] The Charlottetown Accord had four main parts, two of primary concern to Quebec: the "Canada clause" and changes to the division of powers. The other two major components of the accord were Aboriginal self-government and the Triple-E Senate, subjects dealt with in Chapters 4 and 15 respectively. (In brief, the accord would have enshrined Aboriginal self-government in the Constitution and reformed the Senate in the direction of being elected, effective, and giving equal representation to all provinces—the "Triple-E"s).

The Canada clause that began the accord would recognize Quebec as a distinct society within Canada as well as enumerate the other fundamental values and characteristics of the country. These included democracy, the rule of law, the parliamentary and federal systems, the Aboriginal peoples of Canada and their enhanced rights, official language minorities, cultural and racial diversity, individual and collective rights, gender equality, and the equality and diversity of the provinces.

The second main issue of interest to Quebec was the federal–provincial division of powers. As in the Meech Lake Accord, provinces could have a larger role in immigration matters. They could also opt out of new national shared-cost programs set up within provincial jurisdiction and receive federal financial compensation if the programs met national objectives. In addition, if they wished, the provinces could have full or partial power over 10 additional fields of public policy: forestry, mining, tourism, recreation, housing, municipal and urban affairs, culture, labour-market training, telecommunications, and regional development.

The accord would be of no effect until ratified by Parliament and the ten provincial legislatures. Before ratification, however, the federal government announced that a national referendum would be held on the new constitutional deal on October 26, 1992. The decision to hold such a nationwide referendum was based on two main points. First, Quebec was already committed to a referendum on constitutional change on that date, while Alberta and B.C. laws required a referendum on constitutional amendments. If these three provinces would be voting on the accord in any case, the opportunity had to be extended to the others. Second, a referendum would avoid the criticism levelled at Meech Lake that it lacked public input, and public approval would lend legitimacy to the agreement and spur the 11 legislatures into speedy affirmative action.

Unfortunately for its sponsors, the referendum on the Charlottetown Accord failed. On a national basis, 55 percent of the people who cast their ballots voted no and 45 percent voted yes. Majorities opposed the accord in Quebec, Nova Scotia, the four Western provinces, and the Yukon. Even though the referendum was not legally binding, there was no point in bringing the constitutional package before legislatures for ratification: the Charlottetown Accord was dead.

Public opinion polls showed that rather than basing their decision on the contents of the accord as such, many of the people who voted no did so to vent their anger and frustration against Prime Minister Mulroney, the premiers, and politicians and governments in general. Voters were not in a generous frame of mind, and rather than seeing the accord as a multisided compromise, they generally felt that it gave too much to others and not enough to themselves. Indeed, while the accord was primarily designed to address the constitutional insecurity of Quebec, Aboriginal Canadians, and Western and smaller provinces, a majority in all three groups believed that their elites had not bargained hard enough on their behalf.[8]

The Chrétien Government Record and the 1995 Referendum

After this disheartening if not traumatic experience, all federal parties decided that it would be wise to leave the constitutional issue alone. In 1994, however, the Parti Québécois was returned to power in Quebec. With the Chrétien regime in Ottawa largely ignoring the issue, the new Quebec premier, Jacques Parizeau, wanted a quick vote on a clear-cut separatist position. Others, including Bloc

Québécois leader Lucien Bouchard, preferred a scheme that retained significant ties to Canada. When the polls showed that Parizeau could not achieve the support of a majority of Quebec voters on the question of his choice, he succumbed to the pressures he faced and promised an extensive list of continuing links to Canada.

What Do You Think?

What is the harm in recognizing Quebec's distinctiveness in the Constitution? Is such a designation unfair in any way to other provinces? Is it the first step toward separation?

Parizeau's referendum was held in October 1995. The proposal involved a convoluted and unclear question incorporating a kind of sovereignty that retained significant ties to the rest of Canada. In the final week of the campaign, Prime Minister Chrétien finally woke up to the possibility of a PQ victory and made a vague promise of reform if the "no" vote prevailed. The result of the referendum could not have been closer: 50.6 percent voted no, while 49.4 percent voted yes. This narrow defeat precipitated Parizeau's abrupt resignation, and Lucien Bouchard moved from leading the BQ in Ottawa to the PQ in Quebec.

Fulfilling his last-minute promises, but not being able to persuade all provinces to make an actual amendment to the Constitution, Chrétien had Parliament pass a resolution recognizing Quebec as a distinct society within Canada. He also promised that regardless of the official constitutional amending formula, no general amendments would be passed without the approval of every region of the country (including Quebec). Labour-market training was then transferred from federal to provincial jurisdiction.

Troubled by Parizeau's claim that a referendum victory would be sufficient ground for the province to separate, in 1997 Chrétien referred a hypothetical question to the Supreme Court of Canada, asking it to rule on the legality of a unilateral declaration of independence by Quebec. In August 1998, the Supreme Court issued its decision in the reference case: under the Canadian Constitution, the secession of a province could not be achieved unilaterally. To separate legally, Quebec would have to use the constitutional amending formula and seek the approval of the other participants in Confederation. Nor did Quebec gain such a right under international law. On the other hand, if the Quebec government obtained a clear majority vote in a provincial referendum on a clear question in favour of secession, it would be hard for the rest of the country to ignore.[9]

In the Words of the Court
The Legality of Quebec's Secession

"Quebec does not meet the threshold of a colonial people or an oppressed people, nor can it be suggested that Quebecers have been denied meaningful access to government to pursue their political, economic, cultural and social development.... [But] a clear majority vote in Quebec on a clear question in favour of secession would confer democratic legitimacy on the secession initiative which all of the other participants in Confederation would have to recognize."

Source: Reference re Secession of Quebec, [1998] 2 S.C.R. 222.

With Bouchard threatening another referendum, Chrétien introduced his controversial **Clarity Act**, which essentially translated the Supreme Court decision into legislation. He believed that such legislation was required because the questions asked in the Quebec referendums of 1980 and 1995 were deliberately vague. Although the act stopped short of articulating what a "clear majority" would be in numerical terms, it specified that the federal government would not recognize a Quebec referendum result that did not involve a clear expression of the will of the population that the province should cease to be part of Canada. In other words, the federal government would not tolerate a question that involved continuing economic or political arrangements with Canada. Such a constitutional amendment would also have to address the division of federal–provincial assets and liabilities; border changes; the rights, interests, and territorial claims of Aboriginal peoples; and the protection of minority rights. While the Quebec government obviously opposed the new rules and passed a law declaring that it alone would draft the next question, the act did not incite the inflammatory backlash in that province that some opponents had expected.

The Future of French–English Relations

Given that francophones constitute over 22 percent of the Canadian electorate, that 86 percent of them are located in Quebec, and that 80 percent of Quebeckers are French-speaking, there is no denying their significance. Moreover, Quebec's political institutions operate somewhat distinctively in many ways, it has pursued many policy differences from other provinces, and it has separate sources of news and entertainment. Justifiably or not, Quebeckers retain something of a siege mentality with respect to language and culture, and language has replaced the Church as the focus of the French-Canadian identity. The Quebec corporate elite is now a francophone group, and it, along with the new middle class in the Quebec public sector, sees itself as bene-fiting from increased provincial autonomy.[10] Ken McRoberts concludes that "for most Quebec francophones, anything less than distinct society would not do justice to the reality of contemporary Quebec as they understand it,"[11] and Canada will always face pressure for more Quebec autonomy no matter which party forms its government.

The PQ government was defeated by Jean Charest's provincial Liberal Party in 2003. With a federalist party in power in Quebec, the rest of the country relaxed to some extent, but a strong core of sovereignty supporters remained. Just about the time that Chrétien retired, however, it was revealed that his government had issued a number of large advertising contracts promoting national unity to Quebec communications firms that had made financial contributions to the Liberal Party. The effectiveness of such advertising was debatable, but even more troubling was that this "sponsorship scandal" sometimes reached criminal proportions. In the 2004 federal election, not surprisingly, the Bloc Québécois gained nearly 50 percent of the vote in Quebec, much of it from people upset by the Chrétien sponsorship scandal rather than from genuine sovereigntists. Prime Minister Paul Martin felt obliged to appoint Judge John Gomery to conduct a judicial inquiry into the whole operation. But Opposition attacks based on revelations before the inquiry led to Martin's defeat on a non-confidence motion in November 2005 and the Liberals lost further ground in Quebec in the January 2006 election.

Stephen Harper had previously opposed Quebec's calls for distinctive treatment, but as he changed his position in that election, the Conservatives won 10 seats in that province based on 25 percent of the vote. The new prime minister developed a congenial relationship with Premier Charest, allowed Quebec to take a formal role in Canada's delegation to UNESCO, and presented a resolution in the Commons recognizing the Québécois as a nation within a united Canada. In the 2007 budget, the Harper government addressed the so-called "fiscal imbalance" about which Quebec in particular had always complained—that Ottawa had too much money and the province not enough—with a huge increase in equalization payments and other transfers to Quebec.[12] Even so, Charest did not achieve a clear victory in the provincial election held a few days later: with the three Quebec parties almost tied in popular vote, his government was reduced to minority status. But in December 2008, Charest regained a majority.

About this time, analysts began to distinguish between "civic" and "ethnic" nationalism in Quebec. As the proportion of allophones increased, a provincial policy of "interculturalism" appeared. New immigrants were told that they could retain their distinctive practices and cultures as long as they agreed to use French as the common language of Quebec public life. Quebec nationalism would no longer be based on ethnicity and restricted to francophones. The new civic nationalism would welcome non-francophones who felt loyal to Quebec and recognized that the use of French was the essential condition for the cohesion of Quebec society. This distinction has left the concept of "Québécois" rather ambiguous—does it refer only to those of French ethnicity or to this wider, more varied group?

On the other hand, many residents were increasingly concerned about the number of immigrants in the province as well as about certain minority religious and ethnic group practices. The bulk of new immigrants settled in city of Montreal, where the proportion of residents with French mother tongue had fallen in the 2006 census to just over 50 percent. In response to complaints about Islamic and other religious dress and symbols, Premier Charest appointed a two-person commission (Bouchard-Taylor) to hold public hearings and make recommendations with respect to the "reasonable accommodation" of such differences. Contrary to many of the briefs they heard, the commissioners believed that newcomers were not a threat to the Quebec way of life. They recommended that the government of Quebec should be totally secular, treating all religions alike but not denying them individual expression, and that people of all cultures and faiths should share in a common, inclusive state defined by the French language. It remains to be seen whether either allophones, especially of non-Christian faiths, or francophone Quebeckers will actually embrace this official policy. In fact, the Quebec government passed a law in 2010 requiring Muslim women to bare their face (remove their niqab) when dealing with provincial government authorities.

SUMMARY

This chapter demonstrated that the French–English problem has always been with us. It discussed the main developments in this relationship before and since Confederation. Then it turned to the evolution of Quebec society and Quebec nationalism, concentrating on the changes resulting from the Quiet Revolution of the 1960s. The chapter showed that two main strategies emerged for dealing with demands for the protection of the French language and culture, one focused on Quebec and the other on the country as a whole. It then examined government responses to these demands in Ottawa and in the various provinces, including Quebec. The chapter concluded with an outline of the successful and unsuccessful attempts at constitutional change since 1980, predicted that demands for more Quebec autonomy would probably never cease, and raised the question of how Quebec would deal with its increasing immigrant population.

DISCUSSION QUESTIONS

1. To what extent should individual provinces operate on a bilingual basis?
2. If Quebec wants more autonomy, should it be treated differently from other provinces, or do you favour a general decentralization of powers to all provinces?
3. Should Quebec be able to leave Canada if a majority in that province ever vote to do so?

KEY TERMS

Act of Union The 1840 act that united the colonies of Upper and Lower Canada into the colony of Canada.

Bill 101 The 1977 Quebec language law that made French the official language of Quebec and put restrictions on the use of English in the public and private sectors, including French-only signs.

Charlottetown Accord The 1992 constitutional agreement that responded to Quebec's demands for distinct society status, Aboriginal demands for self-government, and the West's demand for a Triple-E Senate, but was defeated in a national referendum.

Clarity Act The 2000 act that specified the conditions under which the federal government would recognize a referendum result in Quebec on the issue of independence.

Conscription crises Two political crises during the two World Wars, in 1917 and in 1944, in which the population and government were divided, largely along ethnic lines, over the necessity of compulsory military service.

Constitution Act, 1867 The new name for the British North America Act, 1867, which united the four original provinces.

Constitution Act, 1982 The act sponsored by Prime Minister Trudeau that contained a made-in-Canada constitutional amending formula and a Charter of Rights and Freedoms.

Constitutional Act The 1791 British law that divided Canada into two separate colonies—Upper and Lower Canada—each with a governor, executive and legislative councils, and assembly.

Distinct society clause A controversial clause in the Meech Lake Accord, and slightly modified in the Charlottetown Accord, claiming that Quebec constituted, within Canada, a distinct society.

Front de libération du Québec (FLQ) The terrorist wing of the Quebec separatist movement in the 1960s and 1970s.

Meech Lake Accord The 1987 package of constitutional reforms intended to bring Quebec back into the constitutional fold but that expired due to lack of unanimity in 1990.

Minority language education rights Rights established in section 23 of the Charter of Rights and Freedoms whereby French-speaking Canadians can send their children to French-language schools wherever their numbers warrant, a principle also extended to English-speaking Canadians where they are a minority.

Official Languages Act The 1969 federal act that established official bilingualism in Canada and gave citizens the right to deal with certain offices of the federal government in either English or French.

Quebec Act The 1774 British law that provided for a system of government for the colony of Quebec that included certain privileges for the French-speaking, Roman Catholic majority.

Quiet Revolution The dramatic change of values and attitudes, especially toward the state, the new collective self-confidence, and the new brand of nationalism in Quebec in the 1960s.

Referendum A populist device in which a public policy proposal is submitted directly to the electorate.

Sovereignty-association The Parti Québécois proposal in which Quebec would be sovereign while maintaining an economic association with the rest of Canada.

War Measures Act The law invoked in both World Wars and during the 1970 FLQ crisis under which the federal Cabinet was given emergency powers to deal with the crisis.

FURTHER READING

Cairns, Alan C. *Disruptions: Constitutional Struggles, from the Charter to Meech Lake.* Toronto: McClelland and Stewart, 1991.

Fraser, Graham. *Sorry, I Don't Speak French: Confronting the Canadian Crisis That Won't Go Away.* Toronto: McClelland and Stewart, 2006.

———. *René Lévesque and the Parti Québécois in Power.* Toronto: Macmillan, 1984.

Hébert, Chantal. *French Kiss: Stephen Harper's Blind Date with Quebec.* Toronto: Knopf Canada, 2007.

McRoberts, Kenneth. *Misconceiving Canada: The Struggle for National Unity.* Toronto: Oxford University Press, 1997.

————. "Quebec: Province, Nation, or Distinct Society?" In Michael S. Whittington and Glen Williams, eds. *Canadian Politics in the 20th Century*, 7th ed. Toronto: Nelson, 2008.

————, and Patrick Monahan, eds. *The Charlottetown Accord, the Referendum and the Future of Canada*. Toronto: University of Toronto Press, 1993.

McWhinney, Edward. *Canada and the Constitution, 1979–82: Patriation and the Charter of Rights*. Toronto: University of Toronto Press, 1982.

Romanow, Roy, J. Whyte, and H. Leeson. *Canada . . . Notwithstanding: The Making of the Constitution, 1976–1982*. Toronto: Methuen, 1984.

Russell, Peter. *Constitutional Odyssey: Can Canadians Become a Sovereign People?*, 3rd ed. Toronto: University of Toronto Press, 2004.

Chapter 4

Aboriginal Peoples, **Ethnocultural** Minorities, and Gender

The French–English question has been a constant of Canadian politics since before Confederation, but until recently Aboriginal and other ethnocultural issues were largely ignored. Similarly, once women achieved the vote around 1920, the system paid little attention to them. About 1970, however, Aboriginal, ethnocultural minority, and gender issues suddenly became prominent items on the political agenda. This chapter explores these three relatively new concerns: the first section examines Canada's Aboriginal peoples; the second discusses ethnocultural minorities; and the last deals with the women's movement and other gender issues.

Chapter Objectives

After you have completed this chapter, you should be able to:

Discuss the historical evolution of Aboriginal–European interaction and the factors that have contributed to the deplorable state of life of many Aboriginal people in Canada

Understand different kinds of Aboriginal land claims, the concept of Aboriginal self-government, and recent developments in both policy areas

Distinguish between pre-1970 and post-1970 Canadian immigration patterns

Trace the evolution of multiculturalism policy

Discuss the implications of Canada's active immigration policy

Enumerate the milestones of women's political participation in Canada, as well as the factors that have inhibited such participation

Discuss the issues that have concerned the women's movement since 1970

Understand the public policy concerns of the gay and lesbian communities

Aboriginal Peoples

History and Numbers

The Native or Aboriginal peoples who have inhabited Canada for as long as 40 000 years are an extremely varied group. In the constitution and census they are officially divided into North American Indians, Inuit, and Métis, but none of these categories is homogeneous. Because the early explorers mistakenly thought they were in India and named the local inhabitants accordingly, Canadian Indians now prefer to be known by the term **First Nations**. It is part of the "politics of identity," that they prefer to use their own terminology rather than labels that were earlier imposed upon them by non-Aboriginal governments.

Terminology

The term "First Nations" came into common usage in the 1970s and can be applied in different contexts. It can refer to the Indian peoples of Canada, both status and non-status, but does not include the Métis or the Inuit. It can also replace the word "band." It can be used as a noun (e.g., "the Whitefish Lake First Nation") or as an adjective (e.g., "life in a First Nations community"). "Aboriginal" is probably the best term to include all three categories of indigenous peoples.

Before Europeans came to the continent, the Aboriginal peoples were self-sufficient and self-governing. They made decisions on the basis of consensus rather than by voting, and in many cases women (sometimes called clan mothers) played a significant role. In their close attachment to the land, they did not think in terms of private ownership; instead, they believed in the shared use of land and saw themselves as trustees of it for future generations. The fur trade, which led to the invasion by Europeans, was devastating for the Aboriginal peoples, totally disrupting their way of life and introducing new diseases that severely reduced their population.

According to the **Royal Proclamation of 1763**, the purchase or settlement of land in a large area called Indian Territory was forbidden without Crown approval, that is, without a treaty between the Crown and the Aboriginal peoples concerned. This policy was not always followed, and Europeans often occupied Indian land without a treaty. Even where treaties were signed, most observers now question the fairness of the negotiations. Later on, the Crown set aside reserves in exchange for the cession of Indian land, in addition to providing benefits such as the right to hunt and fish on unoccupied Crown land.

The 1867 Constitution Act gave jurisdiction over Indians and lands reserved for the Indians to the federal government. In 1876, Parliament passed the **Indian Act**, providing for federal government control of almost every aspect of Aboriginal life. The Indian Act aimed to assimilate Aboriginal people into the new white majority and represented a colonialist mentality—the exploitation, domination, and subjugation of a people by an imperial power. One of its provisions allowed for "enfranchisement," which encouraged Indians to give up their Indian status. Thus began the distinction between "status Indians," those registered with the federal government according to the terms of the Indian Act, and "non-status Indians," those not so registered.

Meanwhile, the treaty-making process continued apace, covering most of northern Ontario and the Prairie provinces. These treaties were designed primarily to clear Aboriginal title so that the transcontinental railway could be built and Western immigrant settlement could begin. In return for surrendering title to the lands involved, Indians received tracts of land for reserves as well as other benefits such as small annuities, schools, hunting and fishing rights, agricultural implements, cattle, and ammunition. In retrospect, almost everyone agrees that the Aboriginal peoples were taken advantage of in these negotiations, and the land given them for reserves was usually small, remote, and lacking in resources. Even worse off, however, were those Indians in much of Eastern Canada, British Columbia, and the Arctic, with whom no treaties were signed at all.

The Métis were the descendants of French or Scottish fur traders and Indian women. Found largely on the Prairies, the Métis combined nomadic hunting with farming. Not covered by the Indian Act or by treaties, they were left to the mercy of new white settlers and provincial and territorial governments. It is not surprising that Louis Riel, leader of the rebellion that led to the creation of Manitoba in 1870, took up their cause in 1884–85 in the second Riel Rebellion in Saskatchewan. After the rebellion was crushed, the Métis found themselves in an even weaker position.

In the 2006 census, some 1.7 million people, or 5.5 percent of the total Canadian population, reported Aboriginal ancestry, but only 1.2 million or 3.8 percent identified with an Aboriginal group. These latter numbers are distributed as follows: 698 000 First Nations; 390 000 Métis; and 50 000 Inuit.[1] Only about 400 000 of Canada's Aboriginals live on a reserve, while over half live in urban areas.

The Living Conditions of Aboriginal Peoples

The above statistics present only part of the picture. Of equal significance are the distressing statistics on Aboriginal poverty.[2] Many reserve families have incomes far below the poverty line and, apart from a few urban professionals, the same is true for most of those who live off-reserve. Related to this level of poverty are alarming rates of Aboriginal alcoholism and other substance abuse, violence, low educational attainment, and high unemployment. The suicide rate among Aboriginal youth is at least five times the national average, and Aboriginal Canadians are much more likely to be murdered or to die from accidents, poisoning, or violence. The incidence of tuberculosis among residents of reserves is seven times that of other Canadians, while cardiovascular disease, diabetes, pneumonia and other respiratory diseases, gastroenteritis, rheumatic fever, ear infections, meningitis, hepatitis, intestinal infections, skin diseases, and disorders of the nervous system are all common. In 2009, several first nations were badly hit by an outbreak of the H1N1 (swine flu) virus. The overall life expectancy of Aboriginal Canadians is about 6.6 years shorter than that of non-Aboriginals, mostly because of poor lifestyles and inadequate health services. Housing on reserves is often sadly deficient, being severely overcrowded and in need of repair, and contaminated drinking water is a common problem.

Much of the current deplorable state of so many Aboriginal peoples in Canada can be traced to the Indian Act and government attitudes behind it. Having lost their land, original livelihood, and culture, and being placed on unproductive reserves, many Aboriginals find themselves with little to do. The resulting unemployment, idleness, and reliance on welfare often lead them to seek solace in substance abuse. In this intoxicated state, they may resort to family and other violence, which in turn brings them into trouble with the law. Not being able to pay their fines, and being subject to discrimination at the hands of

First Nations leaders struggling to break the cycle of joblessness and poverty complain that their efforts are hamstrung by crumbling facilities such as this school in Saskatchewan.
(The Canadian Press/Troy Fleece)

the police, the courts, and other aspects of the justice system, they then go to jail, where they become even more alienated, depressed, and abused. As noted below, they constitute a disproportionately large share of prison inmates.

Aboriginal peoples have suffered from untold discrimination and indignity at every turn. In the past, the Indian Act required non-Aboriginal bureaucratic approval for almost any band decision. Aboriginal babies were frequently removed from the reserves to be adopted by non-Aboriginal parents, and until the 1970s, many Aboriginal children were forced to go to residential schools, where they were punished, sometimes to the point of assault, for speaking their Aboriginal language or engaging in Aboriginal customs. It has recently been revealed that a large number of such children actually died of tuberculosis at such schools due to poor sanitation and medical care. Aboriginal languages and cultures have been systematically discouraged, and traditional forms of government and medicine have been outlawed. Registered Indians did not even have the right to vote in federal elections until 1960, and between 1927 and 1951, the Indian Act made it an offence for them to hire a lawyer to bring a claim against Canada without government consent. Another factor contributing to the disruption of their lives is the exploitation of Aboriginal lands by mining, petroleum, forestry, and hydroelectricity companies. To a large extent, Canadian Aboriginals share such problems with indigenous peoples in other countries; indeed, an almost simultaneous realization occurred across the world to do something about their situation.

Aboriginal Political Issues Since 1970

Once Aboriginals were put down after the Riel rebellions, their struggle against public policies was virtually ignored until 1970 or so. Aboriginals were particularly vocal in their opposition to the Trudeau–Chrétien **White Paper on Indians** of 1969 that called for their complete integration into the wider Canadian society. That paper proposed the repeal of the Indian Act and treaties and discontinuation of reserves, such that Aboriginals would become ordinary, undifferentiated Canadian citizens. On the other hand, Aboriginal peoples finally sensed support in the sympathetic Berger Inquiry into the proposed Mackenzie Valley gas pipeline in 1977. By this time, their problems had become so serious that they simply could no longer be ignored, and the incidence of sit-ins, roadblocks, rallies, court cases, hunger strikes, and international protests increased. Several Aboriginal organizations came into existence, including the **Assembly of First Nations**, to spearhead the demand for change. Post-1970 Aboriginal issues are related primarily to land and to governance.

Land Issues

As noted earlier, in much of the country North American Indians signed treaties with the Crown under which they ceded the land to the government in return for protected reserves. But in Eastern Canada, British Columbia, and the North few such treaties were signed, leaving Indians and Inuit in these regions without a land base, similar to the Métis, who never legally possessed any land. This situation gives rise to the issue of **Aboriginal title**, that is, a claim to land on the basis of traditional occupancy and use rather than treaty. The existence of such Aboriginal title was first recognized in the Calder case in 1973 in connection with the Nisga'a band in British Columbia. In response, the government of Canada announced its intention to negotiate Aboriginal title. A great many Aboriginal land claims have been launched in the past 40 years. They fall into two categories: "comprehensive claims" based on Aboriginal title (i.e., traditional occupancy and use of land) that have not been dealt with by treaty or other legal means, and "specific claims" arising from misinterpretation or non-fulfillment of the terms of Indian treaties and other lawful obligations.

Such claims have moved relatively faster in the North than in the south, since north of the 60th parallel the federal government has jurisdiction over the land as well as over the Aboriginal peoples. In fact, agreement has been achieved in several comprehensive land claims in the North. Besides providing land and money, such comprehensive agreements clarify Aboriginal hunting, fishing, and trapping rights and clear obstacles to future economic development.

In the south, because the federal government has responsibility for Aboriginal peoples and Indian reserves but the provinces have jurisdiction over public lands, such claims have moved more slowly. Aboriginal peoples have generally found provincial governments even less sympathetic to their issues than Ottawa, and conflict has often developed between Indian bands and large natural resource companies as well as with non-Aboriginal people who now live on the land in question. Ottawa insists that the provinces be party to such settlements and contribute to their costs. Thus far, relatively few comprehensive land claim successes can be reported below the 60th parallel.

The first major provincial comprehensive land claim settlement was the 1975 **James Bay Agreement** between the Cree and Inuit and the government of Quebec.

In return for allowing Quebec to construct a giant hydro development project in the area, the James Bay Agreement gave the Aboriginal peoples exclusive use of 13 700 square kilometres of land and additional territory of hunting, fishing, and trapping rights, along with $225 million in cash. One terrible side-effect of the development, due to an unanticipated chemical reaction between water and rock in the flooded land, was the mercury poisoning of the fish and of the Aboriginal people who ate them. This problem, the disruption of the migration patterns of the caribou, and the growing perception that the deal may otherwise have been less generous to the Aboriginal community than originally thought, led the Cree of Quebec to reject the second, "Great Whale" phase of the James Bay project in the 1990s.

Since the province of British Columbia contains a large proportion of First Nations who have not signed treaties, the comprehensive land claims issue has been particularly significant there. Progress was slow until, in the 1997 *Delgamuukw* case, the Supreme Court of Canada established a definition of Aboriginal title and approved the admissibility of oral history evidence in making such a claim. The Nisga'a tribe in northwest British Columbia, which had been seeking recognition of their Aboriginal title for over 100 years, finally arrived at an agreement-in-principle in 1996. The treaty, which was ratified by the federal and provincial governments in 2000, provided the Nisga'a with 1 930 square kilometres of land and $190 million in cash.

Specific land claims are those resulting from dissatisfaction with treaties—especially when bands did not receive the full amount of land that the treaties promised. Since 1973, Canada has settled hundreds of specific land entitlement claims, although not always to First Nations' satisfaction, while leaving as many others under negotiation.

Another dimension of land issues concerns the activities that treaties allow Aboriginal peoples to pursue on public or Crown lands. Aboriginal treaty rights, especially hunting and fishing rights, frequently conflict with provincial law. After many court cases, some progress has been made on this front, including on the issue of logging. However, the issue of Aboriginal peoples' right to fish out of season erupted in 2001–02 in Burnt Church, New Brunswick. In the *Marshall* cases, the Supreme Court of Canada recognized a treaty right of local Aboriginals to make a moderate livelihood from the sea, but it also acknowledged that the Department of Fisheries and Oceans could regulate the fishery in the interests of conservation. The Supreme Court of Canada has also decided that the Métis have a constitutional right to hunt for food, just as other Aboriginal peoples do.

Yet another aspect of the land question arose in the most violent Aboriginal–government conflict of modern times—the crisis at Oka, Quebec, in the summer of 1990.[3] The municipal council's decision to expand a golf course on land claimed by resident Mohawks as sacred ground led to an armed standoff between Mohawk warriors and the Quebec Provincial Police, during which one police officer was killed. The Canadian Armed Forces were later brought in, and Aboriginal demonstrations took place across the country. Then, in 1995, an unarmed Aboriginal demonstrator, Dudley George, was killed by a police officer in a peaceful land claims demonstration at Ipperwash, Ontario. The judicial inquiry into the death blamed the federal and provincial governments for their actions and inaction, as well as the Ontario Provincial Police. In 2006, another incendiary dispute began in Ontario over the development of a residential subdivision on what the Six Nations at Caledonia claimed as their land.

GOVERNANCE ISSUES

Canada's Aboriginals have long demanded improvements in government health, social, and educational services, and some minor improvements have been made over the years. Many Aboriginal peoples began to feel, however, that they were too constrained by the Indian Act and that their problems required Aboriginal solutions. They were tired of living at the mercy of non-Aboriginal politicians and bureaucrats. Yet most Aboriginal peoples did not want to gut the Indian Act and existing government programs until they had something better to put in their place. Thus, shortly after their rejection of the 1969 White Paper, many Aboriginals began to argue that they should have much wider powers to govern themselves.

The specific structures of demands for **Aboriginal self-government** are not clear-cut, and an array of self-government arrangements and institutional models has been developed within the existing constitutional setup. Some advocates would accept a kind of super-municipality, and some progress has been made toward greater community-based control at the local level. Other Aboriginal peoples have more ambitious plans that would be harder to fit into the Canadian constitutional framework.

The first improvement in the constitutional recognition of Aboriginal rights occurred in the Constitution Act, 1982. Section 25 guaranteed that Charter rights would not be construed so as to interfere with any Aboriginal, treaty, or other rights or freedoms that pertained to the Aboriginal peoples of Canada, including any rights recognized by the Royal Proclamation of 1763 and any rights or freedoms "that now exist by way of land claims agreements or may be so acquired." Section 35 recognized and affirmed the existing Aboriginal and treaty rights of the Aboriginal

Manitoba MLA Elijah Harper with-
held assent for the Meech Lake Accord
because it did nothing for Canadian
Aboriginals. (Free Press/Wayne
Glowacki)

peoples of Canada. Inspired by the equality rights clause in the Charter, the Indian Act was amended to rescind the clause that had previously removed Indian status from Aboriginal women who married white men but granted such status to white women who married Indian men. Bill C-31 led to the rein-statement of some 100 000 Aboriginal women and their children, but since bands were allowed to con-trol who could actually live on the reserve, many of those reinstated in status had difficulty returning. In general, the Charter of Rights and its interpretation by the courts have been of some help to Aboriginal peoples, given their inclination to take their claims to court when dealing with uncooperative politi-cians and bureaucrats.[4]

THE MEECH LAKE AND CHARLOTTETOWN ACCORDS

After mid-1980s constitutional talks on Aboriginal self-government broke down, Canadian Aboriginal peoples were understandably opposed to the 1987 Meech Lake Accord, which addressed Quebec's constitutional demands but completely overlooked their own. Even supporters of the accord empathized with Elijah Harper when he blocked it in the Manitoba legislature in 1990. This action, together with the Oka affair, precipitated a dramatic breakthrough in constitutional concern with Aboriginal issues and in the participation of Aboriginal leaders in consti-tutional negotiations. Aboriginal leaders were given the same status as premiers in the talks leading up to the 1992 Charlottetown Accord, and that document responded to Aboriginal concerns in a more extensive and satisfactory way than it did the demands of Quebec.

The Charlottetown Accord would have recognized the inherent right of Aboriginal peoples to self-government within Canada and would have regarded such Aboriginal governments as a third order of government in Canada, analo-gous to provinces. The document also provided for self-government agreements to be negotiated among the three levels of government. Federal and provincial laws would remain in place until superseded by Aboriginal laws, but the latter would have to be consistent with the preservation of peace, order, and good government in Canada. As mentioned in Chapter 3, the Charlottetown Accord was turned down in a national referendum, but the Aboriginal section of the accord was not primarily to blame.

Canada has made few constitutional changes since 1992, and activity in the area of Aboriginal governance has been limited to the legislative and administrative levels, such as delegating federal or provincial government powers to First Nations communities, and to self-government agreements. In 1995, the Chrétien government declared that in its view the inherent right to Aboriginal self-government was already incorporated in section 35 of the Constitution Act, 1982. In consequence, a ministerial statement formally launched a negotiating process to implement that right, with arrangements varying from one group to another.

RECENT DEVELOPMENTS IN ABORIGINAL ISSUES

Much hope for the solution of Aboriginal problems was placed in the Royal Commission on Aboriginal Peoples, appointed in 1991 and reporting in 1996. The commission endorsed Aboriginal self-government in its widest sense and the basic separation of Aboriginal and non-Aboriginal societies. Among other things, it proposed an independent lands and treaties tribunal, an Aboriginal development bank, an action plan on health and social conditions, and an Aboriginal-controlled education system. Although these recommendations were not immediately implemented, Aboriginals came to control over 80 percent of the Department of Indian Affairs' program funding, and Aboriginal authorities increasingly deliver education, language and culture, police, health care, social, housing, and adoption and child welfare services. The Chrétien government also issued a Statement of Reconciliation apologizing for past wrongs, especially the horrors of the residential school system.

Comprehensive land claims and self-government agreements are now often negotiated simultaneously, and two prominent examples should be mentioned. A plebiscite in 1992 ratified the division of the Northwest Territories, and a land claim in the eastern Arctic was finalized in 1993. As a result, in 1999 the territory of **Nunavut** was created and separated from the Northwest Territories. It has all the governmental institutions associated with a province or territory; however, it represents a kind of Aboriginal self-government in the sense that the population is almost completely composed of Inuit. Like the Northwest Territories, Nunavut's legislature operates on a consensual basis without political parties. The previously mentioned **Nisga'a Treaty** incorporated self-government powers somewhat beyond those of municipalities and was secured by federal–provincial–Aboriginal agreement. It includes sections on forestry, mining, wildlife and the environment, the administration of justice, finance, and taxation (including Aboriginal peoples' surrender of their tax-exempt status).[5] Other recent comprehensive claim/self-government agreements south of the 60th parallel were mainly located in Labrador, Quebec, and British Columbia.

When Paul Martin took over as prime minister in 2003, he declared Aboriginal issues to be a high priority for his government, and its main accomplishment was the Kelowna Accord of 2005. Martin announced that Ottawa would contribute some $5 billion over five years in a dedicated effort to closing the gap in the quality of life between Aboriginal peoples and other Canadians, with particular reference to health, education, housing, and economic development. Provincial premiers around the table promised their own contributions.

The Harper government distanced itself from the Kelowna agreement, however, much to the annoyance of premiers and Aboriginals. On the other hand, Harper finalized the compensation package relating to residential schools that Martin had developed, and made a full official and historic apology in the House of Commons in June 2008. Harper also introduced a new system to address the backlog in the settlement of specific land claims, but contaminated water on reserves and Aboriginal fishing rights continued to be serious issues.

While large numbers of Aboriginal groups are involved in various negotiations and progress is being made on many fronts—such as land claims settlements, self-government agreements, and Aboriginal involvement in new northern mining developments—fundamental problems remain. Many of these are on reserves, as noted, but as difficult as it will be to deal with them, attention must also be directed at the majority of Aboriginals who now live in urban areas and who often constitute part of the inner-city poor. Aboriginal women are concerned about issues of day-to-day survival in a harsh urban environment, such as housing, education, and the future of their children. Given the high Aboriginal birthrate, such problems are likely to assume increasing importance in the future.[6]

ABORIGINAL JUSTICE

Aboriginal peoples constitute only about four or five percent of the Canadian population but comprise between 15 and 20 percent of the inmates in Canadian correctional institutions. Among several tragic cases was that of Donald Marshall, a Nova Scotia Micmac who was imprisoned for over ten years for a murder he did not commit. These cases, and the

Shawn A-in-chut Atleo, newly elected National Chief of the Assembly of First Nations, 2009. (The Canadian Press/Jeff McIntosh)

inquiries they precipitated, illustrate the misunderstanding, prejudice, harassment, abuse, and brutality inflicted on Aboriginal people by police, courts, and jails. At the same time, crimes *against* Aboriginals are often not taken seriously. Many have called for a parallel Aboriginal justice system in which Aboriginal convictions and sentences would be based on Aboriginal values and community traditions.

While governments have generally ruled out a wholesale parallel Aboriginal justice system, several provinces have allowed experimental judicial processes involving Aboriginal input. More Aboriginal peoples have been hired as police officers, some reserves have their own Aboriginal police force, and a few even maintain their own correctional facilities. Judges dealing with Aboriginal defendants increasingly follow Aboriginal traditions such as sentencing circles or consulting with elders in imposing sentences that can involve restitution or banishment. With the high rate of Aboriginal incarceration in mind, Parliament amended the Criminal Code in 1995 to read: "All available sanctions other than imprisonment … should be considered for all offenders, with particular attention to the circumstances of Aboriginal offenders."

Ethnocultural Minorities

A third aspect of ethnic cleavage and identity involving other ethnocultural minorities and multiculturalism increasingly vies with the French–English and Aboriginal questions on the political agenda. The 2006 census showed the presence of people of over 200 different ethnic origins in Canada, the largest of which are listed in Table 4.1. The three principal issues in this area are immigration policy, preserving and promoting the identity of ethnocultural minorities (or multiculturalism), and ensuring that individuals belonging to such groups are treated equitably under the law and in society. On the other hand, when minority ethnocultural or religious traditions are at odds with Canadian law, the question sometimes arises of how far they should be accommodated, leading to problems of integration and inclusiveness.

Canadian Immigration Patterns

Beyond the French and the British, the first dramatic surge of immigrants arrived in Ontario and the Prairies during the 1880s. It included Danes, Dutch, Icelanders, Poles, Ukrainians, Finns, Norwegians, and Swedes. In British Columbia, on the

TABLE 4.1 LARGEST ETHNIC GROUPS IN CANADA, 2006 CENSUS (SINGLE AND MULTIPLE RESPONSES)

Canadian	10 066 290	Chinese	1 346 510
English	6 570 015	North American Indian	1 253 615
French	4 941 210	Ukrainian	1 209 085
Scottish	4 719 210	Dutch	1 035 965
Irish	4 354 155	Polish	984 565
German	3 179 425	East Indian	962 665
Italian	1 445 335	Russian	500 600

Source: Adapted from Statistics Canada, Ethnocultural Portrait of Canada Highlights Tables, 2006 Census 562-XWE2006002 Census year 2006. Released April 2, 2008.

other hand, Asians were a leading group: between 1881 and 1884, nearly 16 000 Chinese were brought in as contract labourers to work on the Canadian Pacific Railway. Nova Scotia and Ontario also became home to a substantial number of blacks, most of whom were escaping from slavery in the United States.

An even larger number and variety of immigrants arrived between 1903 and 1914, and the prosperous 1920s was another active decade on the immigration front. After the Second World War, a further huge wave of immigrants came to Canada, largely from southern Europe, supplemented by postwar refugees from around the world. The numbers have swelled further in the past 30 years.

Overall, Britain was the leading source of immigrants between 1900 and 1965. During that period, immigration policy favoured British, American, and European newcomers, since they were considered well educated and skilled and, being predominantly Caucasian, better able to assimilate. After the Immigration Act was significantly amended in 1967, however, Canadian immigration patterns changed radically, as Figure 4.1 shows. In 1957, over 90 percent of immigrants were from Britain or continental Europe, a figure that fell to about 15 percent by 2007. In contrast, Asian immigrants constituted less than two percent of the total in 1957, increasing to about 50 percent in recent years. Table 4.2 lists the top ten source countries in 2008.

As a result of this immigration pattern, the term **visible minorities** came into usage. Members of visible minorities are defined in the Employment Equity Act as "persons, other than Aboriginal peoples, who are non-Caucasian in race or non-white in colour." According to the 2006 census, they now constitute 16.2 percent of the Canadian population—that is, over five million people. Well over

Figure 4.1   Principal Sources of Immigrants to Canada in Selected Years (Percentages)

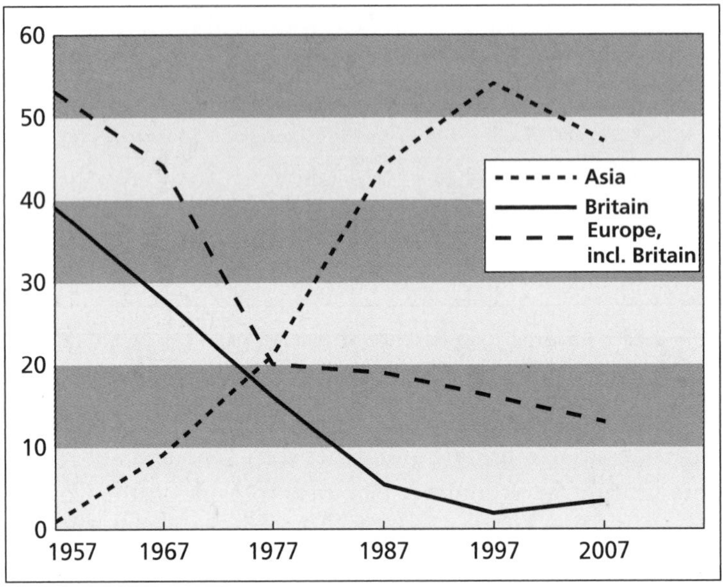

Legend:
- .... Asia
- —— Britain
- — — Europe, incl. Britain

(X-axis years: 1957, 1967, 1977, 1987, 1997, 2007; Y-axis: 0 to 60)

Source: Citizenship and Immigration Canada, Facts and Figures, 2007, available at http://www.cic.gc.ca/english/pdf/pub/facts/2007.pdf. Calculations by author (retrieved March 10, 2009). Adapted and reproduced with the permission of the Minister of Public Works and Government Services Canada, 2010.

three-quarters of the members of visible minorities in Canada reside in the six largest cities, especially Toronto, Vancouver, and Montreal. Indeed, over 43 percent of the residents of Toronto and Vancouver belong to visible minorities. Some public policies, such as employment equity, apply only to visible minorities, while others, such as multiculturalism, include both visible and "invisible" ethnic groups.

In any year, immigrants can be divided into several categories. Economic immigrants are those admitted on the basis of the points they earn (occupational and language skills, etc.) or those who have a large net worth (business-class immigrants). Family-class immigrants, on the other hand, are those related to persons already residing here; most of the remainder are refugees.

Multiculturalism, Equity, and Inclusiveness

After the revision of the Immigration Act in 1967, the composition of the Canadian population changed significantly. Moreover, as their numbers grew, ethnocultural minorities became more self-confident in their distinctive identities, leading them

TABLE 4.2 TOP TEN SOURCE COUNTRIES FOR PERMANENT RESIDENT IMMIGRATION TO
         CANADA, 2008

Country	Number of Immigrants
China	29 336
India	24 549
Philippines	23 724
United States	11 216
United Kingdom	9 243
Pakistan	8 052
Korea	7 245
France	6 384
Iran	6 010
Colombia	4 995

Source: Citizenship and Immigration Canada, "Facts and Figures 2008: Immigration Overview: Permanent and Temporary
Residents," http://www.cic.gc.ca/english/resources/statisticsfacts2008/permanent/10.asp, retrieved April 22, 2010. Adapted and
reproduced with the permission of the Minister of Public Works and Government Services Canada, 2010.

to engage in the "politics of recognition" with more leverage to push for policy
changes in areas where they encountered indifference or discrimination.

Due largely to pressure from Ukrainian Canadians, the 1963 Royal Commission
on Bilingualism and Biculturalism was ultimately asked to examine the contribution made by other ethnocultural groups to the cultural enrichment of Canada and
the measures that should be taken to safeguard that contribution. While focus-
ing primarily on the English and the French, the commission recommended that
increased government attention be given to other groups, including public funding
in certain areas. With this encouragement, such ethnocultural minorities began to
demand public financial assistance in addition to verbal or moral support, and the
term "multiculturalism" came into use.

In 1971 the Trudeau government announced a new policy of multiculturalism
within a bilingual framework. **Multiculturalism** is the official recognition of the
diverse cultures in a plural society; it involves encouraging immigrants to retain
and foster their linguistic heritages and ethnic cultures instead of abandoning
them. The government argued that the Canadian identity would not be under-
mined by multiculturalism; on the contrary, cultural pluralism was the very essence

of that identity. Multiculturalism is based on the idea that having a population of diverse origins makes Canada a more interesting place to live. By providing links to virtually every other country in the world, such a population also enhances Canada's international image and influence.

Basic Objectives of Multiculturalism Policy

- To assist cultural groups in retaining and fostering their identity
- To assist cultural groups in overcoming barriers to their full participation in Canadian society
- To promote creative exchanges among all Canadian cultural groups
- To assist immigrants in acquiring at least one official language

---

The policy of multiculturalism legitimized demands for many other changes both in terms of promoting ethnocultural identities and removing barriers to equity. A federal multiculturalism ministry emerged in the 1970s, and the Canadian Human Rights Commission was created in 1978 to complement equivalent bodies at the provincial level. Another advance for multiculturalism was the 1982 Charter of Rights and Freedoms, which provided constitutional protection against discrimination by federal and provincial governments in the equality rights clause, section 15. Moreover, the Charter endorsed affirmative action programs in order to overcome past discrimination. Under pressure from various ethnocultural groups, another section was added to the effect that the Charter would be interpreted "in a manner consistent with the preservation and enhancement of the multicultural heritage of Canadians" (section 27). In 1988, the Mulroney government passed a new Canadian Multiculturalism Act.

On a different front, the 1986 federal Employment Equity Act designated visible minorities—along with women, people with disabilities, and Aboriginal peoples—as groups that could benefit from affirmative action programs with respect to hiring in the public service. While some group leaders criticized the lack of specific goals and timetables in the legislation, those not included complained about reverse discrimination. The act was strengthened in 1995, but removing legal barriers to equity and/or giving visible minorities an occasional boost does not ensure that they will be free from discrimination in the daily interactions of life. Besides instances of personal abuse, they still encounter situations in which their skills are underused and not fairly remunerated, and many live in poverty.

In 1988, the Mulroney government also took action to compensate Japanese Canadians for their mistreatment during the Second World War. Unjustly suspected of being loyal to Japan, Canadian citizens of Japanese background were uprooted from the west coast, interned in "relocation centres," and had their property confiscated. The Japanese Redress Agreement provided $21 000 for each of the surviving internees.

Recent Developments in Multiculturalism and Immigration

If the responses to demands from the multicultural community were largely positive in the 1970s and 1980s, such was not entirely the case in the 1990s. Opposition surfaced toward immigration in general and visible minority immigration in particular, as well as to multiculturalism, employment equity, and other policies and practices.[7]

Such opposition was partly in response to the recession of the early 1990s and the continuing high unemployment rate afterwards. Whatever the real merits of immigration in economic terms, ordinary voters saw recent immigrants in jobs that they felt would otherwise have gone to Canadian residents of longer duration. As for the source of immigrants, while the level of Canadian acceptance and tolerance of non-traditional immigrants is high, it is not unlimited. The Reform Party was the first to break rank with an all-party consensus on this issue and called for a sizable cut in annual immigration levels, with a greater emphasis on skills. For a time, even the pro-immigration Chrétien government responded to these pressures, such as charging new immigrants a $975 right-of-landing fee.

The policy of multiculturalism has been criticized even by members of the multicultural community, such as writer Neil Bissoondath, who maintains that official multiculturalism is divisive, ghettoizes visible minorities, fosters racial animosity, and detracts from national unity.[8] Critics also argue that it is not appropriate for the government to be fostering the maintenance of foreign traditions while starving Canadian cultural institutions; they say that the money might be better spent teaching immigrants about basic Canadian values.

Less opposition to visible minorities was evident at the beginning of the new century, even as the number of visible minorities increased. This could have been the result of a more prosperous economy and/or the growing recognition that immigration was essential to economic growth. The number of MPs from visible minorities continues to increase, and the Conservative party is making gains in its appeal to recent immigrants, who used to give the bulk of their support to the Liberals. The wearing of turbans and carrying of kirpans by Sikh Canadians has

Kindergarten children in Toronto represent the changing face of urban Canadian schools. (The Canadian Press/Frank Gunn)

been authorized by the Supreme Court, the number of minority-language news-papers and radio and television stations is increasing, and the Harper government halved the immigrant landing fee. Although parts of the country are desperate for certain kinds of workers, it is never simple to gear immigration to the specific needs of the economy, and some well-educated immigrants continue to encounter difficulty in obtaining recognition of their professional credentials. One promis-ing approach to these problems has been to give the provinces a larger role in the immigration process.

After the Japanese Redress Agreement, other groups demanded that they be similarly compensated for wartime discrimination in Canada—Ukrainian Canadians in the First World War and Italian Canadians in the Second. Recent governments have signed redress agreements with them, as well as with Chinese immigrants who had to pay a head tax between 1885 and 1923.

On the other hand, because of the heightened concern about terrorism after the events of September 11, 2001, the government increased security measures at Canada's borders. Indeed, after 9/11, many Canadian Muslims and Arabs were victims of a backlash. Some innocents, such as Maher Arar, suffered grievously at the hands of U.S. authorities, while a few Islamic extremists have been convicted as terrorist suspects.

More generally, many observers are worried about the integration of such large numbers of visible immigrants into Canadian society. On one side are the problems of immigrant poverty, unemployment and underemployment, and discrimination. On the other side are the concerns of long-time residents that newcomers should adapt to Canadian values and practices rather than try to change them. The niqab worn by a small proportion of Muslim women has been of particular concern in Quebec. Racial tensions have arisen in some larger cities, including ethnic-based gangs, and some immigrants are excessively involved in homeland politics. It will take more effort on all sides to promote social cohesion and social inclusiveness and to avoid the social disruption caused by marginalized immigrant communities.

Gender

Evolution of Women's Rights to 1970

Men and male-oriented issues virtually monopolized Canadian politics before 1900. In those early years, when all women were expected to marry and become chattels of their husbands, they first had to fight for educational and occupational rights, such as admission to universities and to the medical and legal professions. Women demanded the right to make contracts and to own property, and they increasingly began to work in factories and offices and to become teachers and nurses, while others continued to make major contributions on the farm. About 1900, farm women in particular became active in reform organizations of many kinds, including those that pressed for the establishment of new public health facilities, better housing, improved working conditions for women and children, and the prohibition of alcohol.

As influential as women were in promoting these causes, many began to feel that their impact would always be limited until they could vote. Thus, in what is sometimes called the "first wave" of the women's movement, women demanded the franchise or vote. After the outbreak of the First World War, proponents of female suffrage had an additional argument: women should be rewarded for their contribution to the war effort. Thus, Manitoba, Alberta, and Saskatchewan, containing some of the most articulate women of the day, pioneered the female franchise in 1916; Ontario and British Columbia joined them in 1917; and all the other provinces except Quebec followed shortly afterward.

At the federal level, the Borden government deliberately manipulated the franchise for the 1917 election, in part by giving the vote to women in the armed services (mostly nurses) and to close relatives of soldiers fighting abroad—women who would likely support the war effort. A year later, the vote was extended to all women (except those excluded for ethnic reasons, such as Aboriginals and Asians); they had their first chance to exercise this new right in the 1921 election.

Two women were elected to the Alberta legislature in 1917, and Agnes Macphail became the first woman elected to the House of Commons in 1921. She served alone until 1935, when a second woman was elected. Macphail stayed on until 1940 and then, in 1943, became the first woman elected to the Ontario legislature. Vigorous and articulate, she promoted radical and progressive causes of many kinds but could do only so much by herself to advance women's issues in such an entrenched male bastion.

It was not until 1940 that Quebec women were enfranchised in provincial elections. Moreover, the legal status of a married woman under the Quebec Civil Code was such that until 1955 she could not seek a separation on grounds of adultery by her husband, and until 1964 she had no right to carry on a trade without her husband's consent.

The number of women who won seats in the House of Commons was minuscule right up to 1970, and many of those elected were the widows or daughters of male members of Parliament. Female political participation was inhibited by many factors. First, people were traditionally socialized into the view that politics was a masculine pursuit and that women should remain in the home. Second, most women were constrained by the responsibilities of homemaking and child-rearing. The long hours and unpredictable schedules of politicians conflicted with most women's family commitments, which prevented them from being away from home for any length of time. Third, homemaking roles had little prestige and prevented women from accumulating the money, contacts, and experience that political careers usually require. Fourth, political parties discouraged female candidacies, and when consciousness of the lack of female candidates increased, parties frequently nominated them as sacrificial lambs against a strong male incumbent.

Until the late 1920s, no women had been appointed to the other house of Parliament, the Senate. When an enterprising group of Western women took this issue to court, the Supreme Court of Canada ruled that women were not "qualified persons" within the meaning of section 24 of the 1867 Constitution Act and were therefore ineligible to sit in the Senate. This decision was appealed to the

Time Line
Milestones in Women's Rights

1916	Women obtain vote in three provinces
1917/18	Women obtain vote in federal elections and in most other provinces
1921	First woman MP
1929	Persons case
1940	Women obtain vote in Quebec provincial elections
1957	First woman federal Cabinet minister
1967–70	Royal Commission on Status of Women
1982	First woman on the Supreme Court
1989	First woman federal party leader
1993	First woman prime minister

Judicial Committee of the Privy Council, which in the 1929 *Persons* case overruled the Supreme Court and declared that women were indeed "persons." After the case was decided, Prime Minister Mackenzie King immediately appointed Cairine Wilson to the Senate, but the second woman was not appointed until 1935, and 18 years would pass before three more received the call.

It was not until 1957 that the first woman, Ellen Fairclough, was appointed to the federal Cabinet; she was followed by Judy LaMarsh in 1963. The advance of women to the Cabinet at the provincial level was generally even slower. Nevertheless, gradual improvements continued to be made in federal and provincial

In the Words of the Court
The Judicial Committee of the Privy Council on the 'Persons Case'

"The exclusion of women from all public offices is a relic of days more barbarous than ours.… [T]heir Lordships have come to the conclusion that the word 'persons' in s. 24 includes members both of the male and female sex."

Source: Henrietta Muir Edwards v. Attorney-General for Canada, [1929] (better known as the Persons case), quoted in Richard A. Olmsted, Decisions of the Judicial Committee of the Privy Council, vol. 2 (Ottawa: Queen's Printer, 1954).

legislation and programs of benefit to women. The federal Family Allowances Act of 1944, for example, provided a small monthly payment to each Canadian mother to help care for her children and often represented the only independent income the woman possessed. In 1952, Ontario passed the first equal pay legislation, to be followed by federal legislation two years later. The birth control pill became available about 1960, amendments to the Criminal Code in 1969 made it legal to advertise birth control devices, and a new Divorce Act made it easier to get out of an unfulfilling marriage.

The Women's Movement Since 1970

By 1970, attitudes had changed sufficiently that it was possible to speak of a women's movement, and the word "feminist" became common. In their most general sense, such terms are used to apply to those who seek to establish complete gender equality, to free men and women from restrictive gender roles, and to end any semblance of the subordination of women. Women were central to the concept of the "politics of identity" from this point onward.

This "second wave" of the women's movement coincided with the Royal Commission on the Status of Women, appointed in 1967 and reporting in 1970. That report "provided a solid statistical base and a framework for most of the feminist action that followed during the 1970s"[9] and made 167 recommendations. Since that time, gender issues have become an important, daily factor in Canadian politics. Most governments now designate a minister to be responsible for women's issues.

Political Representation

In the post-1970 era, women's participation in politics and government increased substantially. Table 4.3 charts this progress in terms of women elected to the House of Commons. Many of the factors mentioned above that inhibited women from becoming politicians before 1970 are still present, although in recent years most parties have created special funds (and sometimes quotas or targets) to support female candidates. The 2008 election was contested by 445 women or 27 percent of all candidates, and 69 women were elected, constituting 22.4 percent of all MPs.

At the Cabinet level, one or two token female ministers were clearly insufficient by the 1980s, and Brian Mulroney made the jump to six women to his 1984 Cabinet. It was also in the post-1970 period that Canada finally saw women elected as political party leaders. Alexa McDonough (NDP, Nova Scotia) led the way in

TABLE 4.3 REPRESENTATION OF WOMEN IN THE HOUSE OF COMMONS, 1921–2008

Election	Number	Election	Number	Election	Number
1921	1	1957	2	1980	14
1925	1	1958	2	1984	27
1926	1	1962	5	1988	39
1930	1	1963	4	1993	53
1935	2	1965	4	1997	62
1940	1	1968	1	2000	62
1945	1	1972	5	2004	65
1949	0	1974	9	2006	64
1953	4	1979	10	2008	69

Source: Women—Federal Political Representation, 1867 to Date, http://www2.parl.gc.ca/Parlinfo/compilations/parliament. Reproduced with the permission of the Library of Parliament, 2010. ParaliWomenRepresentation.aspx, retrieved 3 April, 2010.

1980, to be followed by a host of others at the provincial level. Audrey McLaughlin made history when she was elected leader of the federal New Democratic Party in 1989, the first woman to lead a major national party. McDonough moved from Nova Scotia to succeed her as federal NDP leader in 1995. Two female party leaders have become provincial premiers and Kim Campbell served briefly as prime minister. Women have evidently had more success as political candidates, however, than as party leaders.

Jeanne Sauvé was the first female Speaker of the House of Commons and first female governor general. Bertha Wilson became the first woman to sit on the Supreme Court of Canada in 1982. Women judges have been appointed at an ever-increasing rate in other courts, and about 25 percent of federally appointed judges are now women. In 2000, Beverley McLachlin became the first female chief justice of Canada, and after 2004, four of nine Supreme Court judges were women.

Within the federal bureaucracy, the first women joined the RCMP in 1974, and the first female deputy minister was appointed in 1975. Women gradually became eligible for full combat roles in the armed forces, and the first female general was named in 1988. In 1993, the first woman was appointed to the top public service position in Ottawa, Clerk of the Privy Council and Secretary to the Cabinet.

EMPLOYMENT ISSUES

Since the majority of women of working age are now in the labour force—of which women constitute about 47 percent—one major feminist concern is employment.[10] Women have traditionally been discriminated against in pay, underrepresented in managerial positions, and discouraged from undertaking nontraditional occupations. Women demanded "equal pay for work of equal value," or **pay equity**, and most Canadian governments now have pay equity laws. While there has been considerable improvement in the situation, women's full-time earnings seem to have plateaued at about 70 percent of men's.

Prime Minister Kim Campbell answers questions at a news conference in Ottawa. (The Canadian Press/Chuck Mitchell)

Beyond pay equity is the broader subject of **employment equity**, that is, the elimination of discrimination in hiring and promoting women. Employment equity is sometimes combined with **affirmative action** programs to give women preference in order to make up for past inequities. In 1983, affirmative action with respect to the hiring of women was made mandatory in all federal government departments and the report of the 1984 Commission of Inquiry on Equity in Employment became the foundation of the 1986 Employment Equity Act. The act extended employment equity requirements to all Crown corporations, all federally regulated companies with over 100 employees, and other large companies in receipt of major government contracts. Nevertheless, while women now constitute 55 percent of the federal government workforce, they occupy only 40 percent of executive-level jobs. Ontario passed an even more extensive Employment Equity Act in 1993, which was quickly repealed by the Conservative government of Mike Harris, but Ottawa strengthened its legislation in 1995.

The area in which women are most severely underrepresented is at the top of private corporations. In 2008, of Canada's top 500 companies, only 30 were led by women, most notably Heather Reisman at Chapters-Indigo Books.

For those women who choose to have children as well as seek employment outside the home, the issue of child care is often a serious problem. Daycare for

What Do You Think?

How do you feel about employment equity and affirmative action laws in support of women, Aboriginal peoples, visible minorities, and people with disabilities? Are they necessary to combat systemic discrimination or do they constitute reverse discrimination? Have they ever benefited or disadvantaged you?

children of such parents, especially children of single mothers, remains one of the major unresolved "women's issues" of the day. Some single mothers or two-parent families are happy to rely on relatives, friends, or unlicensed facilities, but those seeking licensed daycare spaces are often out of luck. Both PC and Liberal governments reneged on promises of a national daycare program, leaving the provinces to fund such programs on their own. The Martin government negotiated individualized childcare agreements with each province and territory to provide significant funding in this field, but the Harper Conservatives cancelled the deals and began to pay families $1 200 annually per child and let them find their own solutions. Statistics also show that regardless of their work outside the home, women perform most of the unpaid work, whether in caregiving, housework, or volunteer services.[11]

LEGAL, REPRODUCTIVE, SEXUAL, AND VIOLENCE ISSUES

As the 1982 Charter of Rights and Freedoms emerged from federal–provincial negotiation, gender equality was lumped into equality rights along with such other factors as race, religion, and age, which governments would be allowed to override with the notwithstanding clause. Such treatment at the hands of 11 male first ministers galvanized the women's movement as never before; as a result of its tremendous pressure, section 28 was added to the final document to give gender equality a place of its own, protected from the notwithstanding clause.[12]

There followed a series of feminist challenges to laws that women believed discriminated against them. The government itself encouraged such legal activity with the Court Challenges Program, under which it subsidized the Legal Education and Action Fund (LEAF) in making such challenges. Women have not won every such case, but among their victories was the right to maternity leave under the Employment Insurance Act, removal of gender discrimination in private disability plans, and a tightening up of discriminatory physical requirements for employment.

One of the main feminist rallying cries of the post-1970 period is that women must be able to control what happens to their own bodies. Many women's organizations supported Dr. Henry Morgentaler in his long fight to reform the Criminal Code's provisions on abortion.[13] The Supreme Court of Canada ruled in 1988 that the abortion law was unconstitutional, leaving Canada with no federal law restricting abortion. Even so, access to abortion varies widely across the country. Prostitution and pornography have also been subject to judicial decision, while sexual stereotyping, sexual harassment, and physical and sexual assault are other major issues of concern to women. Women gained a partial victory in "rape-shield" sexual assault cases, when questions to defendants about past sexual history were somewhat restricted and when the Supreme Court ruled that "no means no." The Harper government cancelled the Court Challenges Program in 2006, making it more difficult to finance such cases in the future.

The Feminization of Poverty

Chapter 2 revealed that there is a relatively high incidence of poverty among women. About 32 percent of sole-support mothers raise their children below the poverty line, and many others are just above it. With or without a male partner, large numbers of women with preschool children find it necessary to work outside the home to support themselves and their families.[14] This has continued to be the case even after the Canada Child Tax Credit was added to the income tax system to replace the Family Allowance for lower-income families. To decrease the incidence of women living in poverty, measures such as pay equity, employment equity, higher minimum wages, increased unionization, and improved job training and literacy programs will be required. Unfortunately, the leading feminist advocacy group in the country, the National Action Committee on the Status of Women, has disintegrated.

Gay and Lesbian Issues

A variety of issues related to homosexuality have arisen in recent years, and these also figure prominently on today's

Hemant Morparia/Artizans.com

political agenda. In most cases, politicians are reluctant to deal with demands coming from the gay, lesbian, bisexual, and transgendered communities, leaving such groups to take their concerns directly to the courts.[15]

One of these groups' first demands was for protection in human rights codes from individual discrimination. Somewhat surprisingly, the breakthrough came in Quebec when the Parti Québécois first formed the government. When the Charter of Rights and Freedoms was adopted in 1982, section 15 prohibited discrimination by government or in law on the basis of sex, but **sexual orientation** was not explicitly included. In the 1995 *Egan* case, however, the Supreme Court of Canada unanimously added sexual orientation to the equality rights clause, although it was still subject to reasonable limits. By the late 1990s, whether by legislation or court action (as in the *Vriend* case in Alberta), sexual orientation had been added to all the human rights codes in Canada. Such federal and provincial legislation primarily protects homosexuals from discrimination in the private sector. The Criminal Code was also amended in 2004 to ban the incitement of hatred against gays and lesbians.

The next phase of the battle for equality in this area centred on gay and lesbian couples. In two cases from Ontario, the courts recognized that same-sex couples should be treated in the same way as opposite-sex couples in pension benefits after death and in financial support after separation. In the latter *M. v. H.* case, the Supreme Court advised Ontario to amend all laws that continued to treat same-sex couples differently from others. Afterwards, both federal and provincial governments passed omnibus legislation to make such amendments across the board. In some cases, however, they continued to define "marriage" as a union between a man and a woman and made a distinction between a "same-sex partner" and a "spouse." A number of same-sex couples challenged such distinctions, as well as restrictions on adoption. Through a series of decisions at the provincial appeal court level, both same-sex adoption and same-sex marriage were authorized on the ground that anything less would violate equality rights.

The Chrétien government chose not to appeal controversial provincial court decisions approving same-sex marriage. Instead, it sent a reference case to the Supreme Court of Canada on this issue, which approved proposed legislation on the subject in 2004. Parliament passed a slightly amended law in 2005 and a large majority voted against reopening the issue in 2006. Regardless of the Constitution and the law, many employers in both the public and private sectors have extended employee benefits (such as health, dental, and retirement plans) to same-sex couples.

SUMMARY

This chapter discussed the political significance of issues relating to Aboriginal peoples, ethnocultural minorities, and gender, all of which have become much more prominent in Canada since about 1970. It established that the quality of Aboriginal life was generally much better before the arrival of Europeans on the continent. The discussion then turned to current Aboriginal demands, primarily involving land claims and demands for more autonomy in daily affairs, and the responses thereto since 1970. The second part of the chapter dealt with ethnocultural groups in Canada other than British, French, or Aboriginal. It tracked their arrival and their changing composition. The chapter then discussed the adoption of a policy of multiculturalism and of related policies designed to remove discrimination and to enhance equality and inclusiveness. It also noted divergent views on the subjects of multiculturalism and immigration. The third part of the chapter traced the evolution of women's political participation in Canada. It also noted the factors that have contributed to the lower level of female, as compared to male, involvement, but it showed that issues of primary interest to women are now firmly on the political agenda. The chapter concluded with the relatively new political issues relating to the gay and lesbian communities, including removal of discrimination in such areas as employment and marriage.

DISCUSSION QUESTIONS

1. To what extent should Aboriginal peoples in Canada be able to govern themselves?
2. To what extent should we require immigrants to conform to established Canadian values and practices?
3. What are the most significant current public policy issues of interest to women?
4. How far should we go in public or private policies recognizing same-sex relationships?

KEY TERMS

Aboriginal self-government A demand made by Aboriginal groups that they be able to govern themselves.

Aboriginal title The Aboriginal claim to land based on traditional occupancy and use rather than treaty.

Affirmative action A law or program that provides preference in the hiring or promotion process to individuals with certain characteristics.

Assembly of First Nations The largest interest group representing status and non-status Indians (who now prefer to be called First Nations peoples).

Employment equity A policy that seeks to guarantee complete fairness in hiring, promotion, or remuneration, regardless of gender, ethnicity, or disability.

Equality rights A category of rights in the Charter of Rights and Freedoms that prohibits governments from discriminating against certain categories of people.

First Nations A term that came into common usage in the 1970s that can refer to the Indian peoples of Canada, both status and non-status, or that can replace the word "band."

Indian Act The act that governed almost all aspects of Aboriginal life in Canada after the 1870s, giving extensive authority to government bureaucrats and minimal discretion to Native people themselves.

James Bay Agreement The 1975 deal signed by the government of Quebec and its northern Aboriginal residents that gave the latter land, cash, and hunting rights in return for surrendering land for the James Bay hydroelectric project.

Multiculturalism A policy of encouraging ethnic and cultural groups to maintain their customs and traditions, often with public financial assistance.

Nisga'a Treaty The 2000 treaty signed by the Nisga'a First Nation and the governments of Canada and British Columbia that incorporated a land claim settlement and powers of self-government; it is considered the first modern-day Aboriginal treaty.

Nunavut The eastern half of the Northwest Territories that was established as a separate, Inuit territory in 1999.

Pay equity An element of employment equity programs designed to ensure that all employees are paid equally for work of equal value and are not discriminated against on the basis of gender or other factors.

Royal Proclamation of 1763 The British policy enunciated after conquering Quebec that in a large area called Indian Territory forbade the purchase or settlement of land without a treaty between the Crown and the Indian peoples concerned.

Sexual orientation One's sexual preference, usually either heterosexual or homosexual. It now constitutes a ground on which discrimination is prohibited.

Treaty rights Aboriginal rights based on treaties signed with the Crown.

Visible minorities Members of ethnic groups, other than Aboriginal peoples, whose skin colour is not white.

White Paper on Indians The 1969 Trudeau–Chrétien policy proposal to do away with the Indian Act and treaties and to fully integrate Aboriginal peoples into Canadian society.

Women's movement The collection of women's groups that mushroomed across the country, starting around 1970, demanding complete equality for women.

FURTHER READING

Aboriginal Peoples

Borrows, John. *Canada's Indigenous Constitution*. Toronto: University of Toronto Press, 2010.

Cairns, Alan C. *First Nations and the Canadian State: In Search of Coexistence*. Montreal: McGill-Queen's University Press, 2005.

Frideres, James S. and René Gadacz. *Aboriginal Peoples in Canada*, 8th ed. Toronto: Pearson Education Canada, 2008.

Irlbacher-Fox, Stephanie. *Finding Dahshaa: Self-Government, Social Suffering, and Aboriginal Policy in Canada*. Vancouver: UBC Press, 2009.

Timpson, Annis May, ed. *First Nations, First Thoughts*. Vancouver: UBC Press, 2009.

Warry, Wayne. *Ending Denial: Understanding Aboriginal Issues*. Toronto: University of Toronto Press, 2007.

Ethnocultural Minorities

Abu-Laban, Yasmeen, and Christina Gabriel. *Selling Diversity: Immigration, Multiculturalism, Employment Equity, and Globalization*. Peterborough: Broadview Press, 2002.

Bissoondath, Neil. *Selling Illusions: The Cult of Multiculturalism in Canada*. Toronto: Penguin, 1994.

Day, Richard J.F. *Multiculturalism and the History of Canadian Diversity*. Toronto: University of Toronto Press, 2000.

Kymlicka, Will. *Finding Our Way: Rethinking Ethnocultural Relations in Canada*. Toronto: Oxford University Press, 1998.

Ryan, Phil. *Multicultiphobia*. Toronto: University of Toronto Press, 2010.

Stasiulis, Daiva. "Unequal Relations and the Struggle for Equality: Race and Ethnicity in Canadian Politics," in Michael Whittington and Glen Williams, eds., *Canadian Politics in the 21st Century*, 7th ed. Toronto: Nelson Education, 2008.

Gender

Andrew, Caroline, and Sanda Rodgers, eds. *Women and the Canadian State*. Montreal: McGill-Queen's University Press, 1997.

Bashevkin, Sylvia. *Women, Power, Politics: The Hidden Story of Canada's Unfinished Democracy*. Toronto: University of Toronto Press, 2009.

Dobrowolsky, Alexandra. *The Politics of Pragmatism: Women, Representation, and Constitutionalism in Canada*. Toronto: Oxford University Press, 1999.

Johnson, Holly. *Dangerous Domains: Violence Against Women in Canada*. Scarborough: Nelson Canada, 1996.

Manfredi, Christopher P. *Feminist Activism in the Supreme Court: Legal Mobilization and the Women's Legal Education and Action Fund*. Vancouver: UBC Press, 2004.

Newman, Jacquetta, and Linda White. *Women, Politics, and Public Policy: The Political Struggles of Canadian Women*. Don Mills: Oxford University Press, 2006.

Smith, Miriam. *Political Institutions and Lesbian and Gay Rights in the United States and Canada*. New York: Routledge, 2008.

Trimble, Linda, and Jane Arscott. *Still Counting: Women in Politics Across Canada*. Peterborough: Broadview Press, 2003.

Chapter 5

The Global Context of
Canadian Politics

Canada does not exist in a vacuum; instead, it is linked to the rest of the world by all sorts of political, economic, defensive, cultural, demographic, individual, and technological ties. In colonial times, all basic governmental decisions for the country were made in Britain. As Canada emerged into a sovereign state, however, the world was becoming increasingly interdependent. Thus, even though Canada gained the legal powers to make decisions for itself, it became particularly susceptible to influence from the United States. The U.S. remains the most constant external pressure, especially as it pursues its own interests as the major superpower in the world. But nowadays the outside forces are much more numerous and could be said to constitute the "global" environment of the Canadian political system. A multitude of states, international organizations, international agreements, and transnational corporations have an ever-increasing impact upon Canada, complicating the efforts of the government to pursue its own policy preferences. Moreover, since September 11, 2001, the forces of globalization have been complicated by those of international terrorism.

Chapter Objectives

After you have completed this chapter, you should be able to:

Trace the evolution of Canadian autonomy from Britain

Discuss the American influences on Canadian defence and foreign policies

Comment on American influences on Canadian economic and cultural policies

Identify policies adopted to promote domestic ownership of the economy and promote and protect Canadian culture

Discuss the concept of globalization and its effects on Canadian policymaking

Comment on the effects of international terrorism on the Canadian political system

The Road to Canadian Sovereignty from Britain

The British North American colonies were largely self-governing in internal affairs even before 1867. Contrary to popular belief, the **British North America Act (BNA Act)** of 1867 (later renamed the Constitution Act, 1867) did not directly advance the cause of Canadian independence. Although the act of confederation made Canada a more respectable and viable entity and ultimately strengthened its case for greater autonomy, it did not alter the British–Canadian relationship. In theory, the British government could still overturn any statute passed by the Canadian parliament, although in practice it rarely did so.

In external relations, Canada had succeeded in claiming the right to control its own tariffs even before Confederation, and between 1867 and 1914 it became increasingly autonomous in making treaties with other countries. At the turn of the century, Canada sent an official contingent to the South African (Boer) War in response to Canadian public opinion more than to British pressure. In the Alaska boundary dispute of 1903, however, the British representative on the Anglo-Canadian half of the judicial tribunal voted with the three American representatives to award the United States a long strip of the northern British Columbia coastline.

The ultimate independence of Canada and several other British colonies is usually attributed to developments connected to the First World War. Although Canada was automatically at war in 1914 as a result of British action, a series of conferences of Dominion prime ministers began in 1917, as Canada and the other Dominions demanded a say in return for their wartime contributions. Prime Minister Robert Borden participated in the Paris Peace Conference and signed the peace treaties, and the Dominions became individual members of the League of Nations. Thus, by 1919, Canada had gained new international status as a result of accomplishments on the battlefield and subsequent demands for recognition at the conference table.

The Imperial Conference of 1926 ended with a proclamation of the complete equality of the United Kingdom and the Dominions in internal, international, and imperial affairs. They were proclaimed

> *autonomous Communities within the British Empire, equal in status, in no way subordinate one to another in any aspect of their domestic or external affairs, though united by a common allegiance to the Crown, and freely associated as members of the British Commonwealth of Nations.*[1]

Besides giving Canada complete autonomy in all policy fields, the developments of 1926 had implications for the position of governor general. This official would no longer be an agent of the British government, but rather only a personal representative of the Crown. These arrangements were constitutionalized in the **Statute of Westminster** of 1931.

After 1931, therefore, Canada was completely independent of Britain but a number of anomalies helped to disguise this fact. First, Canada continued to share a head of state with Britain although, from the Canadian perspective, that person was the king or queen of Canada. Of more importance, since Canada had not been able to decide how to amend the BNA Act within Canada, such amendments still had to be passed by the British parliament, albeit only at Canadian request. Also of great significance, due to Canadian inaction, the Judicial Committee of the Privy Council remained Canada's final court of appeal until 1949.

Canada made an autonomous decision to take part in the Second World War, after which British–Canadian ties declined. As time went on, Canada's population became more diversified in its ethnic origins, Britain occupied a diminished role in world affairs, and Canada drew closer to the United States.[2] The 1982 Constitution Act removed the Constitution from any kind of British custody, with a new formula for amending it in Canada. After that, Canada shared only the Queen with Britain (and several other states), but in her capacity as Queen of Canada she provides no official link between the two countries.

Time Line
Canadian Independence

1919	Member of the League of Nations
1926	Imperial Conference confers autonomy on Dominions
1931	Statute of Westminster confirms independence from Britain
1949	Supreme Court of Canada becomes final court of appeal
1982	Made-in-Canada constitutional amending formula

The American Sphere of Influence

Even before becoming fully autonomous from Britain, Canada began its slow but steady absorption into the U.S. sphere of influence. The United States serves as a model for many Canadians in various ways, but it also pressures Canada on a daily basis to follow its lead. Its influence can especially be seen in such areas as defence and foreign policy, economic policy, and culture.

Defence and Foreign Policy

After the Second World War, the United States became increasingly obsessed with containing Soviet communism. In 1949 it persuaded Canada and most Western European countries to form a new military alliance, the North Atlantic Treaty Organization (NATO). Commitments to NATO required a considerable increase in the size of the Canadian armed forces. The United Nations military intervention in the war between North and South Korea in the early 1950s was effectively a U.S. effort to which Canada made a significant military contribution, sacrificing 1 550 lives.

The next phase of the North Americanization of Canadian defence was a series of radar screens built across the United States and Canada during the 1950s to intercept anticipated Soviet bombers. These arrangements logically led in 1958 to what is now called the North American Aerospace Defence Command (NORAD). The agreement provided for a joint Canada–U.S. air defence system with headquarters in Colorado. A Defence Production Sharing Program was added to these collaborative schemes in 1959.

Prime Minister John Diefenbaker encountered two serious missile crises with the United States in the 1957–63 period. When U.S. President John F. Kennedy used the establishment of Soviet missile bases in Cuba as an excuse to announce a naval blockade of that country, the Canadian Cabinet waited three days before putting its armed forces in a state of highest alert. Kennedy's anger at this delay was compounded by American annoyance at Canada's stand with respect to Bomarc missiles. These had been established by the United States at two bases in Canada as part of the NORAD Agreement and were intended to be armed with nuclear warheads. With some Cabinet ministers arguing that placing the warheads on Canadian soil would accelerate the nuclear arms race, the Diefenbaker government fell apart over the issue in 1963 and was defeated on a non-confidence motion. The Canadian–American defence relationship thus became a prominent issue in the 1963 election campaign, which the Liberals won under Lester Pearson. The new prime minister had the warheads installed as part of Canada's international commitments.

Pearson's successor, Pierre Trudeau, removed the warheads, cut military spending, and—in a new emphasis on protecting domestic sovereignty—halved

Canada's NATO contingent. Nevertheless, the NORAD Agreement was repeatedly renewed. Trudeau then allowed the United States to test yet another new weapon, the cruise missile, over Canadian territory because of the resemblance of its terrain to that of the Soviet Union.

The Mulroney government promised to make defence a much higher priority and published a hawkish white paper on the subject in 1987. Public opposition and budgetary considerations prevented the paper's implementation, however, a decision that appeared to have been farsighted when the Cold War effectively ended about 1990.

Canada participated in the U.S.–led Gulf War coalition when Iraq invaded Kuwait in 1990, and then in the various phases of the Balkan war. Canada also responded quickly to the call to join the American-led "war on terrorism." While the Chrétien government declined to take part in the second Iraq war in 2003 and the Martin government resisted pressure to participate in the new U.S. Ballistic Missile Defence (BMD) system, the degree of "interoperability" between the armed forces of the two countries increased.

Independently of, but consistently with, U.S. pressure, both the Martin and Harper governments strengthened the Canadian military, and both promised to put more effort into defending Canadian sovereignty in the Arctic. Even though the NORAD agreement was renewed in 2006, the United States also established a unified command within its armed forces (Northcom) with responsibility for coordinating activities of U.S. forces throughout North America. Most significantly, Canada more or less withdrew from its traditional peacekeeping contributions to the United Nations and became increasingly engaged in a NATO-led fighting role in Afghanistan, suffering many casualties. One of the many controversial aspects of that mission was how Canadian troops treated the enemy Afghan fighters they captured, called detainees. After our combat role in Afghanistan ended in 2011, some 1000 Canadian troops would remain to train the Afghan army until 2014.

It is clear that for over 50 years the United States has exerted significant pressure on Canadian defence policy. Even though Canada did not always respond as energetically as the U.S. wished, such external demands influenced many Canadian political outcomes. Some Canadians were satisfied with the arrangement because the country was essentially protected by the U.S. military arsenal and had to pay relatively little for its own defence. Others did not like the U.S. pressure and the loss of control of a vital aspect of public policy.

To the extent that foreign policy can be distinguished from defence policy, the degree of U.S. influence in this field has also been a controversial question. Canada traditionally saw itself as a "middle power" that staked out an independent position

Troops of the Royal Canadian Regiment battle group hold an orders meeting in April 2007 in the bleak desert of Kandahar province. (CP PHOTO/John Cotter)

on recognizing and/or trading with countries such as Cuba, China, and the Soviet Union. On the other hand, the United States expected Canadian support of its initiatives to be automatic. The Canadian government was quick to respond to U.S. demands to contribute to its military efforts in Kuwait (like Korea, theoretically a UN operation) and its peacekeeping mission in Somalia, also ostensibly in the name of the United Nations.

More independently, Canada responded to international pressure and made a major humanitarian contribution in the Bosnian civil war, as well as in Rwanda. Canada was also a leader in the campaign to ban antipersonnel landmines and to establish an International Criminal Court. Prime Minister Chrétien made aid to Africa one of Canada's top foreign policy priorities and then, as noted, stayed out of the second Iraq war because it lacked legitimacy in the eyes of the United Nations.[3] The Harper government's foreign policy was undistinguished, more oriented toward the Americas, and a 2007 Strategic Counsel public opinion poll indicated that Canadians generally felt it was too heavily influenced by the U.S. during the George W. Bush regime. In 2010 Canada lost its bid for election to the U.N. Security Council.

Economic Policy

The economic influence of the United States on Canada is even more pervasive than its impact on defence and foreign policy. This influence is felt in almost every aspect of Canadian life, including investment, trade, the environment, and energy. In many ways, Canada constitutes a zone within the American economy rather than a distinctive national economy.

FOREIGN INVESTMENT

A new country is not likely to produce enough domestic capital to finance all the development projects desired. Therefore, in the early years of Canadian history a great deal of investment came from Britain. Some of this foreign capital consisted of British companies operating in Canada, such as the Hudson's Bay Company, but to a large extent it took the form of Canadian borrowing in the London bond market. Interest had to be paid on such loans, but ownership remained largely in Canadian hands.

Later, the main source of foreign investment shifted from Britain to the United States. Moreover, the form of investment switched from loans to "direct" or "equity" investment, that is, control through the ownership of shares. Figure 5.1 indicates the shift from British to U.S. investment in Canada between 1900 and 1967. To a large extent, the Canadian economy has come to consist of branch plants of U.S. parent corporations; since these companies typically operate in many other countries, too, they gain the label of "multinational" or "transnational" corporations.

This pattern of economic development was fostered in the first instance by the **National Policy** of 1879, which put a tariff on imported manufactured goods. Rather than export to Canada from the United States and pay the tariff, U.S. companies set up branch plants within Canada behind the tariff wall. This was advantageous for the creation of employment in Canada and contributed to the general prosperity of the country, especially Ontario. Despite the fact that considerable capital was generated within Canada as time went on, the degree of foreign ownership continued to increase.

In addition to manufacturers, foreign companies also moved into Canada to exploit our natural resources. "A large proportion of the investment in resource exploitation reflected the needs of the United States investors for raw materials for their processing and manufacturing plants in the United States." This integration often had the practical impact of "reducing the likelihood of further processing activity of Canadian natural resources in Canada."[4] In fact, Canada has more foreign ownership than any other advanced industrial country, although the sources

....

Figure 5.1   Percentage of British, U.S., and Other Foreign Investment in Canada, 1900–1967

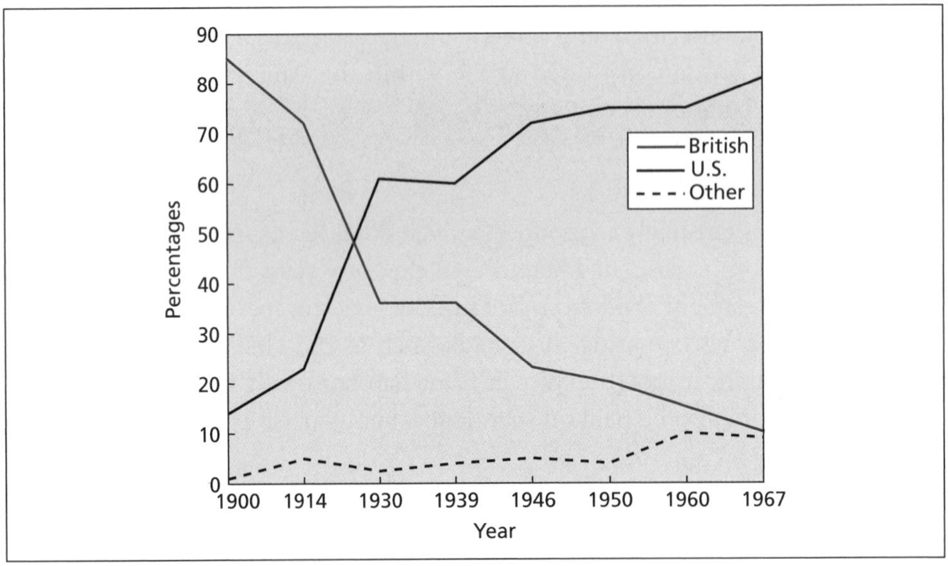

Source: Foreign Direct Investment in Canada, 1972, p. 15. Reproduced with permission of the Minister of Public Works and Government Services, and the Privy Council Office.

of recent international investment in Canada are more diversified than in the past. Some of the largest multinationals operating in Canada are identified in Table 5.1.

Most advocates of the free market system are enthusiastic boosters of unlimited foreign investment. They claim that maximum efficiency results from capital being able to flow to wherever it will yield the greatest returns. In this case, defenders of foreign investment argue that Canada still needs foreign capital and that such investment creates jobs, which in turn raise the Canadian standard of living. They also claim that efficiency is enhanced when multinationals transfer state-of-the-art technology as well as well-trained managers and management techniques to their branch plants.

Others take the view that these advantages are short-term or short-sighted. First, multinationals are likely to purchase supplies and component parts from the parent company or parent country, rather than buying them and creating employment in Canada. Second, their plants usually remain small and inefficient because they are designed only to serve the Canadian market, rather than being encouraged to compete in export markets with the parent plant or with branches set up in other countries. Third, critics claim that a branch-plant economy suffers because

TABLE 5.1 LARGE FOREIGN-OWNED COMPANIES IN CANADA

Imperial Oil Ltd. (U.S.)	Sears Canada Inc. (U.S.)
Walmart Canada Ltd. (U.S.)	Toyota Canada (Japan)
Husky Energy Inc. (China)	ConocoPhillips Resources Corp. (U.S.)
Novelis Inc. (India)	IBM Canada Ltd. (U.S.)
Costco Wholesale Canada Ltd. (U.S.)	Nova Chemicals Corp. (U.A.E.)
Direct Energy Marketing Ltd. (U.K.)	Hewlett-Packard (Canada) Co. (U.S.)
Honda Canada Inc. (Japan)	Sysco Food Services Ltd. (U.S.)
Ford Motor Co. of Canada Ltd. (U.S.)	Dow Chemical Canada ULC (U.S.)
Ultramar Ltd. (U.S.)	Standard Life Assurance Co. (U.K.)
Canada Safeway Ltd. (U.S.)	HSBC Bank Canada (U.K.)
Cargill Ltd. (U.S.)	Staples Business Depot (U.S.)
Best Buy Canada Ltd. (U.S.)	Pratt & Whitney Canada Corp. (U.S.)
Home Depot Canada (U.S.)	Siemens Canada Ltd. (Germany)

Source: *Financial Post Business*, FP 500 (June 2010). Material reprinted with the express permission of "The National Post Company," a division of Postmedia Network Inc.

most of its research and development (R&D) is done in the parent plant in the parent country. This limits the number of challenging jobs in science, engineering, and technology located in Canada. As convenient as it is to import such technology, this process hinders Canadian innovative efforts to develop distinctive export products and increase productivity. Fourth, many observers of the situation also worry that if layoffs or shutdowns are necessary, these are usually slated for branch plants first, and that domestically owned companies are generally more likely to operate in Canada's national interest.

The policies that Canadian governments have adopted to counter this threat of U.S. or other foreign ownership of the Canadian economy can be divided into four main categories. First, **Crown corporations**—government-owned enterprises— have been established to ensure that the company involved remains in Canadian hands. Atomic Energy of Canada Ltd. and Petro-Canada, for example, were created by the federal government in response to demands that a Canadian presence in strategic industries be retained.

Second, while leaving other corporations to function privately, the federal government often created **regulatory tribunals**. The main such agency was the

Foreign Investment Review Agency (FIRA), established in the early 1970s. FIRA screened foreign takeovers of large Canadian companies and new ventures by foreign firms, approving the deal if it involved "significant benefit to Canada." In fact, FIRA rarely disallowed any such initiatives and imposed minimal conditions; even so, it became a major irritant to the United States, and the Mulroney government replaced it with Investment Canada. In this new form, the agency's goal was to *attract* increased foreign investment to Canada. Other regulatory agencies include the National Energy Board and the Canadian Nuclear Safety Commission, which were designed to protect the Canadian national interest in certain important respects.

Third, ownership restrictions and tax incentives have been introduced. Maximum foreign-ownership limits exist in fields such as broadcasting, financial institutions, and newspapers and publishing. Incentives to Canadian ownership were exemplified by the **National Energy Program** (NEP) of 1980, under which, largely via tax write-offs, several oil companies in Canada were purchased from their American owners. Finally, the government has established funding agencies such as the Business Development Bank of Canada, whose mandate is to encourage Canadian entrepreneurs when the commercial banks are not interested in lending them money.

Many of these policies were half-hearted and others were diluted under U.S. pressure. Many were weakened or withdrawn by the Mulroney government, both to increase foreign investment and to remove irritants in the Canada–U.S. relationship. As a result, the proportion of foreign control increased after 1984. Thus, economic nationalists regard the situation as more critical than ever, while others remain indifferent or take the opposite side of this issue, seeing foreign investment as the source of badly needed jobs and a natural aspect of globalization. A spate of major foreign takeovers occurred in 2006–07, including Hudson's Bay Company, Molson, Labatt, Domtar, Inco, Falconbridge, Dofasco, Fairmont Hotels, Alcan, Four Seasons' Hotels, Algoma Steel, Ipsco, LionOre Mining, North American Oil Sands, Stelco, and AbitibiBowater. The prospect of Chinese state-owned companies buying Canadian corporations concerned even the Harper government, and it later disallowed two takeover attempts, including an Australian bid for the Potash Corp. of Saskatchewan.

TRADE

Because of geographic proximity, it is only logical that Canada and the United States are closely linked by trade. It is even more likely because of their complementary resources and industries—the abundance of primary resources in Canada and the extent of manufacturing in the United States. Thus, Canada maintains a

TABLE 5.2 Canada's Exports from and Imports to its Leading Trading Partners, Merchandise Trade, 2009

	Exports	Imports
United States	75.0	51.2
United Kingdom	3.4	2.6
China	3.1	10.9
Japan	2.3	3.4
Mexico	1.3	4.5
Germany	1.0	2.9

Source: Foreign Affairs and International Trade Canada, Office of the Chief Economist, available at http://www.international.gc.ca/ economist-economiste/index.aspx

heavy dependence on the United States as a market for its exports and as a source of its imports. Indeed, most provinces now trade more with neighbouring states than with each other, although much of this trade is of an intra-firm character rather than truly international, such as in the automobile industry.

Canadian exports to the United States exceeded those to the United Kingdom after 1921 and edged up to over 80 percent of all exports after 1990. Imports from the United States constituted nearly 50 percent of the Canadian total from the start and rose to the 70 percent range before falling back in recent years. The 2009 proportions can be seen in Table 5.2, in which the increasing trade with China, both on the import and export sides, must be emphasized. Canada's free trade agreements with the United States are discussed later in the chapter.

Given the degree to which Canadian prosperity depends on export trade, it is advantageous to have ready access to the U.S. market; it is also convenient to have such a close supply of goods that are not produced in Canada. On the other hand, to have so many eggs in one basket means that in times of U.S. recession, such as 2008–09, demand for Canadian goods falls off and the Canadian economy declines, whereas in prosperous periods, U.S. inflation also tends to increase prices in Canada. Furthermore, protectionist pressure in the United States for new or increased tariffs or quotas against Canadian exports can have a devastating effect on certain industries, such as softwood lumber. Although the Harper government signed an agreement with the United States on that issue, American lumber producers continued to complain. The rare incidence of Mad Cow Disease is another example of American restrictions on imports from Canada resulting from pressure from U.S. producers. The relative value of the Canadian and U.S. dollars can also be an important factor and, at least from a strictly import–export point of view, it is good for Canada if our dollar has a lower value. There is also the potential that U.S. security concerns might delay "just-in-time" cross-border shipments and impede the cross-border movement of tourists and other business, as well as the threat that the United States might retaliate economically if Canada does not support it on foreign policy and security issues.

THE ENVIRONMENT

Canadians have seriously damaged their own environment over the years, but the situation has been aggravated by proximity to the United States and by some of its even less restrictive anti-pollution laws. The largest transboundary environmental issue is that of acid rain. Canadian research generally shows that about 50 percent of the acid rain falling north of the border comes from U.S. sources, primarily coal-fired power plants in the Midwest. These emissions fall into Canadian lakes and rivers, killing plant and animal life and damaging trees, cars, and buildings.

The pollution of the Great Lakes is the other serious bilateral environmental problem. Here again, each side is partly to blame, but most of the chemicals are discharged from the larger number of factories and waste dumps situated on the U.S. shores of the lakes. Phosphorous levels were reduced in the 1970s, but the Great Lakes are still in a critical state because of toxic pollution. Devils Lake in North Dakota is a somewhat similar threat to the Red River system in Manitoba.

An external influence of a different kind was the Kyoto Protocol, which Canada signed in 1997. It is a multilateral agreement in which countries committed to reduce the emissions of greenhouse gases, widely believed to cause global warming and climate change. While many Canadians welcomed Kyoto, those industries most affected, such as coal and petroleum, demonstrated considerable concern. Opposition was heightened when the United States decided not to ratify the treaty, leaving Canadian corporations at a comparative disadvantage. The Liberals failed to implement Kyoto and the Harper government abandoned it entirely, finding the much less stringent 2009 Copenhagen Agreement more to its liking. In fact, the Harper environmental policy was to mimic whatever happened south of the border.

ENERGY

In the energy sector, the voracious U.S. industrial complex usually wants to import Canadian electric power, oil, and natural gas. Governments in Quebec, Manitoba, and B.C. have been eager to export electricity, and those of Alberta, Saskatchewan,

President Barack Obama visits
Ottawa in February 2009: sometimes
Canadians appreciate U.S. influence.
(The Canadian Press/Jake Wright)

B.C., Nova Scotia, and Newfoundland want to supply oil and/or natural gas. The federal government has normally approved these sales with little hesitation, although the National Energy Board is charged with ensuring that long-term Canadian needs will not be compromised in the process. Aboriginal and environmental groups in some provinces have not been so favourably disposed toward the dams necessary to produce the electricity, however, and Canadian nationalists worry about the future supply of petroleum for domestic purposes, as well as rising prices and environmental damage because of such exports. George W. Bush's obsession with energy pleased Alberta petroleum exporters, especially in the oil sands, and put the issue of pipelines to transport northern petroleum to the United States back on the political agenda.

The degree of U.S. ownership of the Canadian petroleum industry has also caused considerable conflict between the two countries. The National Energy Program of 1980 set a target of 50 percent Canadian ownership of the oil and gas industry by 1990 and gave certain preferences to Petro-Canada and private Canadian firms. U.S. petroleum companies in Canada protested, and their government pressured Canada to remove these incentives to Canadianization. The Mulroney cabinet dismantled the NEP completely and began the privatization of Petro-Canada; more recently, there have been many foreign takeovers of Canadian oil companies.

TRADE UNIONS

Historically, Canadian trade unions have been just as closely allied with those in the United States as the corporations for which their members worked. Many unions in Canada, such as the United Steelworkers of America and the United Food and Commercial Workers, are part of "international unions" with their headquarters in the United States. The Canadian union movement justified the relationship by arguing that as long as it had to bargain with multinational corporations, it needed the support of international unions, especially because of their larger strike funds. Membership in international unions peaked in 1965 at 67 percent of all union members in Canada. Since then, a nationalist trend has been apparent in the Canadian labour movement, of which the creation of an autonomous Canadian Auto Workers union is the most striking example. Thus, by 2007, only 28 percent of Canadian union members belonged to international unions,[5] and the current president of the United Steelworkers of America is a Canadian.

American Influence on Canadian Culture

People around the world enjoy U.S. popular culture. Canadians are a particularly captive market, given their geographical proximity, their linguistic similarity, their small domestic market, their chronic feeling of dependence and inferiority, and the degree of economic integration between the two countries. The general public has little consciousness of the origin of most pop culture fare, and even less concern that so much of it comes from the United States. But many nationalists among the intellectual elite are disturbed by the high proportion of television programs, magazines, movies, books, and music in Canada that emanates from the United States. They claim that this cultural invasion stifles the development of a distinctive Canadian national identity, worry about its influence on Canadian attitudes and values, and wonder how long a separate political system can be maintained in these circumstances.

Television was the most significant cultural institution of the second half of the 20th century. Today, the average Canadian watches about 22 hours of television per week; for anglophones, 72 percent of that is foreign programming, compared to francophones' 29 percent foreign content.[6] Some Canadians live close enough to the U.S. border to receive U.S. channels directly; failing that, most Canadian stations, except for the CBC, broadcast a large proportion of U.S. programming. In addition, over 85 percent of Canadian households have cable television or satellite dishes that offer them all the U.S. networks, as well as pay and specialty channels of various origins.

Canadian private television networks broadcast so much U.S. programming for two reasons. First, it is much cheaper to buy a U.S. show or series than to produce a Canadian one—about one-tenth the cost. Second, although Canadians generally prefer their own news, public affairs, and sports programs, U.S. programs otherwise attract a larger audience. They therefore command higher advertising rates than the Canadian programs. In fact, Canadian television has a higher reputation abroad than it does at home, and those few Canadian series that are produced—like *Little Mosque on the Prairie*—are readily sold to foreign networks.

Magazines are perhaps the second most important vehicle of popular culture, and this Canadian industry is also permeated by U.S. content. While Canadian magazines lead foreign magazines in subscriptions in Canada, foreign magazines account for the bulk of English-language newsstand sales. Overall, Canadian magazines constitute about 50 percent of the total circulation, but as with television, the picture is much more positive in French-speaking Canada than among English-speaking residents.

The Canadian motion picture industry is even weaker than television or magazines, and the average Canadian moviegoer has rarely, if ever, seen a Canadian feature film. Less than five percent of screen time in Canadian movie theatres is devoted to Canadian films, and most of that is in the large Toronto and Montreal markets or at film festivals. U.S. movie producers make many feature films in Canada every year, taking advantage of its lower prices, scenic locations, and technical expertise, but these are almost always disguised as U.S. movies. The problem has many causes, including the fact that the film distribution system is U.S.–controlled, the undeniable Canadian fascination with Hollywood, the small Canadian market, and a shortage of funds for both production and marketing.

When it comes to books, the Canadian market is also amply supplied with U.S. content, and it is estimated that a majority of the books bought in Canada are imported.[7] Both Canadian-owned companies and foreign-owned publishers operating in Canada sell foreign as well as Canadian titles, for books are like television shows: they are cheaper to import than to make domestically. Moreover, most Canadian bookstores make no special effort to sell Canadian books.

Sound recording is another cultural industry dominated by external firms and content. Although the Canadian music industry is stronger than most other areas of culture, it depends for support on CRTC regulations and financial assistance from government sources.

In short, in the five cultural industries of television, magazines, movies, books, and sound recordings, Canadian-owned companies produce virtually all of the Canadian output. But these companies are marginal players in a market dominated by subsidiaries of large, mainly U.S., multinationals. That there is a Canadian presence at all in such industries is primarily the result of demands made by the upper-middle-class nationalist minority for protection from U.S. domination and for promotion of Canadian content.

COUNTERING THE U.S. INFLUENCE

As in economic matters, the Crown corporation is a nationalistic instrument in the cultural field. The **Canadian Broadcasting Corporation (CBC)**, in its radio and television networks, and Radio-Canada, its French-language equivalent, is perhaps the most crucial agent of Canadian cultural expression. Today, CBC radio has virtually 100 percent Canadian content and can be heard in almost every part of the country. Its programs are widely regarded as crucial links in keeping the country together. CBC television is less successful, mainly because the television medium is so expensive. The Mulroney and Chrétien governments slashed millions of dollars from the CBC budget, making the corporation's task even harder. Conservative governments, including that of Stephen Harper, have shown particular hostility to the CBC.

Another Crown corporation, the National Film Board, has also had an illustrious existence, making impressive Canadian films and winning many international awards. It has two serious disadvantages, however: insufficient funding to make feature films, so that it has specialized instead in documentaries and shorts, and no effective mechanism for giving the general public access to its films.

A second policy instrument to protect and promote Canadian culture is a regulatory tribunal called the **Canadian Radio-television and Telecommunications Commission (CRTC)**. This agency issues broadcasting licences and Canadian-content regulations, the latter being more stringent for the CBC than for private stations and networks. CBC television now airs a virtually all-Canadian line-up in prime time, whereas news, public affairs, and sports take up most of the required Canadian time on the private television networks, which produce very little Canadian drama. The CRTC also requires that radio stations play 35 percent Canadian music, a regulation that is generally seen as the catalyst for the explosion of the Canadian music industry over the past 45 years.

Because the CRTC has been under strong industry and popular pressure to allow more U.S. outlets in Canada, it permitted cable and pay television that diluted the audiences of Canadian channels. In 1995, the CRTC also authorized direct-to-home satellite services. Many nationalists fear for the fate of Canadian content in the not-too-distant future when the largely American 500-channel universe is beamed directly into Canadian homes.

A third policy instrument consists of Canadian ownership restrictions and financial incentives. Ownership restrictions in the cultural field apply to radio, television, newspaper, and book publishing companies in Canada. In addition, Canadian magazine policy from 1965 allowed firms to deduct magazine advertising expenses from their income tax only if those advertisements were placed in Canadian magazines. The same policy also prohibited the entry into Canada of split-run editions of foreign magazines containing advertisements directed at Canadians. In the 1990s, however, Sports Illustrated started to produce a Canadian split-run edition that challenged the law because such editions could now be physically printed in Canada via satellite. Capitulating to U.S. pressure and a World Trade Organization ruling, the Chrétien government allowed foreign magazines sold in Canada to carry up to 18 percent of Canadian ads without any Canadian editorial content and raised the limit on foreign ownership of a Canadian magazine from 25 to 49 percent.

A fourth device to promote Canadian culture is the funding agency. The Canada Council for the Arts, set up in 1957, gives lifesaving grants to hundreds of individual writers, artists, musicians, and playwrights, as well as to almost every orchestra, theatre centre, art gallery, and ballet and opera company in the country.

Cutbacks Crimp CBC reporter's style (Fred Curatolo/Artizans.com)

Telefilm Canada subsidizes the production of feature films, and the Department of Canadian Heritage offers special funding to most cultural industries—television, magazines, books, and music.

Globalization

In the 21st century, Canada has to contend with many external influences beyond those of the United States. These can be lumped together under the label of **globalization**. Globalization is usually understood as a deepening of supraterritorial interaction around the world characterized by the following new developments:

- comprehensive free trade agreements, involving removal of state controls on corporate behaviour;
- massive diffusion of computerization and other technological change, including the Internet, permitting instantaneous communication around the globe;

- megamergers of large transnational corporations, cross-border capital and investment flows, and worldwide corporate competition;
- closure of transnational plants in developed countries and migration to the developing world; and
- widespread movement of people through immigration and the permeability of borders.

Such globalization can be discussed under four headings—foreign governments, international organizations, international agreements, and transnational corporations—with an addendum regarding international terrorism.

Foreign Governments

Foreign governments make decisions every day, in both foreign and domestic policy, which can have some effect on Canada. Sometimes this impact is deliberate, but often it is unintentional. It is the responsibility of our foreign affairs department to put pressure on such governments so that their decisions are not harmful to Canada. The case of the United States has already been discussed, but such influences now come from all directions. For example, the European Union frequently raises objections to Canadian policies. It bans the import of most seal products, it used to reject Canadian lumber exports because of concerns about Canadian forestry practices, and it contested the use of words such as "champagne" on Canadian labels. The pressure that the United States, the European Union, and many other foreign governments apply to Canada to change its policies is often made on behalf of their own multinational corporations. On the other hand, Canada has complaints of its own, especially with regard to the overfishing by a number of European countries in Canadian territorial waters and the unmatchable subsidies that European and American governments pay their wheat farmers. China is an increasingly important player on the international scene, but it took the Harper government several years to give it much attention.

International Organizations

As Table 5.3 shows, Canada has joined a multitude of international organizations with the aim of taking advantage of opportunities to influence other countries' policies, to expand its external trade, and to promote joint objectives with other states. Nevertheless, such membership often entails obligations that influence

TABLE 5.3 LEADING INTERNATIONAL ORGANIZATIONS TO WHICH CANADA BELONGS

United Nations	The Commonwealth
World Trade Organization	La Francophonie
Organization of American States	NATO and NORAD
International Monetary Fund and World Bank	The G8 and G20
Asia-Pacific Economic Cooperation Council	The OECD

Canadian domestic or foreign policies. The United Nations is probably the most important of such organizations. It gives a middle-ranking country such as Canada a platform to promote both its altruistic and its self-interested objectives. But the UN also makes claims on Canada, such as to answer the call whenever it decides to set up a peacekeeping force in trouble spots around the world. Moreover, the UN has criticized several domestic Canadian policies, including Quebec language legislation; federal and provincial laws on labour, Aboriginal peoples, and women; and the deterioration of social programs. Of course, many Canadians welcomed these criticisms as contributing to the effort to change such laws.

In 1947, Canada was among the signatories of the General Agreement on Tariffs and Trade (GATT), under which countries pledged to remove trade restrictions on a multinational basis. The successor to GATT, the **World Trade Organization (WTO)**, can actually order its members to change their trading practices. The WTO has disallowed a large number of Canadian laws and policies in recent years in connection with agricultural marketing boards, magazines, dairy products, drug patents, aircraft company subsidies, and even the Canada–U.S. Auto Pact. The WTO has thus become a huge impediment to the pursuit of Canadian government policies, that is, to Canadian **sovereignty**, in a wide range of sensitive fields. The WTO has attracted opposition around the world from those who feel that its decisions prevent countries from making reasonable policies in their own national public interest, acting instead in the interests of transnational corporations.

Other international organizations also have an effect on Canadian policy, including the International Monetary Fund, and even those to which Canada does not belong, such as the Organization of the Petroleum Exporting Countries (OPEC). The leaders of the G8 (the group of eight leading industrialized countries) meet annually to try to come to a consensus on economic and other matters, supplemented by the new G20.

Prime Minister Stephen Harper hosts the June 2010 G8 Summit in Huntsville, Ontario. (The Canadian Press/Fred Chartrand)

International Agreements

Canadian policymakers had been concerned for some time that the country was being left out of the regional trading blocs being formed, especially the European Union. Then, in the early 1980s, a protectionist mood descended upon the U.S. Congress, and new barriers to many Canadian exports were imposed: on shakes and shingles, softwood lumber, potash, potatoes, fish, and specialty steel. Such protectionist measures were among the factors that converted Brian Mulroney to the concept of free trade. Mulroney found an ally in the White House, so he and Ronald Reagan set the negotiations in motion. The **Canada–U.S. Free Trade Agreement (FTA)** took effect on January 1, 1989. It was a wide-ranging pact covering almost every aspect of the relationship between the two countries—far more than "trade."[8] It was clearly designed to enshrine neoconservative and neoliberal values, give corporations more leeway under government regulation, and prevent the recurrence of such nationalistic measures as FIRA and NEP.

The agreement removed almost all barriers to the flow of goods and services between the two countries over a ten-year period. Firms in each country could henceforth send their products to the other without tariffs, quotas, or other impediments. Each country had to treat the other's firms the same as its own (the "national treatment" principle), but each continued to apply its own tariffs to imports from other states.

Investment, energy, agriculture, and cultural industries were four of the other most controversial sections of the agreement. U.S. businesses would now be able to start new operations in Canada without restriction (and vice versa), and Investment Canada could screen only acquisitions of firms with a value over $150 million and could not impose any performance requirements. A North American energy pool was created in which Canada had to sell oil, gas, or electricity to the United States at the Canadian domestic price; if cutbacks were ever necessary, domestic sales had to be reduced by the same proportion as exports. In agriculture, Canada had to remove import restrictions on chickens, turkeys, and eggs, as well as tariffs on processed food. In theory, the agreement did not affect existing cultural programs; however, any new support of cultural industries could be met by retaliation of equivalent value by the other country.

For any future conflicts in trade between the two countries, a complex dispute-settlement mechanism was set up that involved binational panels and binding arbitration. If either country refused to abide by the final decision of the arbitrators, however, the other could retaliate ("countervail"), as before.

The free trade debate went on for many years, with proponents regarding the agreement as the solution to all Canadian economic problems and the source of perpetual prosperity, and opponents seeing it as leading to the complete integration of Canada and the United States.[9] Some 20 years later, the results seem to be mixed. Ontario did lose 200 000 manufacturing jobs in the early 1990s, but how much of this was due to the free trade agreement as such and how much to the recession and other globalizing factors is hard to determine. More significantly, the number of conflicts under the agreement has been large. Some of the same issues that precipitated the Free Trade Agreement have continued to be problems, especially Canadian exports of softwood lumber. On the other hand, trade between the two countries has expanded enormously in both directions, and few of the most dire predictions have come to pass. That the agreement did not affect the actions of state and provincial governments became clear when the U.S. created its "Buy American" stimulus spending program in the Great Recession of 2008–09. Its prohibition of money going to Canadian firms was eased somewhat after most of the money had been spent.

The ink was hardly dry on the Canada–U.S. Free Trade Agreement when the Mulroney government entered talks with the United States and Mexico that produced the 1994 **North American Free Trade Agreement (NAFTA)**. It essentially extended FTA to Mexico; most provisions in the two agreements were identical. This initiative was not so much of Canada's choice; Canada entered into it mainly to preclude the other partners from endangering its position, although some corporations saw the agreement as a means of enhancing the efficiency of their operations. Opponents feared that companies would move from Canada to Mexico because of the low wages and environmental standards in that country, and they complained that Mexico was able to negotiate a stronger energy clause with the United States than Canada had under the FTA.[10]

As an illustration of how such agreements are drafted to benefit corporations, Chapter 11 of NAFTA allows a foreign company to sue a country on the grounds that a government policy reduced its profits. Canada lost at least two multimillion-dollar lawsuits in this connection, the most infamous involving the gasoline additive MMT. Ethyl Corporation of Virginia used such NAFTA rules to force Canada to roll back its ban on this ingredient, which is widely regarded as a health hazard. Stephen Clarkson has advanced the interesting notion that the two North American trade agreements plus the WTO constitute an external or "supraconstitution" for Canada, which is just as constraining on the operation of government as the internal Constitution. At the same time, Clarkson adds that it is hard to know whether government decisions between 1990 and 2000 were the result of globalization, or of its companion ideologies, neoliberalism and neoconservatism, espoused by most governments over that decade.[11]

After several years of experience with NAFTA, many observers agreed that it had failed all three signatories: it had not ended Canada–U.S. trade disputes, it had not brought prosperity to Mexico, and it had not stopped the flow of illegal immigrants from Mexico into the United States. While some Canadians try to persuade themselves that a new North American identity has emerged, Stephen Clarkson basically answers "no" to the question: does North America exist?[12] In any case, Canada has subsequently signed free trade deals with Chile, Costa Rica, Israel, Peru, Jordan, Colombia, and the EFTA countries (Iceland, Norway, Switzerland, and Liechtenstein).

Transnational Corporations

As noted, the pressures exerted by a foreign government are often made on behalf of corporations with head offices in that country, and comprehensive trade agreements are basically about removing government controls on corporate behaviour. Indeed, at the heart of globalization is the changed role of **transnational corporations**. More and more companies are outgrowing their domestic state; they are introducing new forms of technology at an incredible rate; they are merging and taking each other over; and they are opening or closing operations strictly on the basis of economic efficiency and without regard to traditional location. The world is increasingly becoming one integrated global economic unit in which national boundaries are much less significant than in the past. Corporate money, banking, finance, and investment flow between countries almost at will. In these circumstances, it is becoming more difficult for national or provincial governments to maintain distinctive labour, tax, or environmental laws because such companies (and their senior employees) regularly threaten to move to other jurisdictions that they find more congenial.

On the other hand, many observers feel that governments do not have to cave in completely to such corporate blackmail.[13] Even those who accept the inevitability of globalization have suggested refinements: the process of globalization should be more open or transparent than it has been to date; it should involve a commitment to democracy and human rights; and it should ensure a fairer distribution of the increased wealth that globalization generates.

International Terrorism

Terrorism, an act intended to cause death or serious bodily harm to civilians with the purpose of intimidating a population or compelling a government to do or abstain from doing any act, can be committed by domestic or external groups. Canada has been happily free of much domestic terrorism, but after the attacks on the U.S. World Trade Center and Pentagon on September 11, 2001, concern with international terrorism greatly increased even in this country. These actions represented a significant addition to the global context within which individual states operate. While they had the greatest impact on the United States, most other governments took actions in response, some of their own volition and some at U.S. insistence. Canada passed a comprehensive piece of antiterrorism legislation that gave sweeping powers to the government, began to arm its border guards, and was persuaded to become part of the military operations in Afghanistan. The appointment of a minister of Public Safety and the mushrooming number of federal agencies in the security field are signs that international terrorism has become a new constant in the Canadian policymaking process.[14] A nascent terrorist cell was discovered in Ontario and several other controversial cases of terrorist charges against individuals have arisen since 2001. Several individuals have been found guilty, but some instances involved a denial of basic legal rights, and at least one case caused a horrible injustice to an innocent person, Maher Arar.

SUMMARY

This chapter concerned the external forces that impinge upon the Canadian political system. It began with a discussion of the period during which Canada was a British colony, officially ending in 1931. It then examined how Canada fell into the American sphere of influence, and discussed U.S. influences on Canadian defence and foreign policies, on economic policies such as investment, trade, the environment, energy, and trade unions, and on Canadian culture. It outlined the four main devices that Canadian governments have used to counter such influences: Crown corporations, regulatory tribunals, ownership restrictions, and funding agencies. The third part of the chapter dealt with globalization, and discussed in turn the impact of foreign governments, international organizations, international agreements, transnational corporations, and international terrorism.

DISCUSSION QUESTIONS

1. What are the advantages and disadvantages of the close defensive, economic, and cultural relationship between Canada and the United States?
2. On balance, have the free trade agreements been good or bad for Canada?
3. How much scope does globalization leave to nation-states to make distinctive domestic policies?
4. What are the implications of international terrorism for Canada?

KEY TERMS

British North America Act (BNA Act) The 1867 act of the British parliament that created Canada by uniting the four original provinces, that provided some of the essential elements of the new country's constitution, and that in 1982 was renamed the Constitution Act, 1867.

Canada–U.S. Free Trade Agreement (FTA) The agreement signed by Canada and the United States in 1987 and taking effect in 1989 that gradually eliminated tariffs between the two countries and otherwise prohibited governments from interfering in the private marketplace.

Canadian Broadcasting Corporation (CBC) The large national Crown corporation with radio and television divisions whose mandate is to promote meaningful communication among all parts of the country.

Canadian Radio-television and Telecommunications Commission (CRTC) The regulatory agency established to police the communications industry, including radio, television, telephones, and telecommunications.

Crown corporation A corporation owned by the government that assumes a structure similar to that of a private company and that operates semi-independently of the Cabinet.

Globalization The pattern of deepening supraterritorial interaction around the world, characterized by comprehensive free trade agreements, massive diffusion of technological change, and worldwide corporate competition or megamergers that challenge the sovereignty of the state.

National Energy Program The 1980 policy associated with Pierre Trudeau which was designed to skim off petroleum tax revenue for Ottawa, keep the price of petroleum below world levels, encourage conservation, and Canadianize the industry, and which met with great opposition in Western Canada.

National Policy The broad nation-building 1879 policy of John A. Macdonald that included tariff protection for central Canadian manufacturing, massive immigration, and the construction of a national transportation system.

North American Free Trade Agreement (NAFTA) The 1994 extension of the Canada–U.S. Free Trade Agreement to Mexico.

Regulatory tribunal A government agency established to regulate an area of public policy, such as transportation or communications, that operates at arm's length from the Cabinet.

Sovereignty Ultimate control or independence, such as Canadian national sovereignty vis-à-vis that of other countries.

Statute of Westminster The 1931 British law that declared Canada and the other Dominions to be fully independent.

Terrorism An act intended to cause death or serious bodily harm to civilians with the purpose of intimidating a population or compelling a government to do or abstain from doing any act.

Transnational corporations Corporations operating simultaneously in many countries throughout the world that often take orders from company headquarters and that individual states find difficult to control.

World Trade Organization (WTO) An international organization to which Canada and most other countries belong that has the power to disallow national policies and practices it deems discriminatory against companies from other states.

FURTHER READING

Axworthy, Lloyd. *Navigating a New World: Canada's Global Future*. Toronto: Knopf Canada, 2004.

Barlow, Maude, and Tony Clarke. *Global Showdown: How the New Activists Are Fighting Global Corporate Rule*. Toronto: Stoddart Publishing, 2000.

Bow, Brian. *The Politics of Linkage: Power, Interdependence, and Ideas in Canada–US Relations*. Vancouver: UBC Press, 2009.

Canada Among Nations. Annual. Montreal: McGill-Queen's University Press.

Clarkson, Stephen. *Does North America Exist? Governing the Continent after NAFTA and 9/11*. Toronto: University of Toronto Press, 2008.

Clarkson, Stephen. *Uncle Sam and Us: Globalization, Neoconservatism, and the Canadian State*. Toronto: University of Toronto Press, 2002.

Doern, G. Bruce, and Brian Tomlin. *Faith and Fear: The Free Trade Story*. Toronto: Stoddart, 1991.

Dyment, David. *Doing the Continental: A New Canadian-American Relationship*. Toronto: Dundurn Press, 2010.

Holloway, Steven. *Canadian Foreign Policy: Defining the Canadian National Interest*. Peterborough: Broadview Press, 2006.

McBride, Stephen. *Paradigm Shift: Globalization and the Canadian State*, 2nd ed. Black Point, N.S.: Fernwood Publishing, 2005.

McDougall, John. *Drifting Together: The Political Economy of Canada–US Integration*. Peterborough: Broadview Press, 2006.

Stein, Janice Gross, and Eugene Lang. *The Unexpected War: Canada in Kandahar*. Toronto: Viking Canada, 2007.

PART 2

Linking People to Government

Having outlined the societal and global contexts in which Canadian politics operates, we are now ready to examine how people are linked to the government. The three traditional elements of Canadian politics are the electoral system, political parties, and advocacy groups. At a minimum, each citizen can have a modest impact on the government by voting in an election. If people wish to have more influence on government policy, they can join or support the political party whose platform is closest to their way of thinking or they can choose the vehicle of social movements and advocacy groups. Each of these three links between people and government is discussed in its own chapter in the following section.

At the same time, in the construction of election platforms and in the making of public policies, political parties and governments actively seek out the opinions of individual experts, important groups, and the public at large.

The context of values, attitudes, opinions (and how they are acquired), and patterns of political participation must also be examined. Moreover, no one can deny the importance of the mass media and public opinion polls in linking people to government. Thus we begin with a chapter on the Canadian political culture, socialization, and participation, followed by a chapter on the mass media and public opinion polls.

Chapter 6

Political Culture, Socialization, and Participation

Understanding how Canadians feel about politics and government, how they develop such attitudes, and how they participate politically provides a useful context in which to study elections, political parties, and advocacy groups. This chapter therefore examines Canadian political values and attitudes— the Canadian political culture; how these values and attitudes are acquired— political socialization; and the related subject of patterns of Canadian political participation.

Chapter Objectives

After you have completed this chapter, you should be able to:

Define democracy and discuss the extent to which Canadians are committed to it

Enumerate other basic Canadian political values

Evaluate the extent to which the traditional political culture remains intact, and comment on the forces that threaten it

Identify the main agents of political socialization

Comment on variations in the voter turnout rate and reasons for voting or not voting

Enumerate forms of non-electoral participation

Political Culture

Political culture can be defined as the sum total of the political values, beliefs, attitudes, and orientations in a society. Values can be defined as principles or what one feels is important in life. Vague and elusive as values and attitudes may be, most political scientists think they are worthy of analysis because they influence what is done within a political system.

Political culture includes feelings people have toward the overall political community of Canada, such as their reaction to national symbols—flag, anthem, Constitution—and feelings of patriotism, nationalism, and pride. It also includes people's feelings toward their province as opposed to the whole country. A second aspect of political culture involves beliefs regarding the role of the state—how large a part do Canadians want it to play in their lives? Another variable consists of orientations to the decision-making apparatus. Are people aware of it, and to what extent do they want to control it? How do Canadians feel, in general, about the police, the bureaucracy, the courts, and the politicians? Do citizens trust them? Do people feel that their participation in the political system can make any difference?

When such values and attitudes are widely shared, they can be said to constitute the collective political culture. While political culture in Canada is usually considered to be fairly stable, this chapter will also examine how it seems to be changing.

Democracy

The first conclusion that emerges from a quest for Canadian political values is that almost all Canadians believe in **democracy**. The preamble to the Charter of Rights and Freedoms acknowledges democracy to be a foremost value in the country when it speaks of Canada as a "free and democratic society," but the Charter is not very specific about what this means. Democracy is derived from the Greek words *demos* (meaning people) and *kratia* (meaning power), and in the modern Western world usually includes:[1]

- popular sovereignty,
- political equality,
- political freedom, and
- majority rule.

POPULAR SOVEREIGNTY

Popular sovereignty means that the people have the final say, which in large, modern political systems usually takes the form of elections at specified intervals. For most Canadians, this is a sufficient opportunity for the exercise of popular sovereignty, although few would be content with anything less. Some states use plebiscites or referendums on a regular basis, but these devices have largely been foreign to the Canadian mentality. Only three national **referendums** have occurred since 1867 (on Prohibition in 1898, conscription in 1942, and the Charlottetown Accord in 1992), although the incidence is slightly higher at the provincial and municipal levels. Popular sovereignty is thus normally exercised in periodic elections that are essentially opportunities to select those who will make the big political decisions over the next four years or so, although any effective democracy also involves popular participation between elections as well. At least in the past, Canadians cherished **representative democracy** in which such elected and appointed authorities made decisions on their behalf.

POLITICAL EQUALITY

Given the significance of elections as the means of implementing the principle of popular sovereignty, a second aspect of Canadian democracy is **political equality**—that is, the idea that everyone is equal on election day. In essence, this means that every person has one vote and every vote has equal weight. It is only in relatively recent times, however, that Canada has met this ideal; at one time or another in the past, several groups were excluded, and there remains some question about the equal weight of all votes.

POLITICAL FREEDOM

The 1982 Charter of Rights and Freedoms provided an explicit constitutional statement of **political freedom** in Canada. It says: "Everyone has the following fundamental freedoms: freedom of conscience and religion; freedom of thought, belief, opinion and expression, including freedom of the press and other media of communication; freedom of peaceful assembly; and freedom of association." The Charter did not create these political freedoms, however; it put into writing the freedoms that Canadians had always enjoyed, and it provided a new means of protecting them—using the courts to invalidate legislation that infringed them rather than having to persuade politicians to do so.

MAJORITY RULE

Canadian democracy also incorporates the notion of **majority rule**. In case of dispute, the larger number takes precedence over the smaller number. This principle is generally accepted in elections and in the legislatures that result from elections.

Canadian students learn about democracy by viewing rowdy Question Period.
(Michael de Adder/Artizans.com)

Of course, if the number of options is greater than two, as in the case of Canadian elections, the winning candidate or party may not actually have a majority (over 50 percent), but just a plurality.

On the other hand, it is sometimes felt necessary to protect minorities from the actions of the majority, so that specific minority rights are given constitutional protection. The Constitution Act, 1867, recognized certain religious and linguistic minority rights, while the Charter of Rights and Freedoms extended constitutional minority rights to a considerable degree.

Identifying Other Basic Canadian Values

Once we get beyond the consensus on democracy, it is difficult to find widespread agreement on other Canadian political values. One approach that bears promise, however, is to identify widely held Canadian values by comparing Canada to the United States. Of course, Canadian and American values are very much alike. But some analysts have found at least subtle differences that have their foundation in the revolutionary origins of the United States and in the Canadian reaction against that revolution.

Many analysts make the point that the American Declaration of Independence lists the objectives of "life, liberty and the pursuit of happiness," while Canada's Constitution Act, 1867, talks about "peace, order and good government." Seymour

Martin Lipset goes on to outline a basic distinction: "Canada has been and is a more class-aware, elitist, law-abiding, statist, collectivity-oriented, and particularistic [group-oriented] society than the United States."[2] Pierre Berton has similarly noted that Canadians are law-abiding, peaceful, orderly, deferential toward authority, cautious, elitist, moralistic, tolerant, diffident, and unemotional.[3] The results of a 1995 Allan Gregg survey of what ordinary Canadians thought was distinctive about Canada included nonviolence, tolerance of minorities, humane treatment of the poor and disadvantaged, official bilingualism, and reluctance to boast.[4] This comparative approach leads us to identify five other basic Canadian values:

- Canadians prefer a closer balance between individualism and collectivism.
- Canadians value diversity more than homogeneity and are more tolerant of minorities.
- Canadians are more deferential toward authority.
- Canadians have a stronger belief in egalitarianism.
- Canadians are more cautious, more diffident, and less violent.

BALANCE BETWEEN INDIVIDUALISM AND COLLECTIVISM

If there is one value other than democracy to which most Canadians adhere, it is probably that of **individualism**, often expressed as the sanctity of private enterprise or individual economic freedom. Canadians generally believe that those with the greatest talent or those who work hardest should reap the benefits of their abilities and/or labour. The extent of such commitment can be best gauged, however, in comparison to attitudes in the United States.

While both countries have "mixed economies" today—that is, a combination of private enterprise and government involvement—the United States remains the world's last stronghold of individualism, with a relatively smaller public sector than other modern states. Canada, on the other hand, has been less hostile toward public intervention and more inclined to rely on government. This is partly because of the distinctive geographic environment of the Canadian political system and the desire to protect Canada from various U.S. influences. But it also stems from the basic Canadian value of **collectivism**, or community, originally derived from the United Empire Loyalists who opposed the American Revolution. They saw society not as a mass of grasping, ambitious, "free" individuals, but as an organic community in which all people had their place and did their respective part to contribute to the welfare of the whole. It is not part of the Canadian psyche to be instinctively suspicious of the state; indeed, most Canadians have not seen the government in terms of an alien imposition but as the authorized agent to respond to their individual and collective demands.

Canada is generally less collectivist than Western Europe, and the difference between the two North American countries should not be overstated, but much concrete evidence of a significant variation exists. The Canadian public health insurance system stands out in great contrast to that of the United States, even after the Obama reforms; the Canadian social safety net is also considered more adequate; and the extent of federal and provincial Crown corporations is unheard of south of the border. Taxes in Canada are generally higher in order to finance such collective activity. In just about every policy field, in fact, the extent of government intervention is greater in Canada than in the United States.

DIVERSITY AND TOLERANCE

A second difference between the basic values of the two countries is commonly expressed in terms of the melting pot and the mosaic: immigrants to the United States are urged to become "unhyphenated" Americans, whereas Canada encourages the retention of cultural diversities. Canada celebrates heterogeneity in society and tolerance of minorities, and it expects its public institutions to accommodate immigrants' practices and beliefs to some extent. The distinctiveness of the French-Canadian Roman Catholic community in Quebec was the original basis of this value, but it has now spread to policies of multiculturalism and recognition of other group rights, including those of Aboriginal peoples. Multiculturalism is seen as a means of enriching and enlivening the country, encouraging new Canadians to feel at home, promoting tolerance and minimizing discrimination, and perhaps enhancing Canada's contribution to world harmony. Will Kymlicka makes the point that Canada was a world leader in constitutionalizing multiculturalism and Aboriginal rights and in accommodating national minorities through territorial autonomy.[5]

Diversity also has a territorial dimension—the fact that Canadian provinces are much stronger than American states relative to the central government. Decentralization in Canada is accompanied by stronger regional or provincial loyalties and identities, due again to the example set by Quebec. Most studies have indicated that Ontarians feel closer to Canada than to their province, while the residents of Quebec, Newfoundland, and Alberta identify more with their province.[6] Even so, the provincial orientations of Albertans or Quebeckers should not be overstated. In another survey, 67 percent of Albertans disagreed with the suggestion that the province should replace national programs with its own, and 87 percent of Albertans had a strong sense of belonging to Canada.[7] Tolerance and diversity can also be seen in greater secularism in Canada that permits a commitment to minority rights, such as same-sex marriage, and in Canadian foreign policy, with its acceptance of differences and emphasis on negotiation rather than brute force.

DEFERENCE TO AUTHORITY

Another fundamental difference between Canadian and American values is the greater **deference to authority** in Canadian society. Canadians demonstrate more respect toward the law, judges, police, religious leaders, and many others with "legitimate power." Peace, order, and good government rather than individual liberty constitute the Canadian ideal, and many observers have noted that Canada is probably the only country where a police officer is a national symbol. Slightly less obsessed with material success than Americans, Canadians are more likely to obey a law even if breaking it would be to their economic advantage. Crime rates are considerably lower in Canada (the homicide rate typically being one-quarter that of the United States on a per capita basis), gun control laws are stronger, and the drug problem is less severe.

EGALITARIANISM

Canadians value **egalitarianism** more than do Americans. That is, Canada is more concerned with removing barriers that prevent individuals or groups from achieving their full potential. One striking example is in the constitutional equality of women. Canada adopted a strong guarantee of gender equality (including affirmative action) in the 1982 Charter of Rights and Freedoms at the very time that a similar proposal failed in the United States. The health and welfare programs that flow from Canadian collectivism similarly ensure a greater degree of socioeconomic equality for the poor and working classes. Studies of income distribution in the two countries consistently reveal smaller disparities between rich and poor in Canada. For example, a 2000 Statistics Canada study showed that the poorest 25 percent of Canadian families have more purchasing power than their U.S. counterparts, while the opposite is the case at the top of the income scale, and a 2005 study confirmed that Canada ranks higher on intergenerational social mobility.[8] In the realm of higher education, the United States has a greater hierarchy of educational institutions than is found in Canada. Moreover, Canada also extends this redistributive egalitarianism to have-not provinces through equalization payments.

CAUTION, DIFFIDENCE, AND NONVIOLENCE

A final difference in values to emerge from this analysis relates to Canadian caution and diffidence, sometimes called a national inferiority complex. It includes a historical dependence on other countries and the absence of a spirit of innovation and risk-taking. Canadians delight in the security of savings and understatement. Of course, there have been many Canadian "winners" in all walks of life in whose

Sidney Crosby of Team Canada celebrates after winning the Gold Medal at the 2010 Vancouver Olympics: international hockey prowess always ignites strong feelings of Canadian nationalism. (The Canadian Press/ Dave Sanford)

accomplishments Canadians vicariously share: Margaret Atwood, Céline Dion, Glenn Gould, Wayne Gretzky, Karen Kain, Bryan Adams, Frederick Banting, Lester Pearson, Stephen Lewis, and others. But Canadians are obsessed with "survival" rather than success; they are especially good at deprecating themselves and almost always think that things American are superior. Canadians tend to be prudent and cautious, sober and solemn, introverted, uncertain, and always questioning themselves. Most Canadians take quiet satisfaction in their achievements—the 1995 survey showed that 89 percent of Canadians felt proud when they saw the Canadian flag or heard the national anthem—but they rarely proclaim it aloud.

Along similar lines, although Canada made major contributions to two world wars, Canadians are not a warlike people and they abhor violence at home and abroad. We have tried to be peacemakers and peacekeepers in international relations, putting special emphasis on the United Nations, trying to reduce the militancy of the foreign policy of the United States in quiet, backroom diplomacy (though perhaps not as hard as we should have), and helping to remove the causes of war through assistance to developing countries. The presence of our soldiers in a combat role in Afghanistan troubled many Canadians who *hoped* they were primarily there to help rebuild the country.

The Changing Canadian Political Culture

As Canada approached the 21st century, many aspects of this traditional value structure seemed to be changing. Different concepts of democracy emerged, and the distinction between Canadian and American values appeared to be in decline. Some of this transformation can be attributed to the presence of the United States, directly or indirectly, and some to a worldwide change in political values, especially the rise of neoconservatism or neoliberalism after 1985.

As far as democracy is concerned, the 1990s saw an upsurge in interest in the means of more direct popular participation in government. The most common prescription in this regard was the referendum, in which legislators would be guided or bound by the frequent referral of policy questions to the electorate as a whole. Quebec used this device repeatedly on the question of sovereignty; certain other provinces now require it for approval of constitutional amendments, and some have prescribed it for other issues such as significant tax increases or electoral reform. With the widespread access to computers in the modern world, many have raised the possibility of "e-democracy," in which people could regularly vote on issues online. Somewhat similarly, British Columbia established a mechanism for the recall of MLAs between provincial elections.

What Do You Think?

Do you think e-democracy—which involves regular consultation with voters by means of the Internet—is a valid or viable idea? On what kind of issues should we hold referendums? On what grounds should it be possible to recall a member of Parliament? (In answering these questions, do not forget that you are probably more computer-literate than the majority of the population and the bearer of superior political knowledge.)

As for the distinctions between Canadian and American values, these are threatened in at least three ways. First, given the widespread U.S. influence over Canada and the Canadian exposure to the United States, values implicit in that country's popular culture, as transmitted by television, movies, books, magazines, and music, are likely to have considerable impact on those living north of the border. It is debatable whether distinctive Canadian values can withstand the homogenizing force of modern technology, especially that emanating from the south. Second, Canadian nationalists see all these influences increasing under free trade agreements with the United States, which restrict government intervention to protect Canadian culture. Third, some observers feel that the adoption of a U.S.-style Charter of Rights and Freedoms further diminishes distinctive Canadian values by challenging rather than deferring to government authority.

In a country that articulates its basic values so diffidently to start with, these powerful threats are not to be taken lightly. There are several indications that support for collectivism and feelings of deference in Canada have declined.[9] The obsession with government debts, deficits, and tax cuts at both federal and provincial levels in the 1990s seriously eroded social programs and shifted the basis of pensions and child benefits from universality to selectivity. Privatization of Crown corporations and deregulation also became rampant. Moreover, Canadians seem

· ·

Figure 6.1   Canada–U.S. Differences

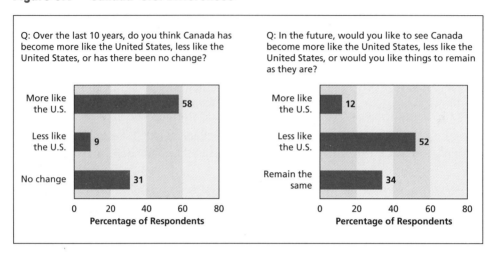

Q: Over the last 10 years, do you think Canada has become more like the United States, less like the United States, or has there been no change?

More like the U.S.   58
Less like the U.S.   9
No change   31

Percentage of Respondents

Q: In the future, would you like to see Canada become more like the United States, less like the United States, or would you like things to remain as they are?

More like the U.S.   12
Less like the U.S.   52
Remain the same   34

Percentage of Respondents

Source: EKOS Research Associates Inc., "Canadian Values and Identities in North America" (July 2002). © 2002. Reproduced with permission of EKOS Research Associates Inc.

increasingly concerned with the legal equality of all citizens, rather than with their socioeconomic equality or well-being. The coming to power of the Harper Conservatives in 2006 might be taken as confirmation of these trends.

Nevertheless, the most authoritative recent study of comparative values finds that Canada continues to be distinctive. Michael Adams argues that "The values and cultures of our two countries remain distinct even in the face of powerful forces of globalization and continental free trade."[10] Stephen Harper had to move his party toward the centre in order to achieve his minority government, and even so, only 41 percent of those who voted for him in 2006 wanted a Conservative government; 54 percent just wanted change.[11] It might be that neoliberalism never really took hold in the Canadian political culture, and as the early 21st century evolved, at least some aspects of it seemed to have run their course. Figure 6.1 indicates that the desire to remain distinct from the United States is still strong.

Political Socialization

Political socialization is the process through which individuals acquire their political values, attitudes, information, and opinions. The process consists in part of direct, individual exposure to political phenomena but is mostly performed by intermediaries or agents of socialization. It is relatively easy to identify the main agents of political socialization in Canada, but evaluating their relative impact is much more difficult. We begin with the four traditional agents—family, school, peers, and the media—and then examine other such influences.

The Family

Despite many modern pressures that have transformed the role of the family, including the increasing incidence of mothers working outside the home and the high divorce rate, the family remains the basic cell of Canadian society. Parents, stepparents, or sometimes grandparents are the first major influence on a child's attitudes and values. Most children absorb attitudes and values, some of which are of political significance, in a kind of osmosis from their family's talk and behaviour. Parents' casual comments about politics, politicians, parties, and police are good examples. Some parents also deliberately try to indoctrinate their children with certain political values or get them to support a particular political party. It seems, however, that what children pick up unconsciously and unintentionally is just as significant as what parents try to teach. For example, if parents talk about politics in the home, with or without attempting to guide their children's orientations, their children will usually develop a higher rate of political interest later on. Nevertheless, the political impact of the family should not be overemphasized, for political socialization is a process that continues throughout one's life.

The School

School is the second main agent of political socialization. All school systems in Canada and elsewhere deliberately attempt to inculcate certain basic values and attitudes, including some of a political nature, such as a feeling of affection or support for the country, the governmental apparatus, the head of state, the police, the flag, and the national anthem. Like the family, the school is an early enough influence that it may shape basic lifelong values. The fact that students are now entering some form of institutionalized educational setting earlier than in previous generations has probably increased the school's importance relative to that of the family; this phenomenon may be of particular significance in immigrant households.

Given the diversity of Canadian society, many questions arise about the role of the school in the political socialization process. Since the provinces and territories have jurisdiction over education, for example, do they deliberately contribute to the development of distinctive political cultures at the expense of the overall country? The radically different accounts of certain historical events found in French- and English-language textbooks are often cited as an example of the biased role of formal education in this process.[12] One point is clear: the forces of dualism, regionalism, and continentalism in Canadian society make it difficult for the school system to develop any pan-Canadian sense of national identity.[13]

Just as happens in the family setting, however, the school also contributes informally and unintentionally to the development of attitudes and values. Such unconscious transmissions occur in teachers' remarks beyond the formal curriculum, in class discussions and excursions, and in extracurricular activities. Moreover, exposure to an authoritarian teacher or principal is likely to produce different attitudes toward participation and dissent than those resulting from a more democratic setting. Corporations are also becoming increasingly involved in the educational system, promoting their own goods, services, and values.

Political socialization in the classroom setting. (© Rand Dyck)

Peers

Peers are the third main agent of political socialization. Peers are simply friends, colleagues, acquaintances, and associates. The concept of "peer pressure" is probably most familiar at the adolescent level and is not usually concerned with political values, attitudes, and opinions. But we are all susceptible to peer influence at any stage of our lives. In any group setting, including peer-group discussions that turn to politics, one person often becomes dominant, whether because of knowledge, position, or strength of character. At this stage, given the likelihood that basic values have already been established, peers are more likely to influence attitudes and opinions.

The Mass Media

The mass media are the fourth main agent of socialization. They are more often instruments of entertainment than enlightenment, however, and personal interaction with family members, teachers, or peers normally carries greater impact than passive, impersonal exposure to the media. When it comes to politics, the media transmit opinions primarily on topical issues and personalities and are less likely to influence lifelong values and attitudes. Nevertheless, there is evidence that Canadians do learn from this coverage,[14] and such short-term stimuli are important in determining how people vote.

Once again, media influence can be divided between the unconscious and the deliberate. In their editorials, newspapers explicitly attempt to influence opinions, while on the other pages of the paper Canadians expect news coverage to be as unbiased and factual as possible. Whether newspapers can keep such a fine line between subjective editorials and objective reporting is an interesting question, and some observers have detected bias in headlines, positioning, pictures, and selection of items to be included or excluded. Even though television does not usually have editorials as such, it has much greater scope for presenting biased news coverage than do newspapers, as noted in the fuller account of the mass media in Chapter 7. Moreover, some observers argue that the images portrayed on television, even in its provision of entertainment, convey powerful messages with political implications.

Other Agents of Political Socialization

Other agents of political socialization in Canada include political parties, religious denominations, interest groups of various kinds, corporations, and the government itself. Political parties practise the art of persuasion and seek to influence opinions and party preferences on a daily basis. Those people who already identify with a particular party find that the simplest means of forming an opinion on any issue is by taking their cue from the party leader.

Various religious groups often take stands on political issues. First and foremost, the Roman Catholic Church strongly influenced political values, attitudes, and opinions in Quebec prior to 1960. It had a close relationship with political authorities and did not hesitate to tell its members how to behave politically. The influence of religion in Canadian society may be generally on the decline, but its political role remains significant, especially perhaps in the form of evangelical Christians and Muslim groups.

Over half the population belongs to an organized group of some kind, and although the orientation of such groups is primarily nonpolitical, all have the potential to influence their members' political views. Some, such as the Canadian Medical Association and the Canadian Labour Congress, are quite determined to do so. As with parties and churches, taking one's opinions from the urging of a group leader obviates the need to make further individual effort to understand the issue. Other groups, such as the Boy Scouts or Girl Guides, try to instill in children an informed affection for the country.

Like political parties, individual corporations are in the business of persuasion, trying to sell their own goods and services. Sometimes, however, companies also try to influence political attitudes and opinions, an effort that is called **advocacy advertising**. Many corporations were involved in the free trade debate, especially during the 1988 election campaign, expressing their support through "speeches, debates, letters, advertisements, information sessions with employees, and inserts in newspapers."[15] On many other occasions, too, employers have tried to influence the voting preferences of their own employees with internal memos about how different parties or policies would affect the firm.

Finally, the government itself is often engaged in efforts to influence public views and behaviour. Sometimes these efforts are widely recognized as legitimate, such as in the cases of encouraging physical fitness and discouraging smoking, impaired driving, racial discrimination, domestic violence, and the use of drugs. Sometimes attempts to influence people are made for broadly acceptable political purposes, such as promoting vacations in Canada and the purchase of Canadian-made goods. Governments are also expected to inform the public about new laws, regulations, and programs, but there is a fine line between providing simple information and extolling the virtues of such initiatives for partisan purposes. The Mulroney government, for example, spent large sums of public funds promoting the merits of the Free Trade Agreement and the Goods and Services Tax in advertising campaigns that most observers felt were excessive and self-serving. The sponsorship of various events in Quebec by the Chrétien government to try to engender greater support for the federal government was not only counterproductive but also resulted in scandal. The Harper government also promoted its stimulus program (Canada's Economic Action Plan) with a tremendous amount of publicly funded advertising.

How Canadians individually and collectively acquire their political values, attitudes, information, and opinions is a complicated question. Because the process is so haphazard and complex, and the stimuli in each person's environment so diverse, no deliberate effort is guaranteed to be successful. Instead, Canadians acquire many of their political values, attitudes, and opinions in a completely unconscious way. Moreover, many Canadians are only semi-socialized: they simply do not have many political values, attitudes, and opinions or much political information. The general level of political awareness is not high, which in turn is reflected in patterns of political participation.

Political Participation

Political participation consists of "those voluntary activities by citizens that are intended to influence the selection of government leaders or the decisions they make."[16] Numerous avenues of political participation exist, but actual participation takes more initiative and effort than many people are willing to exert. Participation is also related to the possession of political efficacy—a sense of political competence and a feeling that one can have some impact on the system. Participation depends on the possession of such resources as time, money, and information, although perhaps not as much as many people think. Regrettably, the opportunities for participation in Canada far exceed actual levels of involvement.

Electoral Participation

Voting on election day is a crucial aspect of democracy and is the most common form of political participation in Canada. The voter turnout rate is also one of the few forms of participation that can be regularly and reliably measured. The overall average national turnout rate between 1900 and 1988 was about 73 percent, or nearly three-quarters of those eligible to vote. These figures disguise the fact that the turnout rate varied considerably from one province to another. The rate for each federal election between 1974 and 2008 is provided in Table 6.1.

TABLE 6.1 PERCENTAGE VOTER TURNOUT IN FEDERAL ELECTIONS, 1974–2008

Year	Turnout (%)	Year	Turnout (%)
1974	71	1993	70
1979	76	1997	67
1980	69	2000	64
1984	75	2004	61
1988	75	2006	65
		2008	59

Source: Elections Canada. http://www.elections.ca/content.asp?section=pas&document=turnout&lang=e&textonly=false

Those who do not vote have consistently been shown to be alienated from or uninformed about the political system, and they primarily include the young, the poor, and the working classes. Other traditional reasons for not voting include lack of interest, finding the alternatives to be unappealing, lacking party identification, possessing passivity engendered by watching television, feeling that government is irrelevant to one's life or is not listening, thinking that to vote for a minor party is wasting one's vote, or believing that the result is predetermined. The voter turnout rate has dramatically decreased since 1990 to an all-time low of about 59 percent in 2008. In general, the largest groups that abstained were poorly educated young people, those who were less interested in politics, and those who were less informed.[17]

It is estimated that only 25 percent of people under the age of 30 voted in the Canadian federal election of 2000. The three most common reasons for not voting given by those in this group were as follows: lack of interest (28 percent); lack of time (23 percent); and lack of appeal on the part of, or lack of faith in, parties, leaders, and candidates (20 percent). Most such young people lack a sense of civic duty and do not feel that voting is either important for its own sake or an essential obligation of living in a democracy. Elections Canada put much effort into a campaign to raise the youth voter turnout rate and estimated that it rose to about 35 percent in 2004.[18]

Another probable factor for the decline in voter turnout rates is the "dismantling of the state," including globalization. Since government performs fewer functions than previously, people have less confidence in it and fewer expectations. Canada's turnout rate falls between the extremes found in other countries; it is well above that in the United States but behind that in most comparable states, including Britain.

Within the group of those who do vote, other degrees of electoral involvement can be distinguished. For one thing, the level of information of the typical voter should not be overestimated. Here is what the leading study of the subject recently concluded:

> The Canadian public contains deep pockets of political ignorance and political illiteracy. Over 40 percent of Canadians were unable to name the leaders of the federal political parties, even though they were being interviewed right after an election in which those leaders had figured prominently. As for the parties' issue positions, 30 percent of Canadians could not identify one single promise with the party making it. And most Canadians were unable to identify which party was on the left and which was on the right.[19]

Beyond those who cast an "informed vote," a smaller proportion of the electorate actually becomes actively involved in the election campaign: attending all-candidates meetings; joining a political party; voting at the party's local nomination meeting; contributing money to a political party; or helping a local candidate to do mailing, telephoning, door-to-door canvassing, and election-day work. A small number in each constituency become totally preoccupied with the local campaign; these people, including candidates themselves, are sometimes called "gladiators," as distinct from the great bulk of the population, who are primarily "spectators."

Non-electoral Participation

The political participation of most Canadians peaks at election time, but many avenues are open between elections in which to make demands or otherwise become involved in the political process. One option is to join a political party. Most Canadian political parties do not maintain reliable lists of their members, but it is estimated that less than three percent of the population belong to a party.[20] It is known, however, that many people sign up before or during the election campaign (often to participate in the nomination of candidates) or before a party leadership contest, and then let their membership lapse.

Another means of political participation is to join an organized interest group, an action that some 60 percent of Canadians claim to do. As seen in Chapter 10, any group, whatever its primary orientation, can become an advocacy group, so that membership in any group is potentially political. Even if the group itself takes a political turn, however, passive members rarely do more than send the occasional pre-printed postcard to their MP or the prime minister.

On the other hand, the purpose of some groups is primarily political, and political activists increasingly seem to prefer involvement in social movements and advocacy groups over joining a political party. Active executive and staff members of such groups may become highly involved in political campaigns and the advocacy-group politics that goes on in Canada every day. Even more initiative is required to form such a group to protest against some political decision or lack of action at the municipal, provincial, federal, or even global level. Such group participation usually involves communicating with the authorities in routine ways, and may actually be solicited by politicians or bureaucrats.

Occasionally, even in Canada, non-electoral participation takes the form of peaceful demonstrations (locally or on Parliament Hill), sit-ins and other types of civil disobedience, and the rare violent protest. As noted earlier, Canadians are generally a peaceful lot, and political violence is uncommon. The main historical

Figure 6.2   Percentage of Canadians Who Engaged in Selected Political Activities over the Previous Year, 2003

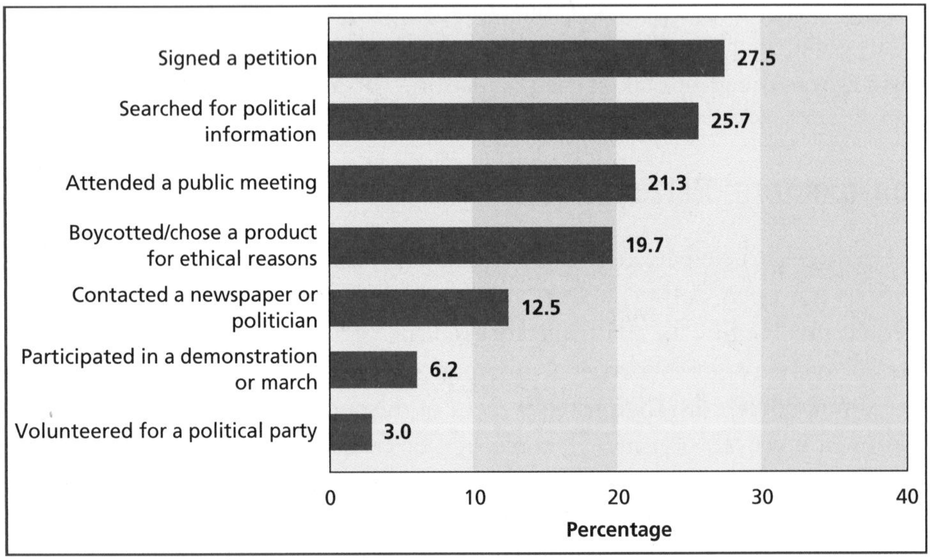

Source: Adapted from Statistics Canada publication, 2003 General Social Survey on Social Engagement, Cycle 17: An Overview of Findings, 2003, Cat. No. 89–598 (July 6, 2004), http://dsp-psd.pwgsc.gc.ca/Collection/Statcan/89-598-x/89-598-XIE2003001.pdf, chart 19, p. 39 (Retrieved December 1, 2010).

incidents of such violence in Canada were the Riel Rebellions of 1870 and 1885, the conscription riots in Quebec City in 1918, the Winnipeg General Strike of 1919, the Regina Riot of 1935, the various FLQ incidents of the 1960s culminating in the FLQ crisis of 1970, and the Mohawks' armed standoff at Oka in 1990.[21]

Canadians can also participate politically between elections as individuals—writing, faxing, or e-mailing letters to MPs, Cabinet ministers, or the prime minister, writing letters to the editors of newspapers, calling radio or television phone-in shows, submitting opinions to online media websites, signing petitions, or telephoning or meeting an MP. Statistics Canada provides some data on the degree of individual involvement in these activities, as shown in Figure 6.2. Hardly more than 25 percent of respondents had signed a petition, an action that does not require much effort, and the degree of engagement declined from there. Moreover, there is probably a large element of overlap among the people who participated in any of these activities.

SUMMARY

This chapter examined political culture, political socialization, and political participation in Canada. After defining political culture, it focused on the adherence to democracy, as well as five other basic political values that distinguish Canadians from Americans. It suggested that while Canadians' political values are undergoing a certain amount of change, they remain quite distinct. The chapter then discussed the concept of political socialization and the principal agents thereof, including family, school, peers, mass media, and government itself. The third part of the chapter dealt with political participation. It showed that the voter turnout rate in Canada has seriously declined in recent years, especially among young people. It also indicated that while various forms of non-electoral political participation are available, the extent to which Canadians avail themselves of these opportunities is not particularly impressive.

DISCUSSION QUESTIONS

1. Are periodic elections a sufficient means of exercising the principle of popular sovereignty? In what situations are referendums appropriate?
2. To what extent are basic Canadian political values still distinct from those in the United States?

3. Thinking about the relative importance of the agents of political socialization in your own life, can you decipher your own socialization process?
4. How high a level of political information and political participation does a democracy require?

KEY TERMS

Advocacy advertising Advertising that advocates a political point of view rather than trying to sell a good or service.

Collectivism As opposed to individualism, an ideology that holds that the public interest is enhanced by substantial collective action, normally via government.

Deference to authority A value considered to be part of the Canadian political culture in which citizens are respectful of government authority and accept its word and orders with little question.

Democracy A political system characterized by popular sovereignty, political equality, political freedom, and majority rule.

Egalitarianism As opposed to elitism, the philosophy or practice of providing everyone with an equal amount of power and/or treating everyone more or less equally.

Individualism An ideology that holds that individuals should have maximum freedom or liberty to do as they please, especially in economic terms, and that governments should not get involved in taxation, regulation, redistribution, or ownership.

Majority rule An element in the definition of democracy that states that in any decision-making setting involving a difference of opinion, the larger number should carry the day.

Political culture The sum total of the politically relevant values, beliefs, attitudes, and orientations in any political system.

Political efficacy The feeling that one has political influence and that one's political participation can make an impact.

Political equality An element in the definition of democracy that entails the principle of "one person, one vote," that is, every citizen has a vote and each counts equally.

Political freedom An element in the definition of democracy that entails freedom of speech, press, assembly, association, etc., such that people can organize and advocate in order to influence election results and public policy.

Political socialization The process whereby individuals acquire their political values, attitudes, beliefs, information, and opinions.

Popular sovereignty An element in the definition of democracy that entails periodically allowing the public at large to exert its will—to have the final say—normally through general elections.

Recall A populist device in which the signing of a petition by a certain proportion of the local electorate to recall their legislative representative means that the representative must resign.

Referendum A populist device in which a public policy proposal is submitted directly to the electorate.

Representative democracy A system of government based on periodic election of representatives to Parliament, as opposed to more direct participation by voters in making public decisions.

FURTHER READING

Adams, Michael. *Fire and Ice: The United States, Canada and the Myth of Converging Values.* Toronto: Penguin Canada, 2003.

———. *Unlikely Utopia: The Surprising Triumph of Canadian Pluralism.* Toronto: Penguin Canada, 2007.

Bell, David. "Political Culture in Canada." In Michael Whittington and Glen Williams, eds., *Canadian Politics in the 21st Century*, 7th ed. Toronto: Thomson Nelson, 2008.

Berton, Pierre. *Why We Act Like Canadians.* Toronto: McClelland and Stewart, 1982.

Friedenberg, Edgar J. *Deference to Authority.* White Plains, N.Y.: M.E. Sharpe, 1980.

Gidengil, Elisabeth, et al. *Citizens.* Vancouver: UBC Press, 2004.

Howe, Paul. *Citizens Adrift: The Democratic Disengagement of Young Canadians.* Vancouver: UBC Press, 2010.

Lipset, Seymour Martin. *Continental Divide.* New York: Routledge, 1990.

Mendelsohn, Matthew, and J. Scott Matthews. "The New Ontario: The Shifting Attitudes of Ontarians toward the Federation." Mowat Centre for Policy Innovation, University of Toronto, February 2010.

Nevitte, Neil. *The Decline of Deference*. Peterborough: Broadview Press, 1996.

Pammett, Jon H., and Lawrence LeDuc. "Explaining the Turnout Decline in Canadian Federal Elections: A New Survey of Non-voters." March 2003. http://www.elections.ca/loi/tur/tud/TurnoutDecline.pdf.

Thomas, David, ed. *Canada and the United States: Differences That Count*, 3rd ed. Peterborough: Broadview Press, 2008.

Chapter 7

The Mass **Media and Public** *Opinion Polls*

The **mass media**, principally television, newspapers, radio, and increasingly the Internet, are the primary source of most Canadians' knowledge and opinions about topical political issues and current political personalities. Public policymakers also depend on the media to provide much of the information they need for their own work as well as to transmit the messages that they want the public to hear. The media thus provide an important two-way communications link between the governors and the governed. A second crucial connector is the public opinion poll. Political parties rely heavily on polls to guide their actions immediately before and during election campaigns, but governments and the media also seek to discover Canadians' opinions on a daily basis. This chapter examines both of these important and interconnected features of the political system.

Chapter Objectives

After you have completed this chapter, you should be able to:

Outline the ownership of different media and evaluate the significance of public, private, and concentrated ownership

Discuss the agenda-setting function of the media

Distinguish between the virtues of newspapers and television as sources of political information

Comment on the new forms of political communication provided by the Internet

Understand the mutually dependent relationship between politicians and the media

Appreciate the extent to which public opinion is not well informed

Enumerate the practitioners of public opinion polling and discuss their techniques

Evaluate the extent to which public opinion polls influence voting behaviour and the policies adopted by governments

The Mass Media

In surveying the newspaper, radio, and television industries today, it should first be noted that the privately owned media exist primarily to make a profit and that whatever political functions they serve are incidental to that purpose. In addition, because the media—even television—usually rely on words and language, and because a majority of Canadians are unilingual, the country is characterized by a "media apartheid," in which English and French are virtually two solitudes.

Newspapers

The Canadian daily newspaper industry has been characterized by chain ownership for several decades, but owners have frequently changed in recent years. An earlier era was dominated by the Ken Thomson and Southam newspaper chains. Then, in the 1990s, Conrad Black, proprietor of the Hollinger chain, added the Southam and most of the Thomson papers to his holdings and established *National Post*. After 2000, the Asper family, proprietors of CanWest Global Television, became active in the newspaper industry and purchased most of Black's Canadian dailies. Meanwhile, Thomson sold majority control of *The Globe and Mail* to BCE (Bell Canada Enterprises), also owners of the CTV television network, although this arrangement was later severed. Table 7.1 shows the leading newspaper chains in Canada in 2009 in terms of number of papers and percentage of total circulation. Pierre Péladeau owns the Quebecor/Sun Media chain with a large presence in Quebec, Ontario, and Alberta; Paul Desmarais's Power Corp. otherwise dominates Quebec; the Torstar chain is the largest in Ontario; and the Irving family's Brunswick News has a virtual monopoly in New Brunswick. In 2010, the CanWest chain was sold to a new ownership group under National Post CEO Paul Godfrey called Postmedia Network. Thus, some of the wealthiest families in Canada control most of the country's newspaper industry. Moreover, one chain or another often has an overwhelming dominance in a single province.

TABLE 7.1 LARGEST CANADIAN DAILY NEWSPAPER CHAINS, 2009

	# of Publications	Total Circulation (%)
Quebecor/Sun Media/Osprey	36	23
CanWest	13	31
Transcontinental	10	3
Glacier	9	1
Power Corp.	7	11
Torstar	4	12
Brunswick News	3	2

Source: Canadian Newspaper Association, http://www.cna-acj.ca/en/aboutnewspapers/ownership.

Such concentrated ownership of Canadian newspapers has always caused considerable concern. Many fear that the owner of several papers will gain an unhealthy degree of influence over public opinion by establishing a common point of view for all papers in the chain. The Trudeau government appointed the Kent Royal Commission on Newspapers to investigate this question but, responding to strong pressure from the industry, abandoned a bill aimed to restrict concentrated media ownership. All conglomerate-owned newspapers are likely to betray a pro-business bias,[1] and most of the newspaper-owning families have substantial holdings beyond newspapers. This leads to the question of whether such media outlets provide fair coverage of the operations of other firms under the same ownership. Especially in the small confines of New Brunswick, for example, it has been suggested that Irving newspapers refrain from critical comment on that family's other holdings. Moreover, many media analysts find the new trend toward companies owning both television networks and daily newspapers to be somewhat troubling. The Asper family's ownership of many daily newspapers across Canada along with the Global Television network illustrated the dangers of chain ownership when a single owner is determined to mould Canadians' thinking on public issues.

Many newspapers can now be read in whole or in part online, while some 35 free daily newspapers are published in Canada with an estimated circulation of over one million copies. Such developments do not bode well for the traditional newspaper industry.

Radio and Television

The radio and television industries are distinct from newspapers in two respects: the degree of public ownership involved and the presence of government regulation of both public and private companies. As for public ownership, the **Canadian Broadcasting Corporation (CBC)** operates radio stations in both official languages nationwide. CBC radio has a relatively large and sophisticated audience, and it plays a major role in transmitting information and opinion among its listeners. The CBC/Radio-Canada television network also has stations across the country, with English-language production centred in Toronto and French-language production in Montreal. These are supplemented by agreements with a number of privately owned affiliated stations, which agree to telecast a certain amount of CBC programming.

Apart from CBC/Radio-Canada, the hundreds of local AM and FM stations used to be independently owned but are now increasingly characterized by chain ownership, just as in the newspaper industry. Ownership changes quite frequently, but some 60 percent of the radio market in Canada is controlled by the ten leading firms. Like newspapers, radio stations must be Canadian-owned. When the limited Canadian content on private radio stations became a problem, the CRTC issued Canadian-content rules, as noted in Chapter 5.

The privately owned CTV network, centred on CFTO in Toronto, consists of some 24 television stations and is now owned by BCE (Bell Canada Enterprises). The Toronto-based CanWest Global system was cobbled together by the Asper family, but ran into financial difficulties in the Great Recession of 2008–10 and was added to the Shaw Communications empire of Calgary. Several major cities also have an unaffiliated, independent private English-language station. Besides the other private companies mentioned, Corus and Astral both own an array of radio and specialty and pay-TV channels. On the French side, the TVA network, whose focal point is Télé-Métropole in Montreal, is owned by the Péladeau family.

The **Canadian Radio-television and Telecommunications Commission (CRTC)** is the federal regulatory agency in this field. The commission requires Canadian television stations to be domestically owned and to telecast 50 percent or more Canadian content. But such regulations are virtually meaningless when almost all residents are within reach, either directly or via cable or satellite, of a large assortment of U.S. television channels. On this point, Fred Fletcher talks of "American images crowding out Canadian ones,"[2] and Ed Black writes of the problem of trying to serve a small population in two language groups "who live in tempting, embarrassing, and almost smothering proximity to [10 times as many]

Peter Mansbridge holds up his Gemini award for Best News Anchor, 2003. Most Canadians get their political information from television. (The Canadian Press/Frank Gunn)

Americans who speak the language of Canada's majority…. They also have the world's most penetrating and effective system for transmitting ideas en masse."[3] Peter Trueman adds, "Think of the overwhelming preponderance of American programming, which in an unobtrusive way pumps us full of American values, American hopes, American history, even American patterns of speech."[4]

CBC television has a strong commitment to Canadian programming but suffers from a chronic shortage of funds. After severe bloodletting under the Mulroney government, the CBC hoped for better treatment under the Chrétien regime. Instead, that government slashed the CBC budget even further, precipitating the resignation of the corporation's president. The public broadcaster was treated in an equally unkind manner by the Harper government.

Private stations and networks realize that profits can be maximized by telecasting as much U.S. programming as the CRTC will allow. Nevertheless, the importance and popularity of CBC, CTV, and Global national newscasts, *CBC News Morning, The Fifth Estate, Marketplace, Dragons' Den, This Hour Has 22 Minutes, Téléjournal, Le Point, Canada AM,* and *W5* should not be underestimated. As mentioned in Chapter 5, the overall percentage of time spent watching Canadian-content programs on Canadian conventional, pay-TV, and specialty channels in 2004 by anglophones was 28 percent, compared to 71 percent for francophones. English-speaking Canadians watch more Canadian than foreign coverage only in the categories of news and public affairs and sports.[5]

The establishment of CBC Newsworld (now CBC News Network) in 1989 and a French-language equivalent in 1995 was another effort to strengthen Canadian television content. These all-news channels cover many political events live and more extensively than regular CBC, with which they work closely, and provide regional coverage, documentaries, and in-depth interview programming. While their audience is small, most members of the political elite tune in regularly. CTV also has a national all-news channel, while several provinces have an educational television channel and/or another that carries provincial legislative proceedings. The national parliamentary channel on cable is called CPAC.

At least 85 percent of Canadian homes are hooked up to (and hooked on) cable television or satellite services; this is more than in any other country. The CRTC regulates which channels they carry, but cable and satellite television bring the major U.S. networks into most Canadian homes and permit subscribers to watch U.S. news, public affairs, and sports programs. The Canadian cable industry is essentially dominated by four regional giants: Rogers Communications, Shaw Cablesystems, Vidéotron, and Cogeco Inc. The variety of other channels on cable and satellite television is constantly increasing, and some of them are of Canadian origin; for example, CBC, CTV, Global, and others have established their own specialty channels. CRTC approval of cable, satellite, and new specialty channels has served to dilute the audience of conventional Canadian television stations.

The Changing Media World: Convergence in Canadian Media Ownership

Probably few aspects of the political system are in such a state of rapid change as the mass media. This change is usually referred to as a **convergence** of technologies and corporations, as television, telephone, satellite, cable, computer, and Internet companies merge.[6] Spectacular media conglomerations have taken place in the United States in recent years (which in themselves have a considerable impact on Canada), but in this respect Canada is not far behind. The multilayered BCE, Quebecor, and Rogers Communications empires represent similar cross-media conglomerates, as shown in Table 7.2. The print and broadcast divisions of CanWest Global Television were severed in 2010, as were the CTV and *Globe and Mail* divisions of CTVglobemedia.

The increased concentration of ownership of such sources of public information is not a healthy development in any democracy that values the maximum diversity of opinions. Moreover, it tends to reduce the resources devoted to news and investigative reporting at the expense of profit-oriented entertainment. On the other hand, the opposite trend toward a fragmentation of audiences allows individuals to ignore broader public questions as they expose themselves to media coverage of only a few personal interests through specialized television channels.

TABLE 7.2 FOUR LARGEST MEDIA CONGLOMERATES IN CANADA, 2010

CanWest Global	BCE	Quebecor	Rogers
conventional TV stations (including E! Channel)	CTV television network	daily newspapers	cable television and telephones
specialty channels	specialty channels	TVA television network	specialty channels
daily newspapers	telephones	Internet services	Internet services
Magazines	CHUM radio and television stations (A Channel)	publishing	Magazines
Internet services	Internet services	cable television	radio stations and telephones
Alliance/Atlantis Communications		magazines	video rentals
news service		video rentals	CITY-TV network

As a result of the breakup of CanWest Global and CTVglobemedia in 2010, Canada was left with less joint ownership of television and newspaper enterprises. On the other hand, communications companies like Bell and Shaw are now concerned to own both the content and transmission of television services.

Many parts of the media industry have recently experienced economic trouble, and most have cut corners in order to stay in business. In this process, political news, which is relatively expensive to gather, is often sacrificed. Moreover, the amount of local news coverage has declined, several local television stations have closed, and a number of daily newspapers have merged or closed their doors.

New Forms of Political Communication

The Internet is starting to rival newspapers, radio, and television as a medium of mass communications. Like them, it can be used as a source of information and entertainment; indeed, as one of its features, the Internet actually provides access to the other three mass media, and has had a negative effect on the newsprint industry. Over 75 percent of Canadians now have access to the Internet at home, work, or school, and those who cannot afford to buy a computer or an Internet service can usually find free online access at university, college, or public libraries.

In addition to providing an alternative source of coverage of topical political developments, the Internet is a vast reservoir of information, including websites of government departments, political parties, advocacy groups, and other actors in the political system. It allows for direct and instantaneous feedback between the sender and receiver, brings together print and electronic communication methods into a single medium, and allows for the targeting of small segments of the population. Politics also lends itself to extensive Internet "blogs" (weblogs) as anyone with intense interest can post commentaries concerning current events on places such as media websites. Blogs can be read by thousands of people and sometimes actually influence political developments, while Internet tools like Facebook, Twitter, and YouTube can be used to avoid the costs and regulations of traditional TV advertising.[7]

The Internet can be a liberating force that permits people to gain information from around the world, connect with others having similar concerns, and provide direct feedback to government. On the other hand, a "digital divide" based on age and class continues to exist, and the Internet can also be used for antisocial purposes.

The Media and the Public

The influence of the mass media on the political system is profound and appears to be constantly increasing.[8] Most of the information Canadians receive about the political process comes from television, newspapers, radio, the Internet, and magazines, rather than from direct observation. Some recipients may be able to separate this information from whatever commentary or biases accompany it, but many are swayed by the particular perspective that the media give to the data they present.

The current consensus on the role of the media is that they set the political agenda for the country. In other words, the media tell people what to think about, what the important issues are, and which political personalities are significant. They help to define what is political.[9] This is a function that the media share with political parties, and while parties may be more important as initiators of issues, these are not likely to remain on the agenda without media attention. The **parliamentary press gallery** seems to have a "herd instinct" or to engage in "pack journalism" in developing a consensus about what these significant issues are.[10] In part, this reflects the influence of the daily oral Question Period in the House of Commons, which provides the media with short, superficial, and controversial issues that are well suited to television coverage.

Figure 7.1 shows the results of a 2003 Statistics Canada survey that asked respondents about their reliance on five different media. Television surpassed

Figure 7.1   Exposure to Different News Sources among "Frequent Consumers" of News

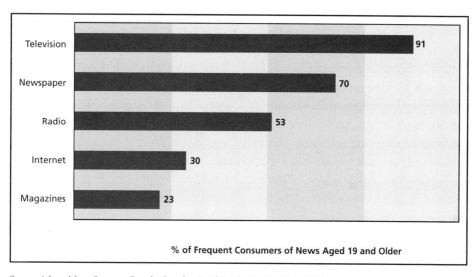

% of Frequent Consumers of News Aged 19 and Older

Source: Adapted from Statistics Canada, *Canadian Social Trends*, 11-008-XIE 2007003 Summer 2007, No. 83. Released June 19, 2007.

newspapers by over 20 percent, although most "frequent consumers" exposed themselves to more than one media source. Other studies have also shown that when asked to choose among the various media, a majority of people say they prefer to get their political information from television rather than newspapers. Those who prefer television feel it is more fair and believable for all kinds of information, as well as more complete, except perhaps for business and economic news.[11]

These results are somewhat distressing to those who know the real advantages and disadvantages of the two main media in question. Because of cost and time constraints, television newscasts must present a shorter and more superficial account of political events than newspapers. Coverage of any item rarely exceeds a 60- to 90-second "news clip" with a 10-second "sound bite" of the voices of political leaders, in which *how* something is said is usually more important than *what* is said. The transcript of a 30-minute newscast would make up about one-third of a single newspaper page.[12] Moreover, because it is a visual medium, television must seek out colourful, dramatic, emotional, controversial, or entertaining pictures. Riots, demonstrations, and political conventions usually make for good television, but the daily routine of politics does not lend itself as well to compelling visual coverage. Witness the efforts taken by politicians, protesters, and the media themselves to find contrived and engaging settings in which to stage political happenings, make announcements, or tape interviews.

Television portrays images and impressions, and it is therefore much better at dealing with political leaders and personalities than with issues. These characteristics make television the most open of the three media to distortion and exploitation, so that it is actually the *least* believable and—however unintentionally—the *most* biased.[13] Television meets the needs of the average citizen with a short attention span who is looking for visual stimulation and does not wish to invest much effort in understanding the political system. Of course, all-news channels like CBC News Network and CPAC, and public affairs programs on other channels, have more time to delve into political issues in depth.

Political parties and politicians increasingly gear their activities to the demands of television rather than those of the other media or the public. Press conferences are now dominated by television lights and cameras; leaders' tours during election campaigns are "photo opportunities" designed to generate a sound bite on the evening news; and party conventions and leaders' debates are scheduled at the television networks' convenience. In preparing for elections, parties put greater effort into designing television commercials and trying them out before focus groups than into devising solutions to the country's problems. The leaders' debate has become the single most important event in an election campaign because elections usually turn more on leader images than issues, policies, local candidates, or other leading figures in the party. The appearance, style, and general image of the party leader, including the ability to perform on television, has become of crucial importance. This emphasis on appearance is often said to trivialize politics.

What Do You Think?

Even if the mass public prefers to get its day-to-day political information from television, is this medium good enough for students of politics such as yourself? Do you try to read a respectable daily newspaper on a regular basis? If you could not afford to buy a newspaper regularly, would you go to your university or college library to read one? Do you read newspapers on the Internet?

It would be too soon, however, to write off the political importance of newspapers. Daily newspapers generally offer more comprehensive coverage of political events, and they excel at covering issues, which they can do at length, in depth, and in detail, presenting both greater factual information and a wider range of interpretation. While the "average" Canadian relies on television for political information, those with political influence, whether in government, parties, advocacy groups, or peer-group situations, are more likely to depend on newspapers. Those who prefer newspapers over television have higher levels of education and higher incomes, and they are better informed. Furthermore, even though print journalists must often defer to the paraphernalia of their television colleagues, the broadcast media and opposition parties tend to take their cues from newspapers.

It should be added that the degree of a person's political participation increases sharply with his or her level of newspaper consumption. In other words, those who make the effort to increase their political information by reading a newspaper (as opposed to sitting passively in front of a TV set) are not only better informed but also more likely to go on to engage in some form of political participation.[14]

The Globe and Mail calls itself "Canada's national newspaper" and publishes a national edition transmitted by satellite to several printing locations, so that it is available every morning in all major centres across the country. It is read by most of the top-level decision-makers and media executives and thus tends to set the agenda for other news organizations. The *Globe* now has competition from the *National Post*, while the independent, nationalistic *Le Devoir* occupies a similarly influential position in French Canada. In fact, all French-language media in Quebec have played a part in communicating a sense of the French-Canadian nation.

The Media and the Politicians

Politicians and their bureaucratic advisers need publicity and therefore have a great interest in how the media cover their behaviour. Even though they have their own direct sources, they also depend on the media to provide information they need about what is happening at home and abroad. The media in turn often rely on government sources for most of their information, and much media reporting of politics is of the "government handout" variety.

OWNERS, EDITORS, AND JOURNALISTS

Canadian daily newspapers are expected to present news coverage in an objective manner and reserve the opinions of the owner or editor for the editorial page. Even so, one can often detect biases in the tone or selection of news items, such as a centre-right slant in *The Globe and Mail* and a centre-left, Liberal inclination in the *Toronto Star*. Conrad Black made such biases more overt when he assumed ownership of the Southam chain, especially in his creation of the *National Post*: a clear-cut preference for the Reform/Alliance party and its right-wing policies pervaded the paper. The newspaper maintained this tradition even after it was purchased by the Asper family and after the Alliance and PC parties merged into the new Conservative Party of Canada. Increasingly, Pierre Péladeau has assumed the mantle of the leader of right-wing media coverage.

In principle, reporters should remain distant from politicians to cover them objectively; on the other hand, it is often necessary to cultivate close relations in order to get the kind of information that those in the media seek. Allan Fotheringham writes that "the narrowest line in journalism is the line between exploiting your sources (without ever destroying them) and being captured by them."[15] Furthermore, since politicians often confidentially seek out the opinions of working reporters, the latter sometimes have to agonize over whether to reveal information that was given to them "off the record," that is, in the expectation that it would not be used.

The media also have to confront the issue of politicians' privacy. When do excessive drinking, sexual infidelity, or family, health, or financial problems begin to interfere with a politician's public functions, and when should they be revealed? Beyond personal privacy is the question of whether the media should transmit information they are not supposed to have, such as when Global Television came into advance possession of a summary of the 1988 budget.

THE GOVERNMENT SIDE: NEWS MANAGEMENT

The increasingly common problem of **news management** and manipulation relates especially to the deliberate timing and selective distribution of government information. It includes exaggerating positive news while keeping secret or delaying release of that which is negative, giving preference to friendly reporters over others, making prime ministerial requests for network television time for less than important announcements, and outright lying. News management also involves putting the best face on a deficient government action or politician's performance by having a partisan official tell the media how successful it actually was, in the hope that the media will transmit this evaluation to their audience. Those involved in such efforts are often called media handlers or **spin doctors**, because they try to put the best face, or "spin," on any event.

One of the most important parts of a Memorandum to Cabinet proposing new government action is the communications strategy. As Fletcher and Everett point out, the 200 members of the press gallery are greatly outnumbered by government communications officers.[16] The Harper government was much less accessible to reporters than its predecessors, maintaining highly centralized control over the flow of information and insisting on choosing which reporters asked questions at rarely held news conferences.

News leaks are another issue in news management. When governments do not know what course to follow, they sometimes leak a proposal to the media as a "trial balloon," hoping for guidance from the public reaction received. Ed Black points out that this practice is helpful in the modern, instantaneous world, where politicians usually have little time to respond to problems or give them comprehensive consideration.[17]

The ultimate problem in media–government relations is political interference with the "freedom of the press," one of the sacred principles of democracy, as discussed in Chapter 6. The most blatant examples of such political interference have occurred at the provincial level. In Quebec between 1935 and 1960, Premier Maurice Duplessis kept the press under control by awarding advertising and printing contracts to newspaper owners and financial gifts to members of the press gallery. In Alberta in the 1930s, the Social Credit Party tried to force newspapers to retract any criticisms of the government. Occasional attempts have apparently been made by the Prime Minister's Office over the years to have the CBC take a certain perspective on a vital national issue. The Trudeau government accused the Radio-Canada network of being riddled with separatists who gave a biased interpretation of federal–Quebec relations. Although there was probably some truth to the charge, it smacked of political interference.

Short of actual government interference or censorship is the highly secretive tradition of Canadian governments. Since 1982, the Access to Information Act made it somewhat easier for the media and other interested parties to obtain access to government information, but the secrecy habit is difficult for politicians and bureaucrats to overcome. Contrary to expectations, Harper's Federal Accountability Act did not provide for greater access to government information, as exemplified by its prolonged refusal to disclose documents related to the handover of Afghan detainees.

Public Opinion Polls

The phrase **public opinion** sometimes implies that a unanimous, informed view on a particular issue is held by all members of the public. In actuality, many opinions are held on any issue, and each issue interests only a certain segment of the population—that is, each issue has its own public. Furthermore, most political opinions are not well informed. They are often based on little information, they are simplifications of complex issues, and they can even be internally contradictory. Indeed, people often form their opinions first and then later look for information to confirm them; at the very least, they "seek out information that conforms to their predispositions ... and avoid or reinterpret any contrary and non-supportive messages."[18] Nevertheless, public opinions about topical issues frequently influence the actions of government.

Measuring Public Opinion

Given this great conglomeration of viewpoints, public opinion is very difficult to gauge. Haphazard methods such as reading editorials or letters to the editor or listening to open-line programs are obviously unreliable, but so are many amateur public opinion surveys. On the other hand, professional polling agencies claim to be able to select a small representative sample of people, ask carefully worded questions, and report with a high degree of accuracy the opinions of the whole population. Such polls have assumed an immense importance in contemporary Canadian politics: "no political party plans campaign strategy without them, no government is prepared to risk major policy initiatives without gauging public opinion, and for major news organizations they are an indispensable reporting tool, both between and during elections."[19]

Man considers political pollsters a threat to nation.
(Graham Harrop/Artizans.com)

Beyond the now common procedure for conducting a **public opinion poll**, two special techniques deserve mention. The first is "tracking," which entails telephoning samples of 100 to 500 people nightly during an election campaign in order to see how day-to-day developments are affecting them. The second is the "focus group," in which a small number of people are gathered together behind a one-way mirror with a group leader who encourages them to voice their "gut" reactions to various leaders, issues, and slogans. Their responses are recorded and then analyzed. The importance of polls and focus groups in constructing a party's campaign message and even picking the language to be used to convey that message can hardly be overemphasized.

Who are these professional pollsters? The leading pollsters all do much non-political polling as well, and a number of lobbying firms also do polling as part of their comprehensive consulting work. Professional pollsters include:

- Nanos Research (formerly SES Research),
- Ekos Research Associates,
- Environics Research Group,
- Ipsos Reid,
- Léger Marketing,
- Angus Reid Strategies,
- Strategic Counsel,
- Pollara Public Opinion and Market Research, and
- Compas Public Opinion and Customer Research.

How accurate are the polls? The only way a survey's accuracy can really be tested is through a comparison of its results immediately prior to an election with the electoral outcome itself. The immediate pre-election findings of most professional agencies have usually been within the range of accuracy claimed—typically plus or minus four percent, 19 times out of 20. This is impressive, considering that results can be influenced by the way a question is worded, the optional responses available, the sequence of the questions, the degree to which respondents are telling the truth, the willingness of respondents to participate, the time frame, and many other variables. In the June 2004 election, however, almost all of the polls underestimated the Liberal vote. Pollsters explained this inaccuracy on a large shift in voter preference that occurred in the last two days of the campaign. On the other hand, Table 7.3 shows the almost perfect 2006 election prediction from SES (now Nanos) Research.

The discrepancies that sometimes occur give rise to a concern that those with ulterior motives can deliberately manipulate polling results by tailoring the sample or the wording of the questions. Moreover, those with significant financial resources can resort to advocacy advertising and then continue polling until the correct "public opinion" is forthcoming.

Impact of Polls on the Public

One of the main issues that arises in the discussion of polls and pollsters is whether their pre-election predictions influence the election results. This question cannot be answered categorically, but it is unlikely that their direct effect is that great.

TABLE 7.3 NANOS RESEARCH POLL ON FINAL FEDERAL VOTING PREFERENCE VERSUS ELECTION RESULTS, 2006

	SES Research Prediction (Percentage of Votes)	Election Results (Percentage of Votes)
Conservatives	36.4	36.3
Liberals	30.1	30.2
NDP	17.4	17.5
BQ	10.6	10.5
Other	5.6	5.5

Source: Nanos research poll released January 22, 2006 and election results January 23, 2006. Reproduced with permission of Nanos Research, http://www.nanosresearch.com

First, most voters do not pay much attention to poll results; second, not everyone believes them; and third, it is not important to everyone to vote for the winning side, even if this is clear in advance. While some voters may want to jump on the victorious bandwagon—the **bandwagon effect**—at least a few are likely to switch to the predicted loser—the "underdog effect"—either out of sympathy or to try to prevent an overwhelming victory for the prospective winner.

On the other hand, the polls probably have a significant indirect effect on the election results. Because the mass media are just as obsessed with the polls as the politicians are, survey results may well entice the media to concentrate on those parties and politicians who are in the lead and to ignore those who are trailing. Furthermore, polls have a considerable impact on party morale. A positive poll usually generates greater enthusiasm and effort, better candidates, and larger financial contributions, while a negative poll saps the spirit of leaders, candidates, and foot soldiers alike. In other words, such poll results affect the momentum of the campaign.

Another issue can be addressed more categorically: polls definitely detract from the discussion of real issues in the election campaign.[20] Because polls are good for business, the media usually emphasize the **horse-race effect** of the contest, tending to spend more time on who is ahead than on comparative analysis of party platforms. They ask leaders to comment on the latest poll results, for example, rather than on how the party would deal with a particular public problem. Now that the media actually hire polling firms, survey results are becoming major news items in themselves. Responding to this problem, the CBC announced at the start of the 2004 federal election campaign that it would not conduct any public opinion surveys, but it has not been above reporting on polls done by others. Polls sometimes also affect the voter turnout rate by generating feelings of either complacency or hopelessness.

Many political losers have blamed their fate on negative public opinion polls, and some have called for the prohibition of polls during part or all of the campaign. Such bans do exist in many countries. Whatever their faults, however, polls enliven the campaign and increase the information available. Prohibiting their publication in the media would not prevent parties, candidates, and others from conducting their own surveys. The main effect of a publication ban would be to give certain crucial information to those who could afford a survey and to deny it to the general public, a rather undemocratic suggestion.

One of the amendments to the Canada Elections Act made in the wake of the Royal Commission on Electoral Reform was to prohibit, in the final three days of the campaign, the broadcast, publication, or dissemination of public opinion poll results. This restriction was soon challenged by the Thomson and Southam newspaper chains as a violation of freedom of the press, and their objection was upheld by the Supreme Court of Canada. A ban on the publication of polls on an election day itself was subsequently enacted, and the law requires polling organizations to provide a full account of their methodology.

Impact of Polls on the Authorities

The other main question in the study of public opinion is the relationship between public opinion and the response of the authorities. For nearly 100 years after Confederation, governments had to act in the absence of a reliable survey, but they now sometimes seem reluctant to make any decision until it can be based on a poll. After criticizing the Liberals for an excessive expenditure on public opinion polling, the Harper government was shown to have spent even more: it commissioned an average of two polls every working day in 2006–07 at a cost to taxpayers of $32 million. Given that opinion is likely to be considerably divided, however, clear-cut guidance from such polling cannot always be found.

Sometimes, even when public opinion is clearly in favour of a certain course of government action, the authorities will decide to act otherwise. This may be the consequence of the politicians' own convictions, the recommendations of the public service, the pressure from lobbyists and advocacy groups, or the rigidity of party discipline. Indeed, some observers hold the view that even in a democracy, politicians are not obliged to follow public opinion; they may also lead it. This is especially true now that we realize how uninformed, superficial, and changeable most public opinions really are. While politicians and bureaucrats may be accused of acting in their own self-interest if they do not follow a clear preference among the public, they may actually be relying on a deeper understanding of the issue, the greater information at their disposal, a more sophisticated analysis of its implications, or a concern for minority rights. For many years, for example, capital punishment was an issue on which public opinion clearly supported one side but on which the authorities repeatedly went their own way. Should Parliament have reinstated capital punishment in response to popular opinion based on a mistaken impression about rising crime rates, a desire for retribution, and a questionable assumption of deterrence? In fact, majority public opinion on this issue has changed, but most political issues are even more complicated than capital punishment, and public opinion is much more divided. Thus the correlation between public opinion and public policy is not as strong as might be expected.

Christopher Page's study of this subject reinforces many of the observations made above.[21] In connection with the Trudeau initiative on constitutional reform in the early 1980s, Page observes that polls had little effect on the content of the Charter, but were useful in maintaining the government's resolve to go through with the reform as well as in designing the way to sell it to the public. Somewhat similarly, the Mulroney government had decided on the GST proposal before it did much polling; indeed, the policy was adopted in defiance of the polls. Nevertheless, government polling helped to decide the details of the policy (e.g., to exempt groceries) and how to reduce its unpopularity as it was communicated to the public. On gun control, the Chrétien government also made the decision to act before it polled the public on the subject. But Liberal polls that indicated a generally favourable public reaction were used to keep dissident MPs and provinces in line as well as in the communications campaign with respect to implementation.

Thus, Page argues that on these three key issues, at least, the government policy was decided before it engaged in polling. Except perhaps on the GST, polling encouraged the government to pursue the policy upon which it had previously embarked, but it mostly affected government communications operations about a policy rather than the substance of the policy itself.[22] Governments appreciate the security of a supportive poll, but they realize the superficiality of many peoples' opinions, and they actually lead public opinion as much as they follow it.[23]

It should be added that the incidence of and government reliance on public opinion polls severely undercuts the argument in favour of referendums. Public opinion polls already provide a quick, cheap, frequent, and accurate picture of the public's views, so there is little danger that the government will not know how the population feels about an issue.

SUMMARY

This chapter considered the political significance of the mass media and of public opinion polls. It began with a discussion of the ownership of the various media in Canada, especially newspapers and television, and an analysis of how much the owner of any medium influences its coverage. This question arises in particular because of the tradition of chain ownership in the Canadian newspaper industry and the more recent emergence of cross-media conglomerates or convergence. The chapter then went on to discuss the important agenda-setting function of the media and the relative merits of newspapers and television as sources of political information. New forms of political communication were also mentioned, especially the Internet, and the section on the media ended with an account of the mutually dependent relationship between the media and politicians. The next section, on public opinion polls, emphasized that each political issue has its own public and that a large proportion of public opinions are not well informed. It identified the leading polling firms in Canada and noted the techniques they use in producing their reports. The chapter considered the extent to which public opinion polls influence voting behaviour as well as the policies adopted by governments, concluding that the impact is not as strong as might be expected in either case.

DISCUSSION QUESTIONS

1. Is there something distinctive about media companies that would justify more restrictions on concentrated ownership than in other industries?
2. What are the advantages and disadvantages of obtaining political information from television and newspapers?
3. To what extent are new forms of political communication replacing television and newspapers?
4. Should public opinion polls be prohibited at some stage of an election campaign?
5. If public opinion polls show a clear policy preference of a majority of citizens, should the authorities always follow it?

KEY TERMS

Bandwagon effect The notion that if and when they know which party or candidate is going to win the election, voters will move en masse in that direction.

Canadian Broadcasting Corporation (CBC) The large national Crown corporation with radio and television divisions whose mandate is to promote meaningful communication among all parts of the country.

Canadian Radio-television and Telecommunications Commission (CRTC) The regulatory agency established to police the communications industry, including radio, television, telephones, and telecommunications.

Convergence The recent phenomenon in the mass media of companies and technologies merging to create multimedia conglomerates, with ownership of newspaper, television, telephone, satellite, cable, Internet, and magazine businesses.

Horse-race effect The notion that election campaigns have degenerated into a "horse race" where everyone, especially the media, is concerned with which party is ahead, not with how parties would tackle serious public issues.

Mass media Sources of information for the mass public—principally radio, television, and newspapers.

News management A variety of techniques used by politicians and governments to ensure positive media coverage.

Parliamentary press gallery Those members of the media who are registered to sit in the press gallery in the House of Commons and who report on its proceedings or on government in general.

Public opinion The sum total of opinions held by members of the public on any subject.

Public opinion poll A survey conducted to ascertain the opinions of the public on assorted matters.

Spin doctors Party officials and ministerial aides who talk to the media and try to influence media coverage by putting the best face on an event from their party's point of view.

FURTHER READING

Barney, Darin. *Communications Technology*. Vancouver: UBC Press, 2005.

Edge, Marc. *Asper Nation: Canada's Most Dangerous Media Company*. Vancouver: New Star Books, 2007.

Gidengil, Elisabeth, et al. *Citizens*. Vancouver: UBC Press, 2004.

Miller, John. *Yesterday's News: How Canada's Daily Newspapers Are Failing Us*. Halifax: Fernwood Publishing, 1998.

Nash, Knowlton. *Trivia Pursuit: How Showbiz Values Are Corrupting the News*. Toronto: McClelland and Stewart, 1998.

Nesbitt-Larking, Paul. *Politics, Society, and the Media: Canadian Perspectives*. Peterborough: Broadview Press, 2001.

Page, Christopher. *The Roles of Public Opinion Research in Canadian Government*. Toronto: University of Toronto Press, 2006.

Taras, David. *Power and Betrayal in the Canadian Media*. Peterborough: Broadview Press, 1999.

Winter, James. *Democracy's Oxygen: How Corporations Control the News*. Montreal: Black Rose, 1997.

Chapter 8

Elections and the
Electoral System

Elections are one of the most important features of a democratic political system and usually one of the most exciting. This chapter examines the formal, legal aspects of the electoral system, as well as the party campaign organization at both the national and local levels. It also contains an evaluation of the electoral system and suggestions for reform, a discussion of party and election finance, and an assessment of electoral behaviour and party support.

Chapter Objectives

After you have completed this chapter, you should be able to:

Outline the process of drawing and redrawing the electoral map

Understand how the formal election machinery is organized at both national and local levels

Comment on how parties organize their election campaigns at both national and local levels

Understand the concern about the proportionality of the electoral system

Enumerate and evaluate the main provisions of the laws on party and election finance, including the problem of third-party advertising

Assess various aspects of Canadian voting behaviour

The Election Organization

Drawing the Electoral Map

Canadian elections are based on single-member electoral districts. Hence, before Canadians go to vote, an electoral map must be established to divide the country into electoral districts, **constituencies**, or ridings. The term **redistribution** is used to describe this process. It involves two stages: first, deciding how many seats in the House of Commons to allot to each province and territory, and second, drawing constituency boundaries within each province.

The Constitution Act, 1867, requires that the readjustment process be repeated after each decennial census, such as after 2001 and 2011. Given the federal character of Canada, with its strong provincial loyalties, the search for a reasonably fair means of distributing seats in the House of Commons among the provinces has been a long and unsatisfactory one. The formula used following the 2001 census and that resulted in a 308-seat House of Commons provided the following distribution of seats: Ontario, 106; Quebec, 75; British Columbia, 36; Alberta, 28; Manitoba and Saskatchewan, 14 each; Nova Scotia, 11; New Brunswick, 10; Newfoundland and Labrador, 7; Prince Edward Island, 4; and Northwest Territories, Nunavut, and Yukon, 1 each. Smaller provinces and those with slowly increasing populations are benefited from two basic rules: each province is entitled to as many House of Commons seats as it has senators, and each province is guaranteed as many seats as it had in 1985—its number cannot decrease.[1]

Because the existing system seriously underrepresented Ontario, British Columbia, and Alberta, the Harper government introduced a reformed process for the post-2011 redistribution. While seven provinces and the three territories are protected by the minimum seat guarantees, the new system would divide the population of each of the three rapidly growing provinces by the national average riding population of 108 000. That would give Ontario an increase of 18 for a total of 124, B.C. an increase of seven for a total of 43, and Alberta an increase of five for a total of 33. The total size of the House of Commons would increase by 30 to 338.[2]

The second phase of the redistribution process, drawing constituency boundaries within each province, was historically the prerogative of the politicians. They regularly engaged in the process of "gerrymandering," that is, manipulating constituency boundaries so as to ensure as far as possible the re-election of the members of the government party. A new system was adopted in the Electoral Boundaries Readjustment Act of 1964, however, so that this task is now performed by nonpartisan commissions. An electoral boundaries commission is appointed for each province, chaired by a judge, with the other two members of each commission appointed by the Speaker of the House of Commons. All commissions draw extensively on the support staff of Elections Canada.

The commissions swing into action as soon as the provincial population figures are available from the census. Theirs is a very delicate task of trying to arrive at a design that will provide constituencies of approximately equal population size throughout the province at the same time as accounting for geographic characteristics or identity and historical patterns (e.g., trying not to divide a town into two separate electoral districts). The most difficult problem is in dealing with sparsely populated rural or northern regions at the same time as concentrated urban centres. In recognition of this problem, the commissions are allowed to deviate from the average population figure in any province to a maximum tolerance of plus or minus 25 percent and even to exceed this limit in extraordinary circumstances. Thus, rural and northern constituencies tend to be below the provincial quotient and southern, urban ones somewhat above it. In general, since it takes fewer votes in smaller provinces and in rural parts of all provinces to elect a member of Parliament, such votes are worth more than those in large provinces or in urban areas, although the post-2011 reforms would reduce the interprovincial disparities.

The Official Election Organization

SETTING THE DATE

The prime minister has normally possessed the prerogative to call the election within five years of the previous one. Largely based on the government party's standings in the public opinion polls, the election has typically been called about four years after the previous campaign. Going into the fifth year, especially to the five-year limit, was usually a sign that the government expected to be defeated. Public opinion polls can be wrong, of course, or public opinion can change between the calling of the election and the actual voting day, since Canadian party preferences are highly volatile. The apparent advantage for the party in power in choosing the date was therefore not absolute, as several prime ministers and premiers have discovered to their chagrin. Nevertheless, allowing the governing party the discretion to choose the election date gave it an advantage in terms of readiness, the ability to "bribe" the electorate at the last minute with new spending and other initiatives, and the opportunity to use government money for advertising. The governor general had to approve the prime minister's request to **dissolve Parliament** in order to call an election, but this was normally automatic. Only once in Canadian history (in 1926), in rather peculiar circumstances, did a governor general refuse such a request.

The defeat of a government in a non-confidence vote in the House of Commons can also precipitate an election, in which case the prime minister's leeway is limited to choosing the exact date. This would not happen in a majority situation, and of course, if a minority government really wanted an election, it could probably engineer its own defeat.

To remove the premier's discretion in this matter, several provinces recently moved to fixed election dates. Then, in 2007, Stephen Harper had Parliament pass a law providing for fixed federal election dates every fourth October (starting in 2009). The law left a loophole for the PM to advise the governor general to call an election before that date, but this was intended to be used in the case of a non-confidence vote, as might have occurred in the minority government situation. Breaking at least the spirit of the new law, Harper employed the escape clause to call the October 2008 election even without the government being defeated. He was thus still able to take advantage of calling an election when it suited his purposes.

ELECTION OFFICIALS

The **chief electoral officer** is responsible for the overall administration of the election and must act with absolute impartiality. **Returning officers**, who organize the election in each of the electoral districts, used to be chosen by the Cabinet on a partisan basis, but are now appointed by Elections Canada. In either case, however, they were expected to function in a nonpartisan fashion. U.S. presidential elections, whose results sometimes remain questionable, reinforce the wisdom of having Canadian federal elections run on a uniform basis by Elections Canada.

THE FRANCHISE

The extension of the franchise (the right to vote) beyond males with substantial property was mentioned in earlier chapters. This process was complicated by the use of different provincial voting rules in federal elections between 1867 and 1917. Moreover, the franchise was manipulated in 1917 so as to maximize support for the incumbent government. On that occasion, the vote was extended to women serving in the war as well as to female relatives of men overseas, but it was denied to Canadian citizens who had come from "enemy alien" countries. In 1918, all women were granted the federal vote, and since 1920 a uniform federal franchise has existed. Even so, until all such restrictions were removed by 1948, most Canadians of Asian ancestry (especially those from Japan, China, and India) were denied the right to vote in federal elections because the federal law disqualified anyone who for reasons of race was denied the vote under provincial electoral statutes. The vote was extended to Inuit people in 1953 and to Registered Indians in 1960. The voting age was reduced from 21 to 18 in 1970, and British subjects who were not Canadian citizens lost their vote in 1975.

By that time, the Canada Elections Act mainly disqualified returning officers (except in the case of a tie), federally appointed judges, prison inmates, those deprived of their liberty by reason of mental disabilities, and those convicted of corrupt or illegal electoral practices. In the course of the 1988 campaign, however, three of these disqualifications were challenged in the courts in terms of the Canadian Charter of Rights and Freedoms, which guarantees the vote to every Canadian citizen. In the case of judges and those with mental disabilities, the provisions of the act were declared unconstitutional and the disqualifications were removed. The courts made a number of contradictory rulings on whether prison inmates should be able to vote, and yet another Supreme Court decision finally resolved the issue: at least in federal elections, all inmates have a right to vote. Returning officers now have a vote, and in case of a tie, a **by-election** would be held in the constituency. By-elections are otherwise necessitated by the resignation or death of an MP between elections.

Time Line
Extension of the Right to Vote in Federal Elections

1918	Women
1948	Asian Canadians
1953	Inuit
1960	Registered Indians
1970	Persons 18 years of age
1988	Judges and people with mental disabilities
1999	Returning Officers
2002	All prisoners

THE VOTERS LIST

The voters list used to be compiled from scratch by means of a door-to-door enumeration after the election writ was issued. Reforms introduced in 1996, however, provided for a permanent National Register of Electors, the base of which was compiled in one last door-to-door enumeration in April 1997. It is automatically updated from such sources as income tax returns and files on citizenship and immigration, drivers' licences, and vital statistics. Although such a permanent voters list is considered less reliable than a door-to-door enumeration, it permitted a reduction in the length of the election period to 36 days. On the other hand, there is no automatic way for first-time voters to be added to the list; they must take the initiative to do so before election day or else at the polling station itself. Even voters already on the list must prove their identity and address by providing a piece of government-issued photo ID or being vouched for by another qualified voter before being issued a ballot. This requirement became especially controversial when it was applied to veiled Muslim women until authorities realized that they could vote by mail without the veil issue even being raised.

NOMINATION

Most candidates are nominated by a political party, but they must submit a $1 000 deposit and formal **nomination** papers endorsed by 100 people on the local voters list. Candidates are now reimbursed for the full $1 000 upon filing their financial statement after the campaign. Official candidates of registered parties must obtain the party leader's endorsement in order to use the party name on the ballot. This requirement was adopted mainly to make it easier for voters to identify candidates with their party, but it effectively gives the leader a veto over nominations, with many implications.

ELECTION DAY

After nomination day, the returning officer arranges for the ballots to be printed and allows people to vote in advance polls or by special ballot. Recent reforms have made voting much more convenient for those not expecting to be at home on election day, including those living or travelling outside the country. The returning officer also hires and trains deputy returning officers and poll clerks to look after each polling station on election day and finds appropriate polling station locations.

Canadian federal elections are held on Mondays, and the polls used to be open from 9 a.m. to 8 p.m. local time. Because voters in the western part of the country complained that the winner was often decided before their votes had even been counted, a system of staggered hours for different time zones was introduced in 1997. This means that the polls close at approximately the same time all across the country, and ballots can be counted and the results announced more or less simultaneously. The media blackout on reporting official results from eastern parts of the country where the polls were still open has been challenged, but upheld by the Supreme

Court of Canada. Voters are entitled to three consecutive hours off work in which to cast their ballot, and the sale of liquor is no longer prohibited during polling hours.

After having proven their identity, voters mark their X in private with a pencil on the ballots provided. When the polls close, the deputy returning officer and poll clerk count them by hand, usually in the company of scrutineers from the various candidates who are allowed to challenge unorthodox markings on ballots and generally keep the whole process honest. Results are announced an hour or two after the polls close, and the candidate with the most votes—"first past the post"—is declared elected. The winner usually does not actually have a majority of the votes cast, only a plurality. If the difference between the first and second candidate in any electoral district is less than 1/1000 of all votes cast, an automatic recount is held.

THE BALLOT

The secret ballot was introduced in federal elections in 1874. The candidates are listed in alphabetical order, and since 1970 the ballot has contained their party affiliation, if any. The chief electoral officer keeps a registry of political parties and, by another decision of the Supreme Court of Canada, a party that runs even a single candidate can place its label on the ballot. Such parties must also register their national and constituency official agents and auditors for the purposes of keeping track of the party's and candidates' finances. Twelve parties were registered for the 1988 election, 14 for 1993, 10 for 1997, 11 for 2000, 13 for 2004, 15 for 2006, and 19 for 2008.

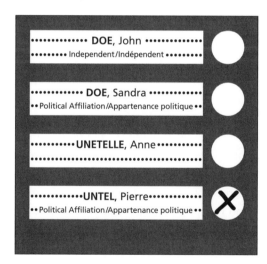

A sample ballot. (Canada Elections Act, 2000, c. 9, Schedule 1. Reproduced with the permission of Elections Canada)

The National Party Campaign

In an era of unstable minority governments, political parties begin thinking about the next election as soon as the last one has passed, and set up a campaign committee long before they expect the election to be called. They start to ponder strategy, policy, image, and budget, and party headquarters conduct public opinion polls to see how the voters perceive the various leaders, parties, and issues.[3] For the party in power, such polls have been central to deciding when to call the election in the first place, and for all major parties, polls serve to guide general strategy, media advertising, and the selection of priority ridings once the campaign begins.

Another national activity that begins before the calling of the election is the search for good candidates. While party headquarters rarely impose a candidate on an unwilling constituency association, they may try to guide the local decision or even parachute a few "star" candidates into safe seats. Most parties try to run a full slate of candidates, so where local organizations are weak, the national level of the party sometimes has to take the initiative to find a candidate for them. In order to ensure a minimum number of candidates of Cabinet calibre, especially women, and to avoid nominations falling into the wrong hands, Jean Chrétien had the party give him the power to appoint candidates in certain cases. Paul Martin and Stéphane Dion also used this power, the latter to significantly increase the proportion of female Liberal candidates. The NDP once hoped to achieve gender parity in its candidates, but it was later content with nearly 50 percent being either women or visible minorities, based on intraparty negotiation rather than the leader's decree.

Party headquarters organize training sessions for campaign managers and candidates (right down to personal deportment) and produce mounds of election material for local campaigns. One of the Liberals' great assets in the 1993 campaign was their election platform, commonly called the "Red Book." It provided a tremendous prop for a leader who was otherwise not overly policy-oriented in his public appearances.[4] Comprehensive election platforms can often be an advantage, but it did the Liberals no good in 2008 when they focused on the Green Shift idea—to raise taxes on those activities that damaged the environment and reduce other taxes proportionally.

The Leader's Tour and Its Media Coverage

Once the campaign begins, party headquarters organize each leader's tour, prepare the party's national media campaign, and gear up for the televised leaders' debate. Each party leader criss-crosses the country over the campaign period in an effort both to give a boost to promising local candidates and to generate daily stories for the national media. The leader is accompanied by a horde of strategists and support staff, as well as by reporters who pay to travel aboard the party-chartered plane or bus. Such "free" coverage is eagerly sought, and parties spare no trouble or expense to obtain it. In general, national television newscasts contain one item per leader per day, but often give greater attention to the parties in the lead. Thanks to modern communications technologies, each leader can now react instantaneously to developments in the others' campaigns.

National Media Advertising

Each party also buys media advertising during (and sometimes immediately before) the campaign, and most parties spend huge amounts of money on the production of television commercials alone. Both major parties have been faulted for their increasing use of negative "attack-style" advertising in recent years. The purchase of broadcast time during the campaign is regulated by the Elections Act, requiring each broadcaster to make available for purchase by registered political parties six and a half hours of prime time. The broadcasting arbitrator allocates time among the parties based primarily on the number of seats held in the House of Commons and on the popular vote received in the previous election. As a result of a Reform Party court challenge, parties can now purchase more than these allotments, subject to their overall expense ceiling, so that the significance of the allocation of time has diminished. In addition to purchasable time, parties are awarded free radio and television time in the same proportions. Table 8.1 reveals the three most expensive items in each of the major parties' 2008 election budgets, and in every case, advertising was at the top.

The Leaders' Debate

The other main aspect of the national campaign is the televised leaders' debate. These debates have become crucial aspects of the campaign because of the combined importance of leaders and television. Separate debates are held in English

TABLE 8.1 LEADING EXPENSES FOR MAIN PARTIES, 2008 ELECTION

Conservatives		Liberals		NDP	
Advertising	$10 595 029	Advertising	$8 031 434	Advertising	$8 444 995
Leader Tour	$2 474 333	Leader Tour	$2 480 327	Leader Tour	$4 043 031
Professional Services	$1 785 037	Salaries/ Wages	$1 181 479	Salaries/ Wages	$1 361 146

Source: Elections Canada, "Election Financing," available http://www.elections.ca/content.asp?section=fin&dir=pol&document=table2_08&lang=e&textonly=false

and French (in 2006, two in each language), putting a premium on a party leader's bilingual capacity.

The debates are not mentioned in the law, so the consortium of television stations that carry them essentially sets the rules. The debates have to fit into the television networks' schedule and are held when least advertising revenue would be lost. In 1993, with a large number of parties in the race, the consortium agreed that only five parties would take part—that is, those represented in Parliament and those that had had a consistent impact in public debates and public opinion. The leaders of the same five parties participated in 1997 and 2000, while in 2004 and 2006, four party leaders participated. In 2006, the leader of the Green Party was excluded under protest because the party had no seats in the Commons, but in 2008 the still seat-less Elizabeth May shamed the other leaders into allowing her to join them in the debate.

The frontrunner in the campaign basically tries to avoid a knockout punch, while the other party leaders attempt to score one. After the debate, each party sends forth its **spin doctors** to persuade reporters that its leader won, but whether the public makes up its own mind on the winner or awaits the verdict of media commentators is not certain. Studies show that approximately half of the voters watch the debates;[5] these tend to be well-informed, peer-group opinion leaders who may well influence others who did not tune in. Although much attention is focused on who "won" the debate, such an advantage may have worn off by election day. Recent debates, at least in English, have not featured a clear-cut winner.

The televised leaders' debate, 2008 election. (The Canadian Press/Tom Hansen)

The Local Candidate Campaign

Nomination

At the local level, each party's first priority is to nominate its candidate. Holding the nomination meeting even before the election is called allows many preparations to be made ahead of time, so the campaign can get off to a strong and early start.

Nominating candidates is one of the most important functions of political parties.[6] It is often a wide-open opportunity for ordinary people to participate in and to influence the direction of the political system, and yet the nomination process does not usually generate much interest. Party leaders often decree that incumbent MPs may not be challenged, but many other nominations are also uncontested. Even if there is a competition, discussion of policy is usually minimal, as those seeking the party nomination recruit hundreds of "instant" party members to turn out to vote for them. The candidate nomination is usually the decision of the local party organization, but as mentioned above, the central party office is often somewhat involved.

The Local Campaign

Once the nomination has taken place, each party sets up a campaign committee under a campaign manager (see Figure 8.1). The official agent is responsible for ensuring that the candidate complies with the Canada Elections Act. In most campaigns, the other key official is the canvass organizer, who organizes the door-to-door "foot canvass" to distribute literature and/or a telephone canvass. Whether canvassers contact voters on the doorstep or on the phone, the object is both to spread the party's message and to seek out its own supporters. Armed with a voters list, canvassers put a positive, negative, or "undecided" mark beside the name of all voters contacted. To cover an entire constituency in this fashion requires a veritable army of volunteers and an elaborate organization. If money is more plentiful than volunteers, the local campaign may rely instead on media advertising. In recent elections, some parties engaged in local polling followed by computer-assisted mail, telephone, or e-mail messages directed to members of key groups. In the past, much of this work was voluntary, but since the opportunity to use "volunteers" paid by a business or union has now been eliminated, parties increasingly engage paid staff. The local campaign is a complex operation requiring ever more sophistication, staffing, and funding.

Figure 8.1   Structure of a Typical Local Campaign Committee

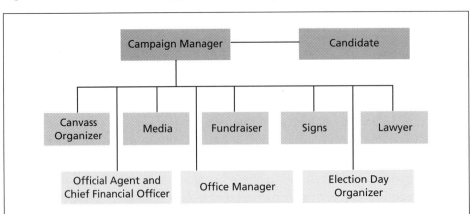

All this activity culminates on election day, when the organization tries to have a party scrutineer placed in each of the polls. Ideally, an inside scrutineer keeps track of which people on the list have cast their ballot, while an outside scrutineer periodically collects this information and heads out to round up all those previously identified as party supporters.

The Proportionality of the Electoral System

In each constituency, the candidate with the most votes wins, even if this is less than 50 percent. Among the advantages of this **first-past-the-post system** are its simplicity, its quick calculation of results, and its provision for each constituency of a clear-cut representative. When all the local results are cumulated nationally, however, the proportion of seats a party wins does not necessarily bear much relationship to its overall share of the total **popular vote**. Take as an extreme, hypothetical example a two-person race in each constituency in which the Liberal candidate beat the Conservative candidate by one vote in every case. The Liberal Party would then win 100 percent of the seats from just over 50 percent of the vote, and the Conservative Party would have 0 percent of the seats from just under 50 percent of the vote. In fact, this example is not so hypothetical: in the New Brunswick election of 1987, the Liberals won 100 percent of the seats with about 60 percent of the popular vote. Many political scientists and other observers are therefore concerned that such overall disparities can occur between percentage of seats won and percentage of popular vote, and advocate a more proportional system.

Overall, in 27 elections starting in 1921, the party with the largest popular vote almost always won more seats than it deserved, while the second party was usually somewhat underrepresented. The system also favoured third parties with concentrated regional support (Social Credit, Reform/Alliance, and the BQ), but those with broad national support usually lost out—the CCF (Co-operative Commonwealth Federation) and the NDP, for example, regularly received only about half as many seats as their popular vote merited.

Some observers tolerate these disparities because the first-past-the-post electoral system usually produces a **majority government**—the leading party obtaining more than 50 percent of the seats—even though a party rarely wins over 50 percent of the popular vote. Table 8.2 indicates that on three occasions (1940, 1958, and 1984) the winning party obtained at least 50 percent of the vote, and this automatically produced a majority government. On 13 other occasions out of 27, this electoral system manufactured a "false" majority government in terms of seats, even though the leading party did not win a majority of the vote. This left 11 occasions when a **minority government** resulted, including the 2004, 2006, and 2008 elections. Moreover, on three occasions (1957, 1962, and 1979) the party with the second-largest popular vote ended up with more seats than the party that came first, and therefore went on to form the government. The possibility of the wrong party winning the election is probably the greatest defect in the first-past-the-post system.

It is worth noting that if parties had received as many seats as their popular vote justified in 1993, the PCs and NDP would have been recognized as official parties in the House of Commons, and the Reform Party, instead of the Bloc Québécois, would have been the official opposition. The 1997 and 2000 elections rectified that situation but continued to underrepresent the PCs and NDP. In 1997, for example, the PCs and Reform were virtually tied in votes, but they were awarded 20 and 60 seats respectively. In 2004 and 2006, the Liberals, Conservatives, and Bloc all got more seats than they deserved, while the NDP and Greens were underrepresented. Table 8.3 illustrates how many seats each party received in the 2008 election compared to how many each would have received in a perfectly proportional system.

As mentioned, one defence of the first-past-the-post system is that it usually produces a majority government out of the winning party's mere plurality of votes. In recent times, it has failed to do so, as the Bloc Québécois siphons off so many seats in Quebec. Moreover, while minority governments have problems of their own, many

TABLE 8.2 Comparison of Percentage of Popular Vote and Percentage of Seats won by Party in Federal Elections, 1921–2008

	Liberal		Conservative		CCF/NDP	
	% Vote	% Seats	% Vote	% Seats	% Vote	% Seats
1921	41	49	30	21	—	—
1925	40	40	46	47	—	—
1926	46	52	45	37	—	—
1930	45	37	49	56	—	—
1935	45	71	30	16	9	3
1940	52	74	31	16	9	3
1945	41	51	27	27	16	11
1949	49	74	30	16	13	5
1953	49	64	31	19	11	9
1957	41	40	39	42	11	9
1958	34	18	54	79	10	3
1962	37	38	37	44	14	7
1963	42	49	33	36	13	6
1965	40	49	33	36	18	8
1968	45	58	31	27	17	8
1972	38	41	35	40	18	12
1974	43	53	36	36	16	6
1979	40	40	36	48	18	9
1980	44	52	33	37	20	11
1984	28	14	50	75	19	11
1988	32	28	43	57	20	15
		Liberal	PC	NDP	Ref/All	BQ
1993	% Vote	41.3	16.0	6.9	18.7	13.5
	% Seats	60.0	0.7	3.1	17.6	18.3
1997	% Vote	38.4	18.9	11.1	19.4	10.7
	% Seats	51.4	6.6	7.0	19.9	14.6
2000	% Vote	40.8	12.2	8.5	25.5	10.7
	% Seats	57.1	4.0	4.3	21.9	12.6

		Liberal	**Conservative**	**NDP**	**BQ**
2004	% Vote	36.7	29.6	15.7	12.4
	% Seats	43.8	32.1	6.2	17.5
2006	% Vote	30.2	36.3	17.5	10.5
	% Seats	33.4	40.3	9.4	16.0
2008	% Vote	26.3	37.7	18.2	10.0
	% Seats	25.0	46.4	12.0	15.9

Source: Data compiled and used to create the above chart was taken from the website of Elections Canada: http://www. elections.ca. It is used with the permission of the Chief Electoral Officer but extrapolation and analysis rest with the author.

observers prefer them to majority governments because the latter tend to demonstrate an arrogance toward and disregard for opposition members of the House of Commons.[7]

Another set of disparities between popular vote and seat figures exists on a province-by-province basis. What is particularly striking is the disparity between the Conservative vote and seats in Quebec (1896–1984) and that between the Liberal vote and seats in Western Canada (since 1957). Alan Cairns has observed that such disparities affect parties in three principal ways: image, strategy, and policy.[8] When the Conservatives had virtually no members from Quebec prior to 1984, they gained an anti-French image, even though they usually obtained at least 13 percent of the popular vote in that province. Similarly, after 1957, the Liberals acquired the image of an anti-Western party because they rarely elected members west of Ontario, even though they normally received over 20 percent of the Western vote.

TABLE 8.3 Seats Won by Party and Seats Deserved on Proportion of Vote, 2008 Election

	Seats Won	**Seats Deserved**
Conservatives	143	117
Liberals	77	80
NDP	37	55
Bloc Québécois	49	31
Green	0	21
Other	2	4

Source: Data from Elections Canada, http://www.elections.ca, retrieved April 15, 2010.

As far as strategy is concerned, when Conservatives despaired of electing members from Quebec and felt they could form a government without much representation from that province, they ignored it. The Liberals often similarly felt that campaigning in the West was a waste of time and money and concentrated their effort elsewhere. In the 2000 election campaign, for example, Jean Chrétien did not bother to make a single campaign stop in Calgary. These strategies are not good for keeping the country together, one of the functions that political parties and elections are supposed to perform.

Finally, since the elected members of the party have a major role to play in the development of party policy, Conservative policy did not reflect the concerns of French Canada when the party lacked francophone and Quebec MPs, just as Liberal policy tended to ignore Western concerns. This is especially serious for the party that forms the government because it has few or no MPs from a province or region to put into the Cabinet. Because of such regionalized party standings between 1962 and 1984, either Quebec or the West was effectively left out of national decision-making at the Cabinet level. Residents of those neglected regions understandably felt that national policy did not reflect their interests and turned to provincial governments to defend these interests or started to think in separatist terms.

Since Cairns first brought these problems to scholarly attention, reform of the electoral system has been frequently discussed. Beyond the basic principle of fairness, many observers would like to overcome the lack of deserved representation of important segments of opinion in party caucuses and the Cabinet, as well as to avoid the sense of regional–ethnic alienation that stems from this situation. In recent years, several provinces have taken electoral reform seriously, and referendums on the issue have been held in British Columbia, Prince Edward Island, and Ontario. None of these results acquired enough support to change the provincial system, but the issue is unlikely to go away.

The most common remedy proposed is the so-called "mixed-member proportional" system which retains single-member electoral districts but supplements them with a number of seats in the legislature based on each party's popular vote. It would give voters a second ballot to register their choice of party, and each party would propose a list of candidates for these proportional seats. Each would be awarded enough of them to provide overall legislative representation proportional to its popular support.

Besides correcting the greatest discrepancies between the proportion of seats and votes that each party receives, and providing the party in power with representation from every province in the Cabinet, it is claimed that such a system would increase voter turnout because people would be less inclined to feel that their vote was wasted.[9] It might also be used to correct gender or minority imbalances. On the other hand, it would rarely result in a majority government, although some observers take that as an advantage, and even first-past-the-post has produced three recent minority governments. Canadian parties might be forced to consider forming coalition governments to provide some stability, as is common in most European countries, and was adopted by Britain in 2010.

Financing Elections

Parties and Candidates

Prior to 1974, Canada had virtually no laws with respect to party and election finance. The Liberal and Conservative parties relied almost completely on contributions from big business at the national level, which usually produced a surplus to be distributed to candidates' campaigns as well. Candidates were otherwise dependent on donations from local small firms. Both parties had fundraisers or "bagmen"—often senators who could exploit their corporate connections and make use of their abundant spare time—assisted by corporate volunteers. Business also made contributions in kind, such as skilled personnel. The CCF/NDP depended primarily on individual membership fees supplemented by union contributions, but in this case the flow of funds was reversed: the local candidates had to help finance the central campaign. Overall, the Liberals and Conservatives raised and spent far more than the CCF/NDP, both at the national and local levels.

The secrecy surrounding party and election finance before 1974 makes it difficult to know exactly how many irregularities and scandals actually took place, but they were probably numerous. Small-scale scandals in the 1960s, together with increasing public expectations of political morality, eventually led to amendments to the Canada Elections Act in 1974. The legislation had six basic provisions:

- a ceiling on candidate spending,
- a ceiling on party spending,
- disclosure of the identity of contributors,
- a tax credit for contributions,
- a public subsidy for serious candidates, and
- a public subsidy for major parties.

The objectives of the legislation were thus to increase the fairness, openness, and participatory nature of the electoral system. While no limit was placed on the size of contributions, fairness was enhanced by limiting national party and candidate spending, as well as by the public subsidy provision; the disclosure clause made it difficult for large secret contributions to be made in return for some favourable government decision, policy, or grant; and the tax credit encouraged individual contributions, reducing Liberal and Conservative dependence on corporations. For all the difficulties and loopholes remaining in the act, it produced a more honest, equitable, and participatory system of election finance.

While the results were fairer than they would have been in the absence of such legislation, the disparities continued to concern many observers. Data from the 2000 election showed that the Liberals and the Canadian Alliance vastly outspent the other parties, and their heavy reliance on the corporate sector gave rise to many suspicions about what those corporations expected from government in return. In fact, the Gomery Inquiry into the sponsorship scandal revealed a significant amount of corruption in Liberal party finance in Quebec. Largely due to these revelations, the Chrétien government introduced a new regime for election finance in 2004, but it was soon supplemented by the Harper government's Federal Accountability Act in 2006. Taking those two sets of reforms together, corporations and trade unions can no longer contribute to elections, nominations, or leadership candidates, but in compensation, parties receive a substantial annual allowance from the public purse. The following are the main features of the new provisions regarding party and election finance.

ELECTIONS

- Individuals are limited to an annual contribution of $1 000 to a party, a constituency association, or a candidate (adjusted for inflation to $1 100 in 2010).
- Corporations and trade unions are prohibited from donating to political parties or candidates.
- Individual contributions are eligible for a 75 percent tax credit for contributions up to $400, with the percentage declining thereafter.
- Candidates have a spending limit based on the number of names on the local voters list.
- A candidate who receives at least ten percent of the votes (down from 15 percent) is eligible to be reimbursed for 60 percent (up from 50 percent) of his or her election expenses.

- National parties have a spending limit based on 70 cents per person in all the constituencies they contest.
- National parties that received at least two percent of the national vote (or five percent in the constituencies they contest) are eligible for an annual public subsidy of $1.75 per vote received in the previous election (adjusted for inflation to $1.95 in 2008 election).
- National parties also are eligible to be reimbursed for 50 percent of their election expenses (up from 22.5 percent).

LEADERSHIP CONTESTS

- Individual contributions are limited to $1 000 (adjusted for inflation to $1 100 in 2010).
- Corporate and trade union contributions are prohibited.
- There is no spending limit, but contributions and expenditures must be disclosed.

NOMINATION MEETINGS

- Corporate and trade union contributions are prohibited; individual contributions are limited to $1 000 (adjusted for inflation to $1 100 in 2010).
- Contributions and expenditures must be disclosed if either exceed $1 000.
- Expenditures are limited.
- Those seeking the nomination can deduct daycare expenses.

Table 8.4 shows the expenses of the main national parties (out of an authorized limit of $20 million) in the 2008 election, but do not include candidate expenses. As mentioned, parties were eligible for reimbursement of 50 percent of these

TABLE 8.4 TOTAL ELECTION EXPENSES FOR MAIN PARTIES, 2008 ELECTION

Party	Total Expenses
Conservatives	$19 418 580
Liberals	14 519 926
NDP	16 754 471
Bloc Québécois	4 876 121
Green	2 795 800

Source: Elections Canada, "Election Financing," available http://www.elections.ca/content.asp?section=fin&dir=pol&document=table2_08&lang=e&textonly=false

expenditures plus an annual allowance of $1.95 per vote in the 2008 election. Thus, even if the Greens did not win any seats, every vote that party received was worth about $1.95 from the public purse, so that such votes could no longer be said to be completely wasted. The Conservatives were so successful in their fund-raising efforts that they tried to repeal this annual allowance for all parties in their ill-fated 2008 fall fiscal update. They also spent a great deal of money before the restrictions of the election campaign period clicked in, often attacking respective Liberal leaders.

Third-Party Advertising

Another problem in the realm of election finance is **third-party advertising**. Legislation in 1983 prohibited all advocacy-group spending during an election campaign that was not channelled through a party or candidate campaign. It was argued by sponsors of the legislation that the only way party and candidate spending ceilings could be effective was if any spending on their behalf was included in the parties' budgets. But more and more groups began to advertise on their own, for or against various parties or candidates. While such advertising was clearly a violation of the spirit of the law as well as its specific terms, the National Citizens' Coalition (NCC) challenged these sections of the legislation in the Alberta courts. The courts initially ruled the clauses unconstitutional as a violation of the freedom-of-expression provisions of the Charter of Rights and Freedoms.

Third-party advertising increased enormously in the 1988 election campaign, especially in the case of the pro-free trade group, the Canadian Alliance for Trade and Job Opportunities. With only the Conservative Party in favour of free trade, any advertising that promoted the Free Trade Agreement also promoted the Conservative Party. Thus the Conservatives benefited from some $5 million in advertising by advocacy groups on top of its own national budget of nearly $8 million. Such third-party advertising made a mockery of party spending ceilings and is widely thought to have helped the Conservatives achieve re-election by turning the momentum of the campaign back in their favour.

In response to widespread criticism of this problem and to address other electoral issues, the Mulroney government appointed a Royal Commission on Electoral Reform and Party Financing shortly after the 1988 election. On this issue, the commission recommended that spending by individuals or organizations other than candidates and political parties be restricted to $1 000 during the election period. The commission argued that to limit paid advertising of such advocacy groups during 36 days every four years was a "reasonable limit" on freedom of expression and would stand up to judicial scrutiny. After further judicial activity, the law was amended in 2000 to allow third parties to spend up to $150 000, of which no more than $3 000 could be spent in each electoral district on advertising for or against candidates. The Supreme Court of Canada finally upheld this version of the law in 2004, and these figures were adjusted for inflation to $187 650 and $3 753 respectively in 2010.[10]

Electoral Behaviour and Party Support

General Patterns of Voting Behaviour

Political scientists put much effort into the study of voting behaviour, often called psephology. One question is whether voters have a feeling of closeness or psychological attachment to a particular political party, that is, a sense of **party identification**. It would seem that between 50 and 60 percent of Canadian voters have demonstrated a consistent party preference, which is lower than in most other Western democracies, while the rest retain considerable flexibility on this count.[11]

Underlying such party identification as does exist are certain socio-demographic characteristics and basic ideological orientations. The former include such factors as region, religion, ethnic background, gender, and class, which relate to the cleavages discussed in Chapters 2, 3, and 4. First, there are wide variations in regional support for different parties. At least before 2006, only the Bloc Québécois and the Liberals were serious factors in Quebec; while the Conservative Party (old and new) has been heavily concentrated in Western Canada. During their era of dominance, the Liberals were strongest in Ontario, but the new Conservatives have made inroads in that province, while the NDP has pockets of strength throughout English Canada. There are also urban–suburban–rural differences in party support, with the Liberals and NDP most urban-oriented, and the Conservatives most suburban and rural. In three elections, the Harper Conservatives won no seats in the core of the three largest cities in Canada—Toronto, Montreal, and Vancouver.

Somewhat surprisingly, a second marked pattern in Canadian voting behaviour has been religion. Roman Catholics have been strongly inclined to vote Liberal, whether they were French, English, or of other ethnic background, and regardless of where they lived in the country. Ethnicity has been a third significant factor in Canadian electoral behaviour. The French-Canadian preference for the Liberal Party is well known and exists outside as well as within Quebec. Among those of non-British and non-French origins, the Liberals also did best, especially among post–Second World War immigrants (largely of Mediterranean and Indian subcontinental origins), who apparently reacted with gratitude to the fact that the Liberal Party was in office when they arrived. The new Conservatives appealed to evangelical Christians, but also made inroads in the Roman Catholic vote. At the same time, their efforts at courting ethnocultural minorities paid considerable dividends by 2008. Gender now seems to be more important than in the past, with women more inclined to vote Liberal or NDP than Conservative.[12]

In terms of class, the expectation would be that upper-class citizens would vote Conservative, the middle class would support the Liberals, and the working and poorer classes would vote NDP. In most Western democracies, such a pattern is quite significant, but it is not borne out well in Canada.[13] The Liberal Party has usually attracted nearly the same degree of support from all classes except farmers. Only a small proportion of the working class actually votes for working-class parties. The NDP, for example, normally gets relatively more support from skilled and unskilled labour than from other groups, but not as much as does each of the other major parties. The low level of **class-consciousness** and class-based voting in Canada is quite striking, and many explanations have been offered.[14]

Despite the absence of much class-based voting, ideology—core values and beliefs—is quite important in Canadian electoral behaviour. At least outside Quebec, there is something of a traditional ideological division between left and right that relates to faith in the free market system as opposed to the desirability of government intervention. Those adhering to market forces tend to vote for the Conservatives, while those more inclined to government intervention choose the Liberals or the NDP.[15]

The voting decision is an extremely complex and subtle one and is not easily explained. Beyond party identification, socio-demographic characteristics, and ideology, such short-term considerations as perception of economic prosperity, opinions on issues, and evaluations of the government's performance and of the respective leaders are highly relevant. For those without a strong party identification, it is usually the leaders and issues that are most important; the local candidate is not normally a crucial factor. Voters often say that they were moved by the issues in their voting decision, but many have trouble identifying the issues that supposedly influenced them. The relative importance of issues and leaders also varies from one election to another. Such flexibility means that about half of the electorate makes up its mind during the course of the campaign and that elections remain highly unpredictable.

These revelations also cast doubt on the question of whether elections provide a policy **mandate** for the successful party.[16] First, Canadian parties rarely present a comprehensive election platform in the campaign. Next, victorious parties do not seem to feel bound by the specific policies that they proposed. In the third place, the limited extent to which issues play a part in the campaign seriously detracts from the claim of any government that it has a mandate to pursue a particular policy. Finally, even on the rare occasion that a single issue figures prominently, the winning party almost never obtains a majority of the total votes cast, and certainly not a majority in all regions of the country. The free trade issue in 1988 provided the closest thing to a policy mandate for any Canadian government in recent times, yet the Conservatives received only 43 percent of the overall popular vote and less than 40 percent in six provinces and territories. The Liberals made much of their "Red Book" during the 1993 campaign, but even though a large part of it was unfulfilled, the electorate returned them to office in 1997.

The 2004, 2006, and 2008 Election Campaigns

The Liberals would probably have won a majority in the 2004 election had it not been for the sponsorship scandal, which angered people both inside and outside Quebec.[17] Even though it happened on Jean Chrétien's watch, many voters thought Paul Martin knew or should have known about it and, in any case, did not handle it well. The new Liberal leader was also hobbled by the deep split within his party as a result of Martin's longstanding challenge to Chrétien.

On the other side, despite his efforts to be more moderate than the Canadian Alliance, Stephen Harper and his new Conservative Party were still seen by many voters in 2004 as too extreme. The Liberals ran "attack" television commercials that helped to reinforce this perception, and Jack Layton's NDP was abandoned by many of his new supporters at the end of the campaign. Some of them were seduced by the Liberal call to vote strategically—for Liberals instead of the NDP—in order to keep the Conservatives out.

In that year, there were essentially two parallel campaigns. In Quebec, it was the Liberals versus the Bloc. Besides the Liberal sponsorship scandal, voters in that province were upset at certain *provincial* Liberal government policies, but nationalists and separatists were also impressed with the performance of Bloc leader Gilles Duceppe. In the rest of Canada, it was a two- or three-party contest. None

Jack Layton campaigns in Quebec City, 2008 election.
(The Canadian Press/Jacques Boissinot)

of the leaders stood out, so most voters were guided by values and issues, such as same-sex marriage, gun control, and social programs. The Liberals tried to differentiate themselves on health care, but in fact the Conservatives and NDP also stressed this issue.

The 2006 campaign was similar in many ways to that of 2004, but produced a different result.[18] By this time, Martin's Liberals were even more on the defensive with respect to the sponsorship scandal, and at first it seemed that the Bloc would sweep Quebec. But as the Conservatives established themselves as the likely winner in English Canada, Quebeckers began to pay more attention to Stephen Harper and his federalist alternative.

In English Canada, Harper ran a well-orchestrated campaign, revealing one moderate policy a day (for a total of five endlessly repeated priorities), departing from some of his neoliberal views and muzzling any extremist candidates. The Liberals did not exploit the fact that the economy was strong, and apart from more ads attacking Harper, ran a lackadaisical campaign that tried to distinguish between Liberal and Conservative values. The many public opinion polls issued during the 2006 campaign basically concluded that a majority of voters felt it was time for a change, for a new government. Voters favoured the Conservatives not so much because of the party's platform as out of anger with the Liberals.

Breaking the spirit of the fixed-election law, the initial 2008 election call was controversial, but did not engage voters very long. The first part of the campaign was dominated by the Liberals' "Green Shift" proposal. With his limited English skills, however, new Liberal leader Stéphane Dion had difficulty defending it, while the Conservatives distorted it and the other parties argued that it was insufficient to deal with environmental problems. Initially, it seemed that the Conservatives might make a breakthrough in Quebec sufficient to give them a majority, but the Prime Minister's musings on culture and crime (along with the realization that that party was offside with Quebeckers on other issues as well) sent many voters back to the Bloc.

The second half of the campaign focused on the negative economic news from around the world. Although the Conservatives declared that Canada had nothing to worry about, voters were increasingly concerned and appeared to favour

Stephen Harper to handle the problem, despite his denial that there was one. In the end, with such unappealing alternatives, many people decided not to vote at all, as the turnout rate dropped to a record low of 59 percent. The dismal Liberal vote precipitated Dion's resignation as leader, while the Conservatives made gains in Ontario, but still finished short of a majority over all.[19]

SUMMARY

This chapter discussed elections and the Canadian electoral system. It began by outlining how the electoral map is redrawn every 10 years in what is called the *redistribution* process. It then set out the operation of the formal election machinery, including the franchise, the voters list, and the ballot. The next two sections dealt with the national party campaign, including the leader's tour, media advertising, and the leaders' debate, and the local candidate campaign, including the nomination process and the effort to get the candidate elected. The chapter then switched focus to analyze the advantages and disadvantages of the first-past-the-post electoral system, noting in particular the unfairness of the system in awarding seats to political parties in relation to their share of the popular vote. It also proposed that an element of proportionality be added to the system. The next part examined how elections are financed, and outlined the many recent changes to electoral financing legislation. Finally, the chapter discussed what we know about Canadians' voting behaviour, including the concept of party identification and the effects of socio-demographic characteristics and ideological factors. The limited extent to which issues figure in the campaign cast doubts on the concept of a mandate for the victorious party.

DISCUSSION QUESTIONS

1. Are fixed election dates a good idea? Should any other aspects of the formal electoral organization be changed?
2. Is the current Canadian first-past-the-post electoral system fair to parties and conducive to national unity? If not, what changes might be made to improve it?
3. Are the recent changes to laws governing party and election finance completely satisfactory? If not, what should be changed?
4. What might be done to give more emphasis to the substance of each party's campaign (i.e., its platform) and less to its presentation (personality, image, and advertising)?

KEY TERMS

By-election An election held between general elections in a specific electoral district due to the death or resignation of the MP or a tie on election night.

Chief electoral officer The independent and impartial official who is in charge of the operation of the whole electoral system.

Class-consciousness An awareness of the social class to which one belongs.

Constituency An electoral district that sends one member to the House of Commons.

Dissolution of Parliament The ending of a parliament, usually after four or more years, by calling an election.

First-past-the-post system The kind of single-member plurality electoral system used in Canada in which the candidate with the most votes wins the constituency.

Majority government A situation in which the party in power has over 50 percent of the seats in the House of Commons.

Mandate The concept that the winning party has an obligation to enact policies it promised during the election campaign.

Minority government A situation in which the government party has fewer than 50 percent of the seats in the House of Commons.

Nomination The act of becoming a candidate in an election, which normally entails being selected to represent a party at a nomination meeting and then completing official nomination papers.

Party identification The tendency of a voter to feel attached to a particular political party over an extended period of time.

Popular vote The percentage of all votes cast for a candidate or party, regardless of who was elected.

Redistribution The process of reallocating seats in the House of Commons among the provinces after each decennial census and then redrawing constituency boundaries within each province.

Returning officer The official in charge of running the election in each electoral district.

Spin doctors Party officials and ministerial aides who talk to the media and try to influence media coverage by putting the best face on an event from their party's point of view.

Third-party advertising Advertising by advocacy groups, as opposed to political parties, during an election campaign.

FURTHER READING

Anderson, Cameron D., and Laura B. Stephenson, eds. *Voting Behaviour in Canada.* Vancouver: UBC Press, 2010.

Blais, André, et al. *Anatomy of a Liberal Victory: Making Sense of the Vote in the 2000 Canadian Election.* Peterborough: Broadview Press, 2002.

Courtney, John C. *Elections.* Vancouver: UBC Press, 2004.

Cross, William. *Political Parties.* Vancouver: UBC Press, 2004.

Gidengil, Elisabeth, et al. *Citizens.* Vancouver: UBC Press, 2004.

MacIvor, Heather, ed. *Election.* Toronto: Emond Montgomery, 2009.

Milner, Henry, ed. *Steps Toward Making Every Vote Count: Electoral System Reform in Canada and Its Provinces.* Peterborough: Broadview Press, 2004.

Pammett, Jon H. "Elections." In Michael Whittington and Glen Williams, eds. *Canadian Politics in the 21st Century,* 7th ed. Toronto: Thomson Nelson, 2008.

———, and Christopher Dornan, eds. *The Canadian General Election of 2008.* Toronto: Dundurn Press, 2009.

———. *The Canadian General Election of 2006.* Toronto: Dundurn Press, 2006.

Young, Lisa, and Keith Archer, eds. *Regionalism and Party Politics in Canada.* Toronto: Oxford University Press, 2002.

Chapter 9

Political Parties

Political parties are integral to the operation of almost every aspect of a modern political system, and are mentioned in almost every chapter of this book. This chapter discusses them in five main sections: the functions of political parties, the historical evolution of Canadian political parties, the number and kinds of parties in Canada, party ideology, and party organization. Party and electoral finance and the role of parties in the electoral campaign, including electoral behaviour and party support, were discussed in Chapter 8.

Chapter Objectives

After you have completed this chapter, you should be able to:

Understand the functions and roles of political parties

Trace the evolution of the Canadian party system

Differentiate between one-party dominant, two-party, two-plus, and multiparty eras

Discuss the pros and cons of broker and class-based or ideological parties

Discuss the various theories accounting for the numerous minor parties in Canada

Enumerate the factors that are contributing to the decline in the importance of parties

Define the concepts of left, right, liberalism, conservatism, social democracy, collectivism, individualism, equality, and inequality, and apply them to Canadian parties

Contrast parties in terms of membership, leadership selection and review, policymaking, and general structures and operations

The Functions of Political Parties

A **political party** can be defined as an organized group that nominates candidates and contests elections in order to influence the policy and personnel of government. Its truly distinctive feature is that it runs candidates in an election campaign. When one sees political parties at their worst (e.g., in the daily Question Period in the House of Commons), it is sometimes tempting to ask why we have them at all or to ask why we cannot make up a government consisting of the best people from each party. Why do we have political parties, and what do they do?

First, parties recruit and train politicians. While many ambitious or public-spirited persons would likely seek public office without them, parties ensure that we have candidates for federal (and provincial) elections. In the best-case scenario, parties provide qualified, representative candidates, nominating the best person they can find and (time permitting) educating that candidate in the issues of the day. In so doing, parties avoid some of the problems of municipal elections: they eliminate acclamations, filter out kooky candidates, and give voters a sense of what the candidate stands for.

Second, political parties provide experienced political leadership. The most able and successful MPs eventually become potential party leaders. Again, in an ideal case, those who seek the leadership of the party and the country will have served in the House of Commons for an extended period of time, so that they are experienced in the operation of the complex government machine. Parties usually serve to preclude the situation where a person will become prime minister out of the blue.

The third function of political parties flows from the earlier points and from the definition above: each provides a united team of people attached to a coherent policy platform. Parties simplify the electoral process as each one aggregates a number of interests together in its platform, thus providing a limited number of alternative packages from which voters can choose. In the process of combining, consolidating, or appealing to many different interests, parties also help to integrate the country and reduce the number of demands to a manageable quantity, sometimes called "issues." In the exchange of election rhetoric, as well as in the partisan crossfire in Parliament, parties educate the public about the issues and help to ensure that the electorate is exposed to a variety of viewpoints.

Besides these electoral functions of parties, they are crucial to the operation of government once the election is over. It is hard to imagine that a cabinet could make efficient, coherent decisions without the shared bond of party loyalty or that the House of Commons could organize its business without a strong element of party discipline. Although coalition governments work well in some countries, a cabinet made up of the best MPs from each party is likely to be unstable, and a parliament of over 300 independents would be a recipe for chaos.

Finally, political parties keep government accountable. One or more opposition parties in Parliament criticize government decisions on a daily basis, providing fodder for media coverage so that the public can remain well informed. Such opposition parties ultimately provide an organized alternative for the voters to support in the next election if they are dissatisfied with the incumbent government's performance.

Of course, political parties rarely live up to the theoretical ideals listed above, and excessive partisanship alienates many citizens. But given the fact that parties are engaged in a serious struggle for power, some inadequacies or excesses are to be expected. That political parties develop in virtually all national political systems in the world, even where not provided for in the Constitution or the law, surely attests to the utility or necessity of such organizations.

Historical Evolution of Canadian Political Parties

When attempting to understand the current Canadian party system, it is helpful to be familiar with the evolution of political parties since the time of Confederation. This evolution can be divided into three periods.

1867–1921

The first 30 years of Confederation were dominated by Sir John A. Macdonald's Conservative party. Hence, the period from 1867 to 1896 is often labelled a **one-party dominant** system. After Macdonald was disgraced in the Pacific scandal over fundraising practices, the Liberals took office between 1873 and 1878 under Alexander Mackenzie, but his government reflected a lack of party cohesion. Although Macdonald returned to power in 1878, his decision to execute Louis Riel caused French-Canadian support to fall away from the Conservative Party, helped by the fact that an appealing French Canadian, Wilfrid Laurier, became leader of the Liberal Party shortly afterwards. Macdonald died in 1891, and his party experienced a period of great instability in the subsequent five years. Thus, with the Liberals finally showing the marks of a well-organized national party, it is not surprising that Laurier won the watershed election of 1896. At that time, Canada moved to a classic **two-party system**, in which Liberals and Conservatives competed on equal terms.

Time Line
Prime Ministers, 1867–1921

John A. Macdonald	Conservative	1867–73
Alexander Mackenzie	Liberal	1873–78
John A. Macdonald	Conservative	1878–91
John Abbott	Conservative	1891–92
John Thompson	Conservative	1892–94
Mackenzie Bowell	Conservative	1894–96
Charles Tupper	Conservative	1896
Wilfrid Laurier	Liberal	1896–1911
Robert Borden	Conservative	1911–20
Arthur Meighen	Conservative	1920–21

Laurier governed quite successfully until he was beaten in 1911 by Robert Borden's Conservatives. The new government was soon confronted with the monumental task of managing Canada's effort in the First World War (1914–18). After three years of war, Borden concluded that conscription—compulsory military service—would have to be adopted. Most English-speaking Liberal MPs agreed to join the Conservatives in a Union (coalition) government in 1917, but Laurier and the French-Canadian Liberals remained in opposition. With conscription, the Conservative Party almost totally alienated French Canada, and at the same time the policies of both parties upset the farming community in English Canada, notably the West. On the other hand, when Mackenzie King succeeded Laurier as Liberal leader, he skilfully pursued party reconciliation.

1921–1993

Mackenzie King led the Liberals back to victory in 1921. That election marked the end of the two-party system in Canada, however, as farmers entered the contest with their own Progressive Party candidates. Because various minor parties made their presence felt but did not seriously challenge the dominance of the Liberals and Conservatives between 1921 and 1957, the Canadian party system during that period can be called a **two-plus party system.**

By the late 1920s most of the Progressive MPs had either become Liberals or been defeated. The Liberals themselves were defeated in 1930, primarily because of the onset of the Depression. Over the next five years, the unlucky victors, the Conservatives led by R.B. Bennett, could not cope with the unemployment, poverty, and general devastation which the Depression wrought. Along with almost every other government in office during this period, they were defeated in the next election.

The Depression was also the catalyst for the creation of a number of new political parties. The Co-operative Commonwealth Federation (CCF) was formed in 1932, an amalgam of farmer and Labour MPs, Eastern intellectuals, and various farmer, labour, and socialist groups and parties, primarily from the West. The party elected several MPs in 1935 and took office in Saskatchewan in 1944 under T.C. Douglas.

The Social Credit Party was born in Alberta in 1935 around charismatic evangelist William Aberhart. The party was originally concerned with the reform of the banking system as a means of dealing with the Depression, but all attempts to do so were disallowed by the courts or the federal government. Alberta soon became prosperous with the discovery of petroleum, and Social Credit transformed itself into an orthodox conservative party under E.C. Manning. The party remained in power in Alberta for 36 years, came to power in British Columbia in 1952, and repeatedly elected several Western MPs.

None of these developments impeded the Liberal Party at the federal level, as Mackenzie King led his party back to power in 1935. King's conciliatory skills were severely tested during the Second World War (1939–45), and the second conscription crisis was much less severe than the first. After also presiding over the initiation of the Canadian welfare state, King retired in favour of Louis St. Laurent in 1948.

The Conservative Party floundered for 20 years after 1935, having previously alienated French Canada and having been blamed, however unfairly, for the Depression. It changed leaders repeatedly, changed party policy to some extent, and changed the party name to Progressive Conservative in 1942, all to no avail. The political climate was suddenly transformed in 1956, however, with the choice of John Diefenbaker as party leader. Benefiting from the public's increasing resentment of Liberal arrogance and complacency, especially over the pipeline scandal, Diefenbaker led the Conservatives to victory in 1957. But after gaining a historic majority a year later, his government fell apart over defence policy in the early 1960s and was defeated in 1963.

Meanwhile, the CCF had seen its fortunes decline throughout the 1950s and decided to combine its efforts with those of the new Canadian Labour Congress. The result was the creation of the New Democratic Party (NDP) in 1961. T.C. Douglas was persuaded to leave the premiership of Saskatchewan to become the first national NDP leader.

Lester Pearson's Liberals were elected in 1963 and re-elected in 1965, but they were always denied a majority of seats. Nonetheless, Pearson tackled many controversial issues, particularly the new nationalism in Quebec, the Canada Pension Plan, medicare, and a new Canadian flag. One opposition party or another supported each of Pearson's measures, so that he was able to continue in office until he retired in 1968.

Time Line
Prime Ministers, 1921–93

Mackenzie King	Liberal	1921–26
Arthur Meighen	Conservative	1926
Mackenzie King	Liberal	1926–30
R.B. Bennett	Conservative	1930–35
Mackenzie King	Liberal	1935–48
Louis St. Laurent	Liberal	1948–57
John Diefenbaker	Progressive Conservative	1957–63
Lester Pearson	Liberal	1963–68
Pierre Elliott Trudeau	Liberal	1968–79
Joe Clark	Progressive Conservative	1979–80
Pierre Elliott Trudeau	Liberal	1980–84
John Turner	Liberal	1984
Brian Mulroney	Progressive Conservative	1984–93
Kim Campbell	Progressive Conservative	1993

The Liberals then gained a majority government under their new leader, Pierre Elliott Trudeau. After 11 years in office, however, the Liberals were defeated in 1979 by the Conservatives, now led by Joe Clark. Nine months later, the Clark government fell with parliamentary rejection of its budget, and Trudeau led his party back to power in early 1980.

After helping to defeat the 1980 referendum proposal of the Parti Québécois, Trudeau patriated the Constitution, together with a Charter of Rights and Freedoms, but without the consent of Quebec. He also alienated the West with his controversial National Energy Program. Upon his retirement in 1984, the Conservatives won a landslide victory under their new leader, Brian Mulroney, which included a startling majority of the seats in Quebec. After the negotiation of the Canada–U.S. Free Trade Agreement and the Meech Lake Accord, Mulroney led his party to a second successive majority in 1988, in which the free trade issue played a pivotal role. But by 1990, Meech Lake failed to acquire the unanimous approval of new provincial governments and, in a 1992 referendum, the successor Charlottetown Accord failed to gain the support of a majority of Canadians.

1993–Present

The Liberal Party's obsession with Quebec was the main reason that the West preferred the Conservatives after 1957. But when the Mulroney Conservatives proved to be primarily concerned with holding on to their unprecedented Quebec support after 1984, many Westerners turned to the new Reform Party, headed by Preston Manning, son of the former Social Credit premier of Alberta. Besides being an expression of Western alienation, Reform was a manifestation of right-wing populism in its opposition to big government, its desire for lower taxes, and its concern with law and order.

With the collapse of the Meech Lake Accord in 1990, sovereigntist sentiment increased in Quebec, giving rise to a second new federal party, the separatist Bloc Québécois. Thus, five parties of considerable strength contested the 1993, 1997, and 2000 federal elections, and produced unusual results: under Jean Chrétien, the Liberals did especially well in Ontario; the Bloc Québécois displaced the Conservatives in Quebec; and the Reform Party/Canadian Alliance usurped the Conservatives in the West. It seemed that a new highly regionalized Canadian-style **multiparty system** had developed.[1] In the 2000 election, the Liberals won seats in every province and territory but lacked depth west of Ontario; the Bloc weakened its grip on Quebec; and the Canadian Alliance, which had replaced the Reform Party, made modest gains east of Manitoba.

Prime Ministers, 1993-present

Jean Chrétien	Liberal	1993–2003
Paul Martin	Liberal	2003–2006
Stephen Harper	Conservative	2006–

The 2000–04 period was characterized by four weak opposition parties—the NDP on the left, the BQ in Quebec, and the competition between the PCs and Alliance on the right. Alliance leader Stockwell Day was replaced by Stephen Harper, and soon afterward Peter MacKay succeeded Joe Clark as leader of the Progressive Conservatives. Harper and MacKay then engineered a merger of the two parties, forming the new Conservative Party of Canada. Paul Martin finally took over the leadership of the Liberals from Jean Chrétien in 2003, and Canada suddenly seemed to possess a four-party system. In 2004, this four-party system (two major parties and two minor parties) translated into a minority Liberal government, and in 2006, a Conservative minority, after which Martin resigned and Stéphane Dion was elected Liberal leader. The 2008 election produced a second minority government for Stephen Harper, and such dismal results for the Liberals that Dion was immediately replaced as leader by Michael Ignatieff.

The Number and Kinds of Parties

Political scientists have proposed several perspectives on the number and kinds of political parties in Canada. They have also theorized about the future of such parties.

Broker Parties

One kind of political party that has been identified is the **broker party**.[2] Those who see the value in such a party focus on the multiple cleavages in Canadian society and the function of parties to aggregate interests. These advocates argue that political parties in Canada should be conciliators, mediators, or brokers among such cleavages as regions, ethnic and linguistic groups, classes, and genders. They suggest that maximizing their appeal to all such groups is not only the best way for parties to gain power but also necessary in order to keep the country together. Thus, in their search for power, parties should act as agents of national integration and attempt to reconcile as many divergent interests as possible. The Liberal party has generally been a good example of a successful broker party and the Conservative party has also been placed in this category.

Throughout most of Canadian history, the two overriding cleavages that have concerned people as well as parties have been region and ethnicity. Thus, broker parties make appeals to the different regions and try to bridge the English–French divide in their election platforms, government policies, and party leadership. Now

Mackenzie King, the longest-serving prime minister, thwarted class politics with his successful pursuit of brokerage politics. (Library and Archives Canada/C-027645)

that other interests have also claimed a place on the political agenda—Aboriginal peoples, other ethnocultural groups, and women, for example—they must also be accommodated. The one cleavage that tends to get overlooked by broker parties is that of class, but defenders of the broker system argue that parties should not foment artificial class conflicts and ideological differences in a country that is already seriously divided; they should bring people together rather than drive them apart.

However appealing the broker system may seem, its negative implications should not be overlooked. By concentrating on regional and ethnic cleavages and identities, parties minimize the role of ideology in Canadian politics. Such parties are opportunistic and pragmatic rather than offering the electorate a choice of principles and genuinely distinctive programs. They are unlikely to generate innovative policy approaches, resting content to respond to public opinion polls and interest group demands. What such parties offer to the electorate in the place of alternative solutions to national problems are alternative leaders and slogans. Especially in a television age, leader images have often become the focus of election campaigns.

Class-Based and Ideological Parties

A second kind of political party is one that is based on a set of principles (an ideology) or that seeks the support of a particular socioeconomic class. There is usually a direct or indirect connection between class and ideology, such that these can be called **ideological** or **class-based parties**.[3] Class analysts expect that in the pre-democratic period of any country all parties will defend the capitalist system, but when the vote is extended to the working class, a new working-class party will emerge. It will generally force politics to take on an ideological and class-based character, an evolution that clearly occurred in Britain.

When the vote was extended to the working class at the end of the 19th century in Canada, some isolated labour, socialist, and communist political activity occurred, and by 1920 new class-based farmer and labour parties existed. But the newly enfranchised working class failed to create a successful class-based party because the Liberals and Conservatives did everything in their power to discourage such a development, using both seductive and coercive techniques. Eventually, the farmers' interest in politics declined, and the working class mostly supported the two old-line parties on ethnic/religious and regional grounds, rendered content by the occasional piece of social legislation.

The Depression represented the collapse of the capitalist system, and the CCF emerged to become the most sustained working-class, left-wing party to that point in time. As unionization expanded significantly in the 1940s, the CCF achieved its highest popular standing. Soon afterward, however, Liberal welfare initiatives helped to draw off working-class support. This decline led to the creation of the NDP in 1961, but even with its organic link to the labour movement, most working-class Canadians continued to vote Liberal or Conservative.

Analysts have proposed many reasons for the lack of class-consciousness among the Canadian working class.[4] Those who defend the lack of such consciousness argue that other divisions legitimately take precedence in Canada, that the system permits social mobility, that most people feel themselves to be middle class, that material benefits are widely shared, and that the Liberal and Conservative parties have accommodated working-class interests along with ethnic, religious, and regional interests in the broker system. Those who decry the lack of working-class consciousness contend that the Liberals and Conservatives were firmly entrenched when the franchise was extended to the working class and had already defined politics around social differences other than class. These two parties diverted attention from class-based issues either by appealing to one or more ethnic/religious and regional groups or by developing pan-Canadian appeals, such as the argument that "national unity" was the primary issue. These parties have been accused of deluding voters into the belief that they belonged to the middle class and of giving them the false impression of inclusion and social mobility.

Advocates of a class-based party system thus point out that the existing system is partially class-based—the upper and upper middle classes are conscious of their class position and vote accordingly; it is just that the working class does not vote appropriately. These advocates claim that a class-based system would provide ideological alternatives in elections that would make them more meaningful. Moreover, when the Liberals and Conservatives are unsuccessful as brokers, the separation of one or more ethnic-regional units is possible. In such circumstances, class and ideology could be the integrating ingredients, uniting the people of various regions and ethnic groups around nationwide poles of left and right.[5]

Class-based parties are one kind of ideological party, but it is possible for a party to be based on a set of principles of some other kind, such as nationalism (e.g., the PQ and BQ) or populism (part of the Reform/Alliance focus). It is also quite likely in real life that some—perhaps most—parties will combine elements of both the broker and class-based or ideological models.

What Do You Think?

Should political parties each establish a fairly clear-cut ideological approach, or should they broaden out and try to be nearly all things to all people? Would you prefer a two-party system with one party on the left and the other on the right?

One-Party Dominance

Until 1993, Canada basically possessed a two-party system, or a two-plus system, as previously mentioned. H.G. Thorburn maintains, however, that the Canadian party system has really been dominated not by two major parties but by one—the Liberals—since about 1900.[6] The Liberals are the "government party," power-oriented rather than issue-oriented, attracting "winners" and "successes" as supporters and candidates, and maintaining themselves in office with the help of public service expertise, public opinion polls, and the chance to choose election day. Writing before 1993, Thorburn saw the Conservatives as the "opposition party," ordinarily having to settle for the role of critic and being elected to office only on those rare occasions when the people got thoroughly fed up with the Liberals. However, with their divisiveness, "opposition mentality," and lack of preparedness to govern, the Conservatives never remained in power very long. Finally, Thorburn termed the NDP the "innovative party," not really having a chance to govern nationally but being responsible for introducing new left-wing ideas from beyond the range of current ideological conformity, often at the provincial level. In the 1993, 1997, and 2000 elections the Liberals continued their dominance, but the PCs and NDP were eclipsed to a large extent by the Reform/Alliance, with its innovations from the right. The instability of the period since 2004 does not provide much guidance with which to evaluate the theory at this time. All three

Why the Green and Marijuana Parties remain minor parties. (Bruce MacKinnon/Artizans.com)

national parties would like to become the "natural governing party" of the future, but their competitiveness in "English Canada," along with the siphoning off of Quebec seats by the Bloc, has thwarted their efforts in this regard.

Minor Parties

Because Canada has had many minor parties, political scientists have developed several theories to account for them. Essentially, these parties can all be explained by the fact that at one time or another certain ethnic, regional, or class grievances have gone unsatisfied by the broker parties. Moreover, new minor parties are to be expected when party identification is weak, and in the context of the ideological stagnation and opportunism of the broker system. In particular, if the working class never managed to establish a major party in Canada, it is not surprising that minor working-class parties would be created. The principal factors responsible for the rise of the various minor parties in Canada involve regional or ethnic alienation, class or ideology, a poor economy, and charismatic leadership. More than one of these factors is often involved.

The Decline of Parties?

Some political scientists, including John Meisel, regretfully detect a decline of political parties.[7] Meisel suggests a number of reasons why this is the case and why traditional party functions have been taken over by other institutions. Perhaps because voters perceive that parties no longer serve their interests very well, people seem to prefer to participate directly in specialized voluntary associations.[8] For example, many feminists felt more effective in the women's movement than in a political party, as did many environmentalists, anti-poverty activists, and students in their respective movements or groups. The result is that advocacy groups have greatly increased in number and strength.

As well, the quantity and complexity of information with which governments must deal renders generalist politicians incapable of coping with it and leaving them increasingly dependent upon the bureaucracy. This culminates in a situation in which advocacy groups confer with bureaucrats to work out policies that the politicians can neither understand nor alter, further reducing the role of political parties in the policymaking process. Federal–provincial conferences and committees have become the forum in which many public policies are ironed out, and once certain political and bureaucratic compromises have been made, there is little that other politicians or parties can do about them.

Meisel also notes that parties now gear most of their activity to the demands of the media, and to the extent that elections are dominated by leader images and leader debates, the need for traditional party organizations diminishes. Similarly, public opinion polls provide better feedback to politicians than their traditional discussions with party activists. Investigative journalism has reduced the role of the opposition in Parliament, direct-mail appeals have replaced traditional forms of party fundraising, and modern transnational corporations are beyond the control of any party or government. Other recent developments that have contributed to the decline of parties are the increasing power of the prime minister, the influence of election strategists and other specialist advisers, and the new role of the courts and the Charter of Rights and Freedoms.

Party Ideology

For the purposes of this discussion, **ideology** can be defined as a coherent set of ideas or principles about how a society ought to function, with particular reference to the role of the state. If Canadian politics has been dominated by broker parties, one would not expect the role of ideology to be of fundamental importance. Nevertheless, it can be argued that genuine ideological differences do exist in Canada, and that such ideologies as liberalism, conservatism, and social democracy can be found to differentiate the three traditional parties.[9] The ideological continuum can be sketched as in Figure 9.1, on the basis of the contending principles of collectivism and individualism on the one hand and egalitarianism and inequality on the other.

This perspective suggests that the overwhelming ideology in Canada is **liberalism**, but that traces of **social democracy** and **conservatism** also exist and that each of the ideologies is represented by a corresponding party. Liberalism seeks to liberate the individual and maximize each individual's freedom and potential, something that almost all Canadians would support. The differences that emerge essentially centre on the role of the state.

Conservatives seek to liberate the individual from the restrictions of the state. Reducing the role of the state to a minimum and allowing capitalistic market forces to determine the distribution of power and wealth is often labelled **individualism**. Minimizing the tax burden on individuals is a key priority, but conservatism also advocates little government regulation and ownership, and leaving people to fend for themselves instead of being supported by public social programs. Conservatives do not cherish inequality, but if such policies result in inequalities or elitism, they are generally unconcerned; inequalities are both natural and deserved—some people are more talented and work harder than others. These attitudes are labelled as

Figure 9.1   The Ideological Continuum in Canada

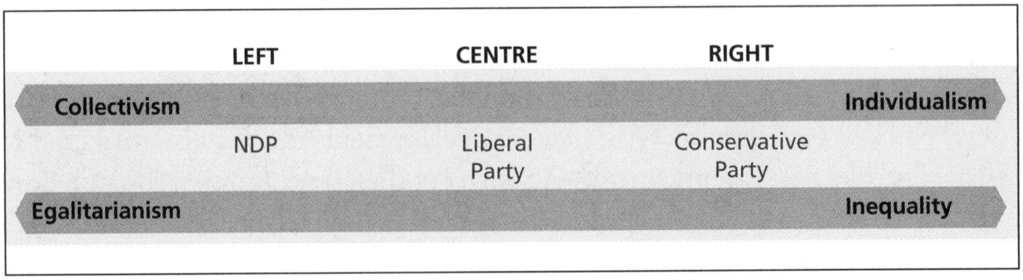

	LEFT	CENTRE	RIGHT	
Collectivism				Individualism
	NDP	Liberal Party	Conservative Party	
Egalitarianism				Inequality

being on the **right**. Historically, those who took this position were found primarily in the Conservative party, and a more extreme faction became the core of the Reform party, and later the Canadian Alliance.

Social democracy, conversely, seeks to liberate the individual from the inequalities and exploitation of the capitalist system. It believes in equality, and prescribes a large element of state action or **collectivism** in order to achieve such liberation and equality. These views are generally referred to as being on the left. In particular, social democracy emphasizes government planning, regulation, ownership of some of the major industries of the country, progressive taxation, and redistribution of income via social programs. Adherents are sometimes subdivided between "democratic socialists" and "social democrats," depending on the extent to which they wish the state to intervene and the extent of equality they wish to effect. Canada's social democratic parties, the CCF and the NDP, take credit for introducing public hospital and medical insurance after forming the government of Saskatchewan, pressing for other social programs, advocating a more progressive taxation system, creating a variety of Crown corporations in the provinces where they held power, and supporting the establishment of new interventionist government bodies in Ottawa.

Liberalism, by default, falls between the other two ideologies. In fact, it has a dual personality and can be subdivided into "welfare" and "business" variants. Business liberals believe that the state inhibits individual self-fulfillment and that its role should therefore be minimized so that individualism can prevail. Welfare liberals, on the other hand, take the view that the state can be a positive agent in liberating individuals from the constraints of other forces, including the private-enterprise economy. Welfare liberals therefore stand for a combination of individualism and collectivism and a combination of equality and inequality that they usually label "equality of opportunity." The Liberal Party is composed of business and welfare liberals, which places it in the centre of the Canadian ideological continuum. While Liberals obviously hold the private enterprise system in greater esteem than does the NDP, Liberal governments introduced old age pensions, family allowances, and many other social welfare programs over the years, although many observers saw a rightward shift after 1993.

To complicate the picture to some extent, a second wing of the former Progressive Conservative Party was the "progressive" element, people who were sometimes called **Red Tories**. These Conservatives combined beliefs in privilege and collectivism, seeing society as an organic whole, emphasizing community values as well as individualism, and standing for order, tradition, and stability. They believed in hierarchy, in which everyone should occupy his or her place, but they also had a paternalistic concern for the condition of all the people. This aspect of conservatism is not unique

As CCF premier of Saskatchewan, Tommy Douglas pioneered public health insurance in Canada and was named "the greatest Canadian" in a CBC contest in 2005. (Globe and Mail/The Canadian Press/Boris Spremo)

to Canada, being found quite commonly in Britain and the rest of Europe; it stands out only in contrast to a lack of such sentiment within American conservatism.

Thus, the ideology of the Progressive Conservative Party was divided as much as that of the other two parties. Furthermore, the Red Tory element overlapped to some extent with welfare liberalism and even social democracy. Except for the environment, the Mulroney government pursued a fairly consistent business-liberal agenda—tax cuts, privatization, deregulation, deficit reduction, and cutting of social programs—but its Progressive Conservative predecessors sometimes exhibited a Red Tory touch, such as in the creation of the RCMP, CBC, CNR, the National Energy Board, the Bennett New Deal, and the Stanfield proposal for government controls on wages and prices.

If liberalism in the United States lacks the collectivist aspect, how does one account for its presence in all three of the traditional Canadian party ideologies? One explanation focuses on the United Empire Loyalists, who removed most of the collectivist tendencies from the U.S. political culture when they migrated to Canada and left behind almost undiluted business liberalism in that country. The United Empire Loyalists legitimized ideological diversity in Canada and, because of their early predominance, made collectivism a respectable and important element in the Canadian political culture. In fact, they added to the collectivist approach already found in the feudal background of French Canada, that is, the ideas of hierarchy, order, stability, and community. Collectivism was reinforced by subsequent waves of British immigrants, whose intellectual baggage included both Red Tory and socialist views, along with the influence of the Social Gospel movement. Such collectivist tendencies were discussed in Chapter 6.

After 1985, the whole ideological spectrum shifted to the right. In Canada, this began with the Mulroney government, which pursued a business-liberal, **neoconservative**, or **neoliberal** agenda in which renewed reliance was placed on market forces and the extent of government intervention was reduced. For the first time in Canadian history, social programs were cut back rather than expanded; Crown corporations were privatized rather than created; regulations were repealed rather than promulgated; public debts and deficits were reduced rather than increased; and public servants were fired rather than hired. The whole phenomenon could be called the "dismantling of the state." The new ideology went beyond one or two parties; it affected governing parties of all ideological persuasions: PCs, Liberals, the Parti Québécois, and even the NDP in Saskatchewan.

The Reform Party was very much part of this shift to the right, and it exerted great influence at both federal and provincial levels, even though it did not form the government. The other leaders of this right-wing crusade, Conservatives Ralph Klein in Alberta and Mike Harris in Ontario, also followed the Reform lead. The Reform/Alliance believed in reducing the role of government, lowering taxes,

What's in a Name?

The terms "neoliberalism" and "neoconservatism" have been commonly applied to the ideology of certain contemporary political parties, especially the Canadian Alliance and perhaps the new Conservative Party of Canada. While the two terms are often used to mean the same thing, a distinction can be made between them. Both neoliberalism and neoconservatism advocate that government withdraw from the private market economy, but sometimes neoconservatism is taken to include a belief in a strong state that can promote certain traditional social values and regulate behaviour in areas such as abortion, same-sex relationships, and freedom of expression.

removing regulations, privatizing Crown corporations, laying off public servants, reducing the debt and the deficit, and cutting back social programs. This is all consistent with a belief in individualism, which is unconcerned about whether it leads to socioeconomic inequalities. What distinguished the Reform/Alliance from other Canadian parties was therefore an almost complete absence of the collectivist value. In this respect, it was almost a clone of the U.S. Republican Party, with which it maintained contact.

A second strand of Reform/Alliance ideology was social conservatism, such as in its opposition to abortion and same-sex rights and its promotion of traditional "family values." This bundle of issues led to internal divisions within the party in the 2000 leadership race and election because to some extent this neoconservative position contradicts the neoliberal one. Social conservatism advocates a strong role for the state in moral regulation by maintaining law and order and upholding conventional values.

A third aspect of Reform/Alliance ideology was its populist streak. It was against political elitism and professed to value the wisdom of ordinary people, giving them direct participation in decision-making via referendums, for example. This emphasis on direct participation, too, is an Americanism, as opposed to the traditional Canadian belief in **representative democracy**. The final concern of the Reform/Alliance was a territorial rather than ideological issue—that the West was getting short-changed within Confederation.

When the Progressive Conservative and Canadian Alliance parties merged, the new Conservative Party of Canada chose Stephen Harper as leader. But even though Harper came from the far right of the spectrum, embodying the essence of neoliberalism, and even though Red Tories have essentially disappeared, party policies over the next few years revealed an increasingly centrist approach. Harper tried to present a platform in the 2004 election that was somewhat more moderate than that of the Alliance, and even more moderate in 2006.[10] Conservative government policies generally brought the party back into the traditional range of the Canadian political culture and the party seemed to have abandoned its more extreme views. Few observers believed that Harper had truly changed his values, but he and others at least realized that they had been out of touch with a majority of Canadians. As the 21st century dawned, the appeal of neoliberalism and neoconservatism decreased across the whole Canadian spectrum,[11] and in the economic crisis of 2008–09, the Harper government engaged in massive deficit-stimulus spending which alarmed many traditional supporters. *Maclean's* magazine proclaimed "the end of Canadian Conservatism." By 2010, however, the Harper government revealed a more right-wing, libertarian streak, including the emphasis on law and order, replacement of the mandatory long-form 2011 Census with a voluntary survey, increased military spending, changes in foreign policy, and a general reduction in the role of the federal government.

The other party, the Bloc Québécois, has one main objective: Quebec sovereignty. The question of nationalism generally overwhelms the left–right ideological approach in Quebec, but the BQ and PQ have usually been placed on the left side of the continuum, somewhere between the Liberals and the NDP.

Protecting the environment has now become one of the leading issues on the political agenda. While all parties have outlined approaches to dealing with this problem, the Green, NDP, and Liberal plans all involve greater government intervention, whether by taxing carbon, placing ceilings on emissions, or both, than the Conservative proposals. Thus, to a large extent, environmental protection falls on the left side of the ideological spectrum, but the Conservatives decided to mimic whatever action was adopted by the Obama administration in the United States.

Party Organization

A political party has been defined as an organized group, but the structure of such a group requires clarification. Two main components of each party can be identified: the parliamentary party or **party caucus**, that is, the party's elected representatives in Parliament, and the **extra-parliamentary party** made up of the party organization, staff, activists, and ordinary members.

Party Membership

All parties strive to sign up members, but most fall far short of their expectations. No more than three percent of Canadians actually carry a party membership card, and only a few make a small contribution of time or money at election time.[12]

The NDP usually takes the concept of party membership more seriously than the other parties, often putting considerable effort into an annual membership drive. New members must take an oath that they support the party's principles, and strict rules apply to the right to vote at nomination meetings. Constituency association representation at party conventions is based on the size of the local membership, and the party is unique in also having affiliated members, that is, members of trade unions that have voted to affiliate with the party.

The Liberals and Conservatives are normally more casual about the annual renewal of party memberships. For the most part, their members sign up in connection with a meeting to nominate a candidate for the next election or to choose delegates to a national convention. It is typical for aspiring Liberal candidates or delegates to recruit large numbers of new members (often from minority ethnocultural groups in large urban centres) just prior to the deadline.

Party Leadership

In the 21st century, there are essentially two methods of choosing party leaders in Canada. The traditional way is at a national convention, to which constituency associations elect delegates.[13] Amid a great abundance of speeches, socializing, and twisting of arms, delegates engage in several rounds of voting until one candidate has gained at least 50 percent of the votes. There is much to be said for a traditional leadership convention: it attracts abundant free media attention, usually raises the morale of party members, and can have a unifying effect on the party as the delegates gradually come together around the successful candidate.

The more recent procedure for choosing party leaders has been to allow every card-carrying member of the party to cast a vote. This avoids much of the party expense of holding a national convention; eliminates the unholy fighting among various candidates for delegates at the constituency level; and ensures that the decision is not left to the more affluent members of the party who can afford to travel. The Parti Québécois was the first party to move to a "one member–one vote" leadership selection process, and many provincial party leaders have now been elected on this basis. At the national level, the Progressive Conservative Party and the Canadian Alliance both used this system, in which party members could vote by telephone, by mail, or in person in local constituencies.

Liberal leader Michael Ignatieff speaks to the Empire Club in Toronto in January 2009. (The Canadian Press/Nathan Denette)

Such procedures have potential problems of their own, however, including techno-logical breakdowns, an unrepresentative electorate, and the involvement of voters who have no knowledge of the candidates or who actually support other parties. Many partisans also feel that the loss of the publicity value of a nationally televised convention carries a high cost; they suggest that by imposing spending limits on candidates and subsidizing delegates' expenses, some of the worst features of con-ventions can be avoided. Moreover, new election legislation regulates the financial aspects of leadership campaigns, making them much more modest events. Parties sometimes try to combine the best of both worlds: giving every member a vote but also having a leadership convention. That is how the Liberals chose Stéphane Dion, for example. After the "emergency" selection of Michael Ignatieff in late 2008 by party notables, however, the Liberals adopted the one-member-one vote system for the choice of leaders in the future.

Most parties also have **leadership review** mechanisms in their constitutions, although these vary in detail. The NDP opens nominations for the position of leader at its national convention every two years, so that an unsatisfactory leader can be immediately replaced. However, in the absence of a concrete challenger, no vote is needed. The other parties generally put the question "Are you in favour of having a leadership convention?" at the first convention following an election.

Party Policymaking

All political parties have difficulty designing their policymaking process. On the one hand, they want to give ordinary party members an opportunity to contribute to party policy. But on the other, every party worries that the issues are too com-plex to be guided exclusively by ordinary members' views, and no party wants to be saddled with unrealistic policy commitments. Thus, they all struggle to combine grassroots input with the influence of the party elite, and none does impressive internal policy research.[14]

Liberal and Conservative national conventions or general meetings usually include a policy session and sometimes focus primarily on policy. But even if spe-cific resolutions are debated and passed, party leaders or cabinets retain the right to determine official party policy. The Liberals' "Red Book," used as the party plat-form in the 1993 election, drew substantially from party policy meetings over the previous two years but was not bound by them, and Michael Ignatieff convened a "thinkers' conference" in 2010. A certain tension existed in the Reform/Alliance between its populist intentions and the dominance of its leader and elite, and it does not seem that the party membership has much say in the formulation the policies of the new Harper Conservative Party.

The NDP always claimed to be particularly distinctive in the realm of party policymaking. It has regular policy sessions every two years, which are the predominant item on the convention agenda. Constituency associations are invited to submit resolutions in advance, and resolutions passed by the convention are considered to be official and binding on the leader and the parliamentary party. Even in the NDP, however, constituency resolutions are now vetted by the party's policy committee with its considerable resources before being transmitted to the council and convention, and in an election campaign the leader has considerable discretion in deciding which issues to emphasize.

Party Conventions

All parties have constitutions that outline their objectives, structures, and procedures. In theory, at least, the ultimate power in each party is the convention that all parties try to hold at regular two-year intervals. The convention agenda normally includes the election of the party executive, constitutional amendments, and policy discussions, but such conventions also serve important social and morale-building purposes. In the Liberal and Conservative parties, each constituency association is entitled to an equal number of delegates, while in the NDP representation is based on the size of the local membership. All parties include certain ex-officio delegates such as MPs; in the NDP, affiliated labour unions also send delegates. Women's, youth, campus, Aboriginal, and ethnocultural groups may also send delegates to certain party conventions.

Federal–Provincial Party Links

The federal nature of Canada and the existence of two levels of government at which political parties seek to influence policy and personnel raise the question of the relationship between national and provincial party organizations. To over-simplify the situation somewhat, the federal and provincial Progressive Conservative parties were essentially independent. There was virtually no formal organizational or financial link between the two wings of the party, and there was no provincial PC party at all in Quebec. Thus, federal and provincial party memberships were usually separate, and a complete set of federal riding associations and executives coexisted with provincial party organizations at the grassroots level.

By contrast, the NDP might be called an "integrated" party because, with the exception of Quebec, one joins the NDP at the provincial level and automatically becomes a member of the national party. Provincial offices of the party serve the needs of both federal and provincial parties, and the two levels of the party are integrated financially. In Quebec, however, federal and provincial wings of the party are quite separate.

The Liberal Party is characterized by two different federal–provincial relationships. In Quebec, Ontario, and the four western provinces, the party is split into federal and provincial wings, each with separate finances, memberships, constituency associations, executives, conventions, and offices. In the other provinces and territories, the party is more "unitary." Where the federal and provincial wings of the Liberal Party are organizationally separate, there is less inclination to ideological compatibility or to be helpful to each other in their respective election campaigns.

Preston Manning wanted to concentrate all of Reform's attention at the national level and persuaded his members to back his objection to provincial party branches. When Reform transformed itself into the Canadian Alliance, it retained the same policy with respect to provincial branches of the party, hoping to cultivate close relations with provincial Conservative organizations, especially in Alberta and Ontario. The new Conservative Party of Canada emerged without formal links to provincial parties from either of its parents, but it developed good relations with most of the parties that had retained the "Progressive Conservative" label in the provinces.

SUMMARY

This chapter discussed political parties in Canada. It made the case that for all their faults, political parties are beneficial, indeed necessary, to the operation of the political system. It traced the evolution of the Canadian party system from two parties before 1921, through a series of additional parties until 1993, following which five parties were represented in Parliament, to the presence of four parties after 2004. The chapter then contrasted the advantages and disadvantages of broker and ideological parties, accounted for the rise of so many minor parties over the years, and asked whether political parties are in decline. The next section analyzed party ideologies, primarily in terms of individualism/collectivism and equality/inequality. It also described where Canadian political parties are situated in relation to three main ideologies: liberalism, conservatism, and social democracy. The last section of the chapter dealt with party organization and looked at differences in the concepts of membership, leadership, policymaking, and general operations.

DISCUSSION QUESTIONS

1. Is Canada likely to have a four-party system for the foreseeable future?
2. Is the new Conservative Party of Canada a broker party, a class-based party, or an ideological party?
3. Is it possible in this complex, information-driven age for ordinary party members to make useful policy suggestions within the political parties to which they belong?
4. How do you categorize yourself ideologically? Why?

KEY TERMS

Broker party A kind of political party that tries to appeal to many different interests and to "broker" compromises among them, rather than having any distinct ideology.

Class-based party A political party that appeals primarily to one socioeconomic class or another.

Collectivism As opposed to individualism, an ideology that holds that the public interest is enhanced by substantial collective action, normally via government.

Conservatism A political ideology generally characterized by a belief in individualism and a minimum of government intervention in the economy and society, as well as by tradition, elitism, and opposition to change.

Extra-parliamentary party That part of a political party beyond its members of Parliament—that is, party members, local and national executives, and party headquarters.

Ideology A coherent set of ideas or principles about how a society ought to function, with particular reference to the role of the state.

Individualism An ideology that holds that individuals should have maximum freedom or liberty to do as they please, especially in economic terms, and that governments should not get involved in taxation, regulation, redistribution, or ownership.

Leadership review A clause in the constitutions of political parties that allows party members or convention delegates to review the leader's performance.

Left That part of the ideological spectrum that believes in equality in society and the intervention of government via collectivist measures such as taxation, regulation, redistribution, and public ownership to effect such equality.

Liberalism An ideology based on a belief in the rationality of the individual and on maximizing individual freedom, liberty, and self-fulfillment. Before 1900, this was assumed to entail a minimal role for government; after 1900, liberalism usually advocated a larger role for the state and was placed on the centre-left of the spectrum.

Multiparty system Typically European in nature, a party system characterized by many parties, usually without any one having a majority in the legislature.

Neoconservatism An ideology originating in the 1980s calling on government to withdraw from its extensive intervention in the private market economy but perhaps still promote certain traditional social values.

Neoliberalism An ideology originating in the 1980s calling on government to withdraw from its extensive intervention in the private market economy—emphasizing privatization, deregulation, balancing of budgets, tax cuts, and trimming of social programs—as well as from regulating society in general.

One-party dominance A party system characterized by the dominance of a single party.

Party caucus The whole body of MPs of any party, together with such senators as choose to attend, who hold a regular weekly meeting to discuss parliamentary strategy and party policy.

Political party An organized group that makes nominations and contests elections in the hope of influencing the policy and personnel of government.

Red Tories A minority faction within the former Progressive Conservative Party that had collectivist leanings akin to those of many British and European conservatives, stressing order, tradition, stability, and a paternalistic concern for the condition of the working class.

Representative democracy A system of government based on the periodic election of representatives to Parliament, as opposed to more direct participation by voters in making public decisions.

Right That part of the ideological spectrum that cherishes individualism and believes in leaving the private sector to operate with minimal government intervention.

Social democracy A moderate leftist ideology that emphasizes the principle of equality and that usually prescribes a large role for government to intervene in society and the economy.

Two-party system A type of party system in which two main parties are of approximately equal strength and alternate in office.

Two-plus party system A type of party system in which two main parties are of approximately equal strength and alternate in office but are accompanied by one or more minor parties of significant strength.

FURTHER READING

Campbell, Colin, and William Christian. *Parties, Leaders, and Ideologies in Canada.* Toronto: McGraw-Hill Ryerson, 1996.

Carty, R. Kenneth, William Cross, and Lisa Young. *Rebuilding Canadian Party Politics.* Vancouver: UBC Press, 2000.

Cross, William. *Political Parties.* Vancouver: UBC Press, 2004.

Flanagan, Tom. *Harper's Team: Behind the Scenes in the Conservative Rise to Power.* Montreal: McGill-Queen's University Press, 2007.

Gagnon, Alain-G., and A. Brian Tanguay, eds. *Canadian Parties in Transition,* 3rd ed. Peterborough: Broadview Press, 2007.

Jeffrey, Brooke. *Hard Right Turn: The New Face of Neo-Conservatism in Canada.* Toronto: HarperCollins, 1999.

Martin, Lawrence. *Harperland: The Politics of Control.* Toronto: Penguin Canada, 2010.

Thorburn, H.G., and Alan Whitehorn, eds. *Party Politics in Canada,* 8th ed. Scarborough: Prentice-Hall Canada, 2001.

Whitehorn, Alan. *Canadian Socialism: Essays on the CCF and the NDP.* Toronto: Oxford University Press, 1992.

Chapter 10

Advocacy Groups,
Social Movements,
and Lobbying

Advocacy groups, pressure groups, or interest groups develop in almost every political system when people with common concerns band together in order to strengthen their cause. At least part of their effort involves interacting with government, which is the emphasis here. This chapter will identify some of the leading Canadian advocacy groups and social movements, outline their targets and methods, assess their resources, and then give an account of the activity of new lobbying firms.

Chapter Objectives

After you have completed this chapter, you should be able to:

Understand the prominence of advocacy groups in the political system

Provide examples of leading advocacy groups in a variety of fields

Distinguish between institutionalized and issue-oriented groups, public interest and self-interested groups, and social movements

Discuss how the structure of government affects the way advocacy groups are organized

Enumerate the targets of advocacy group activity and the methods used to reach them

Analyze the importance of different group resources

Discuss the rise of new forms of lobbying and enumerate the provisions of the Lobbying Act

Comment on unsavoury aspects of the professional lobbying scene

The Functions of Advocacy Groups and Lobbying

An **advocacy group**, **interest group**, or **pressure group** (the terms are used interchangeably here) can be defined as any group that seeks to influence government policy without contesting elections, that is, without putting forward its own candidates. Alternatively, advocacy groups have been defined as organizations whose members promote their common interest by acting together to influence public policy.[1] The term **lobbying** is generally used to refer to any organized attempt to influence the decision makers, an activity that is most commonly undertaken by advocacy groups but could also be done by individuals, companies, or other political actors. Increasingly, however, advocacy groups have been joined by professional lobbying firms in this activity.

Advocacy groups are involved primarily in the function of "interest articulation"; they normally have a narrow focus and are organized around a single interest that they try to impress upon those in authority. As society becomes more complex, Canadians increasingly demonstrate a preference to form or join such specialized, functional groups in order to transmit their demands to government, rather than rely on the broader and largely territorial representation of parties and elections. Thus, in the promotion of interests, advocacy groups provide a supplementary kind of "functional" representation, especially between elections.[2] The term "civil society" is often used to refer to such institutions and organizations that exist between the individual and family on the one hand and the government or state on the other—religions, unions, charities, athletic organizations, recreational groups, social movements, and especially advocacy groups.

The Array of Canadian Advocacy Groups

The number of advocacy groups operating in Canada is in the thousands. If a distinction can be made among these terms, it could be said that an interest group *becomes* a pressure group when it actively pursues an objective with government, while advocacy group is a more generic label. Thus only some of the largest and most influential such groups are listed in Table 10.1.

TABLE 10.1 LEADING NATIONAL ADVOCACY GROUPS

Business	Canadian Council of Chief Executives
	Canadian Manufacturers & Exporters
	Canadian Chamber of Commerce
	Canadian Federation of Independent Business
	Canadian Bankers Association
	Canadian Home Builders' Association
	Canadian Association of Broadcasters
	Canada's Research-Based Pharmaceutical Companies
	Canadian Association of Petroleum Producers
Agriculture	Canadian Federation of Agriculture
Labour	Canadian Labour Congress
Professions	Canadian Bar Association
	Canadian Medical Association
	Canadian Federation of Students
Ethnic	Assembly of First Nations
	Canadian Ethnocultural Council
	National Congress of Italian Canadians
Religious	Canadian Council of Churches
	Canadian Conference of Catholic Bishops
	Canadian Jewish Congress
	United Church of Canada
Causes	John Howard Society
	Canadian Civil Liberties Association
	Sierra Club of Canada
	National Action Committee on the Status of Women
	Mothers Against Drunk Driving
	Non-Smokers' Rights Association
	Council of Canadians
	Canadian Council on Social Development

Business Groups

In the case of business, nothing prevents individual companies from lobbying on their own behalf for grants, subsidies, tariff protection or free trade agreements, loan guarantees, tax write-offs, government contracts, or policy changes, and many firms do so on a regular basis.[3] In addition, the firms within almost every industry have organized a common pressure group to promote the interests of the industry as a whole, such as the Canadian Bankers Association. It is estimated that more than 600 business groups are active in Canadian politics.[4] Superimposed upon these industrial groupings are such "peak" organizations as the **Canadian Council of Chief Executives**, the Canadian Manufacturers and Exporters, the Canadian Chamber of Commerce, and the Canadian Federation of Independent Business. They each represent a wide range of business interests. In agriculture, nearly 100 active organizations vie for influence, the leading group being the Canadian Federation of Agriculture.

Profile

The Canadian Council of Chief Executives: A Business Pressure Group

The Canadian Council of Chief Executives, formed as the Business Council on National Issues (BCNI) in 1976, comprises the chief executive officers of the 150 leading Canadian corporations. Since these firms possess over $4.5 trillion in assets, the organization bills itself as "the senior voice of Canadian business on national and global issues." Both the council and its observers give it credit for setting the agenda for all recent Canadian governments. First, it promoted the idea of free trade between Canada and the United States, then pressured the government to balance the budget, and then advocated tax cuts. Each of these high-pressure campaigns resulted in a reduction in the size and role of the state. For more information on the council, go to http://www.ceocouncil.ca.

Non-business Groups

The Canadian Labour Congress (CLC) functions as a common voice for organized labour, but only about 75 percent of union members in Canada belong to unions affiliated with the CLC. The CLC maintains a link to the New Democratic Party, as do many of its individual unions, a unique relationship among Canadian pressure groups.

Many of the minority ethnocultural groups in Canada have their own organized associations, such as the National Congress of Italian Canadians. Most of these have been brought together, with government support, in the umbrella organization called the Canadian Ethnocultural Council. The largest of several Aboriginal groups is the **Assembly of First Nations**. The English and French are organized only where they are minorities—the anglophone Alliance Quebec and the Fédération des communautés francophones et acadienne du Canada, incorporating provincial units such as the Assemblée de la francophonie de l'Ontario (AFO). Religious denominations in Canada also function as advocacy groups from time to time, with the Canadian Conference of Catholic Bishops, the United Church of Canada, the Canadian Council of Churches, and the Canadian Jewish Congress probably being most influential. Most professions have organizations that speak for their members on relevant issues, the Canadian Medical Association and Canadian Bar Association being two of the oldest and most important. A large proportion of postsecondary students belong to the Canadian Federation of Students.

Other Categorizations of Advocacy Groups

However much any of the previously mentioned groups claim to be pursuing the public interest, they can be generally categorized as "self-interested" groups because in most cases their principal concern is to improve their own, usually economic, position. The true "public interest" group exists to promote causes that it sees as beneficial to society as a whole and that do not directly benefit its own members, such as the John Howard Society (improving prison conditions and the lot of ex-inmates), the Canadian Council on Social Development (promoting better social policy), the Canadian Civil Liberties Association (protecting civil liberties from government infringement), and a variety of environmental groups.

With some exceptions, those named above and many others are called **institutionalized groups** because they are permanent, well-established, formal organizations. Almost all maintain a head office in Ottawa with a full-time staff, a sizable budget, and a reasonably stable membership. Most have developed continuous links with the authorities and represent their members' interests on a daily basis, year after year.

In contrast, some groups spring up spontaneously around a specific issue, and once the issue is resolved, they fade away. Such **issue-oriented groups** lack the institutionalized groups' permanence, office, staff, budget, membership, and access to the authorities. Instead, they are more likely to resort to attracting public attention to their cause through media coverage of such actions as demonstrations.

Examples of issue-oriented groups include the Stop Spadina group, which opposed extension of the Spadina Expressway in Toronto in the early 1970s, and Bread Not Circuses, which objected to Toronto's bid to host the 1996 and 2008 Olympic Games. Rural Dignity was another spontaneous national group that sprang up to fight against the deterioration of rural and small-town life in general, and of its mail service in particular. If the issue that concerns them is not resolved, or if they anticipate further challenges, such groups may become a more permanent fixture.[5]

Political scientists often find it useful to distinguish between advocacy groups and social movements. Many of the issue-oriented groups referred to are, in fact, part of larger unstructured social movements, of which the environmental, women's, and peace movements have been most prominent historically. More recent examples include the Aboriginal, gay, animal rights, anti-poverty, and anti-globalization movements. A **social movement** has been defined as an informal network of organizations and individuals who, on the basis of a collective identity and shared values, engage in political and/or cultural struggle and undertake collective action designed to affect both state and society.[6] Social movements begin at the margins of the political system, possess an alternative vision of "the good life," and usually consist of coalitions of small local groups that have not yet hardened into a cohesive national organization.

The National Action Committee on the Status of Women (NAC) is a somewhat institutionalized coalition of several hundred women's groups, while the Canadian Environmental Network is a looser coalition of hundreds of environmental groups. The Council of Canadians is a citizens' movement that provides a critical voice on key national issues such as safeguarding social programs, promoting economic justice, renewing democracy, asserting Canadian sovereignty, preserving the environment, and promoting alternatives to corporate-style free trade. The Council is part of an international network called the Blue Planet Project that seeks to protect the world's fresh water from the threats of trade and privatization. It also works closely with other groups, such as the CLC, the CFS, the Sierra Club, NAC, and the Canadian Centre for Policy Alternatives.

The Internet facilitates both national and international grassroots political campaigns, and such social movements and networks are often seen as one of the few counterweights to corporate globalization in the modern world.[7] In fact, opposition to globalization in the form of new free trade agreements that primarily benefit transnational corporations is the very issue that increasingly inspires social movements.

Such movements run into much bureaucratic and political party resistance because of a reluctance to consider radical new ideas, and they often do not achieve immediate success. In the long run, however, they widen the scope of public discourse, and parties and other mainstream political institutions eventually respond. Take recent improvements in legislation with respect to women and the environment, for example, and changes in public attitudes toward war, Aboriginal peoples, gays and lesbians, and the treatment of animals.

Other categorizations are also sometimes useful in discussing advocacy groups. Most groups are "autonomous" in the sense that they develop without government initiative, although they may later seek government financial support. But politicians or bureaucrats are sometimes involved in the creation of advocacy groups, whether for personal gain or in the hope of promoting a certain public policy objective. In the late 1960s, for example, the federal government began to fund anti-poverty, women's, minority official language, Aboriginal, and other ethnic groups to ensure that these interests would be heard in the political marketplace.[8] The Trudeau, Mulroney, and Harper governments all cut back on grants to many such groups for both fiscal and ideological reasons or when a particular group became too critical of the hand that fed it. Canada has been something of a world leader in government support of critical advocacy groups, but such grant reductions reveal the dangers that arise if a group becomes too critical and too dependent.[9]

Profile
The Canadian Federation of Students

The Canadian Federation of Students was created in 1981 to provide post-secondary students with an effective and united voice. It now represents more than 500 000 students from more than 80 university and college student unions in all provinces. It is well equipped to represent student interests at the federal level, from which much of the funding of universities and colleges comes, and must also deal with provincial governments, which actually administer most postsecondary education policy. The CFS maintains a provincial wing in Ontario, Manitoba, and British Columbia, and otherwise coordinates the efforts of student union campaigns in other provinces as the need arises. It employs researchers to prepare analyses of government policy and maintains regular contact with elected officials and bureaucrats at both levels of government. It also organizes mass demonstrations from time to time to raise public awareness of its issues.

Advocacy Group Structures

As far as the structure of advocacy groups is concerned, issue-oriented groups can burst forth anywhere an issue arises—at the international, federal, provincial, or municipal level. Institutionalized groups, on the other hand, tend to be organized wherever government decisions regularly affect them. The federal nature of the country means that authoritative decisions are made at two or more levels of government, and most institutionalized groups parallel the federal structure of government. They find it advantageous to be organized at both levels because the division of powers between the federal and provincial governments is so blurred. The Canadian Medical Association is composed of 10 autonomous provincial divisions (such as the Ontario Medical Association) and the Canadian Chamber of Commerce has strong provincial branches (such as the Alberta Chamber of Commerce), as does the Canadian Labour Congress (such as the Nova Scotia

Catherine Swift of the Canadian Federation of Independent Business, John Manley of the Canadian Council of Chief Executives, and Perrin Beatty of the Canadian Chamber of Commerce talk to Prime Minister Harper at an economic round table meeting in Ottawa in 2010. (CP Photo/Pawel Dwulit)

Federation of Labour). These latter two groups in particular also maintain municipal organizations—local chambers of commerce or boards of trade and local labour councils in every sizable community across the country.

Many advocacy groups, including those representing the interests of teachers and nurses, are actually more strongly organized at the provincial level than in Ottawa. This is because they are more affected by decisions of provincial governments than by federal ones. Some, such as the medical and legal professions, are even delegated powers by provincial governments to regulate themselves.

Already vocal in dealing with national and provincial governments, students may even organize protests at the campus level to try to change university or college decisions. In recent years, such protests have often focused on increases in tuition fees or exclusive rights contracts granted to individual corporations (like Coke or Pepsi) to advertise or provide a service on campus.

Targets and Methods of Advocacy Group Activity

Besides being affected by federalism, Canadian interest groups are very much influenced in their operations by the fact that they exist in a parliamentary system. This system, despite its name, places most of the decision-making power in the hands of the bureaucracy and the Cabinet, as will be made clear in Part 4 of this book. Advocacy groups that understand this basic truth direct most of their attention to these two branches of government.

In this connection, the concepts of **policy communities** or **policy networks** should be mentioned.[10] These concepts are based on the premise that each field of public policy is discrete and specialized, with its own constellation of participants. Each policy community consists of a grouping of government agencies, politicians, advocacy groups, corporations, institutions, media people, and individuals who have an interest in that particular policy field and attempt to influence it. These actors initially attempt to establish their legitimacy with the lead government agency, and if they achieve such recognition and status, they may be made part of the agency's information flow. Once such groups are given the privilege of consultation and access to strategic information, they normally behave quite cooperatively, and the whole policy community becomes cohesive and mutually supportive. All the actors involved, including the lead agency, prefer to keep the issues that concern them within the "community" and have a strong incentive to resolve any problems there rather than open the issues up to Cabinet discussion or, even worse, public debate and confrontation.

The Bureaucracy

As will be discussed in Chapter 14, the bureaucracy or public service advises the Cabinet on almost all of its decisions. It drafts legislation and regulations according to the Cabinet's general instructions; it proposes budgets and spends government money; and it implements policies and programs once they have been given Cabinet and/or legislative approval. All of these areas hold considerable scope for bureaucratic discretion. It is for this reason that institutionalized groups in particular direct the bulk of their messages at the bureaucratic target. Many group demands involve technical matters that only the bureaucracy understands and that it may be able to satisfy without reference to the politicians.

Such groups try to cultivate close relationships with senior public servants, hoping to be able to contact these officials on an informal, day-to-day basis via telephone calls, faxes, meetings, letters, e-mails, and business lunches. Although bureaucrats are likely to be suspicious of these groups' motives, the relationship between an advocacy group and its most relevant government department may ultimately become a reciprocal one, as desirable for the public service as it is for the group.

In return for the various ways in which the bureaucracy responds to group demands, the group may pass on information that the department needs or desires in order to do its work. A major contributing cause of this development was the downsizing of government departments in the budget-balancing effort of the 1990s, which cost them crucial analytical capacities. While becoming more dependent on outside sources, however, governments began to pay them millions of dollars to produce such knowledge. Thus, policy network analysis emphasizes the role of information and expertise rather than only the articulation of interests.

Many problems become too complex for politicians—ministers or MPs—to understand, especially as larger numbers of issues, constituents, and obligations eat up their time. As a consequence, legislation is increasingly drafted in skeletal form with the specifics delegated to the bureaucracy to be added later in the form of **regulations** or "delegated legislation." Bureaucrats regularly consult institutionalized groups as they draft legislation, design programs, and draw up regulations. The group may also be a valuable ally in persuading other bureaucratic agencies or ministers to do what the department wants. Although advocacy groups are usually seen in terms of their "input" function of making demands, they also perform various "output" functions. A group may be better equipped to inform its specialized membership about new laws, regulations, or programs than a department that is restricted to the media or other regular channels of communication. In addition, the cooperation of the group might be indispensable to the successful execution of a program. In some cases, as noted, certain groups are even delegated powers of self-regulation.

The Cabinet

The Cabinet is the second most frequently targeted branch of government because it makes the major governmental decisions in a parliamentary system. Since it is now virtually impossible to meet the prime minister and Cabinet as a whole, groups often find it productive to submit single-issue representations to individual ministers, who spend much of their time in meetings with such groups. If a minister stays in one position long enough, a group may be able to construct a more personal, informal relationship, as the Canadian Federation of Agriculture did with Jimmy Gardiner, who served as minister of agriculture for 22 years. The social scene in Ottawa should also be mentioned, for parties and receptions provide excellent opportunities for cabinet ministers, deputy ministers, and established group representatives (especially corporate ones) to meet and mingle.

It is sometimes claimed that most public decisions in Canada emerge from the interaction of three agents—the Cabinet, the senior public service, and advocacy groups, especially in the business field—in a process called "elite accommodation."[11] The individuals who occupy the top positions in these sectors are elites in two senses. First, they are small numbers of people with disproportionate amounts of power, compared to ordinary citizens. Second, they have exclusive socioeconomic backgrounds, coming from families of higher social class, higher incomes, and higher educations. Robert Presthus thus postulates that the common backgrounds and values of political, bureaucratic, and corporate leaders help to facilitate agreement among them. Commanding the heights of these sectors of society, they easily accommodate each other in the working out of public policies. Lobbyists from professional lobbying firms also fit perfectly into this arrangement.

Parliament

The third main branch of the government is the legislature or Parliament, but as will be discussed in Chapter 15, it largely legitimizes decisions previously taken by the executive. That being the case, the House of Commons is not as often the target of advocacy group activity, but it does remain the object of considerable attention, especially for groups lacking access to the executive branch. One of the main reasons that a bill is usually sent to a legislative committee during its passage is to allow groups to make representations on it. The Standing Committee on Finance, with its pre-budget hearings, is now integrated into the expenditure management system and provides an excellent opportunity for advocacy groups, such as the Canadian Federation of Students, to make their case.

Especially in a majority government situation, however, ministers have traditionally been reluctant to accept amendments proposed at the legislative stage, so that groups are better advised to make their case at the executive level before the bill is made public. It has even been said that the sight of a pressure group at the legislative level in Canada is a sign that the group already failed at the level of the bureaucracy and the Cabinet. Nevertheless, groups often converge on MPs in their offices or inundate them with letters, e-mails, or postcards. For example, although not ignoring the Cabinet and bureaucracy, the Canadian Chamber of Commerce is particularly adept at applying pressure on MPs through its base in almost every constituency across the country. Advocacy groups sometimes meet with individual party caucuses, and certain MPs may already belong to a group, in which case they can be expected to speak on its behalf. A minority government situation undoubtedly gives such groups more leverage at the Parliamentary level.

Other Targets

Advocacy groups have many targets beyond these three main branches of government. If they can find a legal or constitutional angle to their demand, for example, such groups may take cases to the courts. Corporations have sometimes challenged federal or provincial legislation in the courts as a violation of the division of powers; francophone groups have used the courts to uphold constitutionally guaranteed minority language rights; and Aboriginal groups are increasingly using the courts to uphold or broaden the meaning of treaty and other Aboriginal rights. The Charter of Rights and Freedoms provides added potential for targeting the courts by actually inviting individuals, corporations, and groups to challenge federal or provincial legislation that they consider to be discriminatory. The tobacco industry, for example, was temporarily successful in arguing that the law banning tobacco advertising violated the companies' freedom of expression, once the Supreme Court decreed that that right applied to corporations.

As mentioned, only the Canadian Labour Congress has seen fit to attach itself formally to a political party—but this strategy may have reduced the group's impact on Liberal and Conservative governments. Other groups remain scrupulously nonpartisan so that they can exert equal influence on whatever party is in power, which is not to say that business groups in particular have any difficulty in gaining access to any party.

Another target of advocacy group activity is the royal commission. These elaborate investigations of public problems normally invite groups and experts to submit briefs in public hearings, supplementing whatever original research the commission itself undertakes.

Besides their direct representations to government, groups and corporations increasingly try to influence public opinion in what is called **advocacy advertising** in the hope that the authorities will respond to a clear message from the public. In 1991, for example, both the Pharmaceutical Manufacturers Association and the rival Canadian Drug Manufacturers' Association took out media advertisements to make their case on opposite sides of the question of patent protection for new drugs, and since then, other groups have used this device regularly. In 2010, Canadians were deluged with an advertising campaign sponsored by the Canadian Association of Petroleum Producers purporting to demonstrate the environmental consciousness of the companies developing the Alberta oil sands.

Many advocacy groups increase their public profile once an election has been called. This phenomenon, discussed in Chapter 8, is usually called **third-party advertising**. Groups often seek the response of parties and candidates to questions of concern and then indicate their support or opposition in media advertising. The National Citizens Coalition was especially active in this respect, while the Canadian Alliance for Jobs and Trade Prospects and its anti-free trade counterpart, the Pro-Canada Network, were particularly visible in 1988. As noted, though, limits on third-party advertising during election campaigns have recently been upheld by the Supreme Court. In addition, national or local groups sometimes target particular politicians, especially ministers, for defeat.

If all else fails, a group may resort to demonstrations, protest marches, tractor parades, sit-ins, and road and bridge blockades. Some of these are peaceful and legal, such as the orderly demonstrations that are an almost daily occurrence on Parliament Hill and frequently greet prime ministers on their travels. But the frustration of Aboriginal, environmentalist, anti-poverty, and other issue-oriented

Protesting Ottawa's lack of financial support for Canadian farmers, a farmer drives his tractor in front of the Parliament buildings. (The Canadian Press/Fred Chartrand)

groups and movements increasingly takes the form of civil disobedience. The 1990 armed standoff at Oka, Quebec, was one of the rare occasions in which a group resorted to violence, but only after governments failed to respond to the Mohawks' verbal protests.

In recent years, globalization and free trade agreements that are seen to benefit only transnational corporations have attracted much violent protest. At the Summit of the Americas in Quebec City in April 2001, for example, hundreds of protesters took to the streets. While most protesters acted in a nonviolent fashion, some were intent on shutting the meeting down. Such demonstrations attract much media and public attention and may be the only way to make a point about certain issues. On the other hand, demonstrations should not be seen as the most common form of advocacy group activity, and in some instances they may be counterproductive.[12] The great majority of Canadians abhor violence, and sincere demonstrations may be infiltrated by thugs, as occurred at the G20 in Toronto in 2010.

Group Resources and Determinants of Success

It is not always obvious why some groups are successful and others are not; however, factors accounting for success and failure include

- sympathy of and access to the government,
- information,
- financial position of government,
- members,
- cohesion,
- money,
- popularity of the cause, and
- absence of opposition.

The sympathy of the government and access to policymakers are probably most important.[13] If a basic correspondence exists between the demands of the group and the government's stated objectives, the group will have greater success than if there is a vast gap in ideological perspective. Contrast the Canadian Council of Chief Executives, which was widely seen as actually setting the agenda of the business-oriented Mulroney government with the Canadian Labour Congress, which was virtually ignored. Similarly, the minister responsible for the status of women in that cabinet repeatedly refused to meet the National Action Committee on the Status of Women because of the group's intense criticism. The government even cut NAC's annual grant and gave the first federal grant to the small rival organization, REAL Women (Realistic, Equal, Active for Life).

The sympathy of the government should normally entail ready access, especially at the political level. But, as the discussion of policy communities and policy networks revealed, groups may be just as concerned to establish their standing with bureaucratic policymakers, regardless of the party in power. A related point is the sharing of a professional orientation between group leaders and the bureaucracy. Many examples could be given of the success of a group because its officials shared the professional norms of the relevant public servants in their reciprocal relationship.

Information is another crucial resource in pressure group politics.[14] Especially at the bureaucratic level, where much of this politics takes place, any vital information that is lacking as the public service drafts technical laws and regulations will be eagerly accepted. Even at the political level, the group may be able to present data and alternative analyses of policy that will lead ministers to rethink their proposals. Closely associated with information is the professional expertise of the group's staff, and in this connection, the large business groups are able to produce mounds of well-researched and glossy documents. The Canadian Bar Association makes frequent representations to parliamentary committees, royal commissions, and government departments, and because of its expertise both in the substance of many issues and in the drafting of legislation, it is often asked for advice.

Since many group demands relate to the spending of public money, the financial position of the government will often influence a group's success. As a result, requests for funds were more likely to be fulfilled in the prosperous and free-spending 1960s and 1970s than in the era of government restraint from about 1985 to 2000 and again after 2008.

The size of the group is usually important, considering that numbers represent votes. The authorities feel comfortable ignoring very small groups, for example, because the electoral consequences would be minimal.[15] In this respect, the Canadian Labour Congress should be regularly successful in having the authorities respond to its demands because, with millions of members, it is the largest advocacy group in Canada.

The fact that the CLC is not overly influential points to the equal importance of the cohesiveness of the organization. First, as previously mentioned, the labour movement as a whole is not very cohesive, and even among those who are members of the CLC, unity, commitment, and militancy are notoriously lacking. Moreover, on those occasions when the CLC "declared war" on the government, the bulk of its members continued to vote for parties other than the NDP. Liberal and Conservative governments apparently feel that the CLC is so incapable of mobilizing its members behind the demands issued by its leadership that it can often be ignored. In recent years, another large group, the National Action Committee on the Status of Women, has been seriously divided in its priorities and has become a basket case financially. In contrast, the Royal Canadian Legion and the Canadian Chamber of Commerce are able to mobilize their members to inundate the authorities with regular demands for concerted action.

As in other aspects of politics, money is an important resource. In the case of advocacy groups, money can buy staff, offices, organization, expertise, publicity, and other useful weapons with which to get the group's message across. The Canadian Council of Chief Executives, the Canadian Manufacturers and Exporters, and the Canadian Chamber of Commerce are all financially strong, which gives them the capacity both to generate information to strengthen their case and to transmit it to relevant targets. Except for those representing big business or highly paid professions, however, most groups have limited financial resources.[16]

It will also help if the cause is supported by public opinion—if it is consistent with the prevailing values of society in general. For example, although Canadian banks are used to getting their way with government, it was largely because of the negativity of public opinion that various governments have rejected bank mergers since 1998.

Finally, a group will be more influential if it has no organized opposition. One of the reasons for the success of the Canadian Medical Association over the years, for example, was that it had medical politics almost all to itself.[17] Contrast that situation with the abortion issue, where for many years the two vehemently opposing sides were evenly divided.

Lobbying in Canada

The tendency of the rich and powerful, including big business, to benefit from pressure group politics and elite accommodation can only be enhanced by recent developments in the practice of lobbying in Canada. If lobbying is the activity of trying to influence the authorities, it is, of course, a perfectly legitimate activity for anyone to undertake in a democracy. Traditionally, individuals, companies, unions, and advocacy groups of all kinds have done their own lobbying, but in recent years Canada has seen the mushrooming of professional lobbying-consultant or government relations firms that lobby on behalf of an individual, company, or pressure group in return for a fee.

Those engaged in the new lobbying industry justify their existence largely in terms of the increasing size and complexity of government. The federal government grew enormously in the 1960s and 1970s, and the policymaking process was restructured such that corporations and advocacy groups could no longer find their way around Ottawa. The early 1980s constituted a period in which new means of influence were being sought, and an expansion of such firms appeared to take place about the time the Mulroney government was elected in 1984. Many of the leading figures in the establishment of the first wave of professional lobby firms were old cronies of the prime minister.

Given that the bureaucracy can satisfy many of the corporations' needs, ex-bureaucrats have also joined or formed lobbying firms in order to capitalize on their inside knowledge and connections. Federal conflict-of-interest guidelines precluded senior government employees from dealing with their former departments for some time after their departure from public employment, but these rules were often broken.

Registration of Lobbyists

After the emergence of such professional lobbying firms, a consensus developed among politicians that legislation, registration, and regulation were necessary. The registration idea was part of the Mulroney government's ethics package, unveiled after its early troubled record of Cabinet resignations due to conflicts of interest and numerous legal charges against Tory backbenchers.[18] Parliament consequently passed the Lobbyists Registration Act in 1989. According to that act, a lobbyist is an individual

> who, for payment, on behalf of any person or organization ... undertakes to arrange a meeting with a public office holder or to communicate with a public office holder in an attempt to influence
>
> a)   the development of a legislative proposal ...
>
> b)   the introduction, passage, defeat or amendment of any bill or resolution ...
>
> c)   the making or amending of any regulation ...
>
> d)   the development or amendment of any policy or program ...
>
> e)   the awarding of any monetary grant or contribution or other financial benefit ... or
>
> f)   the awarding of any contract.

The legislation acknowledged that lobbying public officeholders is a legitimate activity, but it required lobbyists to register because it is desirable that officials and the public know who is attempting to influence government and because paid lobbyists should not impede free and open access to government. With certain exceptions, lobbyists had to file a return including the name and address of the lobbyist and the lobbying firm, the name and address of the client, and the subject matter of the solicitation. Many critics felt that the 1989 legislation was very weak: some lobbyists did not register, and even when they did, the disclosure provisions were minimal. The law did not even require revelation of the specific object of the representations; moreover, the act was almost totally lacking an effective enforcement mechanism.

What Do You Think?

Do you think professional lobbyists are a positive or negative force in Canadian politics? Do you think their activities are sufficiently regulated? Do they make government more or less democratic?

The whole procedure provided a lucrative living to those who claimed to be intimates of ministers or ministries, and it favoured those who could afford to hire such professional lobbyists. In what John Sawatsky calls "one of the most odious lobby campaigns in the history of Canada," the fight of the Pharmaceutical Manufacturers Association to extend drug patent protection, "Gerry Doucet handled the PMAC file in GCI's [Government Consultants International's] office; his brother Fred handled the issue in the Prime Minister's Office."[19]

A parliamentary committee reviewed the Lobbyists Registration Act in 1993 and made many recommendations to strengthen the act. Not surprisingly, the lobbyists lobbied ferociously against greater transparency in their operations, and the amendments that were finally adopted in 1995 were a pale imitation of what had been recommended by the committee and promised by the Liberals during the 1993 election campaign. The new act recognized three categories of lobbyists: Tier I (consultant lobbyists who lobby for clients) and two types of Tier II lobbyists, in-house lobbyists (corporate) and in-house lobbyists (organization)—that is, employees of corporations or advocacy group organizations for whom lobbying was a significant part of their duties.

The new law was somewhat more rigorous in what had to be reported. Rather than merely explain the general object of lobbying, lobbyists had to identify the specific legislative proposal, bill, resolution, regulation, policy, program, or contract in question, as well as the name of each department or other governmental institution lobbied. As well, coalition and grassroots lobbying had to be registered. Contingency fees (fees based on the successfulness of the lobbying effort) were not outlawed, but any such fees had to be disclosed to the registrar. As for enforcement, the six-month limitation of proceedings on contraventions was extended to two years. The ethics counsellor previously appointed by the Liberal government to administer the Conflict of Interest Code for cabinet ministers was required to work with interested parties to develop a code of conduct for lobbyists, which came into effect in 1997. Perhaps the most positive aspect of the 1995 changes therefore was the electronic registration of required information and public accessibility to the registry through the Internet.

In 2009, some 873 consultant lobbyists registered, in addition to 1 454 in-house corporate lobbyists and 2 217 in-house lobbyists for other organizations, for a grand total of 4 544. Some of the largest consultant lobbying firms and a sample of some of their principal clients are given in Table 10.2. Some companies engage the services of more than one lobbying firm in addition to their own in-house lobbyists.

While this revised law was an improvement on the original, it remained highly defective. "By leaving vague the definitions of lobbying, and by excluding any lobbying associated with a consultative exercise, the government ... left much

TABLE 10.2 SELECTED CONSULTANT LOBBYING FIRMS AND PRINCIPAL CLIENTS, 2010

Firm	Clients
Global Public Affairs	Shell Canada, Tech Resources, Canadian Association of Petroleum Producers, Vale Inco
Hill & Knowlton	Bell Canada, Merck Frosst, Canada's Research-Based Pharmaceutical Companies, Talisman Energy
Earnscliffe Strategy Group	Microsoft, General Motors, CIBC, EnCana

Source: Prepared by the author from the website of the Officer of the Commissioner of Lobbying at http://www.ocl-cal.gc.ca/eic/site/lobbyist-lobbyiste1.nsf/eng/home, retrieved April 15, 2010.

room for those sincerely wishing to avoid disclosing their activities or their aims to do so."[20] In other words, much lobbying is simply not recorded. The law did not require lobbyists to disclose positions currently or recently held in national political parties, ministers' offices, or the federal public service; it did not actually prohibit the use of contingency fees; and it did not require disclosure of the global cost of each lobbying campaign. At the same time, the industry was invaded by associates of the Liberal Party, and Paul Martin, as Minister of Finance and later Prime Minister, developed a close connection to the Earnscliffe Strategy Group.

The sustained criticisms of the advocacy group Democracy Watch and the recommendations of the Gomery Report on the Quebec sponsorship scandal led to significant alterations in the control of the lobbying industry. A new Lobbying Act was incorporated within the Harper government's Federal Accountability Act, which included the following provisions:

- a ban on contingency fees;
- the appointment of a commissioner of lobbying as an independent agent of Parliament;
- a prohibition on ministerial staffers, ministers, and senior public servants from registering as lobbyists for five years after leaving office;
- a requirement that lobbyists record telephone calls and in-person meetings with senior public officeholders; and
- the extension of the period during which infractions can be investigated to 10 years.

Nevertheless, certain gaps remain, including the secrecy over lobbyists' fees and the cost of a lobbying campaign. Although recent public office holders cannot function as "lobbyists," they can be employed by lobbying firms. Thus, most lobbying firms in Ottawa were happy to take on new Conservative partners who would

Lobbyists admit: "We've got to be a little more subtle."

(© Graham Harrop)

undoubtedly prove to be positive additions. Although a small number of non-corporate interests have employed lobbyists, it is generally true that the only actors who can afford them are corporations or business pressure groups. That partisan ties continue to play a significant part in the lobbyist process makes the system doubly objectionable.[21] Statistics from the Commissioner of Lobbying show that the four government institutions most actively lobbied were Industry Canada, Finance Canada, the Privy Council Office, and the Prime Minister's Office. Such figures indicate that most lobbying is done with respect to economic interests (i.e., by business interests) and reveal the centralized operation of the Harper government.

SUMMARY

This chapter discussed advocacy, interest, or pressure groups, social movements, and lobbying. Since such groups are not an official part of the political system, their importance is often overlooked, but the first part of the chapter showed how prominent and significant they are. The chapter then listed examples of some of the principal advocacy groups in various fields, provided different categorizations that are often useful, and differentiated advocacy groups from social movements. The chapter also demonstrated how the federal structure of government in Canada affects the organization of advocacy groups—usually requiring their presence at both levels of government. The targets of group activity were outlined, including the four institutions of government: bureaucracy, Cabinet, Parliament, and the courts. The next section tried to account for the relative success of group efforts in terms of the different resources possessed by such groups. The final part of the chapter dealt with lobbying. It identified certain lobbying firms, their clients, and their modes of operation; it discussed the attempt to regulate lobbying activity via legislation; and it revealed continuing problems in this area that the political system should address.

DISCUSSION QUESTIONS

1. Do business groups have more influence than other kinds of groups, and if so, why?
2. Why are student advocacy groups often ignored by federal and provincial governments?
3. Would groups that lack close links with the authorities (e.g., anti-poverty, pro-environmental, and Aboriginal groups) be better advised to work through regular political channels or to opt for more confrontational tactics in order to try to influence public policy?
4. How democratic is the sort of lobbying that goes on, often behind closed doors? Does the Lobbying Act provide adequate transparency?

KEY TERMS

Advocacy advertising Advertising that advocates a political point of view rather than trying to sell a good or service.

Advocacy group/interest group/pressure group Any group seeking to influence government policy without contesting elections; an organization whose members promote their common interest by acting together to influence public policy.

Assembly of First Nations The largest interest group representing status and non-status Indians (who now prefer to be called First Nations peoples).

Canadian Council of Chief Executives The most powerful peak business pressure group in Canada, representing the 150 largest firms in the country.

Canadian Labour Congress The largest labour pressure group in Canada; the political voice of over three million members.

Institutionalized advocacy group A kind of advocacy group characterized by permanence, resources, governmental recognition and acceptance, and well-developed links with the authorities.

Issue-oriented advocacy group A kind of advocacy group that springs up around an issue and disappears once that issue has been resolved.

Lobbying Any organized attempt to influence the authorities, now often performed by professional lobbyist firms.

Policy communities and policy networks Loose communities that form for the purpose of shaping public policy, taking the form of discrete and specialized clusters of government departments and agencies, advocacy groups, politicians, corporations, and interested individuals.

Regulations The detailed rules drafted by the bureaucracy under the authority of laws passed by Parliament that are too voluminous and technical to put into the legislation itself.

Social movement An informal network of organizations and individuals who, on the basis of a collective identity and shared values, engage in political struggle intended to expand the boundaries of the existing system, such as the women's and environmental movements.

Third-party advertising Advertising by advocacy groups, as opposed to political parties, during an election campaign.

FURTHER READING

Ayers, Jeffrey M. *Defying Conventional Wisdom: Political Movements and Popular Contention against North American Free Trade*. Toronto: University of Toronto Press, 1998.

Coleman, William, and Grace Skogstad. *Policy Communities and Public Policy in Canada*. Mississauga: Copp Clark Pitman, 1990.

Conway, Janet M. *Contesting Globalization: Social Movements, Identity, Place and Knowledge*. Black Point, N.S.: Fernwood Publishing, 2004.

Hale, Geoffrey. *The Uneasy Partnership: Politics of Business and Government in Canada*. Peterborough: Broadview Press, 2006.

Pal, Leslie. *Interests of State: The Politics of Language, Multiculturalism, and Feminism in Canada.* Montreal: McGill-Queen's University Press, 1993.

Phillips, Susan. "Interest Groups, Social Movements, and the Voluntary Sector: En Route to Reducing the Democratic Deficit." In James Bickerton and Alain-G. Gagnon, eds. *Canadian Politics*, 4th ed. Peterborough: Broadview Press, 2004.

Sawatsky, John. *The Insiders: Government, Business, and the Lobbyists.* Toronto: McClelland and Stewart, 1987.

Smith, Miriam. "Interest Groups and Social Movements." In Michael Whittington and Glen Williams, eds. *Canadian Politics in the 21st Century*, 7th ed. Toronto: Thomson Nelson, 2008.

———, ed. *Group Politics and Social Movements in Canada.* Peterborough: Broadview Press, 2008.

Young, Lisa, and Joanna Everitt. *Advocacy Groups.* Vancouver: UBC Press, 2004.

PART 3

The Constitutional Context

If "politics" and "government" can be separated, the first half of this text dealt with politics and the second half considers government. Chapter 1 provided an overview of government, but this second half of the book goes into more depth and is itself divided between the constitutional context and the process of governing. The Constitution forms the framework of the whole political system and is analyzed in the following two chapters. Chapter 11 outlines the historical development of the Canadian Constitution, its ingredients and principles, and the addition of the Charter of Rights and Freedoms in 1982. Since one of the most important aspects of the Constitution is the relationship between the federal and provincial governments, Chapter 12 examines all aspects of Canadian federalism.

Figure 11.1   Evolution of Canadian Pre-Confederation Political Institutions

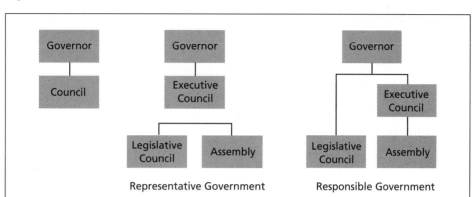

Discord subsequently developed between the locally elected assembly and the executive, composed of the governor and his appointed executive council. The assembly represented the people and could articulate their views, but it had no real power over the appointed councils. This situation was complicated by the cultural division in Lower Canada—a French assembly and an English executive—with "two nations warring in the bosom of a single state."[2] Reformers demanded **responsible government**, in which the members of the executive council would come from and reflect the views of the elected assembly. This problem eventually erupted into the Rebellions of 1837 in both Upper and Lower Canada, led by William Lyon Mackenzie and Louis-Joseph Papineau respectively. The British government put them down by force and then appointed Lord Durham to investigate the situation.

The 1839 **Durham Report** recommended that the principle of responsible government be implemented, so that the executive branch would govern only as long as it retained the confidence of the assembly. Durham outlined a division of powers between local and imperial authorities such that in local matters the governor would follow the advice of colonial authorities, but in matters of imperial concern he would act as an agent of the British government. Overcoming British resistance, responsible government was adopted in Nova Scotia, New Brunswick, and the colony of Canada in 1848, and three years later in Prince Edward Island. Thus, by 1851, all the pre-Confederation colonies operated on the basis that the Cabinet or executive council had to resign if it lost the confidence of the elected legislative assembly.

Durham also recommended that Upper and Lower Canada be united into a single colony of Canada, partly as one last attempt to submerge and assimilate the French. The colonies were amalgamated by the 1840 **Act of Union**, but when it became clear that the objective of assimilation would not be achieved, French was recognized as the second official language of the legislature. Moreover, most governments of the period had joint English and French leaders.

The Road to Confederation

Economic, political, and military factors soon drove the British North American colonies to consider uniting.[3] Because the British had discontinued colonial trading preferences, and because a reciprocity treaty with the United States had expired, the colonies hoped to establish a new free trade area among themselves. This large internal market would be enhanced by a railway link between the Maritimes and central Canada, also providing the latter with a winter Atlantic port. The future prospect of annexing and developing the West was seen as a further source of economic prosperity.

Meanwhile, the colony of Canada had experienced political deadlock between its two parts, then called Canada East (Quebec) and Canada West (Ontario), as well as between French and English component groups. Public decisions had to be made in one combined set of governmental institutions, yet the needs and demands of the two parts were often quite different. This led to the practice of requiring a "double majority" (a majority of members from each part of the colony) for the passage of bills. Confederation would grant greater autonomy to the two parts, because provincial governments would handle distinctive internal matters on their own, while a central government would deal with common problems. Such a two-tier structure also appealed to the Maritime provinces, which did not wish to turn all decisions over to a distant central government.

The individual colonies also felt vulnerable in a military sense. The United States had a powerful army on their doorstep, and the British government no longer seemed interested in providing military protection. By joining together, the colonies would make American aggression more difficult.

In the 1860s, Nova Scotia, New Brunswick, and Prince Edward Island began to consider forming a Maritime union and called the Charlottetown Conference of 1864 for this purpose. When delegates from the colony of Canada arrived, however, the idea of a larger union was put up for debate. The essentials of the **Confederation** scheme were agreed upon at the Quebec Conference later that year, and the London Conference of 1866 fine-tuned the agreement, leaving Prince Edward Island temporarily on the sidelines. Thus, the four provinces of Nova Scotia, New Brunswick, Quebec, and Ontario were officially united on July 1, 1867, by the **British North America Act (BNA Act)**, later renamed the **Constitution Act, 1867**.

Components and Principles of the Canadian Constitution

The Canadian constitution would be easier to comprehend if it consisted of a single document by that name. In the absence of such a document, we can define a **constitution** as the whole body of fundamental rules and principles according to which a state is governed. Canada's constitution provides for the basic institutions of government and relations between them, relations between national and provincial governments, and relations between governments and citizens.[4] Such a comprehensive definition suggests that the final product may not be neat and tidy and that some of it may not be written down at all.

In the search for the components that fit the definition of a constitution provided above, it will be seen that the Canadian constitution is a great hodgepodge. It essentially consists of the following:

- the Constitution Act, 1867, and its amendments;
- British and Canadian statutes;
- the Constitution Act, 1982, principally the Charter of Rights and Freedoms;
- judicial decisions; and
- constitutional conventions.

The Constitution Act, 1867, and Its Amendments

We turn first to the formal, legal documents, the most important of which is the Constitution Act, 1867, as mentioned above. That act provided for much of the basic machinery and institutions of government and established a federal system.

Part III of the act deals with the executive power, for example, and section 9 declares that the executive authority over Canada is vested in the Queen. Subsequent clauses refer to the governor general and to the Canadian Privy

Council, which is "to aid and advise in the Government of Canada." Section 13 observes that the "governor general in council" refers to the governor general acting by and with the advice of the Canadian Privy Council. Note that the prime minister and Cabinet are not explicitly mentioned.

Part IV establishes the legislative power—the Senate and House of Commons. The act requires that money bills (bills that involve the raising or spending of money) originate in the House of Commons, and within it, from members of the executive branch.

Part V concerns provincial constitutions, including the position of lieutenant governor. Since the 1867 act created the provinces of Ontario and Quebec, it had to establish their legislatures, whereas the legislatures of Nova Scotia and New Brunswick continued in their pre-Confederation form.

Part VI, the "Distribution of Legislative Powers" or **division of powers** between the central and provincial governments, is probably the most important part of the document. The core of Canadian **federalism** in a constitutional sense consists of section 91, the federal powers; section 92, provincial powers; section 93, education; and section 95, concurrent powers.

Part VII is concerned with the judiciary. It is a short section that gives the governor general the power to appoint superior, district, and county judges. It also provides for judges' retirement and removal, and it allows Parliament to set up a general court of appeal. Note that the 1867 act does not explicitly establish the Supreme Court of Canada.

Part VIII deals with the division of provincial revenues, debts, and assets at the time of Confederation. It makes clear that the provinces have possession of their own lands, mines, and minerals. Part IX is a miscellaneous collection, including section 132, the treaty power, and section 133, regarding English and French languages. The final section provides for the admission of other colonies.

The Constitution Act, 1867, was thus very brief on the executive and judicial branches of government and included virtually nothing about limiting the powers of government in relation to the people. The act also lacked any mention of the means to amend it, but since it was a statute of the British parliament, most formal changes to the act until 1982 were made by that parliament at Canadian request.

Such formal amendments to the 1867 act are also part of the Canadian constitution, some more important than others. They were often termed "British North America Acts," of whatever year in which they were passed, but in 1982, they were mostly renamed "Constitution Acts" of the appropriate year. For example, the BNA Act, 1940, which is now called the Constitution Act, 1940, transferred jurisdiction over unemployment insurance from the provincial to the federal level of government.

British and Canadian Statutes

The second major component of the Canadian Constitution is a collection of British statutes and orders in council and Canadian statutes. Chief among acts passed by the British Parliament that are of constitutional status for Canada is the **Statute of Westminster**, 1931, which declared Canada to be totally independent of Britain. Henceforth, no British law would apply to Canada unless (as in the case of constitutional amendments) Canada requested it. Orders in council are decisions made by a cabinet as distinct from acts of Parliament, and it was by means of British orders in council that the Northwest Territories and the colonies of British Columbia and Prince Edward Island were added to Canada. Therefore, such orders in council must be considered another ingredient of the Canadian Constitution.

So are the Canadian statutes that carved provinces out of the Northwest Territories—the Manitoba Act of 1870, and the Saskatchewan and Alberta Acts of 1905. Other Canadian statutes of constitutional significance include the Supreme Court Act, an ordinary law that fleshes out the provisions of the 1867 act with respect to the judicial branch of government, the Federal Court Act, the Parliament of Canada Act, the Bill of Rights, the Canada Elections Act, the Citizenship Act, the Emergencies Act, the Canadian Human Rights Act, the Yukon Act, and the Nunavut Act. Such statutes are sometimes are called "organic laws" to distinguish them from those of non-constitutional status.

The Constitution Act, 1982

Although the **Constitution Act, 1982**, was in a sense the last amendment to be passed by the British parliament to the Constitution Act, 1867, it is worthy of separate mention. Canada was completely self-governing after 1931, but most amendments to the 1867 act still had to be made by the British parliament because no formula had been developed to do so in Canada. The Constitution Act, 1982, contained such a domestic **constitutional amending formula**, and the Canada Act passed by the British parliament at the same time finally terminated all British authority over

Canada. Part V of the act provided five different amending formulas, depending on the subject matter of the amendment:

- unanimous consent of federal and provincial legislatures,
- consent of Parliament and seven provincial legislatures representing at least 50 percent of the population,
- consent of Parliament and one or more provinces affected,
- consent of Parliament alone, and
- consent of a provincial legislature alone.

Because of subsequent dissatisfaction with this formula, Parliament passed a law in 1996 to the effect that in the case of amendments falling in the second category above, the federal government would not agree to any constitutional amendment that did not have the consent of Ontario, Quebec, British Columbia, Alberta, and a majority of Atlantic provinces.

The second main part of the Constitution Act, 1982, was the Charter of Rights and Freedoms, a significant addition to the Constitution discussed in detail later in the chapter. The 1982 act also contained statements on Aboriginal peoples' rights and equalization payments to have-not provinces. As far as the division of powers was concerned, a new section, 92A, was added to clarify and extend provincial powers over natural resources. The 1982 document did not alter the position of the monarchy in Canada; Elizabeth II continues to be recognized as Queen of Canada, having no connection to the British government in this role.

Queen Elizabeth signs Canada's constitutional proclamation in Ottawa on April 17, 1982, as Prime Minister Pierre Trudeau looks on. (The Canadian Press/Ron Poling)

Judicial Decisions

The fourth ingredient of the Canadian Constitution consists of judicial decisions that have clarified or altered provisions of the 1867 act or other parts of the Constitution. The largest body of such decisions consists of the judgments of the British **Judicial Committee of the Privy Council**, Canada's final court of appeal until 1949. It was John A. Macdonald's intention to create a strong central government, but the Judicial Committee interpreted the 1867 act in such a way as to minimize federal powers and maximize those of the provinces. The court decisions that effected such a wholesale transformation of the federal nature of the country must be considered a part of the Constitution alongside the actual provisions of the original act. The very power of the courts to invalidate legislation in this manner— **judicial review**—has become a basic principle of the Constitution. Numerous judicial decisions regarding the Charter of Rights are also included in this category.

Constitutional Conventions

Thus far, all the ingredients listed can be found in written form, although not in one place. The final component of the Constitution, on the other hand, has never been committed to paper. It consists of **constitutional conventions**, that is, unwritten rules of constitutional behaviour that are considered to be binding by and upon those who operate the Constitution but that are not enforceable by the courts.[5] Constitutional conventions develop from traditions, and through constant recognition and observance they become as established, rigid, and sacrosanct as if they were written down. Many of these informal rules have been inherited from Britain, some have been modified in the Canadian environment, and others are unique to Canada. Many relate to the operation of the executive branch of government that was given such slight attention in the 1867 act. The dominant position of the prime minister and Cabinet, the subordinate place of the governor general, and the principle of responsible government are three of many conventions that are part of the Constitution.

Recent Constitutional Amendments

As mentioned, a formula to make formal constitutional amendments in Canada was finally adopted in 1982. But, as discussed in Chapter 3, the two attempts at "megaconstitutional" change, the Meech Lake and Charlottetown Accords, were unsuccessful. In fact, the amending formula has proven to be almost unworkable, and was rendered even less viable with the Constitutional Amendments Act of 1996.

On the other hand, several amendments confined to a single province have been made, including those related to the name of Newfoundland and Labrador, denominational schools in that province and Quebec, bilingualism in New Brunswick, and the Confederation Bridge replacing the ferry service to Prince Edward Island. Given the fact that the constitutional amending formula has only been used for such narrow questions, Canadians may have to find non-constitutional means to make reforms on wider issues.

Principles of the Constitution

The preceding discussion has identified three basic principles of the Canadian constitution: responsible government, federalism, and judicial review. At least three other fundamental principles are also embedded in our Constitution: constitutional monarchy, the rule of law, and democracy.[6]

In terms of its head of state, Canada is a **constitutional monarchy**. This is not a principle that attracts much attention, largely because the monarch herself lives in another country and because her actual power, as well as that of her Canadian representative, the governor general, is not extensive. Nevertheless, the monarchical system underlies a great deal of the operation of government in Canada, largely in the form of the Crown, as discussed in Chapter 13.

The **rule of law** is another constitutional principle inherited from Great Britain that rests largely on convention and judicial precedent. In essence, it means that all government action must be based on law and that governments and government officials must obey the law. In other words, the law is supreme and no one, including the lawmakers, is above it. Courts in Canada as well as in Britain have had occasion to overturn government decisions and actions that were not based on law. The sixth principle, democracy, was analyzed fully in Chapter 6.

The Charter of Rights and Freedoms

In the eyes of some observers, the pre-1982 Canadian constitution was deficient in lacking a statement of **civil liberties**, that is, the rights and freedoms that individuals enjoy beyond the reach of the government or the state. Such rights and freedoms are an integral part of a democratic political system and represent territory into which the government is not allowed to enter. In typical British manner, however, the fact that they were not written down did not mean that they did not exist.

Political systems that value civil liberties have adopted two principal methods to protect them. The British approach is to make Parliament supreme, but on the presumption that neither the legislature nor the executive would infringe such rights and freedoms because both branches of government are held in check by public opinion, tradition, the political culture, and self-restraint. In such a system, civil liberties are so deeply ingrained in the values of the people and politicians alike that they do not need to be written down; the authorities would never think of infringing them, even though, in theory, Parliament could do so. While the courts could not overturn legislation in Britain—that is, they lacked the power of judicial review—they have always had wide **judicial discretion** in the interpretation of laws, and many safeguards of civil liberties have been introduced into the law as canons of interpretation. Thus, even in the British system, judicial precedents accumulated into the **common law** offer some protection against arbitrary government action. So does the basic constitutional principle, the rule of law.

The American approach, derived in reaction to an imperial government that *did* encroach upon colonial liberties, is to provide for a written statement of civil rights in the constitutional Bill of Rights. Then, if legislation is passed or the executive takes action that is felt to violate a person's rights, such acts can be challenged in the courts. It is up to the courts to determine whether the government has infringed rights and freedoms as defined in the Constitution. The courts thus have the power of judicial review, and they can overturn offensive legislation or executive actions. In such a system, the substance of civil liberties basically depends upon judicial interpretation of the Bill of Rights.

In Canada, federal and provincial governments often discriminated against various groups—Aboriginals, women, and several immigrant minorities—and occasionally violated other civil liberties. The federal government's internment of Canadian citizens of Japanese extraction during the Second World War was particularly outrageous. Quebec's Padlock Law blatantly interfered with freedom of speech and assembly, while that province's treatment of Jehovah's Witnesses violated freedom of religion, and the Alberta Press Bill infringed freedom of the press. Such actions persuaded Prime Minister Diefenbaker to enact the **Canadian Bill of Rights** in 1960. The bill's apparent intention was to allow the courts to invalidate legislation that they found to conflict with the Bill of Rights, but this aim was not clearly articulated. Other serious gaps in the bill were that it applied only to the federal government, not to the provinces; that it allowed legislation to be passed that overrode the bill, as long as this was acknowledged (i.e., a notwithstanding clause); that as an ordinary piece of legislation, the bill could be amended

Pierre Elliott Trudeau, father of the Charter of Rights and Freedoms. (The Canadian Press)

in the routine way; and that it was superseded by the War Measures Act at the very time when it might be needed most.

Not surprisingly, the courts made very limited use of the Bill of Rights. In only one case, the *Drybones* case of 1970, did they decide that a clause of an act violated the Bill of Rights and was therefore inoperative. The bill was more useful in clarifying legal rights and was referred to in several cases to fill in gaps in definitions of such concepts as the "right to counsel," the "right to an interpreter," and the "right to a fair hearing."

Prime Minister Trudeau recognized the limitations and ambiguities of the Canadian Bill of Rights and wanted to incorporate new kinds of rights into the Constitution, especially linguistic rights. Finally, in 1982, with the adoption of the **Charter of Rights and Freedoms,** he accomplished his objective. The Charter was entrenched in the Constitution, and it is increasingly the task of the judiciary to determine if and when governments have encroached upon the following rights and freedoms:

- fundamental freedoms,
- democratic rights,
- mobility rights,
- legal rights,
- Aboriginal rights,
- equality rights,
- language rights, and
- minority language education rights.

Trudeau was determined to protect bilingualism and official minority language education rights across the country in an effort to undercut Quebec's claim that it alone represented French Canada. Moreover, he hoped to counter centrifugal forces throughout the land and pressures for decentralization to the provinces by creating an instrument that the courts could use to cut down self-serving provincial laws. As a new national symbol, the Charter would also function to increase the allegiance of all citizens to the national government.

The Charter is generally a much stronger document than its predecessor. Besides being broader in scope, it applies equally to both federal and provincial governments. Entrenched into the Constitution, it is difficult to amend. It also states very clearly that the courts are to invalidate any legislation or executive acts that they find to conflict with the provisions of the Charter. We will briefly examine the provisions of the Charter and note some of the prominent court decisions it has inspired.[7]

Reasonable Limits on Rights and Freedoms

It must first be said that the rights articulated in the Charter are not absolute. Section 1, the **reasonable limits clause**, indicates that these rights are subject to "such reasonable limits, defined by law, as can be demonstrably justified in a free

Case Study

Use of Reasonable Limits in the *Sharpe* Case Regarding Child Pornography

In the *Sharpe* case, in 2001, the Supreme Court ruled that the law prohibiting the possession of child pornography infringed Robin Sharpe's freedom of expression. But the Court went on to uphold the law as a reasonable limit on his Charter right because

- the objective of the law that criminalized the possession of child pornography was pressing and substantial,
- the means chosen by Parliament were rationally connected to the objective,
- allowing minor and reasonable exceptions (e.g., innocent photographs of a baby in the bath) showed that the law was a minimal impairment of the Charter right, and
- the benefits of prohibiting such materials outweighed any costs to the right of freedom of expression.

and democratic society." The courts are thus allowed to find that while a piece of legislation violates certain rights, it is still acceptable according to their definition of reasonable limits. In order to decide which restrictions can be justified in a free and democratic society, the Court developed guidelines in the *Oakes* case that have come to be called the **Oakes test**. The objective of the government in limiting a Charter right must be pressing and substantial, and the means adopted must be proportional to that objective. That is, the means must be rationally connected to the objective; they must impair the right as little as possible; and the benefits of the restriction must exceed its costs. In fact, the Supreme Court has made extensive use of section 1, upholding many laws that it considered to be in violation of Charter rights but that were saved because the infringements were reasonable.

Fundamental Freedoms

At least from a political point of view, section 2 of the Charter is probably most important. It lists the following **fundamental freedoms**: freedom of conscience and religion; freedom of thought, belief, opinion, and expression, including freedom of the press and other media of communication; freedom of peaceful assembly; and freedom of association.

With respect to freedom of religion, the Supreme Court threw out the Lord's Day Act as an infringement of freedom of religion because its restrictions on Sunday activities were clearly related to the Christian Sabbath and discriminated against other religions. On the other hand, the Court upheld Ontario's Retail Business Holidays Act, an act designed to limit Sunday shopping and preserve Sunday as a day of rest on a secular rather than a religious foundation. The courts also decided that public schools may no longer hold a compulsory and exclusively Christian school prayer. Ontario's publicly funded Roman Catholic separate school system was upheld as a pre-Charter constitutional right, however, and does not discriminate against other private religious schools for which public funding is not guaranteed. Child welfare authorities can authorize blood transfusions for a child despite the parents' religious beliefs, and Sikh students can carry their *kirpans* (ceremonial daggers) to school, as long as they are sheathed.

Freedom of expression has brought a wide range of issues before the courts. Perhaps most controversial was the Supreme Court's rejection of the French-only sign provision of Quebec's Bill 101, which also violated Quebec's own Charter of Rights. The Court decided that freedom of expression not only included the freedom to express ideas but also the freedom to choose the language in which to express them. Moreover, the concept of freedom of expression incorporated "commercial expression," such as a company's right to erect a sign or engage in advertising. Similarly, the federal government's first attempt at prohibiting tobacco advertising was also deemed a violation of tobacco companies' freedom of expression. But a majority of the Court concluded that a partial ban on such advertising and prohibiting the dissemination of hate literature were both acceptable as reasonable limits on freedom of expression.

Obscenity also falls into the category of freedom of expression. In the *Butler* case, the Court divided pornography into different categories, saying portrayal of sex with violence and sex that is degrading or dehumanizing can be restricted by the authorities, but portrayal of explicit sex that is neither violent nor degrading is generally acceptable unless children are involved. In later cases, an artist's depiction of children in various sexual activities was deemed to be art rather than pornography, and customs officers were instructed not to differentiate in the standards they applied to homosexual and heterosexual materials. In the 2001 *Sharpe* case, as mentioned, the Supreme Court unanimously upheld the provisions of the Criminal Code that prohibit the possession of child pornography as a reasonable limit on freedom of expression. As for prostitution, the Court upheld the prohibition on communicating for the purposes of sidewalk solicitation.

Freedom of expression and freedom of the press in connection with election campaigns have also fostered several constitutional cases. The Supreme Court decided that the three-day blackout period before election day in which newspapers could not publish public opinion polls was too long, and was later limited to election day itself. As mentioned in Chapter 8, repeated efforts by Parliament to restrict third-party advertising during election campaigns were thwarted by the lower courts in Alberta but ultimately upheld by the Supreme Court in 2004.

Overturning an earlier decision, the Supreme Court ruled in a 2007 case that freedom of association protects collective bargaining, although whether that includes the right to strike was not addressed. In other words, at least in certain circumstances, freedom of association prevents federal or provincial legislatures from passing back-to-work legislation or otherwise interfering in the collective bargaining process.

Democratic and Mobility Rights

Under **democratic rights** in sections 3 to 5, the Charter guarantees that every citizen of Canada has the right to vote in federal and provincial elections; that no Parliament can continue for more than five years, except in time of real or apprehended war, invasion, or insurrection; and that Parliament must sit at least once every year. Section 3 has been used in several cases dealing with federal and provincial electoral laws that denied the vote to certain categories of people. One of the most controversial decisions in this respect stated that all prisoners have the right to vote in federal elections; another established that the privilege of listing a candidate's political affiliation on the ballot cannot be restricted to parties running a large number of candidates. Rather unexpectedly, the democratic rights section has also been used to assess the validity of electoral maps that determine the size of constituencies.

Under section 6, **mobility rights**, every citizen of Canada has the right to enter, remain in, and leave Canada, and every citizen or permanent resident has the right to take up residence and pursue a livelihood in any province. On the other hand, laws establishing reasonable residency requirements for receiving public services are acceptable, as is giving preference to local residents if the unemployment rate in that province is higher than the national rate. Trudeau included mobility rights because of his concern that some provinces were restricting the entry of residents of other provinces, as in the case of cross-border employment, but these clauses have not featured frequently in judicial interpretation.

Legal Rights

Legal rights are contained in sections 7 to 14. In section 7, everyone has the right to life, liberty, and security of the person and the right not to be deprived thereof except in accordance with the principles of fundamental justice. "Security of the person" was used to invalidate the abortion provision of the Criminal Code in the famous *Morgentaler* case in 1988. A majority of the Court ruled that the law, with all its arbitrary and bureaucratic procedures, violated the security of the person of the woman concerned and constituted a "profound interference with a woman's body." Sue Rodriguez, dying of Lou Gehrig's disease, was not so fortunate in arguing that security of the person provided her with the right to assisted suicide—only a minority of judges agreed with her. In a controversial split decision regarding wait times for medical services, the Court decided in the *Chaoulli* case that the Quebec law banning the purchase of private health insurance for core medical services was unconstitutional according to the right to the "life, liberty and security of the person." Many observers feared that this would lead to the end of the public medical care system in the whole country. In the *Singh* case, "security of the person" required that the Immigration Department provide an oral hearing for refugee claimants when their lives could be in danger if deported. "Fundamental justice" also necessitated giving such claimants an opportunity to state their case and to know the case against them.

In cases of sexual assault, the Supreme Court has grappled with the right of the accused to use evidence about the victim's previous sexual activity against the right of the victim not to be unnecessarily hounded on the subject on the witness stand. To some extent, the result of several such cases was to tighten up the concept of consent in sexual matters: "No means no." The Supreme Court has upheld the existing Criminal Code provisions with respect to the moderate spanking of children against the claim that it violated security of the person.

Increasing concern about terrorism since 9/11 has raised serious questions about the balance between national security and many legal rights, including life, liberty, and security of the person, and right to counsel, as well as several fundamental freedoms. In the 2007 *Charkaoui* case, the Supreme Court ruled that the use of secret testimony to imprison and deport foreigners as possible terrorist suspects violates the Charter's guarantee of fundamental justice and a fair hearing. The Court suspended its ruling for a year, allowing parliament to draft a new law compatible with the Charter. Then, in June 2008, Charkaoui won a second Supreme Court decision when it ordered CSIS to stop systematically destroying interview notes and other evidence gathered during national security probes. In the fall of 2009, most of the surveillance restrictions on Charkaoui and some of the others involved in stalled security-certificate cases were eased when the Crown said it would rather drop the case than reveal how CSIS had obtained its information against them. Meanwhile, in May 2008, the Supreme Court ruled that Omar Khadr, detained by the U.S. at Guantanamo Bay, was entitled to see the documents relevant to the charges against him, including the records of CSIS interviews in the possession of the Canadian Crown. In another case, the Federal Court decreed in April 2009 that the government must demand that U.S. authorities return Khadr to Canada on the basis of fundamental justice. When the Harper government appealed the decision, the Supreme Court of Canada agreed that the 15-year-old's Charter rights had been violated, but then backtracked to say that it was not appropriate for the Court to give the government direction regarding the breach of such Charter rights.

Section 8 establishes the right to be secure against unreasonable search and seizure. In dismissing the charge of collusion between the Southam and Thomson newspaper chains, the Court extended this right to corporations and decided that the search of Southam's offices by anti-combines officials had indeed been unreasonable because it had not been authorized by a judge. This section has also come into play in cases involving police officers making spot checks, taking blood or

DNA samples, or entering houses; customs officers performing strip searches at border points; guards frisking prisoners; and police officers frisking people on the street.

Section 9 grants the right not to be arbitrarily detained or imprisoned, and section 10 states that on arrest or detention, everyone has the right to be informed promptly of the reasons, as well as the right to contact a lawyer without delay and to be informed of that right. The Court has ruled that random police spot checks, often called R.I.D.E. programs, are a reasonable limit on the right not to be arbitrarily detained, and that roadside breath tests do not include the right to retain counsel. However, a person who fails that test and is asked to accompany the police officer to a police station has a right to retain counsel before the breathalyzer test is conducted there. Moreover, the Court has ruled that a person has the right to be told of his or her right not only to a lawyer but also to legal aid, and must have a reasonable opportunity to exercise these rights.

Section 11 includes a variety of rights available to a person charged with an offence. "To be tried within a reasonable time" has been extremely controversial after the *Askov* decision found that a delay of almost two years between a preliminary hearing and a trial had been excessive. The lower courts took this to mean that everyone had a right to a trial within six to eight months of being charged, and some 34 500 cases were thrown out in Ontario alone.

Persons charged cannot be compelled to testify against themselves, cannot be denied reasonable bail without just cause, and are presumed innocent until proven guilty according to law in a fair and public hearing by an independent and impartial tribunal. The presumption of innocence was addressed in the *Oakes* case. Under the "reverse onus" clause of the Narcotics Control Act, a person proven to be in possession of a narcotic was also presumed to be guilty of trafficking, and it was up to the person charged with possession to prove his or her innocence on the trafficking charge. The *Oakes* case invalidated this clause as an unreasonable limit on the presumption of innocence. Persons charged with an offence are guaranteed a trial by jury if the maximum punishment for the offence is imprisonment for five years or more; as well, whether they are finally acquitted or found guilty and punished, they cannot be tried for the offence again.

Everyone has the right not to be subjected to any cruel and unusual treatment or punishment. In the 2001 *Latimer* case, the Supreme Court rejected the claim that the minimum mandatory sentence of 10 years in jail constituted cruel and unusual punishment in the case of a father who took the life of his severely disabled daughter because he could not bear to see her in such pain. Section 14 stipulates that a party or witness in any proceeding who does not understand or speak the language in which the proceeding is conducted or who is deaf has the right to the assistance of an interpreter.

Equality Rights

Equality rights are contained in section 15, which reads as follows:

> *Every individual is equal before and under the law and has the right to the equal protection and equal benefit of the law without discrimination and, in particular, without discrimination based on race, national or ethnic origin, colour, religion, sex, age or mental or physical disability.*

In the *Andrews* case, the Supreme Court laid down a two-step process for interpreting equality rights. The Court first determines if there has been a violation of the equality rights listed in section 15 (or of others analogous to them), and then whether there has been a harmful or prejudicial effect. In other words, inequalities and distinctions are permitted if no negative discrimination is involved.

Canadian Supreme Court agrees to gay marriage. (Bado/Artisans.com)

According to Ian Greene, the Court made it clear that "it intends to interpret section 15 to help clearly disadvantaged groups in society."[8] Moreover, the second part of the section permits **affirmative action** programs that give preference to those who have been discriminated against in the past. Equality rights are subject to reasonable limits, and on this basis the Supreme Court has allowed several kinds of discrimination to continue. In the case of mandatory retirement at age 65, for example, the Court ruled that such laws and policies were a violation of equality rights and did involve discrimination but could be allowed as reasonable limits.

Perhaps the most innovative use of section 15 has been in connection with sexual orientation and same-sex rights. In 1995, the Supreme Court ruled unanimously that the Charter prohibited discrimination on the basis of sexual orientation, even though this ground was not explicitly listed in section 15. After "reading in" this addition to the list in section 15, the Court made the same order with respect to the Individual's Rights Protection Act in Alberta. Then, in 1999, the Court moved on to same-sex partnerships, finding that in most situations, laws could not discriminate between same-sex and opposite-sex couples. This prohibition on discrimination eventually included same-sex marriage, and Parliament passed a law confirming the change.

Language Rights

Sections 16 to 22 of the Charter constitutionalize the federal and New Brunswick Official Languages Acts. These sections guarantee that certain government agencies will operate on a bilingual basis, as discussed in Chapter 3. Section 23 provides constitutional protection for **minority language education rights**, and some would argue that this was the part of the Charter with which Pierre Trudeau was most concerned. The clause guarantees these rights to Canadian citizens who constitute English- and French-language minorities in all provinces in areas "where numbers warrant." The Supreme Court can decide when the number of francophone students warrants a French-language school, and it has also ruled that such a school must have a "distinct physical setting" and that French-language parents must have a say in the "management and control" of it. The Supreme Court struck down the provision in Quebec's Bill 101 that limited access to the English-language school system in Quebec to the children of parents who were themselves products of that system (the "Quebec clause"). Indeed, section 23 (the "Canada clause") was deliberately drafted so that it would conflict with Bill 101, in order that Canadian citizens who moved to Quebec could also send their children to the English-language schools.

Other Provisions

Section 24 makes clear, where the Bill of Rights did not, that the courts have the power to interpret the Charter and to invalidate laws that conflict with it. The Charter does not actually bar illegally obtained evidence, as in the United States; the admission of such evidence is acceptable as long as it does not bring the administration of justice into disrepute.

Sections 25 through 30 relate to specific groups in society. Section 25 reads that the rights and freedoms in the Charter shall not be construed so as to override any Aboriginal, treaty, or other rights or freedoms that pertain to the Aboriginal peoples of Canada, including any rights or freedoms that have been recognized by the Royal Proclamation of 1763 and any others that may be acquired by the Aboriginal peoples of Canada by way of land claims settlements.

Section 27 asserts that the Charter shall be interpreted in a manner consistent with the preservation and enhancement of the multicultural heritage of Canadians, and section 28 ensures that the rights and freedoms referred to in the Charter are guaranteed equally to male and female persons. The women's movement considered the addition of section 28 to be essential so that governments would not be able to use the notwithstanding clause (section 33) to override the gender-equality provision of section 15. According to section 29, the Charter is not to override any rights or privileges guaranteed by or under the Constitution of Canada in respect of denominational schools. This section thus protects section 93 of the 1867 Constitution Act, which guaranteed existing Protestant and Roman Catholic separate schools.

Section 32 clarifies that the Charter applies to the Parliament and government of Canada, to the legislature and government of each province, and to the northern territories. By implication, it also applies to the municipal level of government. Thus all legislation in Canada must be consistent with the Charter, as must all actions of government executives, including ministers, public servants, and police officers. The Charter is not intended to apply to the private sector, but certain institutions occupy an ambiguous position. The Charter has been applied to community colleges, for example, but more autonomous semi-public institutions such as hospitals and universities are exempt. Federal and provincial human rights codes are intended to prevent discrimination in the private sector, but since such codes take the form of laws, they must also remain consistent with the Charter.

The Notwithstanding Clause

As mentioned above, the "reasonable limits" clause in section 1 allows the courts to exempt certain laws from the application of the Charter. The second limitation on Charter rights revolves around the **notwithstanding clause** in section 33. In the areas of fundamental freedoms, legal rights, and equality rights, either level of government is allowed to pass legislation contrary to the Charter. On the other hand, the legislation cannot be used to circumvent democratic rights, mobility rights, or linguistic rights. The notwithstanding clause would normally come into play when legislation was introduced to override a judicial decision regarding a Charter right. Such a bill can be exempted from the provisions of the Charter only for a five-year period, however, after which it becomes inoperative if not passed again.

What Do You Think?

In cases dealing with abortion, same-sex marriage, assisted suicide, euthanasia, or public health care, do you think the federal Parliament or a provincial legislature should use the notwithstanding clause to override a Supreme Court decision if a majority of legislators disagree with it? Why or why not?

Despite the number of times the Supreme Court has invalidated federal or provincial legislation since 1982, governments have rarely re-enacted such provisions under section 33. Over the first 25 years, it was used in a significant way only in Saskatchewan and Quebec. The Saskatchewan government used section 33 (unnecessarily, as it turned out) to pass back-to-work legislation to end a public service strike in 1986. The first Parti Québécois government in Quebec (1976–85) routinely applied the notwithstanding clause, as a matter of principle, to all new legislation. The next Liberal government discontinued that practice, but when the Supreme Court ruled that French-only store signs violated their owners' freedom of expression, Premier Bourassa invoked section 33 (and the equivalent clause in the Quebec Charter of Rights) and then passed what he considered to be a compromise law that allowed certain bilingual signs inside the store. While this incident in particular gave the notwithstanding clause a negative reception in most of English Canada, section 33 is often defended as a general principle. It allows democratically elected legislators, if they choose, to have the final say in many areas.

Provincial politicians in Alberta have occasionally threatened to invoke the notwithstanding clause. That province probably contains the leading critics of judicial activism in the defence of minority rights, and federal members of the Alberta-based Reform/Canadian Alliance also advocated the use of section 33 on occasion.[9]

Implications of the Charter for the Political System

The Charter of Rights and Freedoms has attracted both passionate support and opposition. Each side agrees, however, that the adoption of the Charter has significantly changed the operation of the Canadian political system. The courts have become involved in almost all of the most difficult political issues that have arisen over the past 30 years: Aboriginal rights, abortion, assisted suicide, euthanasia, French-only signs, gender equality, impaired driving, mandatory retirement, minority language schools, official bilingualism, political rights of public servants, pornography, prostitution, public health care, redistribution of constituency boundaries, the right to strike, same-sex relationships, separate schools, sexual assault, sexual orientation, Sunday shopping, terrorism, testing the cruise missile, and tobacco advertising. Such cases have enmeshed the courts in considerable political controversy and, as Peter Russell says, the Charter has "judicialized politics and politicized the judiciary."[10] Most Canadians seem pleased with the courts' involvement (some of them ignorant of the fact that most rights and freedoms were equally enjoyed before 1982). When asked in a 2000 survey whether courts or legislatures should have the final say, 60 percent of respondents preferred judges, compared to 26 percent who had more faith in legislators.[11]

On the other hand, representatives of both the left and the right have made scathing attacks on the "legalization of politics" in Canada. Michael Mandel, for example, argues that judges make highly political decisions but disguise this fact through legal interpretations and abstract principles that are unintelligible to the general public. Mandel challenges the generally accepted view that politicians make decisions that are popular, political, and self-serving, while judges' decisions are impartial, objective, technical, rational, and in the public interest. Their invocation of the reasonable limits clause, for example, has been highly discretionary.[12]

Mandel's second argument is that while the Charter has been sold as enhancing democracy and the power of the people, it has really reduced the degree of popular control over government. It has transferred power from representative, accountable legislatures and politicians to unrepresentative, unaccountable, and unrestrained judges, courts, and an elitist legal profession.

Third, legalized politics enhances individual and corporate rights against the collective welfare of the community. The adoption of individualistic American values in the Charter, as opposed to traditional Canadian collectivism, is strengthened by the tendency of the courts to cite American precedents when making their decisions.

Mandel's fourth point is that legalized politics is conservative, class-based politics that defends existing social arrangements and undermines popular movements. For a variety of reasons—including the cost of litigation, the background and attitudes of judges, and the biases in the law and the Charter—the socially disadvantaged and labour unions were better off without it.

The attack from the right focuses on the claim that women and minorities have benefited from Charter decisions at the expense of the majoritarian views of elected legislatures and the general public.[13] It is true that an implication of adopting the Charter is that minority groups increasingly ignore the usual political processes—legislatures, cabinets, and bureaucracies—and take their demands to the courts instead. To some extent this happened when such groups were unable to accomplish their goals through traditional political activity, in which case it could be argued that this alternative avenue is advantageous. The Charter does serve to protect certain minority rights against the tyranny of the majority. On the other hand, few observers would welcome a general transformation of political activity into legal activity with the attendant loss of political skills and organization that traditionally characterize a democracy. Seymour Martin Lipset fears that the Charter will remove one of the last traits that distinguish Canadians from Americans by increasing the litigious character of citizen–state relations, and that it will bring about a "rights-centred" political culture.[14]

The main nonpolitical effect of the Charter has been to restrict the behaviour of police officers and others engaged in law enforcement. The manner in which they deal with those suspected or accused of committing an offence is subject to rigid Charter rules. Many apparent cases of guilt have been thrown out because, according to a judge, police officers' collection of evidence brought the administration of justice into disrepute. This was commonly because the accused gave a confession in unusual circumstances, because the accused was denied the right to retain and instruct counsel without delay, or because police (or anti-combines) officers did not comply with a judge's interpretation of Charter restrictions on search and seizure. Thus, law enforcement officers often complain that they are expected to do their job with their hands tied behind their backs.

Greg Hein has shown that it is corporations, not women or minority groups, that are the single biggest interest taking Charter cases to the courts.[15] This is partly because of the enormous cost of pursuing a case all the way to the Supreme Court—only corporations and wealthy individuals can afford it. But if we focus on winners rather than users, it is more difficult to generalize. Official-language minorities, criminals, the gay and lesbian communities, and corporations would probably top the list.

In any case, such analysts and critics at least offer a salutary reminder to question the face value of court decisions; to refrain from glorifying the Charter, judges, lawyers, and courts; and to remember traditional ways of making public decisions and of protecting rights and freedoms. Parliament and the courts each have their own understandable and legitimate perspectives on Charter issues, and the best approach is to hope for some kind of dialogue between them.[16]

Reflecting the fact that it was born of political compromise, the Charter retains one main limitation on judicial interpretation, the notwithstanding clause. Any legislature may pass an act violating certain aspects of the Charter, as long as it says explicitly that it is doing so. Canadians are left with a strange system under which the courts can overrule the legislatures but the legislatures can overrule the courts. Canadian political compromise that it is, this system of protecting rights and freedoms may turn out to be superior to either total legislative supremacy or exclusive judicial review. The truth of the matter, however, is that politicians are now afraid to use the notwithstanding clause because of an anticipated public backlash.

SUMMARY

This chapter focused on the Canadian constitution and an important recent addition thereto, the Charter of Rights and Freedoms. The first part of the chapter outlined the evolution of Canadian constitutional development up to Confederation. It showed that the Constitution is not a single document, but rather consists of many different documents—British and Canadian statutes and judicial decisions—and unwritten constitutional conventions. It enumerated the basic provisions of the Constitution Act, 1867, and the Constitution Act, 1982, and the six basic principles of the Canadian constitution. Turning to the Charter of Rights and Freedoms, the chapter demonstrated that a written charter is not the only way to protect civil liberties. It then discussed the major parts of the Charter together with examples of definitive judicial decisions relevant to each clause. Charter rights are not absolute, and the two loopholes in the document, the reasonable limits and notwithstanding clauses, were both examined. At the end, the chapter considered the major impact that the Charter has had on the operation of Canadian politics and looked at advantages and disadvantages of this influence.

DISCUSSION QUESTIONS

1. Would it be possible or advisable to incorporate all the ingredients of our Constitution into a single document?
2. What were the symbolic, legal, and political consequences of adopting the Constitution Act, 1982?
3. Is the increase in judicial power in the Canadian political system as a result of the adoption of the Charter of Rights and Freedoms an asset or a liability?

KEY TERMS

Act of Union The 1840 act that united the colonies of Upper and Lower Canada into the colony of Canada.

Affirmative action A law or program that provides preference in the hiring or promotion process to individuals with certain characteristics.

British North America Act (BNA Act) The 1867 act of the British Parliament that created Canada by uniting the four original provinces, that provided some of the essential elements of the new country's Constitution, and that in 1982 was renamed the Constitution Act, 1867.

Canadian Bill of Rights An act of the Canadian Parliament passed in 1960 that outlined basic civil liberties but whose defects caused judicial confusion and limited the bill's effectiveness.

Charter of Rights and Freedoms Part of the Constitution Act, 1982, that guaranteed fundamental freedoms and legal, democratic, linguistic, mobility, and equality rights.

Civil liberties Freedoms or rights, including the freedoms of speech, press, religion, and assembly, that citizens enjoy and that cannot be infringed upon by government.

Common law The basis of the British and Canadian legal systems that consists of the accumulation of judicial precedents, which guide judges in the absence or interpretation of a legislature-made law.

Confederation The foundation of Canada in 1867 with the union of four provinces.

Constitution The whole body of fundamental rules and principles according to which a state is governed.

Constitution Act, 1867 The new name for the British North America Act, 1867, which united the four original provinces.

Constitution Act, 1982 The act sponsored by Prime Minister Trudeau that contained a made-in-Canada constitutional amending formula and a Charter of Rights and Freedoms.

Constitutional Act The 1791 British law that divided Canada into two separate colonies—Upper and Lower Canada—each with a governor, executive and legislative councils, and assembly.

Constitutional amending formula The process for making formal amendments to the Constitution.

Constitutional conventions Unwritten rules of constitutional behaviour that are considered to be binding by and upon those who operate the Constitution but that are not enforceable by the courts.

Constitutional monarchy The official designation of the Canadian form of government, characterized by a monarch who is head of state but who rules according to the Constitution, which confides almost all governmental power into other hands.

Democratic rights A category of rights in the Charter of Rights and Freedoms that, among other things, guarantees the vote to every Canadian citizen.

Division of powers The distribution of legislative powers between the federal and provincial governments, largely contained in sections 91 and 92 of the Constitution Act, 1867.

Durham Report The 1839 report by Lord Durham that recommended the union of Upper and Lower Canada and the granting of responsible government to the colony of Canada.

Equality rights A category of rights in the Charter of Rights and Freedoms that prohibits governments from discriminating against certain categories of people.

Federalism A system of government characterized by two levels of authority (federal and provincial) and a division of powers between them such that neither is subordinate to the other.

Fundamental freedoms Political freedoms—of religion, speech, press, assembly, association, etc.—that governments are not supposed to encroach upon and that are guaranteed by the Charter of Rights and Freedoms.

Judicial Committee of the Privy Council A committee of the British Parliament that functioned as Canada's final court of appeal until 1949.

Judicial discretion The leeway inevitably bestowed on the courts when they interpret laws, even when they do not, or have no power to, overturn them.

Judicial review The power of the courts to overturn legislation or actions of the executive branch of government.

Legal rights The rights of a person suspected or accused of committing a crime, now listed in the Charter of Rights and Freedoms.

Minority language education rights Rights established in section 23 of the Charter of Rights and Freedoms whereby French-speaking Canadians can send their children to French-language schools wherever their numbers warrant, a principle also extended to English-speaking Canadians where they are a minority.

Mobility rights A category of rights in the Charter of Rights and Freedoms guaranteeing the freedom to move from one province to another and seek employment there.

Notwithstanding clause Section 33 of the Charter of Rights and Freedoms that allows federal or provincial governments to pass laws that violate certain sections of the Charter.

Oakes test The strategy outlined in the *Oakes* case for interpreting the reasonable limits clause of the Charter of Rights and Freedoms.

Quebec Act The 1774 British law that provided for a system of government for the colony of Quebec that included certain privileges for the French-speaking, Roman Catholic majority.

Reasonable limits clause Section 1 of the Charter of Rights and Freedoms, which allows the courts to uphold a law even if it violates a Charter right.

Representative government A form of government including an assembly elected by the citizens but not necessarily incorporating the principle of responsible government.

Responsible government A form of government in which the political executive must retain the confidence of the elected legislature and resign or call an election if and when it is defeated on a vote of non-confidence.

Royal Proclamation of 1763 The British policy enunciated after conquering Quebec that in a large area called Indian Territory forbade the purchase or settlement of land without a treaty between the Crown and the Indian people concerned.

Rule of law The constitutional principle that all government action must be based on law and that governments and government officials must obey the law.

Statute of Westminster The 1931 British law that declared Canada and the other Dominions to be fully independent.

FURTHER READING

Bateman, Thomas M.J., et al. *The Court and the Charter: Leading Cases*. Toronto: Emond Montgomery, 2008.

Borovoy, Alan. *When Freedoms Collide: The Case for Our Civil Liberties*. Toronto: Lester & Orpen Dennys, 1988.

Forcese, Craig, and Aaron Freeman. *The Laws of Government: The Legal Foundations of Canadian Democracy*. Toronto: Irwin Law, 2005.

Hiebert, Janet. *Charter Conflicts: What Is Parliament's Role?* Montreal: McGill-Queen's University Press, 2002.

Jhappan, Radha. "Charter Politics and the Judiciary." In Michael Whittington and Glen Williams, eds. *Canadian Politics in the 21st Century*, 7th ed. Toronto: Thomson Nelson, 2008.

MacIvor, Heather. *Canadian Politics and Government in the Charter Era*. Toronto: Thomson Nelson, 2006.

Mandel, Michael. *The Charter of Rights and the Legalization of Politics in Canada*, rev. ed. Toronto: Wall and Thompson, 1994.

Morton, F. L., and Rainer Knopff. *The Charter Revolution and the Court Party*. Peterborough: Broadview Press, 2000.

Potter, Andrew. *The Politics of the Charter: The Illusive Promise of Constitutional Rights*. Toronto: University of Toronto Press, 2010.

Reesor, Bayard. *The Canadian Constitution in Historical Perspective*. Scarborough: Prentice-Hall Canada, 1992.

Romanow, Roy, J. Whyte, and H. Leeson. *Canada … Notwithstanding: The Making of the Constitution, 1976–1982*. Toronto: Methuen, 1984.

Russell, Peter. *Constitutional Odyssey*, 3rd ed. Toronto: University of Toronto Press, 2004.

Sharpe, Robert J., et al. *The Charter of Rights and Freedoms*, 3rd ed. Toronto: Irwin Law, 2005.

Chapter 12

The Provinces and the
Federal System

The adoption of a federal system was one of the crucial decisions taken in the creation of Canada, and the shape of the federal–provincial relationship remains at the heart of contemporary Canadian politics. After introducing the role of the provinces, this chapter outlines the federal system in Canada at its creation and then traces the evolution of that system, especially through changes in the division of powers and federal–provincial financial relationships. The chapter concludes with a discussion of Canadian federalism today and an enumeration of recent developments.

Chapter Objectives

After you have completed this chapter, you should be able to:

Define federalism and distinguish it from other forms of intergovernmental relations

Enumerate the ingredients of the Confederation Settlement

Distinguish the intended division of powers between federal and provincial governments from the actual judicial interpretation of these sections

Discuss the evolution of federal–provincial finance, including taxation agreements, different kinds of grants, and equalization payments

Explain how the centralized federation of 1867 became the decentralized Canada of today

Discuss the concepts of executive and bureaucratic federalism, and outline the major features of Canadian contemporary federalism

The Provincial Political Systems

Canada is composed of ten provinces and three territories (see Figure 12.1). The provinces are autonomous within the powers given them by the Constitution, but the territories are constitutionally subordinate to the federal government. Although the territories increasingly function as provinces, exercising similar powers, these powers could theoretically be revoked; moreover, the territories are heavily dependent on Ottawa for their finances.

Each of the provinces can be considered a separate political system. Each has a full complement of governmental institutions and a somewhat distinctive political culture, party system, and array of advocacy groups. The distinctiveness of each province is the principal reason for establishing Canada as a federation, yet their governmental operations bear a striking resemblance to those at the federal level.

Figure 12.1   Canada's Provinces, Territories, and Capitals

Each province is formally headed by the lieutenant governor, the equivalent of the governor general, who represents the Queen and primarily performs ceremonial and social functions. The effective head of the provincial government is the premier, analogous to the prime minister, along with the Cabinet, who are officially called the executive council. As in Ottawa, the provincial cabinet sets priorities, especially financial; determines policies; gives direction for the preparation of legislation; oversees departmental administration; and makes order in council appointments.

The provincial legislatures consist of the elected representatives of the people, usually called MLAs (Members of the Legislative Assembly). Each provincial legislature has only one chamber, which is divided between government and opposition members, and functions quite similarly to the House of Commons. A number of provinces have opted for fixed election dates at four-year intervals.

Given the expansion of provincial government operations, at least until 1990 or so, provincial politicians are increasingly dependent on the bureaucracy or public service to advise them on their decisions and the implementation of their programs. The most important provincial responsibilities are health and education, and those two departments consume the largest share of each province's finances. Provinces have their own sources of revenue, but as noted later in this chapter, they also depend heavily on transfers from the federal government. In fact, despite the division of powers between the two levels of government, there is a great deal of interaction between them, especially at the ministerial and bureaucratic levels.

Each province also establishes its own hierarchy of courts and its own system of municipal government. Since the province determines the structures, responsibilities, and financial powers of its local governments, the latter are constitutionally subordinate. In theory, there is no connection between municipal authorities and the federal government—those two levels of government communicate via the provinces. In practice, however, actions of the federal government often have serious consequences for municipalities. More and more observers are recommending that large cities in particular be somehow brought into the ambit of Canadian federalism.

Federalism and the Confederation Settlement

In a formal sense, **federalism** can be defined as a system of government characterized by two levels of authority—federal and provincial—and a division of powers between them, such that neither is subordinate to the other. This definition distinguishes the relationship between provincial and national governments from that between municipal and provincial governments, for in the latter case the municipalities are clearly subordinate entities. This federal–provincial equality of status is provided for in the constitutional division of powers between the two levels of government that is found primarily in sections 91 and 92 of the Constitution Act, 1867. Other aspects of federalism are also important, however, such as federal–provincial financial relations and joint policymaking mechanisms. The recent tendency of federal and provincial governments to download their responsibilities illustrates the increasingly significant role of municipalities.

The fundamentals of Canadian federalism, often called the **Confederation Settlement**,[1] were incorporated into the **Constitution Act, 1867**. As noted in Chapter 1, the principal architect of Confederation was Sir John A. Macdonald, who intended the new country to be a highly centralized federation, with Ottawa retaining most of the power. In fact, the Confederation Settlement was not consistent with the modern definition of federalism because in certain respects the provinces were made subordinate to the central government.

The Confederation Settlement consisted of five principal components:

- the division of powers between federal and provincial governments,
- the division of financial resources,
- the federal controls over the provinces,
- the provincial representation in central institutions, and
- cultural guarantees.

The Fathers of Confederation gave the provinces 16 specific **enumerated powers** in section 92 (e.g., hospitals and municipal institutions) and then left everything else—the **residual powers**—to Ottawa in section 91. For greater certainty, however, they also listed 29 federal powers such as trade and commerce and national defence (see Table 12.1). Two **concurrent powers**—agriculture and immigration—were listed in section 95, and the treaty power in section 132 gave the federal government the power to implement Empire treaties, regardless of their subject matter.

In the division of financial resources, federal dominance was even more apparent. The 1867 settlement gave Ottawa the power to levy any mode or system of taxation, including both direct and indirect taxes. Since the only tax widely used at the time was the customs duty, an indirect tax, the provincial power over direct taxation was not considered to be significant. Instead, the provinces were expected to raise their revenues from the sale of shop, saloon, tavern, and auctioneer licences, as well as to rely on federal subsidies. The federal government was to

Table 12.1   The Core of the Federal–Provincial Division of Powers

Federal Powers	Provincial Powers
Trade and commerce	Direct taxation within the province
Any form of taxation	Public lands
National defence	Hospitals and health care
Banking	Municipal institutions
Indians	Education
Criminal law	Property and civil rights
Interprovincial transportation and communication	Administration of justice

pay each province an annual per capita grant of 80 cents plus a small subsidy to support its government and legislature. The act also stated that the federal government would assist the provinces by assuming their pre-Confederation debts. It should be added that the provinces were authorized to raise revenues from their natural resources, but this source was not taken seriously at the time because few such resources had yet been discovered.

In addition, in a clear departure from what is now regarded as the federal principle, Ottawa was given several means of controlling the provinces. As an alternative to granting royal assent, the lieutenant governor, a federal appointee, was permitted to "reserve" provincial legislation for the consideration of the federal Cabinet, which could then approve or reject it. Even if the lieutenant governor gave assent to a piece of provincial legislation, however, the federal Cabinet could subsequently "disallow" it. As well, the federal government could declare any local work or undertaking to be for the general advantage of Canada and unilaterally place it within federal jurisdiction. These three controls are respectively referred to as reservation, disallowance, and the declaratory power.

Given the highly centralized nature of the division of powers, the limited financial resources of the provinces, and the federal controls, it is clear that the Confederation Settlement of 1867 placed the provinces in a subordinate position, somewhat akin to municipalities, rather than giving them the equal or coordinate status provided for in the modern definition of federalism.

In the light of the federal government's dominant position, it is not surprising that the smaller provinces were concerned with their representation in Ottawa.

The fourth aspect of the 1867 Settlement, therefore, dealt with provincial representation in the House of Commons and the Senate, a question of much more concern at the time than the division of powers. The great compromise that allowed Confederation to go forward was the agreement that the provinces would be represented according to population in the Commons but that regional equality would prevail in the Senate. Thus, each of the three original regions—the Maritimes, Quebec, and Ontario—received 24 senators, appeasing smaller provinces that could be easily outvoted in the lower chamber.[2]

Confederation was more than just a union of provinces; it was also seen as a union of two cultural groups, English and French. Thus, the fifth aspect of the Confederation Settlement might be called cultural guarantees. Considering the anxiety of French Canadians about the preservation of their language and culture, these guarantees were surprisingly minor. Section 133 of the 1867 act made French and English official languages in the federal Parliament and federal courts as well as in the Quebec legislature and Quebec courts—but nowhere else. At the time, religion was probably of greater concern than language, so existing separate school systems in the provinces (especially Ontario and Quebec) were guaranteed by allowing the federal government to step in to restore them, if necessary. French Canada was also protected by giving power over property and civil rights to the provinces, so that Quebec could maintain certain cultural particularisms, including its civil law system.

Of the five components of the Confederation Settlement, only three relate directly to the relationship between federal and provincial governments. This chapter will therefore proceed to track the evolution of the division of powers, financial resources, and federal controls. In discussing this evolution, it is critical to understand how the very centralized federation created in 1867 became the highly decentralized Canada of today. This trend is apparent in all three areas.

John A. Macdonald, the architect of a centralized federal system. (William James Topley/Library and Archives Canada PA-027013)

Division of Powers

If changes to the **division of powers** between federal and provincial governments have resulted in the provinces being more important today, there are two ways in which this could have happened. First, formal constitutional amendments could have altered the division of powers in the provinces' favour; second, judicial decisions interpreting sections 91 and 92 of the Constitution Act, 1867, could also have had this effect.

Since 1867, only four formal constitutional amendments have been adopted that directly affected the division of powers. In 1940, unemployment insurance was added to the list of federal powers in section 91 after the courts had earlier declared that it belonged to the provinces. In 1951, old age pensions were made a concurrent power, allowing the federal government into this area as well. In 1964, Ottawa's jurisdiction was enlarged to include widows' and survivors' benefits and disability pensions. In 1982, the new section 92A increased provincial jurisdiction over natural resources, while at the same time the Charter of Rights and Freedoms generally reduced the powers of both levels of government. Thus, in the first three cases, the net result was a slight increase in federal powers, but this increase was accomplished with the unanimous consent of the provinces. The 1982 amendment was the only formal constitutional amendment that in any way increased provincial powers at the expense of the federal government. Formal constitutional amendments, therefore, do little to explain the more powerful provinces of today.

Judicial interpretation of the federal and provincial powers in the 1867 act is a much more complicated and significant subject. Before 1949, the **Judicial Committee of the Privy Council (JCPC)** in London was Canada's final court of appeal, and its decisions had a major impact in transforming Canadian federalism from a centralized to a decentralized system. The most important JCPC decisions related to the federal "peace, order, and good government" clause as opposed to the provincial power over "property and civil rights."

The **peace, order, and good government (POGG) clause,** one of two parts of section 91 in the 1867 act, says that all powers not given to the provinces in section 92 are left with the federal government. This clause is also known as the residual clause. The second part of section 91 provides, "for greater certainty," a list of 29 examples of federal powers. In the course of its judgments, the Judicial Committee drove a wedge between these two parts of section 91, deciding that the 29 specific items listed were the *real* federal powers rather than just examples, and ignoring the peace, order, and good government clause except in cases of national emergency. But in times of national emergency, as determined by the JCPC, federal powers were almost unlimited. This became known as the **emergency doctrine**, and how the courts managed to transform the residual clause into an emergency power is a very long story. In normal times, on the other hand, the JCPC gave an extremely broad interpretation to section 92-13, property and civil rights in the province, finding that almost any matter that was the subject of a federal–provincial constitutional dispute could be incorporated within this provincial power.[3] That is why so little was left over for the federal residual clause.

The effect of the judicial interpretation of the peace, order, and good government clause, along with other clauses such as the trade and commerce and treaty powers, was to reduce significantly the intended dominance of the federal government. The complementary broad interpretation of property and civil rights increased substantially the scope of provincial powers. This influence has been very controversial in political, judicial, and academic circles, because it was clearly contrary to John A. Macdonald's conception of Canadian federalism in not permitting Ottawa to take initiatives that centralist advocates often desired.[4]

Other observers contend, however, that the Judicial Committee's line of interpretation was consistent with the increasing size and distances that characterized the country as time went on, as well as with societal forces and public orientations, at least outside Ontario. They argue that the provincial bias pervading so many of the JCPC's decisions was "in fundamental harmony with the regional pluralism" of the federal, decentralized, diversified nature of Canadian society. However desirable centralization may have seemed at the outset, it was inappropriate in the long run "for the regional diversities of a land of vast extent and a large, geographically concentrated, minority culture."[5]

What Do You Think?

Are you a centralist or a decentralist? Would you give more power to the federal or provincial level of government? What are the advantages and disadvantages of each approach to Canadian federalism?

Federal–Provincial Finance

In the Confederation Settlement, the federal government was given the power to levy any kind of tax, while the provinces were restricted to direct taxation.[6] The federal government was also committed to pay the provinces small annual grants.

While the intention was thus to create a highly centralized federation, the financial factor also ultimately contributed to the increased power of the provinces. This situation came about because the provinces levied direct taxes that they were not expected to use, such as income taxes; because the provinces successfully lobbied for larger federal grants; and because some provincial revenues, such as those from natural resources, turned out to be more significant than anticipated.

Provincial revenues proved to be inadequate from the beginning, and it did not take long for the provinces to begin levying their own direct personal and corporate income taxes and to demand larger sums from Ottawa. With both levels of government taxing the same personal and corporate incomes, but in a totally uncoordinated fashion, and with provinces always lining up for more federal funds, the federal–provincial financial situation became very complicated. This muddied state of affairs worsened with the advent of the Depression, when even fewer funds were available to go around. As a result, Prime Minister Mackenzie King appointed the Rowell-Sirois Commission, officially the Royal Commission on Dominion–Provincial Relations, in 1937. One of its recommendations was immediately implemented: the costly responsibility for unemployment insurance was transferred to the federal government.

Before 1940, therefore, the two levels of government were relatively independent on both the taxation and expenditure sides of public finance. Since the Second World War, on the other hand, they have become intimately intertwined, and Ottawa has taken the lead (sometimes with provincial encouragement) in coordinating the various ingredients of the financial relationship. The complicated federal–provincial financial situation since 1940 might be simplified somewhat by considering three aspects separately: taxation agreements, conditional and block grants, and equalization payments.

Taxation Agreements

Between 1942 and 2001, the taxation side was characterized by a series of five-year federal–provincial taxation agreements. The name and terms of the agreements changed over the years, but the basic objective was the same: to effect a degree of coordination in the field of federal–provincial taxation. The main taxes in question were personal and corporate income taxes. While the federal personal income tax was standard across the country (except for Quebec), each province was able to determine its own rate as a percentage of the federal tax, so that the provincial portion varied widely. Except for Quebec, all personal income taxes were collected

FISCAL IMBALANCE

PROVINCES

OTTAWA

Provinces' view of Fiscal Imbalance teeter-totter.
(Michael de Adder/Artizans.com)

by Ottawa in the first instance, after which the provincial portion was transferred back, an arrangement that was found to be satisfactory to all concerned. Quebec has always collected its own personal income tax, so that its residents complete two separate income tax forms. By 2001, however, all provinces had separated their provincial income tax from the federal income tax system, meaning that the provincial tax is no longer necessarily calculated as a percentage of the federal tax, although Ottawa still collects both portions.

Conditional and Block Grants

The second aspect of the federal–provincial financial picture was **shared-cost programs**. These expanded considerably after 1940 in the joint development of a **welfare state**. The most important shared-cost social programs were postsecondary education (1952), hospital insurance (1957), the Canada Assistance Plan (1966), and medical insurance (1968). Hospital and medical programs were later combined as health insurance or "medicare." These programs are termed the "major" federal transfers to the provinces, but a large number of smaller transfer programs also exist.

Federal grants for postsecondary education have always been of a **block grant** variety, that is, a sum of money given to each province for the operating costs of universities and colleges but without any conditions or strings attached. Such a grant significantly helped to fund universities and colleges and allowed provinces to keep tuition fees relatively low. The other major shared-cost programs originally fell into the **conditional grant** category. The usual pattern here was for the federal government to pay approximately 50 percent of the cost of each program provided that the provinces met Ottawa's conditions. For example, Ottawa would fund half of any provincial health care program that was comprehensive (covering all necessary health services provided by hospitals and medical practitioners), universal (covering the whole population), portable (covering the costs of provincial residents while temporarily absent from the province), accessible (not impeding or precluding reasonable access to services by extra charges), and publicly administered. Under the Canada Assistance Plan, Ottawa similarly provided half the funding for almost any provincial or municipal program that provided social assistance and welfare services to persons in need. In this case, the main condition was that anyone in need had to be included, and no one could be forced to work for welfare. Without federal contributions to health and social assistance programs, many provinces would not have been able to finance them.

Most of these programs fell constitutionally within provincial jurisdiction, but Ottawa maintained that its **spending power** allowed it to make payments to individuals, institutions, and other governments in fields over which Parliament did not necessarily have the power to regulate. The federal government even claimed that it could attach conditions to such spending and often did so. In the exercise of its spending power, Ottawa was able to establish national standards in a number of social programs.

While a combination of provincial pressure and federal political and bureaucratic expansionism inspired most of these programs, the provinces often criticized the federal conditions attached to them as being out of place in areas of provincial jurisdiction. Quebec in particular took this point of view in the early 1960s. In response, the Pearson government allowed the provinces to opt out of certain conditional grant programs and continue to receive federal funding as long as they maintained an equivalent program.

Then, in the 1970s, Ottawa became upset at the rapidly escalating costs of many of these programs and its commitment to finance 50 percent of whatever the provinces spent on them. In 1977, therefore, the federal government removed the detailed conditions attached to the health insurance programs, as many provinces wished. But in return, it no longer felt obliged to pay 50 percent of the provincial program costs. The federal grants took the form of tax transfers (giving the provinces more room to levy their own taxes) as well as cash, and henceforth Ottawa would increase its funding of such programs only by a certain annual percentage. Removing the conditions from health insurance grants, however, led to problems such as hospitals introducing user fees, doctors practising double- or extra-billing, and provinces using health care funds for other purposes.

Unhappy with these developments, the federal government consequently passed the **Canada Health Act** in 1984. The act resurrected the five earlier conditions connected to health care and provided for penalizing those provinces that permitted extra charges. At the same time, the federal share of such programs fell below 50 percent, and the 1990s saw a progression of freezes and cuts in funding.

Finance Minister Paul Martin's 1994 federal budget announced a freeze on all major federal transfers except equalization payments, and his 1995 budget inaugurated a significant transformation of federal–provincial transfers. Beginning in 1996–97, postsecondary education, health insurance, and the Canada Assistance Plan (social assistance and welfare services) were combined into a block grant called the **Canada Health and Social Transfer (CHST)**.

The CHST was a combination of cash payments and tax points (federal withdrawal from joint tax fields), but it represented a significant reduction from previous amounts. It was at this time that postsecondary education fees began to skyrocket, as provinces in turn reduced university and college funding. As a block grant, the CHST did not contain the conditions of CAP, nor were Ottawa's expenditures driven by provincial costs. The only condition on welfare transfers was that provinces not impose a minimum residency requirement. As a result, many provinces reduced social assistance programs and/or brought in workfare. Despite the protests of almost all social reformers, who did not trust provincial governments to provide adequate social assistance programs, Ottawa felt that it could not retain such conditions when it was reducing its contributions. On the other hand, the federal Liberal government continued to defend the principles of the Canada Health Act and fought with provinces that appeared to be in violation of the act.

Equalization Payments

The third aspect of federal–provincial finance consists of **equalization payments**. In 1957, the federal government began to pay these unconditional grants to have-not provinces based on provincial need so that all provinces could offer a relatively equal standard of services. The essence of equalization payments was to bring the have-not provinces up to the national average tax yield per capita. Typically, Ontario, British Columbia, and Alberta were above the national average and did not receive equalization payments, while the other seven provinces received an annual payment based on the per capita shortfall of tax revenues multiplied by the province's population. In the first decade of this century, however, provincial rankings changed: in particular, Saskatchewan and Newfoundland and Labrador rose above the national average, while Ontario fell below it. In 2004, the Canada Health and Social Transfer was divided into two separate parts—Canada Health Transfer and Canada Social Transfer. Table 12.2 shows the major federal transfers to the provinces in 2010–11.

TABLE 12.2 MAJOR FEDERAL TRANSFERS TO PROVINCES/TERRITORIES, 2010–11 ($ MILLIONS)

	Health Transfer	Social Transfer	Equalization	Other	Total
Newfoundland/ Labrador	439	167	—	397	1 003
Prince Edward Island	110	47	330	3	490
Nova Scotia	725	308	1 110	477	2 620
New Brunswick	580	246	1 581	80	2 488
Quebec	6 093	2 587	8 552	—	17 232
Ontario	9 965	4 321	972	214	15 472
Manitoba	953	405	1 826	175	3 359
Saskatchewan	829	350	—	7	1 186
Alberta	2 071	1 238	—	—	3 309
British Columbia	3 582	1 482	—	—	5 064
Yukon	26	11	—	653*	691
Northwest Territories	25	14	—	920*	959
Nunavut	28	11	—	1 091*	1 130
Total	25 426	11 186	14 372	4 018	55 002

*Territorial Formula Financing
Source: Department of Finance Canada, Major Transfers to Provinces and Territories—2010–11, available at http://www.fin.gc.ca/fedprov/mtpt-ptfp10-eng.asp, retrieved April 20, 2010.

Provincial Finances

In addition to their grants from Ottawa, the provinces have levied over 30 forms of direct taxation that were unanticipated in 1867. The enormous natural resource revenues that some provinces (especially Alberta) receive on top of direct taxation and federal contributions are also significant. A comparison of federal transfers and the provinces' own revenues (taxes plus natural resource and other revenues) is shown in Figure 12.2.

Thus, the combination of unanticipated federal grants, direct taxes, and natural resource revenues has contributed significantly to the enhanced status of the provinces in the Canadian federal system. It should also be reiterated that the two

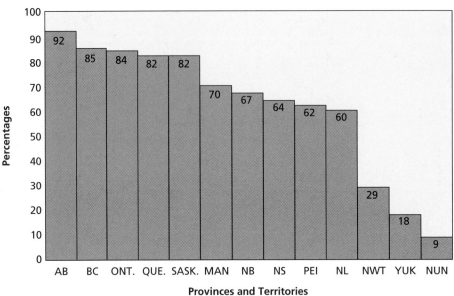

Figure 12.2 Provincial and Territorial Own-Source Revenue as Percentage of Total Revenue, 2008

levels of government began by operating more or less independently of each other, taxing and spending in different areas, with federal grants being unconditional in nature. Then, from about 1940 onward, the federal and provincial governments became closely intertwined by taxation agreements on the revenue side and by conditional and block grant programs in terms of expenditures. At the beginning of the 21st century, however, the degree of integration declined somewhat, especially with the disengagement of federal and provincial personal income tax systems. The richest and most autonomy-minded provinces continue to argue for greater decentralization of powers and more tax room, but the have-not provinces are not capable of increasing their own tax revenues, so they have a stake in keeping a strong central government that can act as a redistributive agency.

Federal Controls

As mentioned, the 1867 Constitution Act contained three specific federal controls over the provinces: reservation, disallowance, and the declaratory power. In the first 30 years after Confederation, all three controls were actively used, and this had the effect of keeping the provinces subordinate to Ottawa. Their use gradually declined and then ceased completely: the reservation and declaratory powers were last used in 1961, and disallowance, in 1943. As these were the federal powers that originally precluded Canada from being classified as a true federation, their disuse has meant that the provinces have shrugged off their subordinate status. Canada is now a genuine federation, and a highly decentralized one at that.

Modern Canadian Federalism

Federal–provincial relations in Canada have gone through many different phases since 1867, depending on shifting attitudes of federal and provincial governments, states of war and peace, and variations in judicial interpretation. In fact, Canadian federalism has experienced pendulum-like swings between centralization and decentralization, and the evolution from a centralized to a decentralized federal system has not been a unilinear process.

Executive Federalism

The phase of Canadian federalism that began after the Second World War might be called **cooperative federalism**. The essence of this concept is that while neither level was subordinate to the other, the federal government and the provinces were closely intertwined rather than operating independently. Here the crucial variable was financial relations. As noted earlier, the post-1945 period has been marked by federal–provincial taxation agreements on the revenue side and a host of shared-cost programs in terms of expenditures.

Cooperative federalism resulted from several developments.[7] First, federal and provincial objectives often had to be harmonized if public policy was to be effective. Second, public pressure forced the federal government to establish minimum national standards throughout the country in certain public services even within provincial jurisdiction such as health care. Third, the two levels of government competed for tax revenues and needed to coordinate these efforts to some extent, at least for the convenience of taxpayers. Fourth, given a generally vague division of powers, federal and provincial ministers and bureaucrats usually sought to maximize their jurisdiction and the programs of the two levels of government eventually overlapped.

Cooperative federalism was made operational by hundreds of federal–provincial conferences at all levels—first ministers, departmental ministers, deputy ministers, and even lesser officials—who engaged in almost continuous consultation, coordination, and cooperation. Cooperative federalism can be conducted on a multilateral basis, involving the federal government and several or all provinces, or on a bilateral basis, in which Ottawa interacts with individual provinces. Since the ministers and bureaucrats involved are all part of the executive branch of government, cooperative federalism is sometimes called **executive federalism**. Two main implications of executive federalism are that legislatures, political parties, and the public at large are not given much role to play in decisions that emerge from the secrecy of such meetings and that federal–provincial conflicts are worked out in conferences or meetings rather than being referred to the courts.

Executive federalism can therefore be defined as "relations between elected and appointed officials of the two levels of government."[8] It is often practised at the level of first ministers, even though the **first ministers' conference**—that is, a conference of premiers and the prime minister—is not provided for anywhere in the written Constitution and rests upon a conventional base. This institution made many significant policy decisions with respect to constitutional issues, shared-cost programs, and taxation and fiscal arrangements. Some of these had to be ratified later by federal and provincial legislatures, but except on constitutional matters, legislative ratification was usually a formality. Such agreements could rarely be altered in any legislature because they would then have to be changed in all 11 legislatures. First ministers' conferences became more elaborate and institutionalized over time. They could be televised, in whole or in part, but it was generally agreed that any serious negotiation had to take place behind closed doors. The prime minister functioned as chair, in addition to representing the federal government, and individual ministers from either level of government were usually allowed to speak as well. Every delegation brought along a host of advisers. After the collapse of the Charlottetown Accord, however, such first ministers' conferences fell into disrepute and were replaced by occasional first ministers' dinners at the prime minister's residence.

Executive federalism conducted at the level of departmental ministers and leading bureaucrats is sometimes labelled "functional" or "bureaucratic" federalism. This form of executive federalism is usually more successful than first ministers' meetings, partly because the officials involved often share certain professional norms and, once they reach a consensus, these experts may be able to "sell" it to their departmental and first ministers.

Canadian federalism between 1945 and 1960 may have been "cooperative" in the sense that the two levels of government were closely intertwined, but it

Prime Minister Paul Martin and his provincial and territorial counterparts participate in session at the First Ministers' Conference on Health in September 2004. (The Canadian Press/Fred Chartrand)

continued to be highly centralized in the immediate postwar period. The ministers and bureaucrats in Ottawa who had almost single-handedly run the country during the Second World War were reluctant to shed their enormous power. Moreover, they had discovered **Keynesian economics**, which prescribed a leading role for the central government in guiding the economy. The Diefenbaker government after 1957 was more sensitive to provincial demands, and the whole picture was increasingly complicated from 1960 onward by the Quiet Revolution in Quebec. This period still manifested an intertwined, non-subordinate relationship between the two levels of government, but with Quebec regularly rejecting federal initiatives, cooperation was sometimes harder to come by. The concept of "opting out" was a hallmark of this phase of federalism, which saw a significant degree of decentralization take place.

Between about 1970 and 1984, federal–provincial relations were racked with conflict. Quebec and the other provinces were more aggressive than ever, but the Trudeau government was not prepared for any further decentralization. Thus, taxation agreements were accompanied by more provincial unhappiness, and block funding replaced conditional grants in important areas, leaving the two levels less intertwined than before. Moreover, especially at the level of first ministers, federal–provincial conferences frequently failed to come to any agreement, and Ottawa often chose to act unilaterally. In this phase, federal–provincial conflicts were more frequently referred to the courts, resulting in a renewed emphasis on the judicial interpretation of the division of powers.

The Trudeau era was characterized by years of federal–provincial discord over resource and energy policies, especially the National Energy Program, conflict with Newfoundland over offshore oil, and conflict with Saskatchewan over the regulation and taxation of that province's oil and potash industries. When these disputes coincided with Trudeau's attempt to unilaterally amend the Constitution and entrench official bilingualism as a national policy, many Western Canadians began to re-examine their place in the federation. Some of the heat was reduced when Trudeau conceded the new section 92A of the Constitution Act, 1982, which enhanced provincial jurisdiction over natural resources. He made this concession in order to secure federal NDP support for his constitutional package and as a peace offering to the West.

Canadian Federalism, 1984–2000

When Brian Mulroney came to power in 1984, he was determined to improve federal–provincial relations and embark on another period of decentralized, genuinely cooperative federalism. In this objective he was somewhat successful, for much of the federal–provincial animosity of the Trudeau years seemed to dissipate. Concerns about energy resources were resolved to a large extent in the 1985 Western and Atlantic Accords. During its second term, however, the Mulroney government increasingly aroused provincial anger, especially as it became obsessed with deficit reduction and cut back on grants to the provinces. The Mulroney government even enforced the Liberals' Canada Health Act, imposing penalties on provinces that allowed doctors to extra-bill or permitted hospitals to charge user fees. The major federal–provincial dispute of the Mulroney years concerned the Goods and Services Tax (GST). To some extent it was just "good politics" for provincial premiers to jump on the anti-GST bandwagon because of widespread popular opposition. Most provinces refused to integrate their sales taxes with the new federal tax, even though many mutual advantages would have accrued from doing so.

The Chrétien Liberals were initially popular with provincial governments in offering funds under the national infrastructure program, and they were somewhat successful in negotiating a reduction in provincial barriers to the free movement of

What Do You Think?

The most persistent federal–provincial issue in recent times concerns health care. If the federal government makes substantial annual contributions to provincial health care programs, is Ottawa entitled to insist that they not be spent to finance health care services that are privately provided or that a two-tier health care system develop? Some provinces contend that as long as people do not have to pay extra for privately provided services, that is, as long as these services are covered by the provincial medicare plan, this is acceptable. Other health care advocates argue that public funds should not leak out into the pockets of profit-making ventures. Should those who can afford to pay for their own health care be allowed to do so and get faster service?

people, goods, services, and capital across the country in the Agreement on Internal Trade. They had only partial success in implementing their promise to replace the GST (in reality, harmonizing it with the provincial retail sales tax in a handful of provinces), and then they angered the provinces with reductions in their transfers, especially after 1995. The provinces' principal complaints included severe reductions in health, postsecondary education, and welfare transfers, although provinces also joined in to protest the cuts to almost every other aspect of federal government operations, such as a wide range of transportation subsidies. On the other hand, Ottawa did not cut equalization payments.

More harmoniously, the Chrétien government transferred responsibility for labour market training to the provinces by means of bilateral deals rather than constitutional amendment and replaced the Child Tax Benefit with a new integrated National Child Benefit system developed through federal–provincial cooperation. It was also during this era that the federal and provincial governments (minus Quebec) signed the 1999 **Social Union Framework Agreement (SUFA)**, a framework on which to construct or modify federal, provincial, or joint social programs.

Canadian Federalism in the 21st Century

Canadian federalism in the 21st century demonstrates aspects of both continuity and change. Despite the fact that the formal Constitution lists only three concurrent powers, the federal and provincial governments continue to be intertwined in programs in almost every area. In other words, Canada is characterized by a large amount of *de facto* concurrent jurisdiction.[9] Moreover, an enormous degree of federal–provincial interaction will be required in the future to come up with solutions to many public problems.[10] While most of the interaction takes place at the ministerial and bureaucratic levels, Paul Martin began his regime by being much more open than his predecessor to talking individually and collectively to provincial premiers themselves.

Meanwhile, at the initiative of Quebec Premier Jean Charest, the annual premiers' conference has been transformed into the Council of the Federation. Its objective is to speak with a strong, united voice for the provinces and territories in their relations with the federal government, at least on issues on which they all agree. Indeed, the whole structure of Canadian federalism has been somewhat transformed by new players and new relationships: Aboriginal self-government, direct contact between the federal government and cities, and relations between provincial governments and foreign states.

Health care continues to be the hottest issue in federal–provincial relations. The Accord on Health Care Renewal in 2003 promised the provinces an increase of $35 billion over five years. About the same time, most provinces agreed to join the Health Council of Canada, an independent body to advise Canadians on the performance of their health care systems. At the September 2004 first ministers' meeting, Ottawa promised the provinces an additional $18 billion over six years to be used to reduce waiting times, and the provinces committed to establish and publish benchmarks and targets to monitor progress in meeting this goal. The ten-year plan allowed Quebec to implement its own plan, a recognition of the principle of asymmetrical federalism. These funds exemplify a new type of transfer, somewhat similar to block grants, sometimes called "targeted funding," which does not require the provinces to meet specific conditions, but which is intended for certain purposes.[11]

Another contentious issue is the formula used to determine equalization payments. Besides a demand from have-not provinces for a general increase in the amount of the payments, Newfoundland and Labrador and Nova Scotia had a specific complaint with respect to their offshore petroleum revenues. They claimed to be losing 70 cents in equalization payments for every new dollar of petroleum revenue they took in. Paul Martin eventually allowed them to retain offshore petroleum revenues with no reduction in equalization payments, which only angered other provinces. Not having Alberta's abundant revenues nor receiving equalization payments, Ontario then complained that the federal government extracted over $20 billion more from the province annually than it returned, and Martin agreed to give it some $6 billion over five years for various purposes.

Martin also promised a "new deal for cities," and established a Ministry of State for Infrastructure and Communities. He exempted municipalities from paying the GST on their purchases and then shared the revenues from the federal gasoline excise tax with the provinces with the aim of having these funds transferred to municipalities to help finance environmentally friendly infrastructure projects.

Aboriginal issues were another priority of the Martin government. Martin convened a meeting of first ministers and Aboriginal leaders in Kelowna in 2005 and announced that the federal government would commit $5 billion over five years to close the gap in the quality of life between Aboriginal peoples and other Canadians. The premiers were enthusiastic participants and pledged to make significant contributions of their own.

Stephen Harper came to power with expectations of being even more generous to the provinces. The 2007 budget was designed to redress the "fiscal imbalance" between Ottawa and the provinces, especially as articulated by Quebec, although some observers argued that it was a myth disguising Quebec's *spending* more per capita than other provinces. The Harper government also brought in a new, more generous equalization formula, but managed to alienate Newfoundland and Labrador, Nova Scotia, and Saskatchewan in its treatment of natural resource revenues.

The Harper government did not honour the full Kelowna commitment with respect to Aboriginal peoples, and it cancelled the early childhood and child care agreements that the Martin government had just signed with all ten provinces. The health care wait-times guarantee Harper signed with the provinces was generally considered very weak. On the other hand, Harper introduced a parliamentary resolution to recognize the Québécois as a nation within a united Canada and allowed Quebec to have a seat in the Canadian delegation to UNESCO. In general, Harper seemed prepared to engage in further decentralization to the provinces, mainly to consolidate his party's support in Quebec, which he labelled "open federalism."

Addressing environmental issues is an increasingly urgent problem and one that is complicated in Canada by the division between federal and provincial jurisdictions. Some observers have anticipated a major constitutional confrontation between the federal and Alberta governments over capping emissions from the oil sands, but the Harper government rejected the Kyoto Protocol in favour of a less stringent approach. No such conflict is expected on his watch unless the U.S. forces Canada to take the environment more seriously.

After the 2008 economic meltdown, infrastructure stimulus spending became a high priority of both federal and provincial governments. By means of the Building Canada Fund, Ottawa not only helped provincial and municipal governments, but also ensured that their infrastructure spending was aligned with federal thinking.

SUMMARY

This chapter examined the relationship between the provinces and the federal government. It began by defining federalism as a system in which neither level of government is subordinate to the other and by setting out the five main provisions of the Confederation Settlement. The heart of the chapter demonstrated how the provinces have become more powerful than originally intended, partly through judicial (mis)interpretation of the division of powers, partly through the enormous increase in provincial financial resources, and partly because the federal government no longer uses its means of controlling the provinces. The evolution of federal–provincial finance is particularly important, replete with taxation agreements, shared-cost programs, and various kinds of grants. The chapter showed that despite the division of powers, the two levels of government are closely intertwined, and that almost all powers, in practice, are concurrent. The chapter concluded with descriptions of developments in Canadian federalism in recent years and of future challenges.

DISCUSSION QUESTIONS

1. Should the federal government increase its financial transfers to the provinces, or should it give them increased taxation room instead?
2. Should the federal government be able to spend money for any purpose, even within provincial jurisdiction?
3. Should Ottawa be able to deal directly with large cities, and should provinces be able to deal directly with neighbouring U.S. states?

KEY TERMS

Block grant A federal grant to the provinces that is given for a specific purpose, such as postsecondary education, but does not contain rigid conditions or standards.

Canada Health Act The 1984 act that re-imposed conditions on federal grants to the provinces for health programs, especially to prevent extra-billing, privatization, or other moves toward a two-tier health system.

Canada Health and Social Transfer (CHST) The annual federal block grant to the provinces between 1996 and 2004 intended to be used for health, postsecondary education, and welfare, now replaced by the Canada Health Transfer and the Canada Social Transfer.

Concurrent powers Powers officially shared by the federal and provincial governments, namely agriculture, immigration, and old age pensions.

Conditional grant A federal grant to the provinces, usually in support of a shared-cost program within provincial jurisdiction, to which Ottawa attaches conditions or standards before the province receives the money.

Confederation Settlement The deal made among the Fathers of Confederation that entailed setting up a new federal system of government with a division of powers, including financial powers, federal controls over the provinces, provincial representation in federal institutions, and certain cultural guarantees.

Constitution Act, 1867 The new name for the British North America Act, 1867, which united the four original provinces.

Cooperative federalism A variant of Canadian federalism since the Second World War in which neither level of government is subordinate to the other and in which there is an extensive degree of interaction between them.

Division of powers The distribution of legislative powers between the federal and provincial governments, largely contained in sections 91 and 92 of the Constitution Act, 1867.

Emergency doctrine A constitutional doctrine invented by the Judicial Committee of the Privy Council that in times of national emergency, the peace, order, and good government clause became an emergency clause, increasing the powers of the federal government.

Enumerated powers The powers of the provincial governments that are explicitly listed in section 92 of the Constitution Act, 1867.

Equalization payments Large annual cash payments made by the federal government to have-not provinces to help them provide a satisfactory level of public services.

Executive federalism A variant of cooperative federalism characterized by extensive federal–provincial interaction at the level of first ministers, departmental ministers, and deputy ministers.

Federalism A system of government characterized by two levels of authority (federal and provincial) and a division of powers between them such that neither is subordinate to the other.

First ministers' conference A federal–provincial conference consisting of the prime minister and provincial premiers (and, increasingly, territorial leaders).

Judicial Committee of the Privy Council A committee of the British parliament that functioned as Canada's final court of appeal until 1949.

Keynesian economics An economic theory that to promote general economic stability, the government should counterbalance the private sector, spending (running deficit budgets) in periods of unemployment when the private sector doesn't spend, and taxing (withdrawing money from the system) in periods of inflation when the private sector is spending too much.

Peace, order, and good government (POGG) clause The words in the opening sentence of section 91 of the Constitution Act, 1867, which state that the residual powers rest with the federal government but which has been often misinterpreted by the courts as providing only an emergency power.

Residual powers Those powers not given to the provinces in the Constitution Act, 1867, that were assigned to the federal government under the POGG clause in section 91.

Shared-cost programs Government programs whose cost is shared by the federal and provincial governments.

Social Union Framework Agreement An overall framework of federal–provincial relations agreed to in 1999 by all governments except Quebec that sought to end long-standing irritants on both sides.

Spending power The unofficial power of the federal government to spend money in any field, including those within provincial jurisdiction.

Welfare state The characterization of most Western democracies from about 1950 to 1985 in which governments functioned as provider and protector of individual security and well-being through the implementation of a wide array of social programs and income transfers to individuals.

FURTHER READING

Bakvis, Herman, Gerald Baier, and Douglas Brown. *Contested Federalism: Certainty and Ambiguity in the Canadian Federation.* Toronto: Oxford University Press, 2009.

Bakvis, Herman, and Grace Skogstad, eds. *Canadian Federalism: Performance, Effectiveness, and Legitimacy,* 2nd ed. Toronto: Oxford University Press, 2008.

Canadian Tax Foundation. *Finances of the Nation.* Toronto: CTF, biennial.

Harrison, Kathryn, ed. *Racing to the Bottom? Provincial Interdependence in the Canadian Federation.* Vancouver: UBC Press, 2005.

Institute of Intergovernmental Relations. *Canada: The State of the Federation.* Kingston: Queen's University, annual.

Rocher, François, and Miriam Smith, eds. *New Trends in Canadian Federalism*, 2nd ed. Peterborough: Broadview Press, 2003.

Russell, Peter. *Constitutional Odyssey*, 3rd ed. Toronto: University of Toronto Press, 2004.

Smith, Jennifer. *Federalism*. Vancouver: UBC Press, 2004.

Stevenson, Garth. "Federalism and Intergovernmental Relations." In Michael Whittington and Glen Williams, eds. *Canadian Politics in the 21st Century*, 7th ed. Toronto: Thomson Nelson, 2008.

———. *Unfulfilled Union: Canadian Federalism and National Unity*, 5th ed. Montreal: McGill-Queen's University Press, 2009.

PART 4

Governing

Having examined the societal context of the political system and the means of linking people to government in the "politics" part of this book, and the constitutional context as the first part of the "government" section, we can now focus on governing itself. Here, therefore, we examine the individual institutions of government in detail. These institutions comprise the executive branch, including the Crown, the Prime Minister, and the Cabinet; the bureaucracy or public service; Parliament, including the House of Commons and the Senate; and the judiciary. The functions and operations of each branch of government are outlined, as are the kinds of outputs or authoritative decisions each makes. Initially, however, these institutions are put into the context of the policymaking process to provide an overview of how they interact with each other in order to produce public policies.

Chapter 13

The Executive

The prime minister and Cabinet constitute the political **executive** and are the key players in the Canadian policymaking process. Their decisions are sometimes overturned by the courts and occasionally even by Parliament, and they are based to a considerable extent on advice from the bureaucracy and other sources. But in the end, the prime minister and Cabinet—often called the **government** of the day—are responsible for making the biggest political decisions in the country. This chapter begins with a brief discussion of the policymaking process and the Crown and then concentrates on the prime minister and Cabinet.

Chapter Objectives

After you have completed this chapter, you should be able to:

Outline the policymaking process in its most comprehensive form

Appreciate the ways in which the monarchy or Crown is engrained in the political system

Understand the ceremonial and symbolic functions of the Crown and assess the rare use of the discretionary powers of that office

Comprehend the importance of the prime minister and Cabinet in the policymaking process and in providing political leadership, as well as the sources of their power

Enumerate the factors that contribute to the pre-eminence of the prime minister

Discuss the factors that influence the composition of the Cabinet

Discuss the principles and processes of Cabinet operation

Enumerate the functions of the four main Cabinet support agencies

The Policymaking Process

The analysis of the individual institutions of government that follows in this and subsequent chapters will be more meaningful if first put in the context of the policymaking process. This section provides an overview of that process, indicating in a general way how the institutions interact with each other in the making of public policy. **Public policy** can be defined as "a course of action or inaction chosen by public authorities to address a given problem or interrelated set of problems."[1]

Chapter 1 contained a model of the whole political system that included such components as demands, authorities, and outputs. If we magnify the "authorities" part of that model, the result would look something like Figure 13.1.

As this model suggests, the actual process can be divided into six phases: initiation, priority-setting, policy formulation, legitimation, implementation, and interpretation. Most policies and decisions do not involve such an elaborate process; indeed, many can be made unilaterally by the prime minister, the Cabinet, the bureaucracy, or the courts. But the model shows the policymaking process in its broadest form, that is, a policy that requires the passage of a new law, or an amendment to an existing law, and that is later interpreted by the courts. Think of the evolution of the laws restricting tobacco advertising or establishing the long-gun registry.[2]

Figure 13.1 The Canadian Policymaking Process

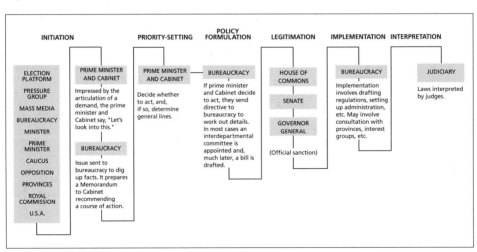

The authorities are bombarded daily with hundreds of demands. These demands emanate from many different sources, and most have no impact. But the policymaking process is set in motion when the prime minister and Cabinet are struck by a particular demand being made and decide to look into it further. On a smaller scale, a single minister may also make such a decision. It is at this point that a demand is sometimes said to become an issue. An issue, therefore, is a demand that has made it onto the public agenda and that is under serious consideration by the authorities.

The second phase of the policymaking process involves the prime minister and Cabinet again, this time in their priority-setting capacity. They decide which of the proposals they have previously selected for consideration are worthy of adoption. In other words, the prime minister and Cabinet (or, on lesser issues, an individual minister) decide whether or not to take action on the issue, and if they decide to act, they determine the general lines of the new initiative. For example, they decided that they would restrict tobacco advertising and that they would require long guns to be registered.

The limited number of projects that have been given the green light by the Cabinet in the priority-setting phase then enter the policy formulation phase. Once the Cabinet has approved a proposal in principle, it sends a directive to the bureaucracy to work out the details. This is usually a time-consuming process requiring coordination among many federal government departments. It may also involve consultation with provincial governments, advocacy groups, and others. Questions may be referred back to the Cabinet for further direction, but eventually a **Memorandum to Cabinet** is submitted, outlining the policy in detail. Assuming the proposal requires legislative action, the policy formulation stage culminates in a bill being drafted on the basis of the Memorandum to Cabinet.

The proposal then enters the legislative arena, as did the bills regarding tobacco advertising and gun registration. The relevant minister may accept technical alterations to the bill as it proceeds through the House of Commons and the Senate, but the main intent or principle of the bill cannot be changed without approval from the Cabinet. The legislative stage is referred to as "legitimizing" the bill, because the proposal is put under the scrutiny of the democratically elected representatives of the people and made legitimate by their approval. The Cabinet and members of Parliament contribute political expertise to the process, but given the shortage of time and limited technical expertise characteristic of the legislative branch, most such bills are passed in "skeletal" form, with details to be added later. The legitimation stage ends with the token approval of the governor general, signifying that the policy has been officially sanctioned.

Royal assent is by no means the end of the policymaking process. Few laws attain any significance just by sitting on the statute books; they must be implemented in order to be made effective. Implementation almost always involves the drafting of detailed **regulations** by the bureaucracy, to add meat to the skeleton of the statute. What wording or pictures will be used on cigarette packages? How or which long guns will be registered? Even though they have the same legal standing as if they were part of the enabling statute itself, the regulations that a law authorizes the executive to make are given only the scarcest scrutiny by either ministers or Parliament and thus are almost the exclusive preserve of the bureaucracy. Implementation normally requires the setting up of new administrative machinery—new staff, agencies, field offices, and operational manuals, among other things. It is therefore not surprising that most legislation does not automatically take effect upon royal assent; it is not "proclaimed" or made operational until the government is ready to implement it. It took more time and money than anticipated, for example, to set up the national gun registry.

The policymaking process may well end, at least for the time being, with the implementation phase. But if new legislation is involved, it is often subject to interpretation by the courts. Thus, it is appropriate to add a sixth phase to the policymaking process, that of judicial interpretation. Judges always have an impact on a law by means of how they interpret it, but in some cases the law's very constitutionality may be challenged in the courts. In such a case, the judiciary must decide whether the provisions of the law are contrary to the Charter of Rights and Freedoms or to the division of powers between federal and provincial governments. The gun control and tobacco advertising laws were both subject to such judicial interpretation.

The Crown

Canada is a **constitutional monarchy**, which essentially means that it is a democracy headed by a king or queen. In other words, the Queen is the Canadian head of state, but she reigns according to the Constitution. Canada is also said to have a dual executive, meaning that the formal and largely symbolic executive powers are given to the Queen, but the effective executive is made up of the prime minister and Cabinet. The prime minister is called the head of government.

The concept of the **Crown** revolves around the head of state and can be defined as the collection of executive powers exercised by or in the name of the monarch. Although the Crown is largely irrelevant to the effective functions of government, many government operations are performed in the name of the Queen or governor general.[3] Moreover, the Crown provides useful functions in the political system that are largely of a symbolic and ceremonial nature.

The Crown also represents the entire state and embodies what belongs to the people collectively. This can be seen in **Crown corporations** (state-owned corporations) or Crown lands (state-owned lands). In addition, the Crown is central to the legal system. Crown attorneys prosecute crimes on behalf of society; court cases are initiated in the name of the Queen (*R.* [for *Regina*, meaning queen] *v. Canadian Newspapers Co.*), or against the government (*Russell v. The Queen*); branches of the judiciary may be called the Court of Queen's Bench; and lawyers are awarded the title of Queen's Counsel (QC). The term "royal" is also widely used in Canada to refer to institutions that function for the advantage of all in the name of the Queen: royal commissions, which investigate problems for the general good, and the Royal Canadian Mounted Police, who are responsible for capturing violators of society's laws. In another branch of government, three important aspects of Parliament reflect the existence of the monarchical system: royal assent, the Speech from the Throne, and Her Majesty's Loyal Opposition. "Loyal Opposition" demonstrates that criticism of the government has been legitimized and institutionalized in the name of the Queen.

Queen Elizabeth in Halifax on her 2010 tour of Canada.
(The Canadian Press/Paul Chiasson)

The Queen of Canada, Elizabeth II, is also the queen of other countries and normally resides in Britain. That means that she needs a local representative in Canada, the **governor general**, who may, in her absence, perform any of her functions and exercise any of her powers. Until 1926, the governor was a double agent: besides being the representative of the monarch, he was an agent of the British government. As long as Canada was a British colony, the governor general exercised authority over Canada on behalf of the British cabinet. Today, the governor general has no connection whatsoever to the British government. The Canadian prime minister nominates the governor general, who, upon appointment by the Queen, serves a term of approximately five years.

Some of the powers of the Crown are provided for in the Constitution Act, 1867, while others, the **prerogative powers**, are left over from the era when the monarch really ruled. Despite this impressive theoretical list of powers, there is no doubt that in a democratic age almost all of them must be exercised on the advice of the government—the prime minister and Cabinet—of the day. The most important prerogative power of the governor general is the appointment of the prime minister, but this must be performed on the basis of constitutional convention. In ensuring that the office of prime minister is never vacant, the governor general normally relies on the operation of political parties and elections, and he or she does not have far to look. On two occasions in the 1890s, however, the governor had to help find a prime minister—John Abbott in 1891 and Mackenzie Bowell in 1894. Political parties are better organized today, and they prefer to choose their own leaders. Thus, if the position should suddenly become vacant, such as through the death or unexpected resignation of the prime minister, the Cabinet and/or government caucus would name an acting leader pending a leadership convention. But in a minority government scenario, the governor general might still be called upon to play a part.

The two most controversial discretionary acts of governors general occurred in 1896 and 1926, when the governors not only acted on their own initiative but also refused the advice of the prime minister and Cabinet. The first occasion concerned the question of making government appointments. Many appointments, such as those of senators and judges, are made in the name of the governor general, even though they are decided upon by the Cabinet. But the Charles Tupper government chose to retain office after it lost the 1896 election (awaiting defeat in the House of Commons) and during that interim period presented a list of several recommended appointments to the governor general, which he refused to endorse.

The second famous case of refusing government advice, the **King–Byng dispute**, involved the dissolution of Parliament. The governor general normally dissolves Parliament to precipitate an election on the advice of the prime minister, but in 1926 Lord Byng refused Mackenzie King's request to do so. In this case, the governor general was primarily influenced by the fact that a motion of censure against the government regarding a scandal in the Customs Department was under debate in the House of Commons. The request to dissolve Parliament appeared to be an attempt to avoid defeat in the Commons. In addition, the opposition Conservatives actually had more seats than the governing Liberals (who had been kept in power with the support of the Progressives), and an election had been held only eight months before. Thus, it seemed logical to Lord Byng to try to avoid an election when an alternative government might be available.

Whether such discretionary action is appropriate today as a check on unconstitutional behaviour by prime ministers and cabinets remains an open question. Everyone agrees, however, that in normal circumstances governors general must act on the advice of the prime minister and Cabinet. Before governors general invoke such emergency powers, "they must be sure they have reached the danger point, and that their actions will stand up to the subsequent judgment of other institutions and the people."[4] The governor general has been called a "constitutional fire extinguisher," whose emergency powers can be used only "when normal controls cannot operate and a crisis gets out of hand." Andrew Heard adds that "governors should intrude into the democratic process only to the minimum extent absolutely required for the basic functioning of Parliamentary government."[5] Since the governor general is intended to function as an impartial symbol of unity, any act that might be interpreted as remotely partisan must be avoided.

On two recent occasions, the question of whether the governor general had the discretion to refuse a prime minister's request for a prorogation of parliament has arisen. The governor general's approval of prorogation, that is, to end a session of parliament, had rarely been an issue until December 2008. On that occasion, when the Harper government introduced an almost universally ridiculed economic update, the three opposition parties signed a coalition agreement, in which they declared their readiness to form an alternative Liberal–NDP government with BQ support. In order to cling to power, Harper delayed a scheduled non-confidence vote, and then pre-empted it with a request to Governor General Michaëlle Jean to prorogue Parliament to avoid the vote altogether. The government argued that they would recall Parliament at the end of January 2009 with a full-fledged budget that would reflect the real economic situation and involve ample public consultation in the interim. The Conservatives also engaged in a powerful propaganda campaign to discredit the coalition, protesting that it would have made Stéphane Dion the Prime Minister when he had been soundly defeated in the recent election campaign, and that it was supported by the separatist Bloc Québécois, although that party would not actually have been included in the Cabinet. Expert opinion was divided as to whether the governor general should have accepted the PM's advice to prorogue because if this request was not a violation of the unwritten rules of the constitution, it came very close. But in the end, she took his advice, perhaps in part because the government had survived a confidence vote on the November Speech from the Throne and because the coalition appeared to be somewhat wobbly. The Liberals lost no time in replacing Dion as leader with Michael Ignatieff, and in early February 2009 they supported the budget (with minor amendments). The parliamentary crisis was resolved, at least for the time being.[6]

The session of Parliament that began in January 2009 was adjourned in December of that year, with the expectation that it would resume where it left off in late January 2010. But Prime Minister Harper declared at the end of December that he had changed his mind. He had telephoned the governor general, a rather disrespectful and presumptuous move in itself, and apparently received approval to prorogue parliament until early March. That meant that the break in parliamentary activity would be over a month longer than planned, but more significantly, that the current session had ended and a new session would begin in March 2010.

Harper gave two main reasons for this change of heart: the government needed more time to prepare its 2010 budget ("recalibrate"), and the whole country wanted to take two weeks off in February to celebrate the Winter Olympic Games. Many observers were surprised that the government did not mind "losing" all the bills that had not yet been passed—some 30 pieces of government legislation would have to start from scratch in the new session. The opposition parties claimed, however, that the government had other reasons for the prorogation. All committees and committee work would have to begin anew in the new session. That would mean that the committee looking into the Afghan detainee question—that had begun to uncover embarrassing information about government policy and practice—would be shut down. It also meant that Senate committees would have to be reconstituted, and with the appointment of five new Conservative senators, the government party would now have a majority on such Senate committees. In 2010 David Johnston succeeded Michaëlle Jean as Governor General.

The Prime Minister and Cabinet

Powers of the Prime Minister and Cabinet

The prime minister and Cabinet have the power to make the most significant governmental decisions. Given their importance, it is ironic that they are not provided for in the written parts of the Constitution, their functions and powers resting instead on custom and convention. What *is* provided for in the 1867 Constitution Act is a **Privy Council** to advise the governor general in the exercise of the powers of that office. In fact, the Cabinet acts as a committee of the Privy Council, but rather than merely advising the governor general, it actually makes the decisions in question. With rare exceptions, the prime minister and Cabinet exercise whatever powers are given to the Queen or the governor general in the Constitution. Such decisions, especially appointments, often take the form of **orders in council**.

Thus, after an election, the governor general calls upon the leader of the party with most members elected to the House of Commons (or the party leader most likely to command the confidence of the Commons) to become prime minister and to form a government.[7] The prime minister assumes the title "Right Honourable" and selects the Cabinet ministers, all of whom are sworn into the Privy Council, which allows them to use the title "Honourable" for life.

In normal circumstances, then, the prime minister and Cabinet exercise the powers of the Crown. These powers include summoning, proroguing, and dissolving Parliament; the pardoning power; and the appointment of senators, judges, other officials, and royal commissions. The prime minister and Cabinet recommend **money bills** to Parliament, and all international acts and the general conduct of foreign relations are the prerogative of the Cabinet, including declaring war and peace, signing treaties, appointing ambassadors, and recognizing foreign governments. The Cabinet may feel it politically advantageous to have Parliament debate declarations of war and may need to submit legislation to Parliament to make treaties effective, but unlike in the United States, such international acts are essentially within the purview of the executive branch of government, not the legislature.

Exercising the powers of the Crown is only a small part of the reason that the prime minister and Cabinet are the centre of gravity in the Canadian political system, however. More importantly, and similarly to the executive of any organization, they have the responsibility for providing political leadership and determining priorities. That is, the prime minister and Cabinet decide which problems to deal with, establish the general thrust and direction of new policies, and determine the spending priorities of the government. In the British and Canadian systems, the responsibility for initiating legislation rests primarily with the Cabinet. As will be seen in Chapter 15, opportunities do exist for other members of Parliament to introduce bills, but most of the time of the House of Commons is set aside for government business. The **Speech from the Throne** provides the Cabinet with an opportunity to outline its legislative program at the beginning of the session. The Cabinet's virtual monopoly over the passage of legislation should ensure coordination among government policies, while its total monopoly over financial legislation is designed to guarantee a close relationship between policies adopted and the funds to make them effective. Such strong executive leadership, based on tradition, necessity, and the Constitution Act, and backed up by vast resources and advice, has generally proven itself to be an effective way to run a country.

Beyond the powers of the Crown and this general leadership function, Cabinet power is also derived from specific acts of Parliament. Almost every law delegates to a minister or the **governor in council** (i.e., the Cabinet) the power to make decisions of many kinds. Similarly, it is largely on the basis of acts of Parliament that individual ministers are charged with supervising the administration of their departments. Ministers provide direction and leadership, establish priorities, and transmit their personal, party, and Cabinet perspectives, all in an effort to ensure that the public servants in their departments remain accountable to democratically elected leaders and public opinion. As mentioned, ministers are also given quasi-legislative powers to issue regulations, sometimes called *delegated* or *subordinate legislation*, that flesh out the bare bones of the statute. In addition, ministers are involved in Parliament, answering questions about the department's operations, defending departmental spending proposals, and piloting bills emanating from the department.

The principle of **individual ministerial responsibility** requires that each minister is responsible to Parliament for everything that goes on in his or her department. It was once thought to entail a minister's resignation over public servants' errors, even those the minister knew nothing about.[8] In an age of big government, however, the principle has lost most of its meaning. Ministers can still be criticized for departmental failures and are expected to correct them, but they rarely resign except for monumental personal mistakes and **conflicts of interest**. In the 1990s, for example, the lax administration of the Human Resources Development department attracted much criticism, but the principle of ministerial responsibility required only that the minister clean up the mess, not resign. Accountability for the dramatic increase in the costs of the gun registry and for the 2003 sponsorship scandal in Quebec was even more elusive.

The Prime Minister

The system of government that Canada inherited from Britain has traditionally been called **Cabinet government**, but such a label does not do justice to the modern pre-eminence of the prime minister. Most observers agree that Cabinet government has been transformed into a system of **prime ministerial government**, and no one doubts that the prime minister has enormous power and should be singled out for special attention.[9] The dominance of the prime minister over Cabinet colleagues can be seen in ten of the PM's principal powers, rights, or responsibilities. In many cases, these relate to the different arenas in which the prime minister must operate, such as Cabinet, Parliament, party, media, federal–provincial relations, international diplomacy, and the economy:[10]

- Cabinet-maker
- Chair of Cabinet meetings
- Party leader
- Chief policymaker
- Leading player in the House of Commons
- Chief personnel manager
- Controller of government organization
- Adviser to governor general
- Chief diplomat
- Public persuader

First, the prime minister is the Cabinet-maker. Prime ministers select their own ministers, subject to certain conventions discussed below, and decide what portfolios to assign to each of them. Ministers thus owe allegiance to the prime minister, who also issues them "mandate letters" that inform them of the PM's policy expectations in their portfolio.[11] In addition, the prime minister promotes and demotes ministers, asks for their resignation, or, if necessary, dismisses them.

Chairing Cabinet meetings is a second main source of the prime minister's power. To start with, the prime minister determines the agenda of such meetings, but in addition to the usual advantages of a chair, the prime minister benefits from the peculiar way in which Cabinet decisions are arrived at. Rather than by motions and votes, the decision is reached when the PM summarizes the discussion and articulates the "consensus"—either by extracting a real consensus from the meeting or by imposing his or her own viewpoint. Ministers who do not agree with this interpretation either keep quiet or resign. Even though many decisions are now made by Cabinet committees, the prime minister decides which committees will be struck, who will chair them, who will sit on them, and which matters will be sent to them, so that this delegation of power from the full Cabinet does not necessarily reduce the PM's control.

Third, the prime minister is the leader of the party, and the PM's pre-eminence has probably increased over the years as political parties have become more cohesive and as election campaigns have come to focus on party leaders. In fact, many ministers may have been elected on the leader's coattails. As leader, the prime minister can control party organization, personnel, strategy, and policy, and in exceptional circumstances impose or veto party candidates. Jean Chrétien, Paul Martin, and Stéphane Dion "appointed" a number of Liberal candidates in recent elections, for example, while party leaders have occasionally refused to sign the nomination papers of a candidate chosen by the local constituency association.

Fourth, the prime minister might be called chief policymaker. The PM has the last word on government policy, whether in personal interaction with individual ministers, within the Cabinet chamber, in Parliament, or in other forums such as the media. Modern government, of course, is too complex for one person to have an active role in formulating all policies, but the prime minister "can play a critical role in problem definition."[12] Recent examples of prime ministerial power are the Clarity Act, which Jean Chrétien bulldozed through despite considerable opposition from Cabinet colleagues and the Liberal caucus, and Stephen Harper's control of virtually every action of his government.

Fifth, the prime minister is the central player in the House of Commons. Even though control of the parliamentary agenda is now delegated to the government House leader, the PM is still expected to be there and speak for the government in the oral Question Period almost every day.

A sixth source of prime ministerial pre-eminence is an enormous power of appointment. This includes the appointment of ministers, senators, Supreme Court judges, deputy ministers, and heads of a wide range of government agencies. Given the extent and power of the bureaucracy today, the prime minister's seventh power, control over government organization, is also significant. Subject to usually routine parliamentary approval, the PM can decide to create new departments and set out their mandates, reorganize government departments, abolish departments or agencies, or privatize Crown corporations. Prime Minister Martin, for example, established new ministries of state for Infrastructure and Communities and for Families and Caregivers.

Eighth, the prime minister personally advises the governor general on such matters as when to call the next election. Chrétien called the November 2000 election against the virtually unanimous advice of Cabinet and caucus, and many Liberals had doubts about Martin's election call for June 2004. The new law on fixed election dates was

Stephen Harper gave new meaning to the concept of prime ministerial government. (The Canadian Press/Tom Hanson)

expected to modify this power to some extent, but had no effect in Harper's election call of 2008.

In an era of summit diplomacy, the prime minister often overshadows the minister of foreign affairs on the world stage, functioning as Canada's chief diplomat. This role can be observed in annual bilateral meetings with the U.S. president, annual meetings of the Group of 8 (or Group of 20) leading industrialized countries, Commonwealth Conferences, meetings of the Francophonie, other summits, and occasional appearances at the United Nations.

The prime minister is also the chief "public relations officer" of the government, or "public persuader."[13] Television has become the main instrument for transmitting the prime minister's message to the party, the government, and the public. Survival in the battleground of media relations "threatens to become the key determinant of prime ministerial success."[14] Stephen Harper took great pains to "stage" his press conferences and was found to have a personal stylist on staff, but was otherwise rather inaccessible to the media.

Given all these powers and a normally deferential majority in the House of Commons, the PM can usually succeed in controlling the policy and personnel of government. In many respects, in fact, the Canadian prime minister is more powerful than the American president, except of course in international clout. In order to get his agenda adopted, the latter must bargain with Congress in which party discipline is not strong, whereas prime ministers can usually count on a disciplined majority to back their measures. Indeed, the expansion of prime ministerial staff, the holding of prime ministerial news conferences, the making of televised addresses to the nation, luxurious travel arrangements, and other conspicuous trappings of power have led many observers to criticize the "presidentialization" of the office of prime minister.[15]

However much ministers may resent the prime minister's dominance, internal attempts to overthrow the PM are rare. Only two Cabinet revolts have occurred in Canadian history (against Mackenzie Bowell and John Diefenbaker), although, as in the case of Jean Chrétien, prime ministers have sometimes been forced by party pressure to advance their retirement plans. Other observers, however, emphasize the restraints on the power of the PM. These theoretically include the media, opposition parties, the Constitution, the party, and public opinion, but more practically they involve financial constraints, opposition from the provinces, international influences, and the limits within which government policy of any kind can effect societal change. Of course, if the government is not supported by a majority in the House of Commons, that is, if it finds itself in a minority position as was the case after the 2004, 2006, and 2008 elections, the prime minister may lose much of this dominance. In such a situation, the PM may have to seek the approval of one or more opposition parties for many of the government's initiatives. On the other hand, if opposition parties are afraid of an election, they will find ways to avoid defeating the government. Even with a majority, the prime minister is often at the mercy of events, which may bring about a fall in public support and a loss of much overall influence in turn. As in other aspects of the political system, any semblance of democratic control requires a vigilant, well-informed electorate. Graham White concludes that the PM has "formidable raw power" but falls short of being an autocrat.[16]

Several incidents of raw prime ministerial power occurred in 2010. These included the cancellation of the mandatory long-form 2011 Census, the refusal to hand over the Afghan detainee documents, the general clamping down of access to information, the refusal to allow ministerial aides to testify before Commons' committees, the inclusion in the budget of several significant non-financial policy decisions, the expulsion of MP Helena Guergis from the cabinet and Conservative caucus, the expansion of the PMO communications budget, and the dismissal of several agency and commission heads and the maligning of several other senior bureaucrats.

Table 13.1, which contains a list of prime ministers ranked by length of tenure, reveals the variations in prime ministerial political fortunes. Stephen Harper was sworn in as PM on February 6, 2006.

TABLE 13.1 PRIME MINISTERS OF CANADA, RANKED BY LENGTH OF TENURE

Prime Minister	Length of Tenure	Prime Minister	Length of Tenure
Mackenzie King	21 yrs., 5 mo.	Alexander Mackenzie	4 yrs., 11 mo.
John A. Macdonald	19 yrs.	Paul Martin	2 yrs., 2 mo.
Pierre Elliott Trudeau	15 yrs., 5 mo.	John Thompson	2 yrs.
Wilfrid Laurier	15 yrs., 3 mo.	Arthur Meighen	1 yr., 8 mo.
Jean Chrétien	10 yrs., 1 mo.	John Abbott	1 yr., 5 mo.
Brian Mulroney	9 yrs., 9 mo.	Mackenzie Bowell	1 yr., 4 mo.
Robert L. Borden	9 yrs., 9 mo.	Joe Clark	9 mo.
Louis St. Laurent	8 yrs., 7 mo.	Kim Campbell	133 days
John Diefenbaker	5 yrs., 10 mo.	John Turner	80 days
R.B. Bennett	5 yrs., 3 mo.	Charles Tupper	69 days
Lester Pearson	5 yrs.		

Composition of the Cabinet

In theory, all Cabinet ministers are equal, although in practice this is far from being the case. All recent PMs, except Stephen Harper, designated one minister as deputy prime minister, although in some cases this title seemed to carry more prestige than any real power.

Next are the regular departmental ministers, each normally in charge of a single department. An informal ranking of these departments may result in variations in influence among this group of ministers, with finance, foreign affairs, justice, industry, health, defence, international trade, Treasury Board, and human resources usually being among the key portfolios. The Cabinet also contains some ministers who do not have full-fledged departments to administer, especially the government leaders in the House of Commons and the Senate. This category may also include junior ministers, variously called ministers without portfolio, ministers of state, or secretaries of state. They might be in charge of small agencies or assigned to assist a senior minister. With the exception of the Chrétien era and the second year of the Harper government, the Canadian tradition has been that all ministers, even these junior ones, were included in the Cabinet.

Since the Cabinet occupies such a central position in the Canadian policy-making process, every interest in the country would like to be represented in its deliberations. This desire alone creates pressure to expand its size. In general, the Cabinet contained about 14 ministers before 1911, and then rose to around 20 until about 1960 when it increased to 30 under Trudeau, and to around 40 in the Mulroney period. Chrétien reduced the Cabinet's size to 23 in 1993, supplemented by nine junior ministers who were part of the ministry but not invited to Cabinet meetings. After the 2000 election, Chrétien's Cabinet grew to 29, along with eight junior ministers. Paul Martin had 39 Cabinet ministers, including many ministers of state, but all with a reserved seat at Cabinet meetings. Stephen Harper started out with only 27, but his Cabinet later grew to 38.

Several conventions have developed to constrain the PM's prerogatives in the selection of ministers. In the first place, reflecting the fact that Canada is a democracy and that the ministers represent the people, all Cabinet ministers must have a seat in Parliament. Ministers sit in the legislative branch of government at the same time as they form the executive. Almost all ministers therefore have a seat in the House of Commons. It is possible for the prime minister to name someone to the Cabinet who has not won election to the Commons, but convention dictates that such a person run in a by-election as soon as possible in order to obtain a seat. This sometimes happens when a PM chooses to appoint a person from outside parliamentary life who possesses greater qualifications than sitting backbenchers. The modern tradition is to include only one senator in the Cabinet, usually serving as government leader in that chamber and having no departmental responsibilities.

The next constraint on the prime minister is the convention that each province be represented in the Cabinet. This flows from the fact that Canada is a federation and that the Senate has never performed its intended role of representing provincial interests in Ottawa. Thus, with the occasional exception of Prince Edward Island, every province that has elected a member to the government side of the Commons has been awarded a Cabinet position. This convention usually results in some ministers being appointed only because their province needs Cabinet representation, rather than on their merits, leaving worthy MPs from other locations excluded. In both the Trudeau and Clark governments, the prime minister chose to appoint senators to the Cabinet to represent provinces that had not elected any or enough government members (the three Western provinces in the former case and Quebec in the latter). That such a practice breaks the modern convention of having only one senator in the Cabinet attests to the importance of provincial representation. In 1997, Chrétien responded to the absence of Liberal MPs from Nova Scotia by choosing his one senator from that province. Stephen Harper's 2006 Cabinet contained two surprises: in order to represent Montreal, Harper appointed Michel Fortier to the Senate and Cabinet simultaneously, and to represent Vancouver he seduced outgoing Liberal Cabinet minister David Emerson to cross the floor and continue his Cabinet service as a Conservative.

It is not only that residents of a province feel more secure if one of their number is in the Cabinet; it is also very useful for the Cabinet itself to have such provincial representation.[17] In fact, ministers essentially wear two hats: they speak for their department as well as for their province. This arrangement is functional for patronage as well as policy purposes: appointments and contracts awarded on a partisan basis in any province will be the responsibility of the resident minister, often called the "political minister" for that province.

Larger provinces are not content with a single minister, of course, and in a Cabinet of 30 or 40 members, Ontario and Quebec have sometimes exceeded ten. In such cases the ministers can be distributed so that each region within the province gains its own representative. Prior to 1984, however, Quebec was usually underrepresented in the Cabinet when the Conservatives were in power, and the West was inadequately represented in the Pearson and Trudeau Cabinets.

The next convention of Canadian Cabinet-making is the need for a balance of ethnic representatives. A proper balance of anglophone and francophone ministers may result almost automatically from the carefully constructed provincial representation. French Canadians were underrepresented even in Liberal governments before 1963, however, and often grossly underrepresented in Conservative Cabinets. It was only in the Pearson, Trudeau, and Mulroney Cabinets that francophone ministers achieved or exceeded the one-third benchmark. Those of other ethnic origins were not proportionately represented in the past, except perhaps in the Clark and Mulroney Cabinets, but now expect fairer Cabinet representation.

As for other social divisions, religion was much more important in the pre-1900 period than it is today. Prime ministers are now more concerned with appointing women to the Cabinet. Since it was difficult to include representatives of all social groups in his 1993 Cabinet of only 23, Chrétien tried to appease some of the others in the appointment of the secretaries of state: three women, one member from Prince Edward Island, one Aboriginal person, and one of Asian background.

The Cabinet therefore provides a location for various segments of society to be accommodated, and William Matheson writes of a representative Cabinet as follows: "in the Canadian context the Cabinet has filled a dual role, for in addition to exercising the usual functions of executive leadership, the cabinet has provided an arena in which the elites may counter the dysfunctional and unstabilizing effects of cultural, regional, and religious fragmentation."[18]

Once the PM has chosen the people who will form the Cabinet, they must be assigned portfolios, that is, departmental responsibilities. It is not normally expected that ministers will be experts in the fields to which they are appointed, partly because the electorate is not likely to furnish the prime minister with members of Parliament having such credentials. Indeed, an argument can be made that a semi-expert is more dangerous than a total amateur, since the latter will have enough sense to listen to the real experts within the department, while the former might try to substitute his or her limited knowledge for theirs. Thus, apart from the minister of justice being a lawyer, there is no necessary relationship between ministers' training or pre-political occupation and their departmental assignment.

What Do You Think?

Is the Canadian system of appointing a minister to head a department that he or she knows virtually nothing about a good way to run a government? Is the concept of "amateur ministers" really sound, or is there just no alternative?

Operation of the Cabinet

CABINET SOLIDARITY AND CABINET SECRECY

The Cabinet is usually considered to be a collective decision-making body. Exceptions to this notion include the prime minister's penchant to make decisions single-handedly and decisions taken by Cabinet committees or by individual ministers. Regardless of which or how many ministers are involved in the making of such decisions, however, the Cabinet operates on the principle of **Cabinet solidarity**, meaning that all ministers must publicly defend all Cabinet policies or else resign. Ministerial resignations because of policy differences are rare in Canada, perhaps only 30 since 1867,[19] suggesting that the thought of giving up the perks of office engenders considerable flexibility in ministers' principles. The most extreme manifestation of Cabinet solidarity can be seen in terms of the annual budget, which is usually the most important government policy statement of the year. Only the finance minister and PM know much about it until the budget is delivered in Parliament, yet all ministers must support it. Cabinet solidarity is related to the principle of collective ministerial responsibility to Parliament. If the government loses the confidence of the legislature, it must collectively resign or call an election.

Cabinet solidarity is also linked to the principle of Cabinet secrecy or confidentiality. Cabinet operations are shrouded in secrecy, and ministers are not supposed to disclose information about its deliberations. Such confidentiality protects state secrets, protects the Cabinet against opposition and media exploitation of ministerial discord, and protects senior civil servants from identification and public criticism. Cabinet documents are not normally made public for 20 years, and, as a result, we do not know as much about how the Cabinet operates as about decision-making bodies that meet in public. In fact, this exception from the Access to Information Act frustrates everyone who wants to understand why the Cabinet makes the decisions that it does. On the other hand, clever ministers are conscious that information represents power and sometimes a well-timed "leak" can be of benefit when involved in a battle within Cabinet.

CABINET BEHAVIOUR

At the time of Confederation, many Cabinet ministers retained positions as corporate directors or other business connections. It is only since about 1960 that ministers have been required to divorce themselves from their former corporate relationships under various versions of conflict-of-interest guidelines. The problem continued to arise from time to time with individual ministers, however, and became critical during the Chrétien era. The prime minister himself was implicated in a dubious business operation in his constituency, while Finance Minister Paul Martin received regular briefings on the activities of his company, Canada Steamship Lines, which had supposedly been placed in a blind trust. Chrétien was forced to tighten the rules regarding prime ministerial and ministerial corporate relationships at the end of his tenure, and under Martin the long-promised independent ethics commissioner was appointed. This commissioner is now an officer of Parliament, no longer reporting to the prime minister, and has a stricter set of conflict-of-interest rules to apply to members of Parliament both inside and outside the Cabinet.

CABINET PROCEDURE

Before 1960 or so, perhaps especially in the Mackenzie King and St. Laurent eras, ministers and departments were largely autonomous. Each developed its own policies and programs with little regard for central coordination and with only minimal prime ministerial interference. Strong ministers could make many decisions and policies without consulting their colleagues, and such ministers tended to remain in charge of a single department for long periods of time. Such autonomous departmental ministers often doubled as strong regional ministers, who were also allowed to handle regional responsibilities on their own. In addition, senior bureaucrats usually served their careers within a single department and became "carriers of the interests, traditions, skills and memories of these particularized bureaucratic organizations."[20]

Despite what has been said previously about collective Cabinet decision-making, the change from autonomous ministers to collegial Cabinet decisions is really a product of the post-1960 period and the enormous expansion of government activity in the following 25 years. As society and its problems became more complex, individual ministers and departments could no longer make decisions and policies in isolation; the policies of one department almost inevitably affected those of another. More consultation and coordination were required with the result that ministerial collegiality replaced departmental autonomy. To some extent the need for policy coordination coincided with the view that Cabinet ministers should have greater control over the bureaucracy; another stimulus was the concern for more rational government decision-making. The Pearson era was transitional in this respect, and the major change was adopted in the Trudeau period.

Prime Minister Trudeau attempted to increase the rationality of government policymaking in a variety of ways.[21] First, the PM and Cabinet gave more attention to setting the overall priorities of the government. Second, the four central agencies—Prime Minister's Office, Privy Council Office, Department of Finance, and Treasury Board Secretariat—were expanded and strengthened so as to provide policy analysis to the prime minister and Cabinet independently of other government departments. Third, to avoid Cabinet overload and to enhance specialization and policy coordination within it, most of the Cabinet's work was done in committees. Fourth, Cabinet procedures were rigidly adhered to, including agendas, advance notice of issues, and advance circulation of background documents. All of these measures tended to render Cabinet decisions more coordinated, organized, and disciplined, hence the term "institutionalized Cabinet."[22]

Historically, the Cabinet as a whole met for about three or four hours once a week, although under Stephen Harper this was reduced to at least once a month. When a meeting is scheduled, the **Privy Council Office (PCO)** prepares an agenda for the prime minister, which is circulated in advance. The PCO will also have prepared a scenario note suggesting issues that the PM may want to raise, including guidance in getting through the meeting successfully, although most PMs prefer that ministers and departments sort out their differences beforehand. Rather than resolving questions by a formal vote, the prime minister sums up the discussion on each item and articulates his view of the consensus arrived at. A handful of senior officials on hand take note of the discussion and decisions and circulate minutes afterward. They are rarely asked to speak, but may pass notes to the PM. Given the demands on the time of those involved, meetings are conducted in a very business-like manner.

As mentioned, since the mid-1960s, more and more such work has been done by Cabinet committees rather than by the full Cabinet, each committee normally meeting once a week. Unlike in full Cabinet meetings, ministers may bring advisers (usually their deputy minister) along to Cabinet committees, so they are less reliant on their own personal resources. In most recent governments, the Priorities and Planning Committee was clearly the most important Cabinet committee. Its special functions included setting priorities, allocating budgets, reviewing other committee decisions, making many important decisions itself, and supervising federal–provincial relations. Being chaired by the prime minister and containing the most important ministers (including the chairs of other Cabinet committees) also added to its significance. In the Harper government, the Operations Committee was the second important executive committee, especially because the full Cabinet rarely met. Harper began with four other policy committees: Treasury Board, social affairs, economic growth and long-term prosperity, and foreign affairs and national security; he later added committees on environment and energy security and on Afghanistan.

Working with the committee chair and the PM, the Privy Council Office develops and distributes an agenda that is largely composed of Memorandums to

Cabinet from various departments. Each committee is supported by a secretariat within the PCO that works with the sponsoring department(s). Much interdepartmental discussion and negotiation takes place in advance, and under Harper's "command and control" management style, policy committees were left little room for unscripted policy deliberation. The committee chair receives a PCO briefing before the meeting and a scenario note. If the committee cannot come to a consensus, the memorandum is returned for further work; if it is approved, it is attached to the agenda of the next meeting of the full Cabinet.[23]

Cabinet Support Agencies

As mentioned, the following four main central agencies exist to support the prime minister and/or the Cabinet as a whole:

- the Prime Minister's Office,
- the Privy Council Office,
- the Department of Finance, and
- the Treasury Board Secretariat.

(Sue Dewar/Artizans.com)

The **Prime Minister's Office (PMO)** handles the prime minister's correspondence, media relations, partisan appointments, public appearances, and speeches, and briefs the PM on legislative proceedings. The office contains nearly 100 people who monitor political developments and offer policy advice from a partisan point of view. The PM usually meets daily with the head of the PMO to be briefed on developments from a partisan perspective. Under every recent prime minister, the PMO has had a powerful influence on virtually all government decisions. Under Stephen Harper, it also controlled most of the words and actions of all government MPs.

The Privy Council Office (PCO) has served several unique purposes since it was recognized as the Cabinet secretariat, and since Cabinet meetings became more businesslike in 1940 due to the pressures of war. First, it provides logistical support for the Cabinet—organizing meetings, preparing agendas, writing and distributing background material, taking and circulating minutes, and communicating Cabinet decisions. In these ways, the PCO is engaged in the coordination of overall government policy. The PCO also performs the same services for Cabinet committees. As mentioned, PCO officials brief Cabinet committee chairs and the prime minister even on the strategy of conducting their meetings. All these functions help the PCO obtain the kind of decisions that it considers best. Another example of its influence is in its detailed strategy notes for the prime minister when he or she meets important people at home or abroad or makes critical telephone calls.

Other sections of the Privy Council Office have responsibility for the machinery of government, the appointment of senior public service personnel, and federal–provincial relations. The head of the PCO, the **Clerk of the Privy Council and Secretary to the Cabinet**, is regarded as the government's highest-ranking public servant. The Clerk meets daily with the prime minister to review problems and render nonpartisan advice and could be called the lynchpin of the government of Canada. Being the closest adviser to the PM, the Clerk has his or her hands on almost everything that really counts: drafting the Speech from the Throne, working with the Department of Finance on the budget, organizing the machinery of government, writing mandate letters for ministers and deputy ministers, appointing and evaluating deputy ministers, chairing the coordinating committees of deputy ministers, keeping an eye on Memorandums to Cabinet, helping to strategize Cabinet and Cabinet committee meetings, and keeping track of federal–provincial relations. The prime minister may be the most important player in the actual making of government decisions, but the Clerk advises on almost every one. To quote the Gomery report, "the Prime Minister sits at the apex of the political hierarchy, while the Clerk sits at the apex of the bureaucratic hierarchy. Together, they wield a great deal of power and influence."[24]

The **Department of Finance** and the Treasury Board Secretariat primarily supply financial information to the Cabinet, and they have historically exercised a cautioning, restraining influence on new program proposals. The role of the Department of Finance is to look at the government's overall revenue and expenditure situation, including its accumulated debt, and to advise on allocations among departments. Under the powerful deputy minister, it is also the chief adviser on taxation policy and on transfer payments to the provinces. While reporting directly to the minister of finance and in that sense being an ordinary department of government, the Department of Finance has a special responsibility of advising the Cabinet collectively on such matters, being incorporated into the process of developing Memorandums to Cabinet, as well as preparing the budget.

The **Treasury Board** is a committee of Cabinet chaired by the minister called President of the Treasury Board, who is in turn in charge of a full-fledged government department, the **Treasury Board Secretariat (TBS)**. This secretariat has the overall responsibility for controlling regular departmental spending, being involved in the development of detailed departmental budgets—the **Estimates**—and overseeing the actual expenditure of funds. The TBS is also in charge of labour relations in the public service and issues policies on personnel, administration, and finance. Although its perspective is more detailed than that of the Department of Finance, the two agencies usually see things in a similar light.

Figure 13.2 illustrates how these central agencies, as well as other relevant departments, have to be persuaded to support any departmental initiative before it can appear on the agenda of a Cabinet committee en route to the Cabinet as a whole.

The most astute student of the political executive in Canada, Donald Savoie, has emphasized the pre-eminence of recent prime ministers over their Cabinet colleagues. Increasingly, however, he now dismisses Cabinet as not overly important and talks of "court government." By court government,

> *I mean that effective political power now rests with the prime minister and a small group of carefully selected courtiers. I also mean a shift from formal decision-making processes in cabinet and, as a consequence, in the civil service, to informal processes involving only a handful of key actors.*[25]

Figure 13.2 Flow of Departmental Initiative to Cabinet

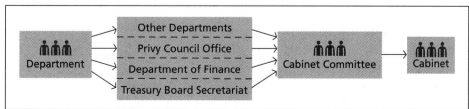

SUMMARY

This chapter examined the executive branch of government. It began by outlining the six phases of the policymaking process—initiation, priority-setting, policy formulation, legitimation, implementation, and interpretation. The second part dealt with the Crown—the place of the monarch and governor general—and claimed that they have a useful symbolic and ceremonial role to play. The chapter then explained the important decision-making functions of the prime minister and Cabinet and sought to discover the sources of their powers. It separated out the prime minister for special attention, enumerating ten roles that establish the PM's pre-eminence over the whole political system, including the Cabinet. The next section revealed the factors that influence a prime minister in the construction of a Cabinet and was followed by a discussion of the principles and processes of the Cabinet's operation. In particular, it highlighted the increased use of Cabinet committees and the heightened concern with ethical behaviour. Finally, the chapter considered the important influence on the prime minister and Cabinet of four main Cabinet support agencies: the Prime Minister's Office, the Privy Council Office, the Department of Finance, and the Treasury Board Secretariat.

DISCUSSION QUESTIONS

1. What are the advantages and disadvantages of recognizing the Queen as the Canadian head of state? Should we confer that title upon the governor general?
2. Does the prime minister have too much power in the Canadian system of government?
3. Should individual departments and ministers have more power at the expense of collective decision-making processes, central agencies, and "court government"?

KEY TERMS

Cabinet government A system of government in which the major political decisions are made by the Cabinet as a whole, as opposed to one in which the prime minister acts with considerable autonomy or dominance.

Cabinet solidarity A convention that all Cabinet ministers publicly support whatever decisions the Cabinet has taken, regardless of their personal views.

Clerk of the Privy Council and Secretary to the Cabinet The head of the Privy Council Office and head of the federal public service; the chief nonpartisan adviser to the prime minister and Cabinet.

Conflict of interest A situation in which any public officeholder places personal benefit (usually financial) before the public interest.

Constitutional monarchy The official designation of the Canadian form of government, characterized by a monarch who is head of state but who rules according to the Constitution, which confides almost all governmental power into other hands.

Crown The collection of executive powers exercised by or in the name of the monarch.

Crown corporation A corporation owned by the government that assumes a structure similar to that of a private company and that operates semi-independently of the Cabinet.

Department of Finance The government department that has overall responsibility for the government's finances and its role in the economy and that has a powerful influence on all government policy.

Estimates The annual spending plans of government departments and agencies.

Executive That branch of government that provides leadership and makes the major decisions.

Government The set of authorities centred around a prime minister, Cabinet, and party that currently occupy the executive offices of the state and provide political leadership.

Governor general The representative of the Queen in Canada who normally performs her head-of-state functions.

Governor in council The prime minister and Cabinet (but *not* the governor general) exercising powers of the Privy Council.

Individual ministerial responsibility The principle that Cabinet ministers are individually responsible to the House of Commons to answer for everything that happens in their department.

King–Byng dispute The 1926 dispute between Prime Minister Mackenzie King and Governor General Lord Byng over King's request for a dissolution of Parliament, which Byng denied.

Memorandum to Cabinet The formal written document that a minister submits to the Cabinet seeking to initiate or change a government policy.

Money bill A bill to raise money for government purposes or to spend public funds.

Order in council A formal, legal decision made by the prime minister and Cabinet (governor in council), including regulations and appointments.

Prerogative powers That small number of residual powers of the Crown that remain from the era of an all-powerful monarch that the Queen or governor general can still exercise on rare occasions at his or her own discretion.

Prime ministerial government The notion that the prime minister is now so pre-eminent that the label "Cabinet government" no longer accurately describes how decisions are made in the political executive.

Prime Minister's Office (PMO) The office that supports and advises the prime minister in partisan terms.

Privy Council A body established by the Constitution Act, 1867, to advise the governor general in the exercise of the powers of that office but that was effectively taken over by the prime minister and Cabinet.

Privy Council Office (PCO) The office that supports and advises the prime minister, Cabinet, and Cabinet committees in nonpartisan terms.

Public policy A course of action or inaction chosen by public authorities to address a given problem or interrelated set of problems.

Regulations The detailed rules drafted by the bureaucracy under the authority of laws passed by Parliament that are too voluminous and technical to put into the legislation itself.

Speech from the Throne The document prepared by the prime minister and Cabinet and read by the governor general at the opening of each session of Parliament that outlines the government's legislative proposals for the session.

Treasury Board A Cabinet committee whose primary responsibility is to restrain government spending.

Treasury Board Secretariat The government department that advises the Treasury Board in its deliberations and that functions as a restraining influence on departmental spending.

FURTHER READING

Campbell, Robert M., et al., eds. *Real Worlds of Canadian Politics: Cases in Process and Policy*, 4th ed. Peterborough: Broadview Press, 2004.

Dunn, Christopher, ed. *The Handbook of Canadian Public Administration*. Toronto: Oxford University Press, 2002.

Forcese, Craig, and Allan Freeman. *The Laws of Government: The Legal Foundations of Canadian Democracy*. Toronto: Irwin Law, 2005.

Goldenberg, Eddie. *The Way It Works: Inside Ottawa*. Toronto: McClelland and Stewart, 2006.

McWhinney, Edward. *The Governor General and the Prime Ministers: The Making and Unmaking of Governments*. Vancouver: Ronsdale Press, 2005.

Russell, Peter H., and Lorne Sossin, eds., *Parliamentary Democracy in Crisis*. Toronto: University of Toronto Press, 2009.

Savoie, Donald J. *Court Government and the Collapse of Accountability in Canada and the United Kingdom*. Toronto: University of Toronto Press, 2008.

Savoie, Donald J. *Governing from the Centre: The Concentration of Power in Canada*. Toronto: University of Toronto Press, 1999.

Simpson, Jeffrey. *The Friendly Dictatorship*. Toronto: McClelland and Stewart, 2001.

Smith, David E. *The Invisible Crown*. Toronto: University of Toronto Press, 1996.

White, Graham. *Cabinets and First Ministers*. Vancouver: UBC Press, 2004.

Chapter 14

The Bureaucracy

Most citizens encounter public servants as providers of services, but the **bureaucracy** is probably even more significant in its advisory role. Modern government is so pervasive and complex that the prime minister and Cabinet ministers hardly make a move without the advice of their permanent, expert staff. In fact, the bureaucracy has become so large and indispensable that many observers wonder whether it can be kept under political control. This chapter begins by examining the functions and powers of the bureaucracy and then deals in turn with the three main kinds of bureaucratic organization. It concludes with a discussion about controlling the bureaucracy and the recent attempts to reform it.

Chapter Objectives

After you have completed this chapter, you should be able to:

Identify the role of the bureaucracy in the phases of the policymaking process

Describe the structure of a government department, the roles of the minister and deputy minister, and the principle of ministerial responsibility

Discuss the links between government departments and central agencies, their provincial counterparts, and advocacy groups

Discuss the merit system and assess the attempts to make the public service more representative of society

Outline the purposes, structures, and operations of Crown corporations

Outline the purposes, structures, and operations of administrative agencies and regulatory tribunals

Enumerate the methods of controlling the bureaucracy

Discuss recent attempts to reform the bureaucracy

Functions and Powers of the Bureaucracy

As Glen Milne observes, "only major decisions require cabinet approval and fewer still require new legislation or amendments. In practice, the vast majority of federal government decisions are made at the bureaucratic level within a hierarchical framework of policies decided by cabinet and individual ministers."[1] But even when the other institutions of government are involved, the bureaucracy is usually there too.

Thus, the significance of the bureaucracy can be demonstrated by examining its presence in the model of the policymaking process presented in Figure 13.1. First, the bureaucracy plays a crucial part in the initiation phase. The bureaucracy may be a source of demands, since administrators of any program may be among the first to recognize its inadequacies. Even if a demand reaches the Cabinet from other sources, once the politicians decide to look into an issue further, the public service will be asked to provide additional information and advice.

If the Cabinet decides to take action at the priority-setting stage, it is rarely without advice from the public service and the bureaucracy is then centrally involved in the policy formulation phase. With its concentration of technical information and experience, the public service spends a great deal of its time formulating policies because the details of such policies are usually beyond the grasp of the politicians. Once the policy, program, or law has received political authorization by Cabinet and/or Parliament, implementation is almost exclusively a bureaucratic responsibility. In today's complex society, the politicians are forced to leave wide discretionary powers to the public service to carry out the general goals that they have identified in laws and their other basic decisions.[2]

Because of the time and informational constraints on Parliament, most bills are passed in rather general or skeletal form, and the real meat or substance of the law is expressed in the **regulations** issued under it. These are published under the authority of the minister or Cabinet in the *Canada Gazette*. A considerable lag often exists between the political approval of a law and its effective implementation, during which time the public service drafts such regulations, sets up new administrative machinery, and hires new personnel. The implementation phase may involve time-consuming negotiations with the provinces or with relevant advocacy groups. Once the date arrives for the start of a new program, it is the bureaucracy again that actually provides the service, does the regulating, or performs whatever other functions are involved. Implementation also requires the bureaucracy to disseminate information to the public about new policies or programs, and it may even involve exercising quasi-judicial powers.

Given its role in almost all phases of the policymaking process, reference to "bureaucratic power" in political science or contentions that the bureaucracy is more powerful than the legislature or even the prime minister and Cabinet should not be surprising. It is more conventional to say that the prime minister and Cabinet make the most important decisions in the political system and that they theoretically control the bureaucracy, but this is not to deny the extent of bureaucratic power in the modern state. The most common forms of bureaucratic operations are government departments, Crown corporations, and administrative agencies and regulatory tribunals.

Government Departments

Most of the operations of the Government of Canada are organized into **government departments**, each of which is created by an act of parliament setting out its responsibilities. A major consolidation of departments took place in 1993, reducing the overall number from 25 to about 20. Minor modifications have been made since, such that as of 2011 the departments were as follows:

- Agriculture and Agri-Food
- Canadian Heritage
- Citizenship and Immigration
- Environment
- Finance
- Fisheries and Oceans
- Foreign Affairs and International Trade
- Health
- Human Resources and Skills Development
- Indian Affairs and Northern Development
- Industry
- Justice
- National Defence
- Natural Resources
- Public Safety
- Public Works and Government Services
- Transport
- Treasury Board Secretariat
- Veterans Affairs

The government department assumes a pyramidal shape with the minister at its apex. Since ministers in this system are chosen from among the politicians elected to Parliament, it is too much to hope that they will be experts in the work of the department. All that is expected is that they have intelligence, ideas, common sense, and an ability to relay government priorities and public opinion to departmental experts as well as to relate expert advice from the department to Parliament and the public. Ministers will naturally develop some expertise if they stay in one Cabinet position for any length of time, but they are often shuffled to another department just as they are getting the hang of it.

Ministers are responsible for their department in the sense that they are expected to provide overall direction and to accept criticism for its faults. In other words, ministers take most of the credit or blame for what the department does, whether or not they know what is going on within it. As pointed out in Chapter 13, the principle of **individual ministerial responsibility** was once thought to mean that ministers had to resign for serious mistakes made by their public servants. But no cases of this occurring have ever been recorded since 1867, and in this age of big government it is not a realistic proposition.[3] What does ministerial responsibility mean today? First, ministers occasionally resign over their personal mistakes or conflicts of interest. Second, they must take political responsibility and answer to Parliament for all actions of their officials. The minister must explain and defend the actions of the department in Parliament, especially during Question Period, and when a bureaucratic error is made, the minister must apologize and promise to correct the mistake. Third, although ministers may discreetly discipline the offender, they should not violate the traditions of public service anonymity, that is, that public servants are not publicly identified.[4] The lax accounting of job-creation funding at Human Resources Development Canada (HRDC) in 2000 is a recent illustration that this is all that ministerial responsibility means.

In the aftermath of the HRDC case and others, the Auditor General wrote in 2001 that "Canada has never modernized its doctrine to distinguish between a minister's area of public responsibility and that of his senior public servants. To me, there is a certain lack of realism in holding ministers ultimately accountable for everything."[5] In a similar vein, Donald J. Savoie notes that bureaucrats have increasingly come to dominate the policymaking process without being responsible for their actions, and he questions whether ministers should be held accountable instead.[6] During the 2004 election campaign, the public was understandably angry that it could not determine who was responsible for the escalating costs of the gun registry or for the sponsorship scandal in Quebec, and the Gomery Report also made recommendations to alter the minister-bureaucratic relationship.

Long-gun Registry clerk wants to know when he can leave. (Vance Rodewalt/Artizans.com)

The more permanent head of the department is the **deputy minister**. Even though they are appointed by the prime minister (on the advice of the Clerk of the Privy Council and Secretary to the Cabinet), "deputies" or "DMs" are usually career public servants. Deputy ministers have two principal roles: they act as chief policy advisers to the minister and function as managers of the department. Over the past 45 years, emphasis in the appointment of deputy ministers has switched from an understanding of a single department to possession of managerial skills that can be applied in any administrative setting. Even though DMs are now frequently shuffled from one department to another, they are usually in place longer than the minister and are thus likely to develop greater knowledge of the department's work. Deputy ministers also interact regularly with DMs in other federal departments, provincial DMs in corresponding departments, and the heads of advocacy groups particularly interested in the department's work.

The relationship between the minister and the deputy minister is of great interest and concern to political science and public administration.[7] Ideally, the minister sets the priorities for the department, while the DM provides a number of options among which the minister can choose to implement them. The deputy should give the minister advice based on administrative, technical, and financial considerations, but the advice must also be sensitive to the political context. The reality of the relationship sometimes approaches this theoretical ideal, but weak ministers may be mere puppets of their bureaucratic advisers. Even strong ministers may be presented only with alternatives favoured by the department; it has been said, for example, that officials in the Department of Finance imposed their ideological bias on one of their most able ministers, Paul Martin.[8] Ministers may encounter bureaucratic resistance to new initiatives, such as in being denied relevant information, having it delayed, or having new policies implemented without enthusiasm.

What Do You Think?

How can we raise the level of accountability or responsibility for serious errors in the operation of government departments, such as the HRDC mess, the gun registry overspending, or Quebec sponsorship scandal? Make the minister resign? Make the deputy minister resign? Make the Auditor General even more vigilant?

It is not easy for a single, solitary, temporary, amateur minister to impose his or her will on thousands of expert, permanent public servants who have established departmental attitudes, values, policies, and procedures. Ministers are allowed to appoint a small, personal, partisan "exempt" staff, but these people are engaged primarily in promoting the image and reputation of the minister. Nevertheless, the minister's political staff is significant. Staff members manage the minister's agenda, correspondence, travel, appointments, media liaison, public appearances, and meetings with lobbyists and advocacy groups.[9]

Under the deputy minister, the department is typically divided into several branches, each headed by an assistant deputy minister (ADM), and the hierarchy broadens out below them. Those divisions of a department that actually carry out services and interact with the public are said to be performing "line" functions. Except for the top managerial posts, most of the line positions in any department are located in the "field"—in local offices in communities across the country. But every department also has "staff" divisions serving internal needs: policy development and research, personnel, financial, information, and legal divisions. The people working for these divisions, as well as the heads of the line divisions, are normally located in Ottawa.

Hundreds or thousands of public servants in the department are ranged in descending levels of authority under the deputy minister and share four basic characteristics: they are expert, permanent, impartial, and anonymous. First, they are chosen on their merits—ability, knowledge, training, and/or experience—for the duties their position entails. Second, they are career public servants, normally remaining within the public service until retirement. Third, they are nonpartisan and expected to serve whichever party comes to power with equal loyalty and enthusiasm. Fourth, bureaucrats are not normally identified in public; instead, the minister speaks for the department and takes responsibility for its performance. Figure 14.1 presents an organizational chart of a hypothetical government department.

Relations with Other Departments and Central Agencies

The operation of a government department is complicated by the necessity of interacting with other departments as well as by the authority of various central bureaucratic agencies to intervene in its affairs. Since almost any law, policy, or program affects a variety of departments, many interdepartmental committees exist. Whenever any new policy is under active consideration, for example, an *ad hoc*

Figure 14.1 Organizational Chart of a Hypothetical Government Department

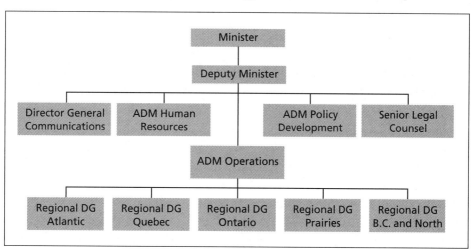

interdepartmental committee is appointed to look into it. The problem must be examined from a number of departmental perspectives and is also subject to considerable bureaucratic politics and territorial claims.

The central agencies that regularly complicate the life of a department include the Treasury Board Secretariat (TBS) and the Privy Council Office (PCO). The **Treasury Board Secretariat's** responsibility for financial and expenditure management was outlined in Chapter 13. The TBS scrutinizes departmental plans, performance, and spending; aims to enhance the financial accountability within the public service; and represents the employer in the collective bargaining process. It is responsible for the preparation of the Estimates, and it issues all sorts of administrative policies such as those on purchasing, contracts, and travel. The Department of Finance is normally allied with the TBS as an opponent of new departmental spending programs.

Relations between the Privy Council Office and government departments primarily arise in connection with policy development and coordination, reallocation of programs between departments, reorganization of departments, and senior management appointments. The PCO drafts the prime minister's mandate letter to the minister of the department and takes a great interest in any new policy proposals emanating from it.

Staffing the Bureaucracy

The Canadian public service originally operated on the "spoils system," under which the party that won an election replaced those holding civil service positions with its own friends and supporters. It was only in the 1930s that the foundations of the modern merit system in Ottawa were laid.[10] Even if **political patronage** was virtually eliminated in the public service, however, there remained considerable scope for partisan appointments in other areas. Senators, lieutenant governors, certain types of diplomats, citizenship judges, and some real judges were still often appointed on a partisan basis, as were those appointed to the boards of Crown corporations, administrative agencies, and regulatory tribunals, and those working in the PMO and ministers' offices.

Almost as soon as the **merit system** was fully effective, people began to demand that the bureaucracy be more representative of the society that it served. Given the power of the public service, many critics argued that the bureaucracy could be responsive to all parts of society only if it included a proportional representation of various groups in the population. The senior levels of the public service had always overrepresented males, anglophones, the middle and upper classes, the well educated, and Ontarians. Thus it was claimed that policy recommendations and implementation reflected an insensitivity to women, the working class, the poor, francophones and other ethnocultural groups, and the peculiarities of hinterland regions.

The first main concerns in this connection were the small number of francophones in the higher reaches of the bureaucracy and the virtual absence of the French language at policymaking levels. The passage of the **Official Languages Act** in 1969 essentially bilingualized the executive branch of government. It gave both English- and French-speaking citizens the right to deal with head offices of government departments (as well as with local offices where numbers warranted) in either official language. It also expanded language-training programs, made recruitment and promotion of francophones a higher priority, and designated certain positions as bilingual. Predictably, the policy ignited a backlash against the preference given to French Canadians and to bilingualism. As of 2008, 40 percent of public service positions had been designated as bilingual, 51 percent as English-essential, four percent as French-essential, and four percent as requiring either official language. As for the people who occupied these positions, about 68 percent were anglophones and 32 percent francophones. Compared to countrywide census statistics, francophones were actually overrepresented in almost every category.[11]

Women were targeted for increased representation in the higher levels of the public service in the 1960s and 1970s.[12] Additionally, the pay equity program of the 1980s and 1990s was designed primarily to ensure that women received equal pay for doing work having the same value as that done by men. It is not easy to compare dissimilar jobs for purposes of compensation, but many occupational groups comprising mostly women have argued that their work was undervalued. In 1999, some 200 000 secretaries and clerks received a pay equity settlement of $3.6 billion.

The next stage in creating a more **representative bureaucracy** came in 1983, when an explicit affirmative action program was adopted for women, Aboriginal peoples, and people with disabilities; two years later visible minorities were added to the list. A stronger Employment Equity Act in 1995 required the adoption of policies and practices that would ensure that people in the four designated groups achieved a degree of representation in each occupational group proportional to their numbers in the Canadian workforce. Table 14.1 shows federal public service employment by employment equity category in March 2008.

TABLE 14.1   PUBLIC SERVICE BY EMPLOYMENT EQUITY GROUPS, 2007–2008

	Women		Aboriginals		People with Disabilities		Members of a Visible Minority Group		Total
	Number	%	Number	%	Number	%	Number	%	Number
Executive	2 042	41.7	165	3.4	278	5.7	326	6.7	4 898
Scientific & Professional	12 385	45.3	697	2.5	1 094	4.0	3 662	13.4	27 350
Administrative & Foreign Service	55 832	61.8	4 121	4.6	5 554	6.2	8 533	9.5	90 284
Technical	5 663	32.5	612	3.5	896	5.1	1 106	6.3	17 422
Administrative Support	21 719	80.9	1 395	5.2	2 093	7.8	2 730	10.2	26 849
Operational	3 948	19.8	1 200	6.0	1 086	5.4	850	4.3	19 951
Total	101 589	54.4	8 190	4.4	11 001	5.9	17 207	9.2	186 754

Source: Employment Equity in the Public Service of Canada 2006–2007 and 2007–2008. Found at: http://www.tbs-sct.gc.ca/rp/0608ee06-eng.asp. Treasury Board of Canada Secretariat, 2008. Reproduced with the permission of the Minister of Public Works and Government Services Canada, 2009.

Interaction with Provinces and Advocacy Groups

Much of the interaction between federal and provincial governments takes place at the bureaucratic level. Because the division of powers is rather vague and because both federal and provincial personnel often try to maximize their jurisdiction, the two levels end up operating programs in the same fields. Limitations on provincial finances have in some cases prompted the provinces to request federal financial assistance. When Ottawa agreed to such demands, it usually attached conditions to the expenditure of the funds, making the two levels of government even more intertwined.

The close relationship between advocacy groups and the bureaucracy was discussed in Chapter 10. Groups wishing to influence either the formulation or the implementation of policies and programs are active in taking their message to the relevant government department. Sometimes public servants resist the efforts of self-interested groups, but the department is generally more receptive if the group has vital, reliable information that may lead to the development of a more effective program or can help muster support for the departmental initiative among other key players in the policymaking process.

Crown Corporations

The second most important form of bureaucratic organization is the **Crown corporation**. Crown corporations are government-owned operations that assume a structure similar to that of private corporations. There are about 40 major Crown corporations at the federal level, including

- Atomic Energy of Canada Ltd. (AECL)
- Business Development Bank of Canada
- Canada Mortgage and Housing Corporation
- Canada Post Corporation
- Canadian Broadcasting Corporation
- VIA Rail Canada Inc.

The largest in terms of employees are Canada Post (61 557), the Canadian Broadcasting Corporation (7 784), AECL (4 728), and VIA Rail (3 017).

One major difference between a Crown corporation and a regular government department is its organizational structure. A Crown corporation includes a board of directors, president, vice-presidents, etc. The Cabinet appoints the president as well as the board of directors, who theoretically set the general policy of the corporation. Many Crown corporation presidents have been appointed on a patronage basis, but after ridding itself of several of them for various reasons, including the sponsorship scandal in Quebec, the Martin government pledged that their replacements would be selected on the basis of merit.

A second distinguishing feature of the Crown corporation is that it is not subject to day-to-day political direction. The statute that creates it sets out its objectives to some extent, and while the Cabinet may issue general policy guidelines, the corporation otherwise operates more or less independently. The Cabinet minister to whom the Crown corporation is attached acts largely as a channel of communication between it and Parliament, passing on answers to parliamentary inquiries but not being held responsible for the corporation in the same way as for a regular department. On the other hand, because the government creates the Crown corporation, appoints its leading personnel, and usually provides some of its funds, the minister and Cabinet cannot avoid complete responsibility for its actions.

Third, Crown corporations are freer of bureaucratic controls relating to personnel and finance than ordinary government departments. As a general rule, the greater the financial self-sufficiency of the corporation, the greater its autonomy. Crown corporations can therefore operate more flexibly than government departments, especially if they are in competition with private firms.

The Crown corporation is thus a logical structure for a governmental operation of a commercial or industrial nature. It may also be used in politically sensitive areas such as broadcasting, and/or if the operation has private sector competition. More specifically, Crown corporations have been created to promote national integration (VIA Rail, Canada Post, and Marine Atlantic), national identity (CBC and Canada Museums), a particular industry (Canadian Wheat Board), and business in general (Business Development Bank). Like other government operations, then, Crown corporations have a public policy purpose. They are created where, for one reason or another, the private sector has not met public needs.

Led by Margaret Thatcher in Britain, the 1980s witnessed a worldwide trend toward the **privatization** of public enterprises, and the Mulroney government happily jumped on the bandwagon. Privatizations were largely made for two ideological reasons: the government had an instinctive preference for the private sector, and the sale of Crown corporation shares helped to reduce the national deficit. Privatizers also argued that such Crown corporations no longer served a public policy purpose and that they would operate more efficiently as private companies. The Chrétien government also did its share of privatization, such that by the beginning of the 21st century, the following major Crown corporations were no

The Trudeau government created Petro-Canada as a Crown corporation and the Mulroney government privatized it.
(The Canadian Press/Chuck Stoody)

longer owned by government: Air Canada, Canadian National Railway, Eldorado Nuclear, Fishery Products International, Petro-Canada, Teleglobe Canada, and Telesat.

Administrative Agencies

Administrative agencies, including **regulatory tribunals**, are the third basic form of bureaucratic organization. Such agencies regulate many aspects of our daily lives. Some of the most important among them are the

- Canadian Nuclear Safety Commission,
- Canadian Food Inspection Agency,
- Canadian Human Rights Commission,
- Canadian Radio-television and Telecommunications Commission (CRTC),

- Canada Revenue Agency,
- Canadian Transportation Agency,
- Immigration and Refugee Board,
- National Energy Board, and
- National Parole Board.

In structure, administrative agencies and regulatory tribunals bear considerable resemblance to Crown corporations. They comprise a chair and board appointed by the Cabinet, and are advised by a permanent, expert staff. The incidence of partisanship in appointments to the chair and board is unfortunately quite large; indeed, these agencies remain one of the last refuges of patronage in the political system. Such agencies and tribunals typically receive policy guidelines from the Cabinet, but as with Crown corporations, ministers are kept at arm's length from their day-to-day operations.

The Harper government had a troubled relationship with many administrative agencies. It cancelled the mandatory long-form 2011 Census and replaced it with a voluntary survey, which precipitated the resignation of the Chief Statistician. It dismissed or maligned several agency, commission, and Crown corporation heads (and other senior bureaucrats) including the heads of the Military Police Complaints Commission, the Nuclear Safety Commission, the RCMP Public Complaints Commission, the Canadian Wheat Board, the Information Commissioner, the Chief Electoral Officer, the Parliamentary Budget Officer, and the Veterans' Ombudsman.

Administrative agencies and regulatory tribunals may make quasi-legislative rules and regulations, such as in the case of the Canadian-content regulations of the CRTC. A typical regulatory agency also makes quasi-judicial decisions based on the Cabinet's policy guidelines and its own regulations. Among other things, regulatory agencies decide contentious immigration cases (Immigration and Refugee Board), review transportation rates (Canadian Transportation Agency), approve exports of natural gas and electricity (National Energy Board), and allow prisoners out of jail (National Parole Board).

These functions could presumably be performed by regular government departments, but they are given to semi-independent agencies in order to divorce them from political and partisan considerations. Such adjudicative functions could also be performed by the courts, but these kinds of decisions demand a technical expertise not expected of judges. Moreover, given the backlog in the court system, it is hoped that the decisions of administrative agencies and regulatory tribunals will be made more quickly and more cheaply than those of the courts.

At the same time, however, regulatory agencies are expected to provide an impartial, court-like hearing, and in many cases lawyers are present in their proceedings in the same capacity as in court. Decisions of such agencies are normally appealable to the courts on procedural grounds but not on the substance of the case; some are appealable to the Cabinet.

Many observers have argued that there are too many regulatory agencies with too much power. Hence, **deregulation** was a companion ingredient to privatization in the neoconservatism (or neoliberalism) of the past 20 years. The Canadian transportation industry in particular was deregulated to a large extent.

Not all government operations fall into the three categories discussed above. Others include central agencies (e.g., PCO), royal commissions, advisory councils (e.g., National Council of Welfare), funding bodies (e.g., Social Sciences and Humanities Research Council), and agents of Parliament (Auditor General, Elections Canada, the Information Commissioner, and the Commissioner of Official Languages). One-of-a-kind agencies include Statistics Canada, the RCMP, the Correctional Service, and the Canadian Security Intelligence Service.

Controlling the Bureaucracy

Given the enormous influence and considerable power of the bureaucracy in the modern state, democracies are understandably concerned about keeping the public service under control. Some of the means of doing so are identified in Figure 14.2.

First, individual ministers and the Cabinet as a whole are supposed to provide political control of the bureaucracy. The minister gives direction to the public

Figure 14.2   Means of Controlling the Bureaucracy

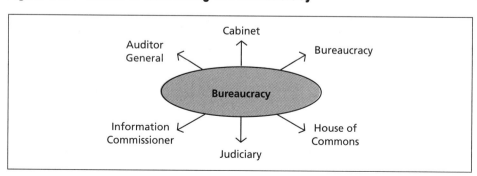

service and has the power to veto any of its proposals. Ministers have provided varied accounts of what happens in practice: some argue that they do control their departments, while others feel that they are manipulated by their public servants. In a more specialized context, civilian control of the military and police is an important principle in a democratic society.

The second line of defence against bureaucratic power is the House of Commons. One principle of parliamentary government is that the executive (Cabinet or bureaucracy) is not allowed either to raise or to spend money without Parliament's approval. In practice, proposals for tax changes as well as spending proposals all originate with the executive. They are rarely altered in the legislative process, and the taxing and spending usually begin before Parliament has given its consent. Examining the Estimates, however, gives the House of Commons an opportunity to question and criticize ministers and deputy ministers about all aspects of their departmental spending, programs, and policies. Furthermore, once the money has been spent, an independent official of Parliament, the **Auditor General**, provides a report on instances where funds were not spent properly.[13] The **Public Accounts Committee** of the House (chaired by an opposition member) goes through the Auditor General's reports and calls onto the carpet those ministers or deputy ministers who have committed the worst financial faults.

The Auditor General's staff function something like spies within the public service, recording any decisions or practices that are illegal, immoral, wasteful, or otherwise ill-advised. They now perform "legislative audits" that go well beyond traditional financial auditing. In the light of the Auditor General's revelation of financial improprieties in the Human Resources Development department, the firearms registry, and the sponsorship scandal in Quebec, the office of the Auditor Genera has now been accorded heroic status. Especially in the absence of other devices to ensure accountability in the spending of public funds, almost everyone is now prepared to give the Auditor General all the resources asked for.

The House of Commons has several other means of exercising some control over the bureaucracy, the first being the daily oral Question Period. In this case, the opposition members in the Commons criticize the minister, who is theoretically responsible for everything the department does. Although the minister is expected to take the blame for bureaucratic errors, public servants seek to avoid bringing such embarrassment or disrepute upon their minister and department. In addition, members of Parliament receive requests on a daily basis from their constituents to intervene on their behalf to speed up or correct bureaucratic decisions. MPs and their staff normally handle such problems with a telephone call or a letter to the public servant or minister concerned. Another aspect of parliamentary control of the bureaucracy is exercised by the Standing Joint Committee on the Scrutiny of Regulations, which attempts to review the reams of regulations that the bureaucracy produces annually.

A third kind of control of the bureaucracy is provided by the judiciary. The power of the courts to overturn decisions of bureaucrats in regular government departments is essentially restricted to cases of breaches of the law or actions taken beyond the public servant's jurisdiction. The Charter of Rights provides more scope for this kind of judicial review than existed in the past. In the *Singh* case, for example, the Supreme Court ruled that the Immigration Department had to provide an oral hearing for all refugee claimants rather than deport such claimants on the basis of written documents alone. Police officers are a special category of bureaucrats who have also had their professional behaviour severely restricted by judicial interpretation of the legal rights section and/or section 24 of the Charter, as noted in Chapter 11.

Regulatory agencies are usually expected to operate in a court-like manner, and their decisions can be overturned by the courts for procedural abuses as well as for exceeding their jurisdiction. The Federal Court of Canada, to be discussed in Chapter 16, specializes in hearing appeals from such regulatory agencies.

Finally, several independent watchdog agencies exist, the most important next to the Auditor General being the **Information Commissioner**. Canadian governments have traditionally functioned under a cloak of secrecy at both the cabinet and bureaucratic levels. This tradition prevented the opposition and the public from knowing what alternative policies had been considered, what kind of public opinion polling was done, or what advice was actually offered by the bureaucracy. The 1983 **Access to Information Act** considerably improved the situation, although the many exemptions in the act mean that it is not entirely effective. If a citizen, journalist, company, or advocacy group is denied access to a desired piece of government information, that person or organization can appeal to the Information Commissioner, who can overrule the department in the matter. The government can, however, appeal to the Federal Court, and in recent years that court has frequently sided with the government, especially the PMO, when the Information Commissioner supported more openness.

The sponsorship scandal and the Gomery Report inspired the Harper government's Federal Accountability Act in 2006, a mammoth document that affected almost every aspect of government operations. It made deputy ministers more accountable for the operation of their departments and created or strengthened independent agents of Parliament that would ensure that the politicians and bureaucrats operated at a higher ethical level than in the past. That included beefing up the "whistle-blower" legislation that the Martin government had introduced, after the public servant who first complained about the sponsorship scandal lost his job. This office is called the Public Sector Integrity Commissioner.

Reform of the Bureaucracy

Apart from the problem of keeping the bureaucracy under some kind of democratic control, three other problems or dysfunctions are often identified. First, from the public's perspective, the bureaucracy is accused of being bound up in "red tape." This generally includes a collection of sins that characterize the behaviour of all large organizations, not only governmental ones, including delays, a multitude of forms, excessive rules and regulations, difficulty in finding the appropriate official to solve a problem, and lack of helpful, personal attention. If these dysfunctions are more characteristic of government than of large private firms, it is primarily because governments are required to operate according to the law and the regulations issued under the law. Government must treat everyone in exactly the same way, and unlike private firms, it cannot show favouritism or make individual exceptions. Delays may be the result of public servants wanting to be certain that their decision is absolutely right because mistakes may be criticized in Parliament or in the media.

A second general criticism of bureaucracy is that it is inefficient because it lacks the profit motive of the private sector. Officials in private firms are said to move more quickly because they are in greater danger of losing their jobs and because minimizing costs is a higher priority. To some extent this is true, or at least may once have been. Given that the essential difference between the public and private sectors is that the bureaucracy is charged with providing a public service, however, it should be judged primarily on the adequacy of that service. Nevertheless, the widespread belief that there is much "fat" and inefficiency within the bureaucracy led both the Mulroney and Chrétien governments to impose severe financial restraints on government departments and Crown corporations, leading them to make across-the-board cuts, terminate programs, lay off staff, freeze hiring, charge user fees, and contract out certain services.[14] As a result, many of those employees left in the public service report higher levels of stress.

From a management point of view, the main dysfunction of the public service is that deputy ministers and other managerial personnel are too hemmed in by rules and regulations and their authority is too limited by central agencies. Several recent reforms have been introduced to provide more autonomy and managerial flexibility to deputy ministers by relaxing some of the detailed rules and reporting requirements.

One aspect of the neoliberalism or neoconservatism that swept the Western world between 1985 and 2000 specifically concerned the public service, and was called the **New Public Management (NPM)**. General factors leading to such proposals for public service reform included concern with debts and deficits, changing public and private sector expectations, globalization, new technologies, growing doubts about the capacity of state institutions to fulfill their mandates, and citizen demands for direct participation.[15]

The 1994 and 1995 federal budgets inaugurated a process generally labelled Program Review. This involved a fundamental rethinking of what government did and how it did it—or redefining the role of government.[16] Through this process, the federal government determined which activities it could continue to deliver or support within a much reduced budget. It also identified which activities it could cease providing, scale back, devolve, or deliver or finance differently. The process involved significant reductions in subsidy programs, increased user fees, and the provision of many government activities on a commercial basis. In the 1995 budget, the minister of finance declared his intention to eliminate 45 000 public service jobs by 1998 to help the government reduce its deficit.

Another part of NPM was called Alternative Service Delivery (ASD). ASD is a generic term covering a variety of innovative means of providing services that involve reducing the size and expense of government, making government more citizen-oriented, involving users in service delivery, providing more flexibility in service delivery, and incorporating new developments in information technology. ASD consists primarily of special operating agencies and developing partnerships with provinces or commercial or nonprofit organizations outside government.

Special operating agencies are units that function with relative autonomy within government departments. In most cases, they have the potential to become self-financing, and their objective is to deliver a service along private sector lines, that is, in a manner more sensitive to client requirements. Two of the first main partnership initiatives were the Canadian Food Inspection Agency and the Canada Revenue Agency (CRA).

The federal government may enter other kinds of partnerships with private firms (sometimes called public–private partnerships or P3s), nonprofit, noncommercial, or volunteer organizations. The government–private company relationship behind the construction and operation of the Confederation Bridge between Prince Edward Island and New Brunswick and the creation of local authorities to operate Canadian airports are prominent examples. Another is NAV CANADA, the agency created to replace the government's air traffic control system. Its board of directors includes representatives of the airlines, government, and employee unions, and it sets its rates so that it breaks even.

It should be said, however, that not everyone thinks the reality of NPM matches its rhetoric, and many observers do not believe it to be a good idea at all. For example, the whole movement stems from a preoccupation with cutting government expenditures, which involved the elimination of thousands of government jobs. Beyond the fact that fewer public servants are now delivering fewer public services is the troubling question of democratic accountability. It can be argued that with semi-independent partners of various kinds supplying public services, any semblance of democratic ministerial responsibility has been lost.

The latest innovation in government operations is "e-government," that is, making government information "electronic" and putting it online. Ottawa intends to be more electronically connected to its citizens than any other government in the world, with Canadians being able to access all government information and services on the Internet. Service Canada is the coordinating agency in this initiative.[17]

SUMMARY

This chapter began by showing that the bureaucracy plays a major part in almost every phase of the policymaking process. Even when the prime minister and Cabinet actually make decisions, the bureaucracy provides advice, and on many other occasions the bureaucracy makes decisions on its own. The chapter then analyzed the operation of the government department, distinguishing the roles of the minister and deputy minister. It showed that the minister, the deputy minister, and many bureaucrats are in regular contact with other departments and central agencies of the federal government as well as provincial departments and advocacy groups. It also discussed a major concern in staffing the bureaucracy: selecting the best people for the job while trying to accurately represent the society at large. The chapter then considered Crown corporations and administrative agencies, distinguishing their purposes, structures, and operations from those of regular government departments. The next section dealt with the methods of keeping the bureaucracy under some degree of democratic control. The chapter concluded with a discussion of other recent bureaucratic reforms.

DISCUSSION QUESTIONS

1. How can financial accountability in the public service be brought to an acceptable level?
2. To what extent should Canada establish a "representative bureaucracy"?
3. Given the necessity of the bureaucracy in the modern state, are the democratic controls on its power sufficient?
4. How do you feel about downsizing of the public service, privatization of Crown corporations, deregulation, and the various initiatives involved in the New Public Management?

KEY TERMS

Access to Information Act The 1983 act that gave citizens, journalists, and others the right to gain access to government documents, with certain exceptions, and established the office of Information Commissioner.

Auditor General The official of Parliament whose staff audit the expenditures of government departments and who reports on instances of funds being unlawfully or unwisely spent.

Bureaucracy The permanent officials employed by the government, also known as the public service.

Crown corporation A corporation owned by the government that assumes a structure similar to that of a private company and that operates semi-independently of the Cabinet.

Deputy minister The public servant who heads each government department, manages the department, and advises the minister.

Deregulation A government policy that removes previous regulations, especially those affecting the corporate sector.

Government department A government organization headed by a minister who is politically accountable for its operations and a deputy minister who is in charge of its hierarchical administrative apparatus.

Individual ministerial responsibility The principle that Cabinet ministers are individually responsible to the House of Commons to answer for everything that happens in their department.

Information Commissioner The official of Parliament who encourages government to operate on a more open basis and makes judgments in cases where departments withhold information under the Access to Information Act.

Merit system A system of hiring and promoting public servants on the basis of their merits (education, experience, etc.) rather than on party preference or other considerations.

New Public Management A movement within public administration since about 1990 that involved the downsizing of government operations, alternative service delivery, and partnerships with private or voluntary sector agencies.

Official Languages Act The 1969 federal act that established official bilingualism in Canada and gave citizens the right to deal with certain offices of the federal government in either English or French.

Political patronage Making appointments to public offices or awarding government contracts on a partisan basis.

Privatization Transferring a government program, agency, or Crown corporation to the private sector.

Public Accounts Committee The House of Commons committee that examines the Auditor General's reports and criticizes government officials for illegal or unwise expenditures.

Regulations The detailed rules drafted by the bureaucracy under the authority of laws passed by Parliament that are too voluminous and technical to put into the legislation itself.

Regulatory tribunal A government agency established to regulate an area of public policy, such as transportation or communications, which operates at arm's length from the Cabinet.

Representative bureaucracy A public service that reflects the composition of the population, with the most usual concerns being gender, ethnicity, and region.

Treasury Board Secretariat The government department that advises the Treasury Board in its deliberations and that functions as a restraining influence on departmental spending.

FURTHER READING

Barker, Paul. *Public Administration in Canada*. Toronto: Nelson Education, 2007.

Dunn, Christopher H., ed. *The Handbook of Canadian Public Administration*, 2nd ed. Toronto: Oxford University Press, 2010.

How Ottawa Spends. Toronto: Oxford University Press, annual.

Inwood, Gregory J. *Understanding Canadian Public Administration: An Introduction to Theory and Practice*, 3rd ed. Toronto: Prentice-Hall Canada, 2009.

Osbaldeston, Gordon. *Keeping Deputy Ministers Accountable*. Toronto: McGraw-Hill Ryerson, 1989.

Pal, Leslie A. *Beyond Policy Analysis: Public Issue Management in Turbulent Times*, 4th ed. Toronto: Nelson Education, 2010.

Privy Council Office. *Accountable Government: A Guide for Ministers and Ministers of State, 2008*. Ottawa: Government of Canada, 2006.

Savoie, Donald J. *Breaking the Bargain: Public Servants, Ministers, and Parliament*. Toronto: University of Toronto Press, 2003.

Chapter 15

Parliament

Although the term theoretically also includes the Queen and the Senate, the word **Parliament** is popularly synonymous with the House of Commons, by far its most important part. Hence, those elected to the House of Commons are called members of Parliament or MPs. The House of Commons is the central link between the public and the government in Canadian democracy; it is where the elected representatives of the people meet in daily, open, verbal combat. This chapter examines the House of Commons from a number of perspectives and later explores the role of the other branch of the legislature, the Senate.

Chapter Objectives

After you have completed this chapter, you should be able to:

Discuss the functions of the House of Commons and of its individual members within and beyond the policymaking process

Comment on the extent to which MPs are representative of the population

Outline the weekly and yearly parliamentary timetables

Evaluate the advantages and disadvantages of strict party discipline

Identify the different stages and kinds of legislation

Identify the various officers of the House of Commons

Discuss the committee system of the House

Comment on the various roles that MPs perform and on members' services

Discuss the balance between government and opposition, distinguishing between majority and minority situations

Enumerate the intended functions of the Senate and assess its performance

Discuss possible avenues of Senate reform

Functions and Powers of the House of Commons

The **Westminster model** of government employed by Canada begins with a bicameral **legislature**—an elected lower house, the House of Commons, with primary legislative powers and answerable to the people through elections, and an appointed upper house, the Senate, with limited legislative powers. The executive is part of the Commons and, through the Cabinet, drives or "energizes" the legislative process. The **government** or Cabinet is in charge of and is responsible for the conduct of parliamentary business, while an institutionalized opposition has the right and duty to criticize the government. This model therefore promises potent government and political stability through the Cabinet, along with political accountability through open debate. MPs can thus be divided into three main groups: those who serve as Cabinet ministers, those who support the Cabinet (government **backbenchers**), and those who oppose the government (the **opposition**).[1]

Historically, the sovereignty or **supremacy of Parliament** has been a basic principle of Canadian government. Apart from interfering in provincial jurisdiction and with other minor exceptions, Parliament could pass laws that were virtually beyond review by any other organ of government, including the courts. With the adoption of the Charter of Rights and Freedoms in 1982, however, this principle was considerably transformed. The courts' power of **judicial review** has been greatly extended and now includes the right to examine both federal and provincial legislation in terms of the Charter and to invalidate such legislation to the extent of any contradiction. On the other hand, rather than overturn a law, the courts have often suggested that the legislation be redrafted to fit within the boundaries of the Charter. As a last resort, the notwithstanding clause allows for the reassertion of parliamentary sovereignty on many points.

In discussing the functions of the House of Commons, it is instructive to examine its role in the chart of the policymaking process illustrated in Figure 13.1. First, Parliament may be involved in the initiation phase by raising issues in the daily Question Period and in general debates, in criticizing existing spending programs, or by means of private members' bills. It is then virtually nonexistent in the priority-setting and policy-formulation phases. However, the Commons dominates the legitimation stage. Whether or not bills are refined in the process, Cabinet proposals are made legitimate by their passage through the formal, authorized, democratic channels of the Commons. The House may not make many significant changes, but it does subject bills to extended debate and publicizes their advantages and disadvantages before converting them into laws or statutes. The legislative stage serves to inform the public of the content of new policies, and out of this "prolonged warfare," consent or acceptance is eventually obtained. This debate essentially prepares the electorate for its decision on how to vote in the next election.

Composition of the House of Commons

The basic principle of representation in the House of Commons is that each province is represented in proportion to its population. Chapter 8 outlined how the 308 seats in the Commons are distributed among the provinces, as shown in the box below. Shortly after the 2011 census, it is anticipated that the size of the Commons will increase to 338, with Ontario, B.C., and Alberta gaining 18, seven, and five seats respectively.

Seats in the House of Commons

Ontario	106	New Brunswick	10
Quebec	75	Newfoundland and Labrador	7
British Columbia	36	Prince Edward Island	4
Alberta	28	Nunavut	1
Manitoba	14	Northwest Territories	1
Saskatchewan	14	Yukon	1
Nova Scotia	11	**Total**	**308**

Even if members of Parliament other than Cabinet ministers have only a limited role in the policymaking process, the social background characteristics of ordinary members merit examination. To the extent that MPs are not representative of the population, certain issues are not likely to be addressed.

Since they are elected to represent territorial units and usually live in or near their constituencies, MPs almost automatically become representative of the population in a geographic sense. MPs are also fairly representative in terms of English and French ethnic backgrounds. The Constitution Act, 1867, required from the beginning that all House documents be printed in English and French, but the absence of simultaneous interpretation until 1958 and the unilingualism of most MPs served to limit interaction between the two linguistic groups.

On the other hand, members of Parliament do not reflect the population very well in terms of other ethnic origins, education, occupation, class, or gender. Although not as exclusive in these respects as Cabinet ministers, MPs have higher educational levels and higher-status occupations than the general population. Historically, the legal profession furnished the largest single group in the Commons, but since 1984 those with a business background have predominated. Next come educators, administrators, lawyers, and consultants. This change still leaves a gross underrepresentation of the working class.[2] Relatively few women have been elected to the House of Commons, although the number has increased in recent years, reaching 53 of 295 in 1993, 62 of 301 in 1997 and 2000, 65 of 308 in 2004, 64 in 2006, and 69 in 2008—just over 20 percent.

What is probably most striking about Canadian MPs, especially compared to members of other legislatures around the world, is their rapid turnover in office. There are relatively few **safe seats** in Canada, so that the proportion of new members after each election averages 40 percent, and the typical MP serves less than 10 years.[3] This is partly a reflection of the low degree of party identification among the electorate, and it means that few members remain in Parliament long enough to develop an understanding of the institution or to stand up to a long-serving prime minister. The 1993 turnover was over 75 percent, as a result of the decimation of the Conservatives and NDP; in 1997, it was over 30 percent; in 2000, 15 percent; in 2004, 35 percent; and 20 percent in each of 2006 and 2008.

The Parliament Buildings, Ottawa—the seat of the Government of Canada.
(The Canadian Press/Peter Bregg)

The Parliamentary Timetable

Perhaps the best way to get an overview of the work of the House of Commons is by examining the parliamentary timetable—the agenda of a typical session and a typical week.

The Typical Session

The normal practice is to have each session of Parliament last about one year. A session begins with the **Speech from the Throne**, prepared by the prime minister and read by the governor general. Its function is to outline the government's legislative plans for the session, and it introduces the Throne Speech debate, a six-day debate in which MPs can talk about anything that comes to mind. Party leaders and Cabinet ministers may use the occasion to articulate their priorities, while backbenchers often expound on the wonders or troubles of their constituency.

The second major event of the session is the **budget** and the budget debate. The minister of finance delivers the budget, a statement chiefly concerned with tax changes (the revenue side of the government's books) but also dealing with government finances in general. Among other things, the budget usually fleshes out the promises of the Speech from the Throne. The budget sets the stage for a four-day freewheeling debate and provides the opposition with a second opportunity to try to defeat the government. Legislation incorporating the specific tax changes mentioned in the budget comes along later, although the changes usually take effect as of budget night.

A third part of the session consists of the government's spending proposals for the next fiscal year, the **Estimates**. Once tabled, however, the Estimates are transmitted to standing committees of the House for scrutiny, so that they occupy little time of the Commons as a whole.

A fourth element of the session consists of the 22 **opposition days**, when the opposition parties choose the subject of debate and the government in turn responds. These are divided proportionally among the opposition parties and distributed throughout the session.

Other than these four components, the time of the House of Commons is taken up with the discussion of bills, and most of that time with bills introduced by the government. Indeed, it is partly because of the volume of government legislation that some sessions of Parliament exceed a year in length. Bills that have not been passed die at the end of the session, tempting governments to allow sessions to continue beyond one year until all current legislation is disposed of.

The Commons sits for about 135 days per year. When the government wishes to take a break within a session, it adjourns the House. When it wants to bring a session to an end, it prorogues the Commons, setting the stage for a new Speech from the Throne to initiate a new session. Finally, an election call results in the **dissolution of Parliament**.

In its routine usage, "prorogation" is not a dirty word. It merely ends one session of parliament and sets the stage for the beginning of another, involving a short break in parliamentary activity. It normally means that the work of the previous session has been completed and that a new Speech from the Throne will inaugurate a new set of government priorities. Like summoning and dissolving parliament, prorogation is a decision made by the government (i.e., the prime minister) of the day, subject to the approval of the governor general in very controversial cases.

Prorogation was hardly ever controversial until December 2008 when Stephen Harper asked the governor general to end a session which had only started a few weeks before; it was an obvious manoeuvre to avoid a scheduled non-confidence vote and to prevent an opposition-party coalition from taking power. It was an unusual situation, and in her wisdom, the governor general reluctantly agreed to the prorogation. As mentioned in Chapter 13, the 2009–10 prorogation was also somewhat questionable.

The Typical Week

The House begins its sessions at 11 a.m. on Monday and meets at 10 a.m. on the other four weekdays. The most exciting part of the day is the 45-minute oral **Question Period**. It is this period that offers the opposition its best opportunity to criticize and embarrass the government, as it grills Cabinet ministers about their deficiencies and faults. Ministers are not given notice of such questions, but before going into the chamber they are briefed by aides who try to anticipate what questions might be asked. Even greater daily effort goes into the preparation and rehearsal of questions by opposition party leaders and their staff. The **Leader of the Opposition** and the leaders of any other recognized parties begin the attack, and the Speaker of the House distributes the opportunity to ask questions to various opposition parties in a rough proportion to their numbers. Since ministers often respond in a deliberately vague manner, several supplementary questions are allowed, but the objective of the opposition is not so much to elicit information as to portray the government in a negative light. Such exchanges, along with corridor interviews and hallway "scrums" based on Question Period, find their way onto the television news and form the backbone of media reporting on the House. Government backbenchers are also allowed to participate, but they usually ask "planted" questions to which relieved ministers give prepared and self-serving replies.

Immediately before Question Period, 15 minutes are set aside for "members' statements," during which individual MPs have 60 seconds to get something off their chests. After Question Period, unless the House is involved in one of the special events—the Throne Speech or budget debates or an opposition day—the regular business is the discussion of government orders, usually government bills. Government bills are those introduced by a Cabinet minister with the full backing of the Cabinet, and these debates are the basic routine of Commons life. At this point in the day most of the **parliamentary press gallery** and MPs leave the chamber in search of more pressing or more interesting activity (often to attend committee meetings). The speeches in these debates are generally dull and boring, and the public and media can hardly be blamed for paying so little attention to them when MPs themselves rarely listen to each other. The few members assigned to make up quorum on any day are more likely to be answering their mail, texting on their Blackberries, reading the newspaper, or working on their laptops.

Only five hours a week are reserved for private members' bills and motions, at the normal rate of one hour per bill. These bills and motions, introduced either by government supporters who are not in the cabinet or by opposition members, are usually of little interest to anyone else.

Finally, the adjournment proceeding is a half-hour opportunity at the end of the daily sitting (6:30 to 7 p.m.) four times a week for opposition MPs to pursue issues that they feel were inadequately answered in the Question Period. Ministers usually send their **parliamentary secretary**—an MP assigned to help them in any way they see fit—to fill in for them when called to account so late in the day.

Given the sharply adversarial nature of Question Period and the dullness of the rest of the parliamentary day, television coverage of the House of Commons does little to enhance the public's support of the government or politicians in general. On the other hand, some defend "the all-consuming ritual of adversarial combat completely dominated by political parties."[4] It serves the functions of keeping government conduct under constant surveillance and presents a clear-cut picture to the electorate of which party is responsible for everything that has been done. In an ideal situation, it also identifies an alternative government.

Party Discipline and the Caucus

The most striking aspect of the operation of the House of Commons is probably that everything is organized along party lines and that **party discipline** is so rigid. Almost all members belong to one party or another, and with rare exceptions, the MPs of each party vote together. Why is it that members of Parliament so consistently toe the party line?

The most obvious reason for party discipline, at least on the government side of the House, is the system of **responsible government**. It is commonly, but mistakenly, believed that if the Cabinet is defeated on a major measure, it must resign or call an election; therefore, its backbenchers must always ensure that Cabinet proposals are passed. Until such time as the principle of responsible government is interpreted more flexibly, government supporters will always be pressured to put party loyalty ahead of their own views or those of their constituents. That kind of reform might be accomplished by regarding a limited number of non-confidence motions as really critical, and then allowing the Cabinet to carry on in spite of the occasional defeat of a piece of legislation—a mode of operation characteristic of Britain.

Several other reasons can be cited to explain why MPs stick together with party colleagues in parliamentary votes. One is the tendency of people who belong to a political party to see things in a similar light—a natural cohesiveness common to most organized groups. Related to this cohesiveness are an equally natural deference to the leadership of the party and a desire to present an image of party unity to the public. In addition, MPs are encouraged to support the party line because of the prospects of promotion. Government backbenchers who are well behaved can become committee chairs, parliamentary secretaries, or Cabinet ministers, while even opposition party members can be moved up to more important responsibilities, such as into their party's "shadow cabinet." Members also want to participate in the distribution of perks available in parliamentary life, especially opportunities to travel at public expense, which are generally in the control of the party whips. Another inducement is to receive full support of the party organization in the next election, including campaign funds and a visit by the party leader. Moreover, given the high turnover rate, many MPs depend on the government to provide them with employment if they suffer defeat. The ultimate sanctions for disloyal behaviour are expulsion from the party caucus and denial of the party label in the next election. For all these reasons, parties vote as blocs and a government with a majority of seats in the Commons feels confident that it can get parliamentary approval for almost anything it wants.

In modern times, Jean Chrétien took a particularly hard line on party discipline. For example, despite concessions made to Liberal dissenters and other opponents of his government's gun control bill, three backbenchers voted against it due to pressure from their constituents. The PM quickly retaliated by removing them from their committee assignments. When veteran MP Warren Allmand voted against the 1995 budget because it dismantled historic Liberal social programs, the prime minister removed him from his committee chair position. Chrétien vowed not to sign the nomination papers of Liberal candidates in the next election if they had voted against government measures.

Jean Chrétien took a hard line on party discipline.
(The Canadian Press/Adrian Wyld)

As Chrétien moved closer to retirement, his power over the Liberal caucus declined. In an unprecedented and humiliating revolt in 2002, 55 Liberal backbenchers broke with the government to ensure the passage of an opposition motion to allow standing committees to elect their own chairs by secret ballot rather than have them imposed by the PMO. This was actually part of a package of proposals to reduce the "democratic deficit" in the operation of the House of Commons put forward by Chrétien's rival, Paul Martin. When Martin became prime minister in 2003, he introduced a new approach toward party discipline in Canada, which consisted of three alternatives for voting in the Commons. A three-line vote indicated that Liberal MPs had to support the government; a two-line vote told MPs how the government wanted them to vote, but private members were allowed to dissent; and a one-line vote was a **free vote**, even for ministers. The assumption was that most bills would fall into the second category, with only votes of confidence and a limited number of matters of fundamental importance to the government being considered three-line votes. When minority governments followed the 2004, 2006, and 2008 elections, with constant threats of government defeat, this initiative was unfortunately discontinued.

Martin's reforms reflected increased pressure to allow greater opportunity for MPs to represent the interests of their constituencies rather than slavishly following the dictates of the party. Rare free votes have been held on such subjects as capital punishment, abortion, and same-sex marriage. While few would argue against a little more autonomy and freedom for the individual MP, free-vote advocates and opponents of party discipline sometimes fail to appreciate the merits of an executive-centred system. Forcing MPs to toe the party line has allowed the executive to pursue a collectivist public interest beyond the narrow interests of constituencies, provinces, and other pressures, and it has permitted Canadian governments to be more activist and welfare-oriented than legislature-centred systems such as that of the United States.[5] Party discipline protects MPs individually and collectively from the threats of single-interest pressure groups and lobbyists, and it promotes the accountability of the government party to the electorate. It also frees the prime minister from time-consuming negotiations with individual MPs. Given the Canadian tradition, it is unlikely that party discipline will ever be loosened excessively, and it remained particularly tight under Stephen Harper, except for a "free vote" on whether to revisit the issue of same-sex marriage. Both the Liberals and Conservatives ejected an MP from their caucus for voting against the party on the 2007 budget.

To balance the public display of party discipline, MPs are allowed to speak their mind in the secrecy of the **party caucus**.[6] The caucus consists of all the elected members of each party (and such senators who choose to attend) who meet behind closed doors on Wednesday mornings. In the case of the government party, the prime minister and Cabinet ministers attend such meetings, unlike in Britain. In a typical government caucus meeting of over 150 MPs the opportunity to make an effective contribution is obviously limited. As in the case of Cabinet secrecy, however, members occasionally "leak" caucus information for their own benefit. Provincial and regional caucus meetings of each party are often held before the general caucus meeting, and caucus committees are sometimes appointed.

Stages and Kinds of Legislation

The great bulk of legislation introduced takes the form of **public bills**. These are general legislative proposals, such as the Income Tax Act or the Employment Insurance Act, that affect all Canadians. Most public bills (and all **money bills**, that is, the bills involving the raising or spending of money) are sponsored by the government and introduced by a Cabinet minister, thereby being titled **government bills**. As noted earlier, most of the weekly and yearly agenda is taken up with such government business.

However, a certain amount of time (now five hours per week) is set aside for members who are not in the Cabinet to introduce legislation and motions of their own. Since these MPs (on whichever side of the House) are private members, their proposals are called **private members' bills**. These bills are still of a general nature, such as those attempting to restore capital punishment, but they rarely reach the statute books. Historically, the most that private members could hope for was that the Cabinet might incorporate their ideas into a government bill. Since 1992, however, provision has been made for a more in-depth examination of a random sample of 30 private members' bills and motions per session. They are each given two hours of debate and can come to a vote. Then, if successful, they can continue in the regular legislative channels. Examples of private members' bills that made it to the statute books include those acknowledging non-smokers' rights, changing the name of Trans-Canada Airlines to Air Canada, designating the beaver as a symbol of Canadian sovereignty, recognizing hockey as Canada's national winter sport and lacrosse as our national summer sport, eliminating the excise tax on jewellery, and changing the names of electoral districts.

Private bills, on the other hand, refer to a specific person or corporation. Certain divorces used to be effected by act of Parliament and took the form of private bills, although today this category consists mostly of bills incorporating companies or other organizations. Private bills now originate in the Senate and occupy very little of the Commons' time.

Turning to the stages of the legislative process, the first requirement is for three readings in each chamber. Most government bills originate in the Commons, although, with the exception of money bills, they may be first introduced in the Senate. First reading simply means that a bill has been introduced—it is tabled, printed, and made public—and may be briefly explained. Some days later, the bill comes up for second reading. This stage involves a debate on the principle of the bill and may last several days. A favourable vote at the end of the second-reading debate means that the bill has been approved in principle.

Even if the opposition has little chance of defeating a bill, it may hope that prolonged exposure of the flaws in the legislation will persuade the government to amend it. Failing that, public opinion can be aroused via media coverage so that the electorate will remember the debate when the next election occurs. Excessive opposition debate is called a **filibuster**, but government and opposition rarely agree on what is excessive. The counterpart of the filibuster is **closure**, a rule allowing a majority government to cut off debate. Although the closure rule has been used quite routinely in recent years, a more civilized procedure is for the government to negotiate with the opposition over the time to be allocated to debating various issues.

Figure 15.1   Legislative Process in the Canadian Parliament

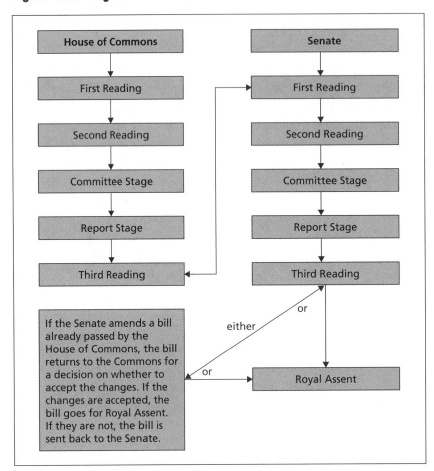

After second reading, a bill goes to committee, where it is examined in detail. In the small, informal confines of a Commons committee, the bill is scrutinized and voted on clause by clause, while ministers, public servants, advocacy groups, and other experts may be called upon for explanations or criticisms. After being approved, sometimes with amendments, the bill is reported back to the House in what is called the Report stage. This gives all members of the House, not just those on the committee, an opportunity to propose amendments. On a few occasions in recent years, hundreds of amendments were moved at the Report stage of a bill (e.g., by the Bloc Québécois in the case of the Clarity Act), resulting in the creation of a new delaying tactic. Once a bill has been approved at the Report stage, it goes to third reading for a final, overall appraisal.

As part of his package of Commons reforms, Paul Martin promised to send most two- and one-line vote bills to committee after first reading, rather than after they had been approved in principle. To allow the committee to debate the principle of the bill would allow more scope for both government backbenchers and opposition MPs to contribute to the shape of the legislation. This reform did not become institutionalized.

Assuming that the bill started in the Commons, it must then go through the same procedure in the Senate. In the rare case that the Senate amends a bill already approved by the Commons, the bill will have to go back to the lower house to see if it is acceptable in its amended form. Once a bill is passed in identical terms by both houses, it is given royal assent by the governor general or a Supreme Court judge acting as "deputy governor general." It then becomes a law or statute, although it may not be immediately proclaimed.

This may seem like an overly complicated process, but each stage has a distinctive purpose, and most bills must be debated for some time before the media and public begin to pay attention to them. Besides being necessary to engender eventual public knowledge of and consent to the law, reasonably lengthy consideration of the merits and faults of the bill serves to help the electorate gradually make up its mind about whether to re-elect the government that introduced such legislation or to opt for an opposition party that criticized it effectively.

Officers and Procedure of the Commons

The Speaker

The leading official of the House of Commons is the presiding officer, the **Speaker**, for whom deputy or acting speakers can substitute in the chair. The Speaker interprets and enforces the written rules of the Commons, called the **Standing Orders**,[7] plus unwritten traditions, practices, and conventions. The powers of the Speaker include recognizing which member can speak, and ruling on whether motions are in order, whether debate is relevant, whether questions are urgent, and whether an unruly MP should be expelled. It is therefore important for the person selected to be competent and impartial. Unfortunately, Speakers used to be chosen by prime ministers from among their party's MPs and thus carried the suspicion of being biased in favour of the government. In 1986, a major change was adopted that allowed MPs to choose their own Speaker by secret ballot. Two years later, the Speaker was given new authority to suspend unruly members from the chamber.

The Speaker can vote only in the case of a tie and cannot articulate the needs of his or her constituency or constituents in the Commons as such. In compensation for this silence, ministers and bureaucrats are especially sensitive to the concerns that the Speaker discusses with them outside the chamber.

House Leaders, Party Whips, and Clerks

From within their ranks, each party selects a House leader and a party whip. The government **House leader** is a Cabinet minister who manages the government's business in the Commons. This minister seeks to work out an agenda for House business with the opposition party House leaders, who function as procedural strategists for their parties. It is a credit to the House leaders that the Commons has functioned as well as it has, seeing that it has been occupied by four or five official parties since 1997, and minority governments since 2004.

Party whips are responsible for ensuring that their party's members are present for important votes and that they vote the right way.[8] Whips must therefore know the whereabouts of all their party's MPs at all times. Whips also distribute members' offices, assign members to parliamentary committees, and line up the order of party speakers in Question Period and debates. It is largely through the whips that party leaders impose discipline on their members. Members' opportunities to speak, to serve on the committee of their choice, and to travel as part of parliamentary delegations are largely influenced by their degree of party loyalty. In return, whips seek out backbench opinion on various matters and transmit it to the party leadership.

The principal permanent official of the Commons is the Clerk of the House, a position analogous to a deputy minister in a government department. As chief procedural adviser to the Speaker and manager of the support staff attached to the Commons, the Clerk is also required to act in a totally nonpartisan manner. Figure 15.2 shows the layout of the Commons chamber.

Procedure in the Commons

Votes in the Commons are taken orally when the Speaker invites members to say "aye" or "nay." When either side wants a formal recorded vote, it requests a **division**. In this case, the division bells ring until the government and official opposition party whips agree that all their available members have arrived, at which time a

Figure 15.2   The Layout of the House of Commons Chamber

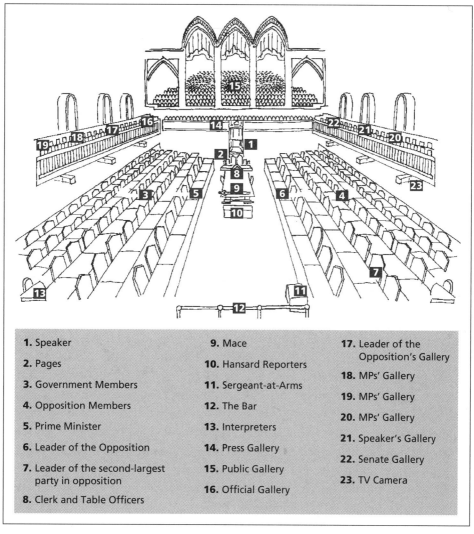

1. Speaker
2. Pages
3. Government Members
4. Opposition Members
5. Prime Minister
6. Leader of the Opposition
7. Leader of the second-largest party in opposition
8. Clerk and Table Officers
9. Mace
10. Hansard Reporters
11. Sergeant-at-Arms
12. The Bar
13. Interpreters
14. Press Gallery
15. Public Gallery
16. Official Gallery
17. Leader of the Opposition's Gallery
18. MPs' Gallery
19. MPs' Gallery
20. MPs' Gallery
21. Speaker's Gallery
22. Senate Gallery
23. TV Camera

Source: Reproduced with permission of the Library of Parliament/Bibliothéque du Parlement.

standing, recorded vote is conducted. It used to be that if either whip refused to give the go-ahead, the bells could ring indefinitely, but after the two-week "bell-ringing incident" of 1982, a 30-minute limit was adopted in 1986. A new procedure in 1994 allowed for divisions to be deferred, with all-party consent, to a more appropriate time of the week.

The length of MPs' speeches has been severely curtailed over the past 20 years. The 1982 reforms generally shortened them from 40 minutes to 20, but this depends on who is speaking, in what debate, and at what stage of the debate. As a debate drags on, the maximum length is reduced to ten minutes.

The Committee System

Much important legislative work of the House takes place outside the Commons chamber in a variety of committees. Committees allow a small number of people to develop expertise in a particular field and to examine proposals in depth; moreover, if several committees operate simultaneously, a greater volume of business can be accomplished. Committees allow private members to make constructive contributions to the governing of the country and sometimes operate in a consensual rather than adversarial atmosphere. Repeated reforms since 1968 have made the Canadian Commons committee system more significant.[9]

Standing committees are set up more or less permanently in most of the substantive areas of government policy, such as health and finance, largely paralleling government departments. They have two principal functions: to peruse the Estimates, that is, the government's spending proposals, and to examine legislation at the committee stage. The Estimates of the Department of Health, for example, are scrutinized by the Standing Committee on Health. In studying bills clause by clause after second reading, committees question ministers, public servants, advocacy groups, and other expert witnesses. Standing committees are also authorized to investigate any aspect of the department with which they are associated. Committees have a budget to hire a clerk, supporting staff, and researchers, and thus to develop independent expertise. The Standing Committee on Finance is perhaps most important, and it now engages in extensive pre-budget consultations.

Standing committees have varied in size over time, most of them currently being composed of 11 or 12 members. Because they often have a number of different issues on their agenda, they may also set up subcommittees. Representation on all committees is proportional to party standings in the House. Although chairs were always elected by committee members, they used to be preselected by the PMO so that most retained more loyalty to the PM than to the committee itself. As mentioned, a procedural change in 2002 allowed committees to elect their chairs by secret ballot, although most still come from the government side. The main exception to this is the **Public Accounts Committee**, which normally has a government majority but has been chaired by an official opposition MP since 1958. It has the important function of examining the report of the **Auditor General**, the official of Parliament who audits the government's accounts.[10]

Special committees are set up temporarily for some specific, special purpose. They usually have an investigatory function—to examine an issue before the government has determined how to deal with it.

In addition to the standing and special committees of the House of Commons alone, the Commons and Senate sometimes work together in joint committees. Joint committees avoid duplication and give senators a chance to get involved at an earlier stage of the process than is usually the case. The most important joint standing committee is that on the Scrutiny of Regulations. It has the vital but unenviable responsibility of scrutinizing the mounds of regulations and other subordinate legislation issued by the executive branch each year, and it can recommend that offensive delegated legislation be rescinded.

Finally, there is the "committee of the whole." This is simply the entire Commons membership sitting in the chamber as a committee. In such a case, the Speaker is replaced in the chair by the deputy speaker, and the rules are relaxed somewhat. This committee is only used to debate appropriation bills (once the Estimates have been approved) and certain non-controversial or emergency bills, preference otherwise being given to smaller committees that can meet simultaneously in rooms outside the Commons chamber.

The transformation of the committee system in recent years has enhanced the position of backbench MPs in the legislative process. Committees that are small and stable in their membership become more expert in their field, and as their members develop greater collegiality, they sometimes shed a good deal of their partisanship. After 1986, for example, many committees developed a consensus on the issues before them that cut across party lines, becoming newly independent sources of power in the legislative system. This led to the acceptance of an unprecedented number of amendments to government bills. After 1993, unfortunately, it was more difficult to gain a consensus among four or five different parties, and many became intensely partisan.

Members' Roles and Services

The roles that members of Parliament perform can be seen in two different lights. First, in terms of how they vote, MPs can be classified as trustees, constituency delegates, or party delegates. "Trustees" are MPs who feel obliged to vote according to their own conscience, their own understanding of the issue in question, or their own conception of the national interest. "Constituency delegates," on the other hand, are MPs who vote the way they think a majority of their constituents want them to. "Party delegates" are those who vote as directed by the party leader and party whip.

Backbenchers sometimes face the dilemma of opposing the party and risking discipline or opposing their constituents and risking electoral defeat. Historically, in this situation, MPs have rarely deviated from the party line: if the party's position conflicted with either their own views or those of their constituents, MPs have almost always been obliged to put the party position first. As mentioned, however, Paul Martin was at least temporarily more lenient in imposing party discipline.

The other way to examine the roles of MPs is in terms of how they spend their time or determine their priorities. The first role in this respect is the "lawmaker"—devoting attention to the legislative process by introducing, amending, and debating legislation. MPs are supported in these tasks by the Research Branch of the Library of Parliament.[11] Since this role is almost irrelevant to their constituents, MPs are more likely to spend time promoting their constituency to bring it public favours in what could be called a "representational" role. These members lobby ministers and public servants for new public buildings, roads, wharves, and other job-creation facilities, so that they will have something "concrete" to show for themselves by the time of the next election. Finally, MPs function as "ombudsmen" or social workers for their individual constituents, intervening with ministers or public servants to hasten administrative decisions, correct bureaucratic errors, and repair governmental injustices. There will always be constituents with passport, immigration, employment insurance, pension, and many other kinds of problems. This "caseload" of MPs is now so heavy that they are provided with considerable administrative assistance in their Ottawa and constituency offices. David Docherty estimates that constituency work takes up about 35 percent of the average MP's time, and recommends that more resources at the local level would free them up for policy and legislative functions.[12]

In 2001, MPs received a pay raise, which increased their salaries and added an annual inflation factor, to about $160 000 by 2011. On top of this basic income, a large number of MPs received additional payments for supplementary responsibilities. Combining these two payments, for example, the prime minister receives about $320 000, and the Speaker, Cabinet ministers, and Leader of the Opposition over $200 000.

In addition to their basic pay, MPs receive many benefits and services at public expense. They are provided with parliamentary and constituency offices, together with equipment and supplies; they have an annual staff allowance of approximately $300 000; and they have virtually unlimited telephone, mailing, and travel privileges. Recognized parties in the House—that is, groups of at least 12 members—receive substantial annual funding for research purposes, the loss of which was a major blow to the Conservatives and NDP between 1993 and 1997.

The MPs' pension plan has raised much controversy because many observers felt that it was too generous, and in 1995 some of its provisions were changed for newly elected MPs. They would have to wait until age 55 to collect, they could not "double-dip" (collect their pension at the same time as a salary from some other government job), and those who thought the plan was too generous could opt out entirely. Few did!

What Do You Think?

How much should members of Parliament be paid? And how should the amount be determined? Should their pay be equivalent to that of truck drivers, professors, nurses, judges, or public servants?

The Government–Opposition Balance and Parliamentary Reform

An objective look at Parliament reveals a basic dilemma: the government wants legislation passed expeditiously, but the opposition must have the time to criticize government proposals in order to make the public aware of their defects, as well as to articulate constituency needs.

When the government has a majority of seats in the Commons, the Cabinet operates as a virtual dictatorship until it has to face the electorate again some four or five years down the road. The opposition can do little more than criticize and delay government legislation, taking advantage of Question Period, media scrums, and the introduction of amendments. The imbalance of resources between government and opposition is dramatic, and the rules of the Commons are stacked in the government's favour. As the Auditor General reported in 2001, the government does not even provide Parliament with enough information to evaluate the results of public programs.

Many observers who deplore the arrogance of a **majority government** and regret that so much opposition talent and so many opposition ideas ordinarily go to waste prefer a **minority government**.[13] In this situation—where the government is outnumbered by opposition members—it may have to negotiate with opposition parties to some extent, such as to amend government proposals, abandon them, or even accept opposition initiatives. Between 1867 and 2011, there were 28 majority governments and 12 minority governments in Canada; few of the latter could have been called weak and indecisive. Many were more active and courageous than the majority governments that preceded or followed them. Some were exceptionally bold and decisive, especially the Pearson governments (responsible for the Canada Pension Plan, the flag, medicare, and cooperative federalism) and the Trudeau minority, which was particularly sensitive to opposition demands with respect to regulating election finance, screening foreign investment, and creating Petro-Canada. Although minority governments admittedly did not last as long as majority governments, not all of them ended in defeat; some ceased when the prime minister

"Stephen Harper pulls Parliament with his tricycle." (John Larter/Artizans.com)

decided to call an election with the hope of obtaining a majority. In the modern era, with the Bloc siphoning off a substantial number of seats in Quebec, and the NDP taking a significant number in pockets across the country, it is unlikely that either Liberals or Conservatives can win a majority government. After the 2004, 2006, and 2008 elections, for example, Canada experienced minority governments led by Paul Martin and Stephen Harper respectively. Harper was able to run his governments as if he had a majority, however, because the opposition parties were afraid of precipitating an election. In 2008, he even managed to out-manoeuvre an attempt by the other parties to form a coalition government.

Because of the imbalance between government and opposition in a majority situation, and because the legislative role of ordinary MPs has been so ineffective, parliamentary reform is never far from the minds of political scientists and politicians alike. Reform proposals are designed to remedy excessive partisanship, Cabinet domination, and private members' lack of influence. These proposals commonly take the form of reducing party discipline, allowing more free votes, and giving greater powers to committees, and as indicated, minor changes in these areas have been made.

The questions of operating in a minority government situation and reforming the House of Commons lead to a discussion of the principle of responsible government, which declares that if the Cabinet loses the confidence of the Commons it must call an election or resign. But it is not always clear whether the Cabinet is required to take such drastic action. In a majority situation, the problem is most unlikely to arise, but when the government is in a minority position, does it have to resign or call an election over any and every defeat? The Standing Orders are silent on this point, and any doubts about it were probably resolved by the 1968 incident in which the Pearson government was defeated on a piece of financial legislation. Pearson argued that the defeat was a fluke and that his government should be able to carry on. In that case, the matter was decided when the cabinet subsequently survived an explicit **non-confidence motion**. Any other case of dispute about whether a government has been defeated should probably be settled in the same manner.[14] In Britain, a majority government carries on despite the occasional defeat of a piece of its legislation, as long as it retains the confidence of the House on its overall performance.

In the Martin minority government, two bills were defeated by the opposition, but since the government did not consider these confidence votes, it ignored their defeat. The government was willing to amend its Speech from the Throne and budget in order to survive non-confidence motions related to them, and did so. This was a result of abstentions in the former case, and the Speaker breaking a tie in the latter, after Belinda Stronach crossed the floor from the Conservative to the Liberal ranks. But in November 2005, the Martin government was ultimately defeated on a straightforward non-confidence motion.

In the first few years of the Harper minority government, it was clear that no party would benefit from an early election call, so strategists for the various parties ensured that the government would not lose a significant vote. When a real threat of losing a non-confidence motion appeared at the end of 2008, Harper persuaded the governor general to prorogue parliament and give him time to prepare a proper budget.[15]

The most contentious government–opposition issue in 2010 concerned the release of documents on Afghan detainees. Opposition parties forced through a Commons motion ordering the Harper government to release uncensored copies of the documents, and when the government refused to do so, the Speaker of the House had to rule on a point of privilege that the government was in contempt of Parliament. Speaker Milliken declared that Parliament had a fundamental and unlimited right to order the production of government documents. But given their sensitive nature, he urged all parties to search for a compromise mechanism by which to make them available, and after weeks of behind-the-scenes wrangling, a small committee agreed on such a procedure, with the NDP dissenting.

The Senate

Purposes and Powers

The ideal of democracy was still not enthusiastically accepted in the 1860s. The Fathers of Confederation thus felt it advisable to provide for an appointed body that would exercise "sober second thought" with respect to measures emanating from the popularly elected House of Commons. The Senate was therefore to be the equivalent of the British House of Lords, an older, conservative influence, with a minimum age of 30, appointment for life, and a relatively high property qualification.[16]

Additionally, the smaller provinces would agree to join Confederation and accept representation by population in the House of Commons only if they were overrepresented in the Senate. The Fathers settled on a chamber that would be based on equal regional representation. Such a system gave the Maritimes and

Quebec (and later, the West) a limited amount of protection against the voting power held by Ontario in the House of Commons. It followed that senators were supposed to represent their regions and provinces within the national policy-making system.

A third function of the Senate, not explicitly provided for in 1867 but that can also be seen as part of the concept of sober second thought, is to improve legislation from a technical point of view. The Senate often acts as a routine revising chamber, picking up on flaws in legislation that have not been noticed during its passage through the busy Commons.

As far as powers were concerned, the Senate was given a veto over all legislation, a power not subsequently restricted as in the case of the British House of Lords. The only point of Senate inferiority to the Commons was that money bills had to be introduced in the lower chamber. Nevertheless, nothing in law prevented the Senate from delaying, amending, or vetoing any bills, whether or not they involved money.[17]

It was not until 1982 that the Senate's power was in any way reduced, and that had to do only with constitutional amendments, not ordinary legislation. According to the Constitution Act, 1982, the Senate can delay a constitutional amendment for only 180 days. If the Senate has defeated the constitutional amendment or not approved it by then, it can be re-passed by the Commons, after which it bypasses the Senate in the ratification process.

Composition of the Senate

Ontario, Quebec, and the Maritimes originally received 24 senators each. When Prince Edward Island joined Confederation, it received four of the 24 Maritime senators, reducing Nova Scotia's and New Brunswick's share to ten each. In a general reform in 1915, the West was designated as a senatorial region with 24 senators (six per province), preserving the principle of equal regional representation. In 1949, Newfoundland was awarded six senators in addition to the 96 already allotted, so as to leave the Maritime contingent intact. Finally, in 1975, the Yukon and Northwest Territories were given one senator each, as was Nunavut in 1999, so that the total became 105.

The 1867 Constitution Act gives the governor general the power to appoint senators, but by convention this is done on the advice of the prime minister. Prime ministers have almost always chosen partisan supporters, such as sitting MPs

Current Provincial and Territorial Representation in the Senate

Ontario	24	Saskatchewan	6
Quebec	24	Newfoundland and Labrador	6
Nova Scotia	10	Prince Edward Island	4
New Brunswick	10	Nunavut	1
Alberta	6	Northwest Territories	1
British Columbia	6	Yukon	1
Manitoba	6	**Total**	**105**

seeking a safer haven, defeated MPs or candidates, those who have served the party organization well, retired premiers or other provincial politicians, and federal Cabinet ministers who have outlived their usefulness. Hence, almost all of those appointed could be called "party hacks." In addition to rewarding faithful service to the party in the past, many appointments were made on the assumption that the new senator would continue to promote the party in the future. Such senators carried on as party fundraisers, party presidents, organizers, election campaign strategists or managers, or in other partisan capacities. Besides the partisan basis of their appointment, many senators have been held in low esteem because of their absenteeism and their corporate connections; occasional convictions for abusing their powers have also occurred.

The Constitution Act, 1867, speaks of "qualified persons" being eligible for appointment to the Senate, a term originally understood to include only men. In one of the most famous court cases in Canadian history, however, an enterprising group of women challenged this interpretation of "persons," and in 1929, the Judicial Committee of the Privy Council decided that "persons" did include women.[18] Thus, in recent years, increased consideration has been given to the appointment of women, as well as representatives of various minority ethnocultural communities.

Senators originally served for life, and many lived to a ripe old age before they died. Lester Pearson had a constitutional amendment passed in 1965 to the effect that incumbent senators could stay on until death (all of them gone by 1997) or retire at 75 with a pension; all subsequent appointees have had to retire at 75, but they do receive a pension at that point.

Operation of the Senate

If the original intentions of the Senate are obsolete or have not been fulfilled, today's senators justify their existence on other grounds. First, they point to the routine revision of bills in which the Senate engages, and some observers support the validity of their claim.[19] In addition to this function, the Senate sometimes undertakes protracted examination of complex legislation, such as the Bankruptcy Act or the Criminal Code. Similarly, bills are occasionally introduced simultaneously in both chambers, so that the Senate can engage in an unhurried "pre-study" of the bill rather than waiting until it has passed three readings in the Commons.

Senators also seek to emphasize other important aspects of their work, such as their consideration of private bills. These concern individuals, companies, religious organizations, professional associations, and other institutions and are a nuisance to a busy House of Commons. Since 1934, almost all private bills have been introduced in the Senate, where the background work can be done so that the Commons can approve them routinely at a later date. This practice does help the Commons, but private bills are not numerous and do not absorb much of anyone's time.

Another kind of work not originally provided for is the study of various public problems by Senate committees in what Colin Campbell calls "social investigations."[20] Senators often have the expertise and certainly the time to conduct inquiries that relieve the pressure on the House of Commons and are cheaper than royal commissions. Among the issues investigated by the Senate over the years were poverty, aging, unemployment, the mass media, science policy, land use, national defence, fisheries, Canadian–American relations, the Canadian Security Intelligence Service, medical care, and the legalization of marijuana. Many of these committee reports have been very useful to government policymakers.

Finally, the Senate reviews regulations issued by various government departments. The Standing Joint Committee on the Scrutiny of Regulations has the responsibility of reviewing the great quantity of subordinate legislation issued every year.

Even with all these activities, the Senate timetable is very lax, and a small group of people does most of its work. There is no doubt, however, that the institution performs more useful functions than in the past, and many of its members deserve their annual paycheque, which is now about $125 000.

The Senate is often considered less partisan than the Commons; however, when it has exercised its veto power, it has usually been motivated by partisanship. In such a case, a Liberal majority in the Senate has obstructed a Conservative majority in the Commons, or vice versa.[21]

Brian Mulroney had considerable difficulty with the Senate between 1984 and 1991, when a Liberal majority in that chamber coincided with a Conservative majority in the Commons. The Senate's changes to the Meech Lake Accord, for example, had to be overridden by the Commons after the expiry of the 180-day limit on constitutional amendments. Then, in mid-1988, at John Turner's direction, the Liberal majority in the Senate held up the Canada–U.S. Free Trade Agreement until the electorate had a chance to express its will on this important measure. After the 1988 election, the Senate bowed to the popular will and passed the Free Trade Agreement, but it later dug in its heels on other measures, especially the Goods and Services Tax (GST). At this point, Mulroney invoked an obscure clause in the 1867 Constitution Act that allowed him to appoint eight additional senators (two for each of the four senatorial regions) to tip the balance in favour of the Conservatives.[22] After the GST passed in an atmosphere of great bitterness, the Senate defeated the government's compromise abortion bill (on a tie vote). This became the first measure in 30 years that the Senate actually defeated, but some Cabinet ministers were probably secretly relieved that the Senate had exercised its rare veto.

By the time the Liberals came to power in 1993, the Conservatives had established a clear majority in the Senate, so positions were reversed, and the Liberals began to pay for their earlier intransigence. The Conservative majority in the Senate was particularly incensed about the Liberal bill cancelling the privatization of Toronto's Pearson Airport, and the bill was defeated (on another tie vote). The PC-controlled Senate then stalled or amended several other Chrétien government bills. Shortly after the 1997 election, a Liberal majority in the chamber was restored, but by then senators of all political persuasions were inclined to play a more active role than previously. Between 2001 and 2004, the Senate amended 11 bills that the Commons later accepted in revised form; the Senate backed down on one amended bill that the Commons would not accept; and the two chambers were stalemated on two bills when the 2004 election was called.

Prospects looked rather dismal when the Harper Conservatives were faced with an opposition majority in both houses of Parliament in 2006. After much political manoeuvring, however, that government got its main electoral priorities through both houses, with some amendments, as both MPs and senators acted responsibly. The Senate was less cooperative with respect to Harper's early proposals to reform that institution, although by early 2010, through a huge invasion of new Conservative appointments, that party outnumbered the Liberals in the chamber.

Senate Reform

Given the limited value of the Senate as it traditionally operated, its reform has always been on the political agenda. All sorts of reform proposals have been made, primarily with respect to how senators are chosen and what they should do. The former category ranges from abolition, to election, to having provinces choose some or all of its members. There is an increasing consensus that senators should be elected to legitimize the Senate's existence in a democratic age. With respect to its functions and powers, many reformers have advocated reactivating the Senate's role of representing regional and provincial interests at the federal level.

In the 1980s, Alberta began pushing its **Triple-E Senate** proposal: "elected, effective, and equal."[23] The government of Alberta felt so strongly about an elected Senate that it held a "senatorial election" in 1989 when, in the spirit of the Meech Lake Accord, Brian Mulroney asked for a list of provincial nominees to fill a vacancy. The Reform Party candidate won the province-wide contest, and Premier Don Getty forwarded his name to the prime minister, who after some delay, reluctantly complied. Alberta held a second senatorial election in 1998 and a third in 2004, but nobody outside that province paid much attention. Triple-E advocates also want each province rather than each region to have an equal number of senators, and want to give the Senate the power to protect smaller, hinterland provinces.

For some time, it seemed that if the Senate was unlikely to be reformed through formal, constitutional amendments, the best that could be hoped for was informal self-reform. To some extent, this has been evident in recent years.[24] Younger, often female senators from a wider diversity of backgrounds are usually prepared to put in more effort than their predecessors. Its more vigorous members want the Senate to become the "think tank of the Canadian government." Although the lack of democratic accountability will always cloud the Senate's work, its members' considerable accumulated political experience can be something of an asset.

Stephen Harper, coming from the Alberta Triple-E tradition, arrived in power determined to reform the Senate. Rather than relying on self-reform or unlikely formal constitutional amendments, he favoured "legislated" reform. He introduced legislation to restrict the term of new appointees to eight years as well as a law that would provide for the prime minister to appoint senators subsequent to senatorial elections. He also appointed one of the previously "elected" Alberta senators to the chamber. Both bills generated much controversy, especially in the Senate, but partly because of their dubious constitutionality. Despite his distaste for appointed senators, Harper made a large number of Conservative appointments in the hope that they might hasten the achievement of his attempt at Senate reform, as well as to ensure the passage of other government bills.

SUMMARY

This chapter discussed the two institutions that make up the legislative branch of government—the House of Commons and the Senate, the former being far more important. The chapter emphasized that, to a large extent, the legislative branch merely ratifies decisions and bills proposed by the executive, although this is less the case in a minority than a majority situation. But even if the government has a majority in the House of Commons, the chamber's role in the policymaking process is significant in many ways, not the least of which is in helping to educate the public about what the government is doing and holding it somewhat accountable. Moreover, MPs have other important functions apart from policymaking, including representing their constituencies and taking care of their constituents. An examination of the background of MPs revealed that they are closely representative of the population in some respects (especially geography) and less so in others (notably gender and class). The chapter then outlined the weekly and yearly timetables of the Commons, emphasizing that most of its time is taken up in the debate of government bills. It discussed the pros and cons of party discipline, the various stages that a bill goes through en route to enactment, the different kinds of bills involved, the key officials in the House, and the committee system. The section on the House of Commons concluded with a discussion of the roles MPs perform, the services available to them, and the relationship between the legislature and the executive in majority and minority situations. The section on the Senate pointed out that the original intentions for the Senate have been replaced with others, that the institution has recently become a much more useful part of the parliamentary system, but that Senate reform remains on the political agenda.

DISCUSSION QUESTIONS

1. If Parliament does not play a significant part in the policymaking process, what are its basic functions?
2. What are the advantages and disadvantages of rigid party discipline in the Commons?
3. Does the Senate do enough to justify its existence? If not, how should it be reformed?

KEY TERMS

Auditor General The official of Parliament whose staff audit the expenditures of government departments and who reports on instances of funds being unlawfully or unwisely spent.

Backbencher A member of Parliament, whether on the government or opposition side, who sits on the back benches and does not have a Cabinet post or equivalent position in other parties.

Budget The annual financial statement of the government issued by the minister of finance that introduces tax changes and gives an overview of government finances for the next fiscal year.

Closure A rule in the House of Commons in which a Cabinet minister introduces a motion to cut off debate.

Dissolution of Parliament The ending of a Parliament, usually after four or more years, by calling an election.

Division A formal, standing, roll-call vote in the House of Commons in which members' names are recorded in *Hansard*.

Estimates The annual spending plans of government departments and agencies.

Filibuster An organized attempt by the opposition in the House of Commons to prolong debate and delay adoption of government measures.

Free vote A rare vote in the House of Commons in which members are not required to abide by the party line.

Government The set of authorities centred around a prime minister, Cabinet, and party that currently occupy the executive offices of the state and provide political leadership.

Government bill A bill introduced by a Cabinet minister on behalf of the whole government.

House leader The person appointed by each party in the House of Commons to deal with counterparts in other parties with respect to scheduling Commons business.

Judicial review The power of the courts to overturn legislation or actions of the executive branch of government.

Leader of the Opposition The leader of the main opposition party in the House of Commons.

Legislature That branch of government whose function is to represent the people and make laws.

Majority government A situation in which the party in power has over 50 percent of the seats in the House of Commons.

Minority government A situation in which the government party has fewer than 50 percent of the seats in the House of Commons.

Money bill A bill to raise money for government purposes or to spend public funds.

Non-confidence motion A motion in the House of Commons, brought by the opposition, inviting MPs to demonstrate a lack of confidence in the government, which, if successful, would require the Cabinet's resignation or the calling of an election.

Opposition Those members of Parliament who do not support the government of the day.

Opposition days Twenty-two days per session of Parliament set aside for the opposition parties to determine the topic of debate.

Parliament Theoretically, the Queen, the House of Commons, and the Senate, functioning collectively, such as in the approval of legislation, but often used to refer to the Commons and Senate or Commons alone.

Parliamentary press gallery Those members of the media who are registered to sit in the press gallery in the House of Commons and who report on its proceedings or on government in general.

Parliamentary secretary A government MP who has been given additional responsibilities to assist a Cabinet minister.

Party caucus The whole body of MPs of any party, together with such senators as choose to attend, who hold a regular weekly meeting to discuss parliamentary strategy and party policy.

Party discipline The convention that all MPs within any party vote together on every occasion, as predetermined by the leader or in the party caucus meeting and as enforced by the party whip.

Party whip An official of each party in the House of Commons whose function is to enforce party discipline and ensure that members are present for all votes.

Private bill A bill introduced in Parliament that affects only a specific individual, company, organization, or group.

Private member's bill A public bill introduced in Parliament by an MP who is not in the Cabinet.

Public Accounts Committee The House of Commons committee that examines the Auditor General's reports and criticizes government officials for illegal or unwise expenditures.

Public bill A bill introduced in Parliament that affects society in general.

Question Period The daily 45-minute period in the House of Commons in which opposition members spar with the prime minister and Cabinet ministers.

Responsible government A form of government in which the political executive must retain the confidence of the elected legislature and resign or call an election if and when it is defeated on a vote of non-confidence.

Safe seat A constituency that a single party can be assured of winning, election after election.

Speaker The presiding officer of the House of Commons.

Speech from the Throne The document prepared by the prime minister and Cabinet and read by the governor general at the opening of each session of Parliament that outlines the government's legislative proposals for the session.

Standing committees Those committees of the House of Commons that are set up semi-permanently and that parallel government departments.

Standing Orders The written rules of the House of Commons.

Supremacy of Parliament The principle that no other organ of government can overrule Parliament or its laws.

Triple-E Senate A proposal for Senate reform in which each province would have an equal number of senators who would be elected and who would be given effective powers.

Westminster model The model of government developed in Britain in which the political executive is given extensive power to provide effective leadership.

FURTHER READING

Andrew, Caroline, John Biles, Myer Siemiatycki, and Eric Tolly, eds. *Electing a Diverse Canada: The Representation of Immigrants, Minorities, and Women.* Vancouver: UBC Press, 2008.

Bejermi, John. *Canadian Parliamentary Handbook.* Ottawa: Borealis Press, annual.

Docherty, David C. *Legislatures.* Vancouver: UBC Press, 2004.

———. *Mr. Smith Goes to Ottawa: Life in the House of Commons.* Vancouver: UBC Press, 1997.

Franks, C.E.S. *The Parliament of Canada.* Toronto: University of Toronto Press, 1987.

Heard, Andrew. *Canadian Constitutional Conventions.* Toronto: Oxford University Press, 1991.

Joyal, Serge. *Protecting Democracy: The Senate You Never Knew.* Montreal: McGill-Queen's University Press, 2003.

Russell, Peter H. *Two Cheers for Minority Government: The Evolution of Canadian Parliamentary Democracy.* Toronto: Emond Montgomery, 2008.

Russell, Peter H., and Lorne Sossin. *Parliamentary Democracy in Crisis.* Toronto: University of Toronto Press, 2009.

Chapter 16

The Courts and the
Administration
of Justice

The **judiciary** or the court system was traditionally of little interest to political science—usually only in terms of its interpretation of the federal–provincial division of powers. Now that the Charter of Rights and Freedoms has catapulted the courts into the midst of many heated political issues, however, political scientists are giving this fourth branch of government much more attention. This chapter examines the judiciary as an institution of government, discussing the function of adjudication, categories of laws, the structure of the courts, the operation of the Supreme Court of Canada, and the appointment, removal, and independence of judges. The chapter ends with a brief account of policing and the correctional system in Canada.

Chapter Objectives

After you have completed this chapter, you should be able to:

Discuss the role of adjudication as exercised by the courts

Distinguish between the powers of judicial discretion and judicial review

Assess the equality of access to the judicial system

Distinguish among various categories of laws

Outline the structure of the Canadian court system

Describe the jurisdiction of the Federal Court of Canada

Discuss the powers and operations of the Supreme Court of Canada

Discuss the appointment of judges in Canada

Understand the principle of judicial independence and how it relates to the removal of judges

Discuss the function of policing in Canada and the operation of the correctional system

Functions and Powers of the Courts

The judiciary has always been associated with the "adjudication" function in the political system. Adjudication can be defined as interpreting the law in case of dispute, settling disputes by applying the law to them, or making a judgment based on the law. Peter Russell defines the term as "providing authoritative settlements in disputes about the law."[1]

The function of the judiciary therefore is to render formal, impartial, authoritative judgments in the case of legal disputes between two parties that cannot be settled otherwise. The judicial process generally relies on the adversarial system, with lawyers representing each side. The judge, clothed with the authoritative powers of the state, acts as an independent referee and decides which of the disputants is legally right. As a result, the process usually culminates in the designation of a winner and a loser rather than in the adoption of some acceptable middle ground, which is more characteristic of political conflicts.

Apart from the civil law system in Quebec, the Canadian legal system operates in the tradition of the English **common law**. The basis of that system is the accumulation over the centuries of judicial precedents, both in England and more recently in Canada. Thus, in a typical court case, the two sides seek to find precedents—previous court decisions—favouring their respective points of view. The judge (and sometimes the jury) has to decide which precedents most closely resemble the case currently before the court. The principle that precedents are binding on successive decisions is called **stare decisis**.

If the law were always comprehensive and crystal-clear, and if the situations to which it applied were always simple and straightforward, adjudication would be fairly routine, and the potential for **judicial discretion** would be limited. The real world is more complex, however, and the law is unlikely to be clear on all points or to provide for every conceivable situation. Russell refers to the "inescapable generality of the law" such that, while judges theoretically settle disputes according to pre-existing law, they actually shape and develop the law in the very process of settling disputes about it. Judges at least establish priorities among competing legal

Chief Justice Beverley McLachlin.
(CP Images/STRCANWEST/Ashley Fraser)

rules and principles, and in this process they "put flesh on the bare skeleton of the law and shape its substance."[2]

Thus, rather than taking place subsequent to policymaking, the judiciary and the function of judicial interpretation were included in the chart of the policymaking process in Figure 13.1. Unlike Americans, Canadian observers have not previously given much recognition to the concept of judicial involvement in this process. Russell argues that this omission "wrongly assumes that all important public policies are expressed in statutes passed by legislatures … and overlooks the extent to which [such] policies … are shaped through the process of being applied in particular cases by judges and administrators."[3] In the course of adjudicating disputes, the courts are inherently involved in policymaking.

Rather than meaning the mere interpretation of laws with discretion, **judicial review** is the power of the courts to declare them invalid. The original Constitution Act, 1867, did not contain any such provision, although the courts soon appropriated this power in one respect. Chapter 12 of this book detailed the extent to which the courts invalidated federal and provincial legislation as violations of the division of powers. In rendering federal or provincial legislation void if either encroached on the jurisdiction of the other, the decisions of the courts had a significant effect on the shape of Canadian federalism. The courts' power of judicial review was greatly enhanced with the adoption of the **Charter of Rights and Freedoms** in 1982, and the effects of the first 30 years of that review were discussed in Chapter 11. Peter McCormick writes:

> We should recognize that judges have always had power, have always affected our society by the decisions they make…. The Charter has simply made a longstanding reality more immediately visible and directed us belatedly to an assessment of the implications of judicial power.[4]

Thus, especially since 1982, the courts are active players in the policymaking process. Whether judges leave a law intact or declare it unconstitutional, their interpretation of any law has a major bearing on its effect. Judicial review also entails overturning executive decisions that the courts find to violate the law or the Constitution.

Access to and Costs of Justice

Many people cannot afford to hire a lawyer to defend themselves in a criminal or civil case, yet the objective of the court system must be the search for truth and the obtaining of justice, goals that have traditionally rested on the adversarial system. To ensure that those without the financial resources have a fairer chance to achieve justice, legal aid programs financed jointly by the federal and provincial governments have been established. These go some way to meet the fairness objective, but they vary in detail from one province to another, do not cover every kind of legal work, and have been cut back by governments that are intent on balancing their budgets. Community legal clinics and publicly paid duty counsel serve a similar function. Many observers, including the Chief Justice of the Supreme Court of Canada, have recently decried this inadequacy in the judicial system.[5]

Related means of reducing the costs of the administration of justice are the practices of plea bargaining and pre-trial conferences. Plea bargaining involves discussions between defence and Crown attorneys with the aim of achieving agreement on charges to be pursued, typically by having the accused plead guilty to one charge when the Crown drops other charges. This practice is routine at the provincial court level and avoids a lengthy, costly trial. In the higher trial courts, it is increasingly common for the judge to hold a pre-trial conference with the lawyers for each side. Such conferences can result in a negotiated settlement or at least a time-saving clarification of the issues involved. Similar conferences have also proven useful in family and small claims courts. Although plea bargaining and pre-trial conferences must not be allowed to subvert justice, as often seems to be the case, they are valuable devices that cut costs for everyone involved (including the public) and reduce the workload of the usually congested court system. Some provinces have tried to save money and remove the adversarial nature of small claims or other civil cases by instituting various mediation services, such as Alternative Dispute Resolution (ADR).

Categories of Laws

The law can be defined as "society's system of binding rules."[6] Laws are commonly divided into different categories, one distinction being between "civil" and "criminal." A **civil law** regulates relationships between two private parties such as individuals or corporations; if private agreement cannot be reached in the case of dispute, one party may take the other to court. Most aspects of civil law in Canada are within provincial jurisdiction, largely based on the provincial power over property and civil rights. Civil cases often involve disputes over commercial contracts or property, and such cases are normally resolved by the court's ordering one party to pay damages to the other. Civil cases are decided on the basis of the "balance of probabilities" of the merits of each side.

Criminal law, on the other hand, is primarily a federal responsibility; it is thus more or less uniform throughout the country and has been consolidated in the **Criminal Code**. In this case, the commission of a crime such as murder, sexual assault, or theft is considered to be a wrong against society as a whole, and the state takes the initiative to bring the suspect to justice by means of the police and Crown attorneys. In criminal cases, judges may impose fines or prison sentences if the accused is found guilty. Such guilt must be proven "beyond a reasonable doubt," which is a considerably higher standard than just a balance of probabilities.

One of the many peculiarities of Canadian federalism is that although criminal law is within federal jurisdiction, it is usually the provincial attorneys general and their agents, the Crown attorneys, who are responsible for initiating proceedings against the person who is charged. This situation has come about because the provinces have jurisdiction over the administration of justice. Sometimes a case contains both civil and criminal elements, such as when a drunken driver does damage to another person's car. The state pursues the violation of the Criminal Code, but the victim's insurance company would have to take the initiative to sue for property damage.

Instead of this basic division between civil and criminal law, a distinction is sometimes made between public and private law.[7] Private law is essentially the same as civil law described above, that is, law that primarily involves private interests. Beyond the contracts and property mentioned, private law includes torts, wills, company law, and family law. Public law, involving the public interest or the government, goes beyond criminal law to include constitutional, administrative, and taxation law. Constitutional law has traditionally involved questions about federal or provincial jurisdiction, and governments themselves have often been the parties to a constitutional case. With the adoption of the Charter of Rights and Freedoms, a whole new aspect of constitutional law in Canada has emerged. Administrative law concerns the operation of government departments, agencies, and tribunals, and as government activity expanded over the years, this branch of law also increased in significance. (Note the later discussion of the Federal Court of Canada.)

By giving the provinces jurisdiction over property and civil rights, the Fathers of Confederation allowed the province of Quebec to retain its distinctive private or civil law system called the **Code Civil du Québec**. The private law system in the other provinces is based on the English common law tradition. The theoretical distinction between the two systems in terms of form is that while the common law consists of a hodgepodge of judicial precedents, the Code Civil is a single comprehensive document. As Gerald Gall puts it, "in a common law system, the courts extract existing principles of law from decisions of previous cases, while in the civil law system, the courts look to the civil code to determine a given principle and they then apply the facts of an instant case to that principle."[8]

Structure of the Courts

Because the provinces that formed Confederation in 1867 already possessed a court system, and because the Judicial Committee of the Privy Council continued to function as a court of appeal for the whole British Empire, it was not necessary to devote much attention to the judiciary in the Constitution Act, 1867. The provinces were given responsibility for the establishment of a provincial court system, and the federal government was allowed to establish a general court of appeal.

As shown in Figure 16.1, the court systems within each province developed into a reasonably uniform three-level hierarchy. At the bottom are "inferior" or provincial courts, whose judges are appointed by provincial governments. Above

Figure 16.1   The Court Structure of Canada

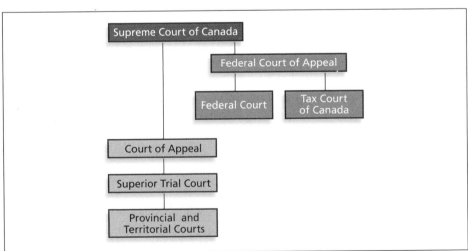

them are two "superior" courts—the superior trial court and the court of appeal—although they go by different names from province to province. Each of the territories has a similar court structure.

Because of the assumption that provinces could not be trusted to make worthy appointments to the two levels of superior courts in the province, the Fathers of Confederation provided that the judges of these courts would be appointed by the governor general, conventionally meaning the federal Cabinet or minister of justice. Such judges are also paid by the federal government. Thus, in another peculiarity of Canadian federalism, each province determines how many superior court judges it needs, but they are appointed and paid by Ottawa. Since these courts and their judges are provided for in section 96 of the 1867 document, they are often called section 96 courts and section 96 judges.

Provincial and Territorial Courts

Whatever their structure or name, provincial and territorial courts generally are responsible for

- summary offences (less serious crimes and provincial and municipal offences);
- most aspects of indictable offences, some mandatory and others optional;
- preliminary hearings for most serious crimes;
- bail hearings;
- youth criminal offences;
- family law, except divorce and proceedings flowing from divorce; and
- small civil cases.

Provincial courts have a monopoly on summary offences except in provinces where this responsibility has been given to lower tribunals such as justices of the peace. Summary offences, as noted, include violations of municipal bylaws, provincial offences, and the least serious Criminal Code offences, such as common assault. More serious crimes, called indictable offences, can be subdivided into three categories. Some, such as murder, are reserved for superior courts in the provinces; others, such as theft, are assigned to provincial courts; and those in an intermediate category can be tried in either section 96 or provincial courts. The federal Youth Criminal Justice Act covers offences committed by those aged 12 to 18, and in some provinces these offences are tried in special youth courts.

Family law is another area of great federal–provincial complexity. Since divorce is a federal responsibility, divorces are dealt with in section 96 courts, and any proceedings flowing from the divorce must also be dealt with there. On the other hand, if divorce is not involved, such matters as custody, access, maintenance, alimony, adoption, guardianship, and protection of children are handled in provincial courts, sometimes called family courts. Several provinces have tried to overcome the problem of the fragmentation of family law with a "unified family court" presided over by a section 96 judge.

Provincial courts, sometimes in a civil division and sometimes called small claims courts, also have jurisdiction over disputes involving small amounts of money. Each province determines the monetary limit for cases that can be considered at that level, with disputes involving larger sums being initiated at the section 96 court level.

Superior Trial Courts

The superior trial court in the province or territory, whatever its name, is responsible for

- some mandatory and other elective indictable offences;
- civil matters over a given monetary amount;
- divorces and proceedings flowing therefrom;
- appeals from lower courts regarding summary convictions, juvenile cases, and family cases; and
- administrative law cases.

Provincial and Territorial Courts of Appeal

Provincial and territorial courts of appeal hear criminal, civil, and other appeals. Although some of these courts' judgments can be appealed to the Supreme Court of Canada, decisions of the provincial courts of appeal are usually final, adding to the significance of this level of court.[9] The basic function of an appeal court is to correct errors or injustices that were made in a lower court, so that an appeal court is primarily interested in legal rather than factual issues.

The second function of the appeal court is to render an opinion in a **reference case**, that is, on a constitutional issue referred to it by the provincial Cabinet. Russell thus speaks of the "lawmaking" role of appeal courts because their legal interpretations have a "creative legislative dimension."[10] Decisions of the court of appeal are binding on all courts below it in the same province and are "strongly persuasive" for trial courts in other provinces. Courts of appeal normally sit in banks of three judges, but these panels can be increased to five for very important cases. Each side of a case submits a brief or *factum* in advance that summarizes its arguments, and lawyers then engage in oral argument.

The Federal Court of Canada

The **Federal Court of Canada** was established in 1971, with trial and appeal divisions. It was intended to relieve the Supreme Court of Canada of routine appeals from certain federal administrative tribunals and to strengthen judicial review of federal administration by developing a more unified and cohesive body of federal administrative law.[11] The main areas of responsibility of the Federal Court are

- citizenship, immigration, and refugee appeals;
- intellectual property cases, including copyright, trademark, and patent disputes;
- appeals from other federal administrative tribunals;
- civil cases involving the federal government;
- cases involving bills of exchange, promissory notes, admiralty law, aeronautics, and interprovincial works and undertakings;
- prerogative writs (e.g., injunctions) applying to agencies of the federal government;
- appeals relating to the Access to Information and Privacy Acts;
- issuance of Canadian Security Intelligence Service warrants; and
- Aboriginal law.

Although the Federal Court deals with cases in all the above categories every year, it is dominated by those involving the Immigration and Refugee Protection Act and the Immigration and Refugee Board. It has recently seen a growth in Aboriginal cases dealing with monetary and constitutional issues, land entitlements, and natural resources. The Federal Court also hears appeals regarding the Access to Information Act and the Privacy Act and decides on requests for warrants from the Canadian Security Intelligence Service in order to plant bugs, open mail, and engage in other surreptitious activities.

The Federal Court consists of a chief justice and 12 other judges on its appeal division and the associate chief justice and 32 other full-time and assorted part-time judges on its trial division. The appeal division judges sit in panels of at least three members, and the individual judges of the trial division sit in cases all across the country.

The Supreme Court of Canada

The **Supreme Court of Canada** sits at the apex of the Canadian court system. The Supreme Court hears appeals from the provincial and territorial courts of appeal in civil and criminal cases and from the appeals division of the Federal Court of Canada in administrative law matters. The part of its work of most interest to political science involves constitutional law, whether in terms of the division of powers or the Charter of Rights and Freedoms. Besides hearing appeal cases from lower courts, the Supreme Court can be asked by the federal Cabinet to give opinions, usually on constitutional matters, in reference cases. A recent example was the case regarding Quebec's right to make a unilateral declaration of independence. Although the Supreme Court hears fewer cases per year than any lower court, it is interested almost exclusively in questions of law. Thus, of all courts, it is the most heavily engaged in a "lawmaking" role, and its decisions are binding on all lower courts.

Until 1949, the Supreme Court was a seriously deficient institution. First, its decisions could be appealed to Canada's pre-1949 final court of appeal, the **Judicial Committee of the Privy Council (JCPC)** located in London, and it was bound by JCPC precedents. But even more humiliating was that appeals could go directly to that Empire court from provincial appeal courts, completely bypassing the Supreme Court of Canada. This weakness in authority was exacerbated by the generally poor quality of judges appointed to it in that earlier period, with some notable exceptions.[12]

Canada could have cut off appeals to the Judicial Committee after obtaining complete independence in 1931, but it was unclear whether the provinces would have to agree to this measure, since their appeals could go directly to the JCPC. By the late 1940s, it was determined that Ottawa could unilaterally curtail all such appeals, and it promptly did so. The Supreme Court of Canada has not been formally bound by Judicial Committee decisions since 1949 and has explicitly overruled them on occasion.

The Supreme Court used to have little discretion in deciding which cases it heard, but since 1974 it has basically controlled its own agenda. Such discretion

The Supreme Court of Canada. (The Canadian Press)

considerably enhances the stature of the institution. Today, only two categories of cases have an automatic right of appeal to the Supreme Court: provincial refer-ence cases and murder cases in which the provincial court of appeal was split on a question of law. Applications for leave to appeal discretionary cases are normally handled in writing by a panel of three judges, but sometimes the panel hears them live. Public law cases, especially criminal and constitutional, now clearly predomi-nate over private law disputes on the Supreme Court docket.

Although an increasingly important institution of government, the Supreme Court rests primarily on the Supreme Court Act rather than being embedded in any constitutional document as such. That act provides for a nine-member court, three of whom must come from Quebec with its distinctive civil law system. Convention dictates that of the other six, three normally come from Ontario, two from the West, and one from Atlantic Canada. The act requires that at least five judges constitute a quorum, with the result that civil law cases from Quebec can be heard by a five-member panel including a majority from the civil law system. The posi-tion of Chief Justice normally alternates between francophone and anglophone members, simultaneous interpretation is available, and Supreme Court judges are now expected to be at least functionally bilingual. The judges hold office during good behaviour until the age of 75.

The Court holds three sessions of about two months' duration each per year, and then adjourns to write up its decisions.[13] As much as possible, the Court tries to hear cases with a full complement of nine. Judges study the lower court proceedings and judgments in advance, along with the written arguments of the lawyers for each side. Oral arguments normally last only two hours, during which time the judges often ask trenchant questions. In some instances, the Court also grants "intervener status" to provincial governments and interest groups that are concerned about a case but not directly party to it. Once the arguments are completed, the judges usually "reserve judgment" and meet in private conference to discuss the case. Each gives his or her tentative conclusion, and one or more draft opinions are prepared. These are later circulated and evoke comments before being revised. Each Supreme Court judge is assisted by a number of outstanding new law school graduates called law clerks. They help the busy judges search for and sift through precedents and other relevant material on the issues involved. So much effort is put into the process of preparing their opinions that a decision is typically not issued until about six months after the Court hears the case, and it has occasionally taken over a year for all members of the Court to make up their minds. The Court tries to come to a unanimous decision, but if this is not possible, majority and minority opinions are issued. Members of the Supreme Court of Canada as of 2011 are listed in Table 16.1.

TABLE 16.1 MEMBERSHIP IN THE SUPREME COURT OF CANADA, 2011

Year of Appointment	Name
1989	Beverley McLachlin (Chief Justice)
1998	Ian Binnie
2000	Louis LeBel
2002	Marie Deschamps
2003	Morris Fish
2004	Rosalie Abella
2004	Louise Charron
2006	Marshall Rothstein
2008	Thomas Cromwell

The Appointment of Judges

As has already been established, judges of the Supreme and Federal Courts of Canada as well as judges of the provincial and territorial superior trial courts and courts of appeal are appointed by the federal Cabinet, while provincial court judges are appointed by provincial Cabinets. There are approximately 1000 judges in each category. All of the first group must be qualified lawyers of at least ten years' standing, as must provincial court judges in Ontario and Quebec. Elsewhere, provincial court judges have to be members of the bar for a minimum of five years.

In a high proportion of cases over the years, Cabinets at both federal and provincial levels have used judicial appointments to reward faithful party supporters, often defeated candidates.[14] Such **political patronage** raises three main problems: unsuitable individuals are appointed because of their connections to the party in power; well-qualified candidates are overlooked because of their lack of service to that party; and partisan judges may favour their former political colleagues.[15] This patronage system of appointing judges is still alive, although it is not as blatant as it once was.

At the federal level, Pierre Trudeau as minister of justice instituted an informal practice of submitting names of potential judicial appointments to the Canadian Bar Association (CBA). Trudeau sullied his own government's record in this field in 1984, however, with the appointment of six high-profile Liberal partisans, several to the Federal Court of Canada. After an even more partisan record of judicial appointments during its first term,[16] the Mulroney government established a somewhat more satisfactory appointment system in 1988 for all "federal" judges except those on the Supreme Court of Canada and then modified it slightly in 1991. An independent Commissioner for Federal Judicial Affairs now maintains a record of those interested in federal judicial appointments—to the Federal Court of Canada, the Tax Court of Canada, and provincial and territorial superior courts. This official then submits such names to one of 16 judicial advisory committees, each including a section 96 judge; one nominee of each of the provincial/territorial law society, the provincial/territorial branch of the CBA, and the provincial/territorial attorney general; and three nominees of the federal minister of justice. The Harper government added a representative from the law enforcement community (police service), a move severely criticized right up to the level of the Chief Justice of the Supreme Court. Many observers feared that besides entrenching partisanship in judicial appointments, the move would add an ideological ingredient—right-wing judges who would be hard on crime—which might compromise the principle of judicial independence. While it is regrettable that partisanship still plays a role

Marshall Rothstein "waxes poetic" during Supreme Court interview. (Bado/Le Droit/Artizans.com)

in this process, party service or legislative experience should not automatically disqualify a worthy candidate from a judicial appointment.[17]

The prime minister chooses the chief justice in each province, almost always from the existing bench, as well as new members of the Supreme Court of Canada. Prime ministers consult widely before making such appointments and have managed to overcome their penchant for partisanship in this area. Patronage has therefore not been much of a problem on the Supreme Court for over 50 years.

Given the significant lawmaking potential of Supreme Court judges, many observers have proposed that nominees be subject to public hearings, such as appearing before a parliamentary committee, before being appointed. In this forum, they might be grilled about their views on a wide variety of issues. This is despite the fact that, without a formal consultation process, Supreme Court appointments have rarely generated much controversy. Jacob Ziegel and the Standing Committee on Justice both proposed an alternative to public confirmation hearings—a Supreme Court nominating commission.[18]

A formal procedure, somewhat similar to those proposed, was adopted in connection with the appointment of Marshall Rothstein to the Supreme Court in 2006. The Minister of Justice conducted widespread consultations from which an initial list of six candidates was developed. Then, he established an advisory committee of nine people, consisting of a representative from each recognized party in the House of Commons, a retired judge named by the Canadian Judicial Council, a representative of the provincial attorneys general and of the law societies of the region involved, and two eminent laypeople nominated by the Minister of Justice. This committee provided an unranked shortlist of three, from which the minister was to make a recommendation to the prime minister. When Paul Martin handed power over to Stephen Harper in the midst of this process, the latter selected one of the three, but then insisted that the nominee be subject to a televised interview by an informal Commons committee. Members of the committee were instructed to use characteristic Canadian reserve in questioning the appointee, and Marshall Rothstein convinced them that he would do a good job. He was thereupon officially appointed by the prime minister, in a process that seemed to please just about everyone.

The procedure to replace Mr. Justice Bastarache in 2008 was supposed to be somewhat similar to the one used to choose Rothstein. But, perhaps because of the election call, it was abandoned, and Mr. Justice Thomas Cromwell was appointed without any parliamentary involvement, although no one objected to his selection.

What Do You Think?

How much public and/or parliamentary input should be added to the process of choosing a Supreme Court judge? Should prospective judges be grilled in public before being appointed so that the public knows their views on controversial issues?

At the provincial court level, the attorney general now usually consults with the provincial judicial council or an equivalent body in making such appointments.

A central nonpartisan nominating commission consisting largely of non-lawyers was established in Ontario in 1988, originally headed by political scientist Peter Russell. It screens judicial applicants on their merits and ranks the candidates from which the attorney general chooses.

Another controversial aspect of judicial appointments concerns the Supreme Court of Canada alone. Because this court must adjudicate federal–provincial disputes, concern has been expressed that all of its members are federally appointed. In theory, once chosen, judges act with total impartiality and their independence is protected in various ways. Nevertheless, it may not appear as if justice has been done in such a situation. The ill-fated Meech Lake and Charlottetown Accords provided for Ottawa to make Supreme Court of Canada appointments from lists provided by the provinces. The latter accord also proposed federal and provincial consultation with Aboriginal peoples in the appointment process.

Even though judges are expected to perform their duties in an unbiased manner, they naturally bring their personal predilections and prejudices to the post. This realization leads us to investigate whether they are representative of Canadian society. Partly as a consequence of equitable geographic representation, judicial appointments have balanced francophone and anglophone origins at both federal and provincial court levels, especially in recent years as provinces have made more French-language court services available. Those of other origins used to be excluded, but judges such as Laskin (Jewish), Sopinka (Ukrainian), and Iacobucci (Italian) have been appointed to the Supreme Court of Canada—and increasingly to lower courts as well. Thus, the most serious aspects of judicial underrepresentation relate to women and the working class.[19]

Just as in the case of different ethnic groups, however, more female and working-class law school graduates are becoming available for judicial appointments, and governments have at least begun to recognize the necessity of appointing greater numbers of female judges. The Supreme Court finally saw its first female member in 1982, and it now has a total of four women out of nine, including Beverley McLachlin, the first female Chief Justice. Such female judges have sometimes used their position to point out the male bias in legislatures, judiciaries, and laws.[20]

As noted in Chapter 4, Aboriginal peoples have serious doubts about the Canadian judicial system, feeling that it discriminates against them at every turn. Many argue that an increase in the number of Aboriginal judges would not substantially improve this situation and therefore advocate the establishment of a parallel justice system to deal with Aboriginal defendants (at least where they did no harm to non-Aboriginals), reflecting their own distinctive concepts of guilt and healing and emphasizing rehabilitation rather than punishment. While it seems unlikely that a separate system will be created in the near future, the regular courts are increasingly recognizing traditional Aboriginal concepts in cases involving Aboriginal people. These include sentencing circles (involving a judge, police, elders, peers, family, and victims), elder sentencing panels, and community mediation processes.

Retirement, Removal, and the Independence of Judges

Whatever the process involved in making judicial appointments, judges are expected to abide by the principle of **judicial independence** or impartiality once they are on the bench. They are supposed to adjudicate without fear or favour with respect to private or political interests and without any incentive to give preference to the government side where it is involved.

The independence of judges is based primarily on security of tenure, and it is difficult for the government to remove judges before their scheduled date of retirement. Judges on the Supreme and Federal Courts of Canada and provincial superior courts have a mandatory retirement age of 75 years, and provincial court judges must retire at 65 or 70. The general rule is that they serve on "good behaviour"—that is, they cannot be removed unless they have been guilty of misbehaviour. Although the meaning of these terms has never been definitively established, judges are certainly removable for serious criminal acts and possibly for reasons of infirmity or incapacity, failure to execute their duties, or bringing the judicial system into disrepute.[21] On the other hand, they cannot be removed merely because the government regards a decision as erroneous or contrary to government policy, nor because they ruled against the Crown.

The process of removing a judge varies with the level of the position, the degree of difficulty increasing with the court's ranking in the hierarchy. Except in Ontario, where legislation is required, provincial court judges can be removed by an order in council of the provincial Cabinet, but only after an inquiry has been conducted by one of the judge's peers or by the provincial judicial council. It is even more difficult to remove judges of the provincial superior courts and the federal courts. In such situations, the Canadian Judicial Council conducts an inquiry and reports to the minister of justice, after which the passage of a joint address of both houses of Parliament is required.

The **Canadian Judicial Council** was created in 1971 and consists of all the chief justices and associate chief justices of courts staffed by federally appointed judges. It is chaired by the Chief Justice of the Supreme Court of Canada. Like the provincial judicial councils, its primary purpose is to deal with complaints raised against individual judges, but it also has a role in the continuing education of judges, provides a forum for developing consensus among its members, and makes representations to government with respect to judicial salaries and benefits.

While a number of judges have been reprimanded by judicial councils, the issue of judicial removal has rarely arisen at the federal level. Several provincial court judges have been removed over the years, a practice that is increasingly common as the public becomes less tolerant of their faults. But only four judges of the old county and district courts met this fate, and not a single superior court judge has been removed from office. Such proceedings were initiated in several cases, but the judges either died or resigned during the removal process.[22]

Besides security of tenure, judicial independence involves financial, administrative, and political independence.[23] Salaries and pensions are fixed in such a way that neither individually nor collectively can judges be intimidated by government threats to reduce them. Some judges did go to court, however, to challenge freezes or reductions in their salaries as part of provincial government restraint programs in the 1990s and again in Ontario in 2004.[24] Superior court judges have seen their salaries increased substantially in recent years, yet still asked for a 17 percent raise in 2004. In addition, judges are increasingly in control of the administration of the court system. Judges must also be able to function without political pressure—from Cabinet ministers, legislators, bureaucrats, or other judges—whether in public or in private. At both federal and provincial levels, many cases have occurred of Cabinet ministers contacting judges; but, however innocent their questions might seem, this must not be done.

It is sometimes thought that the prospect of promotion from one court to another might bias a judge's decisions, but no evidence has been found to justify this fear. On the other hand, judges are not supposed to make public speeches that might compromise their impartiality. For example, when Tom Berger of the B.C. Supreme Court publicly criticized the 1982 Constitution Act for its omission of Quebec and virtual neglect of Aboriginal peoples, certain highly placed opponents of his views brought him before the Canadian Judicial Council. Although its recommendation was not to dismiss him, he resigned to protest the process employed.[25]

Policing and the Correctional System in Canada

Policing in Canada

In Chapter 14, police officers were categorized as a special kind of public servant. Police can be employed by the federal, provincial, or municipal governments. The Royal Canadian Mounted Police (RCMP) is the national police force with many appropriate central functions, such as operating a criminal information system and a forensic laboratory and maintaining international policing linkages. Ontario and Quebec possess their own provincial police forces, Newfoundland and Labrador retains the Royal Newfoundland Constabulary for certain purposes, and larger municipal governments have local police services. Eight provinces, three territories, about 200 municipalities, and nearly 200 First Nations communities—all jurisdictions without their own police services—have signed contracts with the RCMP to provide policing functions. But even where separate provincial and municipal police exist, and where they enforce the Criminal Code, the RCMP enforces federal non-Criminal Code statutes such as the Narcotics Control Act.

The basic functions of police officers of any kind are to prevent crime, to maintain order in the community, and to detect and apprehend offenders. In order to perform these important functions, police officers are given special powers, such as to question suspects, conduct searches, make arrests, and carry guns. On the highways alone, where the bulk of Canadians are most tempted to break the law, police officers can use concealed or unmarked patrol cars, photo radar or radar traps, and spot checks and breathalyzer tests for impaired driving. As mentioned in Chapter 11, however, judicial interpretation of the Charter of Rights and Freedoms has served to restrict such police powers in many circumstances and to augment the rights of a person suspected of or charged with committing a crime.

Besides being subject to Charter restrictions, police must obey civilian authorities. While police services are deliberately designed to operate at arm's length from politicians, police officers are subject to the general supervision of provincial or municipal civilian police commissions or, in the case of the RCMP, the minister of Public Safety.

RCMP use random breathalyzer for flat tire. (Graham Harrop/Artizans.com)

The Canadian Correctional System

Since it is judges and the courts that put people into correctional institutions, it is appropriate to add a final word about the Canadian correctional system. As in many other aspects of the judicial system in Canada, there is an important federal–provincial dimension to this subject. Those adult offenders sentenced to two years or more are sent to federal penitentiaries, while those serving less than two years find themselves in provincial prisons or reformatories. In other words, both levels of government maintain correctional institutions, and the distinction between the two is based on the length of the sentence, not on whether the offender broke a federal or provincial law.

Federal legislation also requires the provinces to establish facilities such that young offenders are kept separate and apart from adult offenders. Youth crime is yet another complicated issue of federal–provincial relations, leading the provinces to make frequent criticisms of federal policy.

The Corrections and Conditional Release Act provides that an individual who has served a portion of his or her sentence may be released early (and conditionally) on parole. Three provinces have set up parole boards to review inmates of their own prisons or reformatories for this purpose, while the National Parole Board performs this function for federal institutions as well as for the other provinces and territories.

SUMMARY

This chapter dealt with the judicial branch of government. It began by discussing its function of adjudication—providing authoritative settlements in disputes about the law. It then distinguished between judicial discretion (interpreting laws) and judicial review (overturning them). It noted the problem of access to the courts and outlined less than satisfactory ways of reducing that difficulty. The chapter went on to distinguish between civil and criminal law, as well as private and public law, and then addressed the structure of the court system in Canada. It discussed, in turn, lower provincial courts, superior trial courts in the provinces, provincial courts of appeal, the Federal Court of Canada, and the Supreme Court of Canada. After outlining the jurisdiction and operation of the two national courts, the chapter focused on the appointment of judges to different levels of courts including the appointment process for the Supreme Court of Canada. The chapter then turned to the principle of judicial independence and the deliberate intention to make it difficult to remove judges. The chapter ended with a note on the function of policing and corrections.

DISCUSSION QUESTIONS

1. Is judicial discretion in the interpretation of laws just as important as the power of judicial review?
2. How can fairness in the judicial system be guaranteed for Aboriginal peoples, the poor, women, and minorities?
3. If the current procedure for appointing judges is less than ideal, how should we reform it?
4. How would you improve the operation of police forces and the correctional system?

KEY TERMS

Canadian Judicial Council An agency composed of the federal and provincial chief justices that disciplines federally appointed judges and provides leadership and coordination among federal and provincial judicial systems.

Charter of Rights and Freedoms Part of the Constitution Act, 1982, that guaranteed fundamental freedoms and legal, democratic, linguistic, mobility, and equality rights.

Civil law A branch of law dealing with relations between private parties, such as individuals and corporations, that do not involve government.

Code Civil du Québec The unique system of civil law used in Quebec that is based on the Napoleonic Code.

Common law The basis of the British and Canadian legal systems that consists of the accumulation of judicial precedents which guide judges in the absence or interpretation of a legislature-made law.

Criminal Code A federal document that codifies most of the criminal law in the country.

Criminal law That branch of law dealing with wrongs committed against others that are considered to be offensive to society as a whole, for which the state takes the initiative to investigate, and for which perpetrators can be fined or jailed.

Federal Court of Canada A court established by the federal government dealing with cases involving that government and other specialized subjects within its jurisdiction.

Judicial Committee of the Privy Council A committee of the British parliament that functioned as Canada's final court of appeal until 1949.

Judicial discretion The leeway inevitably bestowed on the courts when they interpret laws, even when they do not, or have no power to, overturn them.

Judicial independence The constitutional principle that the courts should function independently of the rest of the government apparatus, especially the politicians, with implications for security of tenure and remuneration of judges.

Judicial review The power of the courts to overturn legislation or actions of the executive branch of government.

Judiciary The court system.

Political patronage Making appointments to public offices or awarding government contracts on a partisan basis.

Reference case A case referred to the courts by a provincial or federal cabinet usually to obtain a ruling on the constitutionality of a law.

Stare decisis The legal principle that precedents are binding on similar subsequent cases, which forms the basis of the common law system.

Supreme Court of Canada The highest court in Canada and the final court of appeal since 1949.

FURTHER READING

Anderson, Ellen. *Judging Bertha Wilson: Law as Large as Life*. Toronto: University of Toronto Press, 2002.

Gall, Gerald. *The Canadian Legal System*, 4th ed. Toronto: Carswell, 1995.

Green, Ian. *The Courts*. Vancouver: UBC Press, 2006.

Green, R.G. *Justice in Aboriginal Communities: Sentencing Alternatives*. Saskatoon: Purich Publishing 1998.

McCormick, Peter. *Canada's Courts*. Toronto: Lorimer, 1994.

———. *Supreme at Last: The Evolution of the Supreme Court of Canada, 1949–1999*. Toronto: Lorimer, 2000.

Russell, Peter. *The Judiciary in Canada: The Third Branch of Government*. Toronto: McGraw-Hill Ryerson, 1987.

Sharpe, Robert J., and Kent Roach. *Brian Dickson: A Judge's Journey*. Toronto: University of Toronto Press, 2003.

Glossary[1]

Numbers in parentheses refer to the chapter(s) containing the main discussion of the term.

Aboriginal self-government. A demand made by Aboriginal groups that they be able to govern themselves. (4)

Aboriginal title. The Aboriginal claim to land based on traditional occupancy and use rather than treaty. (4)

Access to Information Act. The 1983 act that gave citizens, journalists, and others the right to gain access to government documents, with certain exceptions, and established the office of Information Commissioner. (14)

Act of Union. The 1840 act that united the colonies of Upper and Lower Canada into the colony of Canada. (3, 11)

Advocacy advertising. Advertising that advocates a political point of view rather than trying to sell a good or service. (6, 10)

Advocacy group/interest group/pressure group. Any group seeking to influence government policy without contesting elections; an organization whose members promote their common interest by acting together to influence public policy. (1, 10)

Affirmative action. A law or program that provides preference in the hiring or promotion process to individuals with certain characteristics. (4, 11)

Assembly of First Nations. The largest interest group representing status and non-status Indians (who now prefer to be called First Nations peoples). (4, 10)

Auditor General. The official of Parliament whose staff audit the expenditures of government departments and who reports on instances of funds being unlawfully or unwisely spent. (14, 15)

Backbencher. A member of Parliament, whether on the government or opposition side, who sits on the back benches and does not have a Cabinet post or equivalent position in other parties. (15)

Bandwagon effect. The notion that if and when they know which party or candidate is going to win the election, voters will move en masse in that direction. (7)

Bill 101. The 1977 Quebec language law that made French the official language of Quebec and put restrictions on the use of English in the public and private sectors, including French-only signs. (3)

Block grant. A federal grant to the provinces that is given for a specific purpose, such as post-secondary education, but does not contain rigid conditions or standards. (12)

British North America Act (BNA Act). The 1867 act of the British parliament that created Canada by uniting the four original provinces, that provided some of the essential elements of the new country's constitution, and that in 1982 was renamed the Constitution Act, 1867. (5, 11)

Broker party. A kind of political party that tries to appeal to many different interests and to "broker" compromises among them, rather than having any distinct ideology. (9)

Budget. The annual financial statement of the government issued by the minister of finance that introduces tax changes and gives an overview of government finances for the next fiscal year. (15)

Bureaucracy. The permanent officials employed by the government, also known as the public service. (1, 14)

By-election. An election held between general elections in a specific electoral district due to the death or resignation of the MP or a tie on election night. (8)

Cabinet government. A system of government in which the major political decisions are made by the Cabinet as a whole, as opposed to one in which the prime minister acts with considerable autonomy or dominance. (13)

Cabinet solidarity. A convention that all Cabinet ministers publicly support whatever decisions the Cabinet has taken, regardless of their personal views. (13)

---

[1] A fuller definition of many of these terms can be found in John McMenemy, *The Language of Canadian Politics: A Guide to Important Terms and Concepts*, 4th ed. (Waterloo: University of Waterloo Press, 2006).

Canada Health Act. The 1984 act that re-imposed conditions on federal grants to the provinces for health programs, especially to prevent extra billing, privatization, or other moves toward a two-tier health system. (12)

Canada Health and Social Transfer (CHST). The annual federal block grant to the provinces between 1996 and 2004 intended to be used for health, postsecondary education, and welfare, now replaced by the Canada Health Transfer and the Canada Social Transfer. (12)

Canada–U.S. Free Trade Agreement (FTA). The agreement signed by Canada and the United States in 1987 and taking effect in 1989 that gradually eliminated tariffs between the two countries and otherwise prohibited governments from interfering in the private marketplace. (5)

Canadian Bill of Rights. An act of the Canadian Parliament passed in 1960 that outlined basic civil liberties but whose defects caused judicial confusion and limited the bill's effectiveness. (11)

Canadian Broadcasting Corporation (CBC). The large national Crown corporation with radio and television divisions whose mandate is to promote meaningful communication among all parts of the country. (5, 7)

Canadian Council of Chief Executives. The most powerful peak business pressure group in Canada, representing the 150 largest firms in the country. (2, 10)

Canadian Judicial Council. An agency composed of the federal and provincial chief justices that disciplines federally appointed judges and provides leadership and coordination among federal and provincial judicial systems. (16)

Canadian Labour Congress. The largest labour pressure group in Canada; the political voice of over three million members. (2, 10)

Canadian Radio-television and Telecommunications Commission (CRTC). The regulatory agency established to police the communications industry, including radio, television, telephones, and telecommunications. (5, 7)

Charlottetown Accord. The 1992 constitutional agreement that responded to Quebec's demands for distinct society status, Aboriginal demands for self-government, and the West's demand for a Triple-E Senate, but was defeated in a national referendum. (3)

Charter of Rights and Freedoms. Part of the Constitution Act, 1982, that guaranteed fundamental freedoms and legal, democratic, linguistic, mobility, and equality rights. (1, 11, 16)

Chief electoral officer. The independent and impartial official who is in charge of the operation of the whole electoral system. (8)

Civil law. A branch of law dealing with relations between private parties, such as individuals and corporations, that do not involve government. (16)

Civil liberties. Freedoms or rights, including the freedoms of speech, press, religion, and assembly, that citizens enjoy and that cannot be infringed upon by government. (11)

Clarity Act. The 2000 act that specified the conditions under which the federal government would recognize a referendum result in Quebec on the issue of independence. (3)

Class-based party. A political party that appeals primarily to one socioeconomic class or another. (9)

Class-consciousness. An awareness of the social class to which one belongs. (2, 8)

Clerk of the Privy Council and Secretary to the Cabinet. The head of the Privy Council Office and head of the federal public service; the chief nonpartisan adviser to the prime minister and Cabinet. (13)

Closure. A rule in the House of Commons in which a Cabinet minister introduces a motion to cut off debate. (15)

Code Civil du Québec. The unique system of civil law used in Quebec that is based on the Napoleonic Code. (16)

Coercion. Power based on authorized physical force, including police, armed forces, and jails, on which government has a near monopoly. (1)

Collectivism. As opposed to individualism, an ideology that holds that the public interest is enhanced by substantial collective action, normally via government. (6, 9)

Common law. The basis of the British and Canadian legal systems that consists of the accumulation of judicial precedents, which guide judges in the absence or interpretation of a legislature made law. (11, 16)

Concurrent powers. Powers officially shared by the federal and provincial governments, namely agriculture, immigration, and old age pensions. (12)

Conditional grant. A federal grant to the provinces, usually in support of a shared-cost program within provincial jurisdiction, to which Ottawa attaches conditions or standards before the province receives the money. (12)

Confederation. The foundation of Canada in 1867 with the union of four provinces. (11)

Confederation Settlement. The deal made among the Fathers of Confederation that entailed setting up a new federal system of government with a division of powers, including financial powers, federal controls over the provinces, provincial representation in federal institutions, and certain cultural guarantees. (12)

Conflict of interest. A situation in which any public officeholder places personal benefit (usually financial) before the public interest. (13)

Conscription crises. Two political crises during the two World Wars, in 1917 and in 1944, in which the population and government were divided, largely along ethnic lines, over the necessity of compulsory military service. (3)

Conservatism. A political ideology generally characterized by a belief in individualism and a minimum of government intervention in the economy and society, as well as by tradition, elitism, and opposition to change. (9)

Constituency. An electoral district that sends one member to the House of Commons. (8)

Constitution. The whole body of fundamental rules and principles according to which a state is governed. (11)

Constitution Act, 1867. The new name for the British North America Act, 1867, which united the four original provinces. (3, 11, 12)

Constitution Act, 1982. The act sponsored by Prime Minister Trudeau that contained a made-in-Canada constitutional amending formula and a Charter of Rights and Freedoms. (3, 11)

Constitutional Act. The 1791 British law that divided Canada into two separate colonies—Upper and Lower Canada—each with a governor, executive and legislative councils, and assembly. (3, 11)

Constitutional amending formula. The process for making amendments to the Constitution. (11)

Constitutional conventions. Unwritten rules of constitutional behaviour that are considered to be binding by and upon those who operate the Constitution but that are not enforceable by the courts. (11)

Constitutional monarchy. The official designation of the Canadian form of government, characterized by a monarch who is head of state but who rules according to the Constitution, which confides almost all governmental power into other hands. (11, 13)

Convergence. The recent phenomenon in the mass media of companies and technologies merging to create multimedia conglomerates, with ownership of newspaper, television, telephone, satellite, cable, Internet, and magazine businesses. (7)

Cooperative federalism. A variant of Canadian federalism since the Second World War in which neither level of government is subordinate to the other and in which there is an extensive degree of interaction between them. (12)

Criminal Code. A federal document that codifies most of the criminal law in the country. (16)

Criminal law. That branch of law dealing with wrongs committed against others that are considered to be offensive to society as a whole, for which the state takes the initiative to investigate, and for which perpetrators can be fined or jailed. (16)

Crown. The collection of executive powers exercised by or in the name of the monarch. (13)

Crown corporation. A corporation owned by the government that assumes a structure similar to that of a private company and that operates semi-independently of the Cabinet. (5, 13, 14)

Deference to authority. A value considered to be part of the Canadian political culture in which citizens are respectful of government authority and accept its word and orders with little question. (6)

Democracy. A political system characterized by popular sovereignty, political equality, political freedom, and majority rule. (6)

Democratic rights. A category of rights in the Charter of Rights and Freedoms that, among other things, guarantees the vote to every Canadian citizen. (11)

Department of Finance. The government department that has overall responsibility for the government's finances and its role in the economy and that has a powerful influence on all government policy. (13)

Deputy minister. The public servant who heads each government department, manages the department, and advises the minister. (14)

Deregulation. A government policy that removes previous regulations, especially those affecting the corporate sector. (14)

Dissolution of Parliament. The ending of a parliament, usually after four or more years, by calling an election. (8, 15)

Distinct society clause. A controversial clause in the Meech Lake Accord, and slightly modified in the Charlottetown Accord, claiming that Quebec constituted, within Canada, a distinct society. (3)

Division. A formal, standing, roll call vote in the House of Commons in which members' names are recorded in *Hansard*. (15)

Division of powers. The distribution of legislative powers between the federal and provincial governments, largely contained in sections 91 and 92 of the Constitution Act, 1867. (11, 12)

Durham Report. The 1839 report by Lord Durham that recommended the union of Upper and Lower Canada and the granting of responsible government to the colony of Canada. (11)

Egalitarianism. As opposed to elitism, the philosophy or practice of providing everyone with an equal amount of power and/or treating everyone more or less equally. (6)

Emergency doctrine. A constitutional doctrine invented by the Judicial Committee of the Privy Council that in times of national emergency, the peace, order, and good government clause became an emergency clause, increasing the powers of the federal government. (12)

Employment equity. A policy that seeks to guarantee complete fairness in hiring, promotion, or remuneration, regardless of gender, ethnicity, or disability. (4)

Enumerated powers. The powers of the provincial governments that are explicitly listed in section 92 of the Constitution Act, 1867. (12)

Equality rights. A category of rights in the Charter of Rights and Freedoms that prohibits governments from discriminating against certain categories of people. (4, 11)

Equalization payments. Large annual cash payments made by the federal government to have-not provinces to help them provide a satisfactory level of public services. (2, 12)

Estimates. The annual spending plans of government departments and agencies. (13, 14, 15)

Executive. That branch of government that provides leadership and makes the major decisions. (1, 13)

Executive federalism. A variant of cooperative federalism characterized by extensive federal–provincial interaction at the level of first ministers, departmental ministers, and deputy ministers. (12)

Expenditure Management System. The process for determining government financial priorities and the annual distribution of public funds. (10)

Extra-parliamentary party. That part of a political party beyond its members of Parliament—that is, party members, local and national executives, and party headquarters. (9)

Federal Court of Canada. A court established by the federal government dealing with cases involving that government and other specialized subjects within its jurisdiction. (16)

Federalism (federation). A system of government characterized by two levels of authority (federal and provincial) and a division of powers between them such that neither is subordinate to the other. (1, 11, 12)

Filibuster. An organized attempt by the opposition in the House of Commons to prolong debate and delay adoption of government measures. (15)

First ministers' conference. A federal–provincial conference consisting of the prime minister and provincial premiers (and, increasingly, territorial leaders). (12)

First Nations. A term that came into common usage in the 1970s that can refer to the Indian peoples of Canada, both status and non-status, or that can replace the word "band." (4)

First-past-the-post system. The kind of single-member plurality electoral system used in Canada in which the candidate with the most votes wins the constituency. (8)

Free vote. A rare vote in the House of Commons in which members are not required to abide by the party line. (15)

Front de libération du Québec (FLQ). The terrorist wing of the Quebec separatist movement in the 1960s and 1970s. (3)

Fundamental freedoms. Political freedoms—of religion, speech, press, assembly, association, etc.—that governments are not supposed to encroach upon and that are guaranteed by the Charter of Rights and Freedoms. (11)

Globalization. The pattern of deepening supraterritorial interaction around the world, characterized by comprehensive free trade agreements, massive diffusion of technological change, and worldwide corporate competition or megamergers that challenge the sovereignty of the state. (1, 5)

Government. (1) The set of institutions that make and enforce collective, public decisions for a society; (2) The set of authorities centred around a prime minister, Cabinet, and party that currently occupy the executive offices of the state and provide political leadership. (1, 13, 15)

Government bill. A bill introduced by a Cabinet minister on behalf of the whole government. (15)

Government department. A government organization headed by a minister who is politically accountable for its operations and a deputy minister who is in charge of its hierarchical administrative apparatus. (14)

Governor general. The representative of the Queen in Canada who normally performs her head of state functions. (13)

Governor in council. The prime minister and Cabinet (but *not* the governor general) exercising powers of the Privy Council. (13)

Horse-race effect. The notion that election campaigns have degenerated into a "horse race" where everyone, especially the media, is concerned with which party is ahead, not with how parties would tackle serious public issues. (7)

House leader. The person appointed by each party in the House of Commons to deal with counterparts in other parties with respect to scheduling Commons business. (15)

Ideology. A coherent set of ideas or principles about how a society ought to function, with particular reference to the role of the state. (9)

Indian Act. The act that governed almost all aspects of Aboriginal life in Canada after the 1870s, giving extensive authority to government bureaucrats and minimal discretion to Native people themselves. (4)

Individual ministerial responsibility. The principle that Cabinet ministers are individually responsible to the House of Commons to answer for everything that happens in their department. (13, 14)

Individualism. An ideology that holds that individuals should have maximum freedom or liberty to do as they please, especially in economic terms, and that governments should not get involved in taxation, regulation, redistribution, or ownership. (6, 9)

Information Commissioner. The official of Parliament who encourages government to operate on a more open basis and makes judgments in cases where departments withhold information under the Access to Information Act. (14)

Institutionalized advocacy group. A kind of advocacy group characterized by permanence, resources, governmental recognition and acceptance, and well-developed links with the authorities. (10)

Interest group. *See* Advocacy group/interest group/pressure group.

Issue-oriented advocacy group. A kind of advocacy group that springs up around an issue and disappears once that issue has been resolved. (10)

James Bay Agreement. The 1975 deal signed by the government of Quebec and its northern Aboriginal residents that gave the latter land, cash, and hunting rights in return for surrendering land for the James Bay hydroelectric project. (4)

Judicial Committee of the Privy Council. A committee of the British Parliament that functioned as Canada's final court of appeal until 1949. (11, 12, 16)

Judicial discretion. The leeway inevitably bestowed on the courts when they interpret laws, even when they do not, or have no power to, overturn them. (11, 16)

Judicial independence. The constitutional principle that the courts should function independently of the rest of the government apparatus, especially the politicians, with implications for security of tenure and remuneration of judges. (1, 16)

Judicial review. The power of the courts to overturn legislation or actions of the executive branch of government. (1, 11, 15, 16)

Judiciary. The court system. (1, 16)

Keynesian economics. An economic theory that to promote general economic stability, the government should counterbalance the private sector, spending (running deficit budgets) in periods of unemployment when the private sector doesn't spend, and taxing (withdrawing money from the system) in periods of inflation when the private sector is spending too much. (12)

King–Byng dispute. The 1926 dispute between Prime Minister Mackenzie King and Governor General Lord Byng over King's request for a dissolution of Parliament, which Byng denied. (13)

Leader of the Opposition. The leader of the main opposition party in the House of Commons. (15)

Leadership review. A clause in the constitutions of political parties that allows party members or convention delegates to review the leader's performance. (9)

Left. That part of the ideological spectrum that believes in equality in society and the intervention of government via collectivist measures such as taxation, regulation, redistribution, and public ownership to effect such equality. (9)

Legal rights. The rights of a person suspected or accused of committing a crime, now listed in the Charter of Rights and Freedoms. (11)

Legislature. That branch of government whose function is to represent the people and make laws. (1, 15)

Liberalism. An ideology based on a belief in the rationality of the individual and on maximizing individual freedom, liberty, and self-fulfillment. Before 1900, this was assumed to entail a minimal role for government; after 1900, liberalism usually advocated a larger role for the state and was placed on the centre-left of the spectrum. (9)

Lobbying. Any organized attempt to influence the authorities, now often performed by professional lobbyist firms. (10)

Majority government. A situation in which the party in power has over 50 percent of the seats in the House of Commons. (1, 8, 15)

Majority rule. An element in the definition of democracy that states that in any decision-making setting involving a difference of opinion, the larger number should carry the day. (6)

Mandate. The concept that the winning party has an obligation to enact policies it promised during the election campaign. (8)

Mass media. Sources of information for the mass public—principally radio, television, and newspapers. (1, 7)

Meech Lake Accord. The 1987 package of constitutional reforms intended to bring Quebec back into the constitutional fold but that was turned down in 1990. (3)

Memorandum to Cabinet. The formal written document that a minister submits to the Cabinet seeking to initiate or change a government policy. (13)

Merit system. A system of hiring and promoting public servants on the basis of their merits (education, experience, etc.) rather than on party preference or other considerations. (14)

Minority government. A situation in which the government party has fewer than 50 percent of the seats in the House of Commons. (1, 8, 15)

Minority language education rights. Rights established in section 23 of the Charter of Rights and Freedoms whereby French-speaking Canadians can send their children to French-language schools wherever their numbers warrant, a principle also extended to English-speaking Canadians where they are a minority. (3, 11)

Mobility rights. A category of rights in the Charter of Rights and Freedoms guaranteeing the freedom to move from one province to another and seek employment there. (11)

Money bill. A bill to raise money for government purposes or to spend public funds. (13, 15)

Multiculturalism. A policy of encouraging ethnic and cultural groups to maintain their customs and traditions, often with public financial assistance. (4)

Multiparty system. Typically European in nature, a party system characterized by many parties, usually without any one having a majority in the legislature. (9)

National Energy Program. The 1980 policy associated with Pierre Trudeau which was designed to skim off petroleum tax revenue for Ottawa, keep the price of petroleum below world levels, encourage conservation, and Canadianize the industry, and which met with great opposition in Western Canada. (2, 5)

National Policy. The broad nation-building 1879 policy of John A. Macdonald that included tariff protection for central Canadian manufacturing, massive immigration, and the construction of a national transportation system. (2, 5)

Neoconservatism. An ideology originating in the 1980s calling on government to withdraw from its extensive intervention in the private market economy but perhaps still promote certain traditional social values. (9)

Neoliberalism. An ideology originating in the 1980s calling on government to withdraw from its extensive intervention in the private market economy—emphasizing privatization, deregulation, balancing of budgets, and trimming of social programs—as well as from regulating society in general. (9)

New middle class. A term from class analysis describing salaried professionals such as teachers, public servants, and nurses. (2)

New Public Management. A movement within public administration since about 1990 that involved the downsizing of government operations, alternative service delivery, and partnerships with private or voluntary sector agencies. (14)

News management. A variety of techniques used by politicians and governments to ensure positive media coverage. (7)

Nisga'a Treaty. The 2000 treaty signed by the Nisga'a First Nation and the governments of Canada and British Columbia that incorporated a land claim settlement and powers of self-government; it is considered the first modern-day Aboriginal treaty. (4)

Nomination. The act of becoming a candidate in an election, which normally entails being selected to represent a party at a nomination meeting and then completing official nomination papers. (8)

Non-confidence motion. A motion in the House of Commons, brought by the opposition, inviting MPs to demonstrate a lack of confidence in the government, which, if successful, would require the Cabinet's resignation or the calling of an election. (15)

North American Free Trade Agreement (NAFTA). The 1994 extension of the Canada–U.S. Free Trade Agreement to Mexico. (5)

Notwithstanding clause. Section 33 of the Charter of Rights and Freedoms that allows federal or provincial governments to pass laws that violate certain sections of the Charter. (11)

Nunavut. The eastern half of the Northwest Territories that was established as a separate Inuit territory in 1999. (4)

Oakes test. The strategy outlined in the *Oakes* case for interpreting the reasonable limits clause of the Charter of Rights and Freedoms. (11)

Official Languages Act. The 1969 federal act that established official bilingualism in Canada and gave citizens the right to deal with certain offices of the federal government in either English or French. (3, 14)

One-party dominance. A party system characterized by the dominance of a single party. (9)

Opposition. Those members of Parliament who do not support the government of the day. (15)

Opposition days. Twenty-two days per session of Parliament set aside for the opposition parties to determine the topic of debate. (15)

Order in council. A formal, legal decision made by the prime minister and Cabinet (governor in council), including regulations and appointments. (13)

Parliament. Theoretically, the Queen, the House of Commons, and the Senate, functioning collectively, such as in the approval of legislation, but often used to refer to the Commons and Senate or Commons alone. (15)

Parliamentary government. A form of government, distinct from the U.S. congressional system, characterized by the dominance of the political executive whose members also sit in parliament. (1)

Parliamentary press gallery. Those members of the media who are registered to sit in the press gallery in the House of Commons and who report on its proceedings or on government in general. (7, 15)

Parliamentary secretary. A government MP who has been given additional responsibilities to assist a Cabinet minister. (15)

Party caucus. The whole body of MPs of any party, together with such senators as choose to attend, who hold a regular weekly meeting to discuss parliamentary strategy and party policy. (9, 15)

Party discipline. The convention that all MPs within any party vote together on every occasion, as predetermined by the leader or in the party caucus meeting and as enforced by the party whip. (15)

Party identification. The tendency of a voter to feel attached to a particular political party over an extended period of time. (8)

Party whip. An official of each party in the House of Commons whose function is to enforce party discipline and ensure that members are present for all votes. (15)

Pay equity. An element of employment equity programs designed to ensure that all employees are paid equally for work of equal value and are not discriminated against on the basis of gender or other factors. (4)

Peace, order, and good government (POGG) clause. The words in the opening sentence of section 91 of the Constitution Act, 1867, which state that the residual powers rest with the federal government but which has been often misinterpreted by the courts as providing only an emergency power. (12)

Policy communities and policy networks. Loose communities that form for the purpose of shaping public policy, taking the form of discrete and specialized clusters of government departments and agencies, advocacy groups, politicians, corporations, and interested individuals. (10)

Political culture. The sum total of the politically relevant values, beliefs, attitudes, and orientations in any political system. (6)

Political efficacy. The feeling that one has political influence and that one's political participation can make an impact. (6)

Political equality. An element in the definition of democracy that entails the principle of "one person–one vote," that is, every citizen has a vote and each counts equally. (6)

Political freedom. An element in the definition of democracy that entails freedom of speech, press, assembly, association, etc., such that people can organize and advocate in order to influence election results and public policy. (6)

Political party. An organized group that makes nominations and contests elections in the hope of influencing the policy and personnel of government. (1, 9)

Political patronage. Making appointments to public offices or awarding government contracts on a partisan basis. (14, 16)

Political socialization. The process whereby individuals acquire their political values, attitudes, beliefs, information, and opinions. (6)

Politics. The activity in which conflicting interests struggle for advantage or dominance in the making and execution of public policies. (1)

Popular sovereignty. An element in the definition of democracy that entails periodically allowing the public at large to exert its will—to have the final say—normally through general elections. (6)

Popular vote. The percentage of all votes cast for a candidate or party, regardless of who was elected. (8)

Poverty line. An amount of income such that anyone who received less would be living in poverty. (2)

Power. The ability of one actor to impose its will on another, usually considered to be the essence of politics and government. (1)

Prerogative powers. That small number of residual powers of the Crown that remain from the era of an all-powerful monarch that the Queen or governor general can still exercise on rare occasions at his or her own discretion. (13)

Pressure group. *See* Advocacy group/interest group/pressure group.

Prime Minister's Office (PMO). The office that supports and advises the prime minister in partisan terms. (13)

Prime ministerial government. The notion that the prime minister is now so preeminent that the label "Cabinet government" no longer accurately describes how decisions are made in the political executive. (13)

Private bill. A bill introduced in Parliament that affects only a specific individual, company, organization, or group. (15)

Private member's bill. A public bill introduced in Parliament by an MP who is not in the Cabinet. (15)

Private sector. That part of the economy operated by individuals and corporations, based on the profit motive. (1)

Privatization. Transferring a government program, agency, or Crown corporation to the private sector. (14)

Privy Council. A body established by the Constitution Act, 1867, to advise the governor general in the exercise of the powers of that office but that was effectively taken over by the prime minister and Cabinet. (13)

Privy Council Office (PCO). The office that supports and advises the prime minister, Cabinet, and Cabinet committees in nonpartisan terms. (13)

Public Accounts Committee. The House of Commons committee that examines the Auditor General's reports and criticizes government officials for illegal or unwise expenditures. (14, 15)

Public bill. A bill introduced in Parliament that affects society in general. (15)

Public opinion. The sum total of opinions held by members of the public on any subject. (7)

Public opinion poll. A survey conducted to ascertain the opinions of the public on assorted matters. (7)

Public policy. A course of action or inaction chosen by public authorities to address a given problem or interrelated set of problems. (13)

Public sector. That part of the economy operated or financed by government. (1)

Quebec Act. The 1774 British law that provided for a system of government for the colony of Quebec that included certain privileges for the French-speaking, Roman Catholic majority. (3, 11)

Question Period. The daily 45-minute period in the House of Commons in which opposition members spar with the prime minister and Cabinet ministers. (15)

Quiet Revolution. The dramatic change of values and attitudes, especially toward the state, the new collective self-confidence, and the new brand of nationalism in Quebec in the 1960s. (3)

Reasonable limits clause. Section 1 of the Charter of Rights and Freedoms, which allows the courts to uphold a law even if it violates a Charter right. (11)

Recall. A populist device in which the signing of a petition by a certain proportion of the local electorate to recall their legislative representative means that the representative must resign. (6)

Red Tories. A minority faction within the former Progressive Conservative Party that had collectivist leanings akin to those of many British and European conservatives, stressing order, tradition, stability, and a paternalistic concern for the condition of the working class. (9)

Redistribution. The process of reallocating seats in the House of Commons among the provinces after each decennial census and then redrawing constituency boundaries within each province. (8)

Reference case. A case referred to the courts by a provincial or federal cabinet usually to obtain a ruling on the constitutionality of a law. (16)

Referendum. A populist device in which a public policy proposal is submitted directly to the electorate. (3, 6)

Regionalism. Strong feelings of attachment to the region or province where one lives that often generate political activity. (2)

Regulations. The detailed rules drafted by the bureaucracy under the authority of laws passed by Parliament that are too voluminous and technical to put into the legislation itself. (10, 13, 14)

Regulatory tribunal. A government agency established to regulate an area of public policy, such as transportation or communications, which operates at arm's length from the Cabinet. (5, 14)

Representative bureaucracy. A public service that reflects the composition of the population, with the most usual concerns being gender, ethnicity, and region. (14)

Representative democracy. A system of government based on periodic election of representatives to Parliament, as opposed to more direct participation by voters in making public decisions. (6, 9)

Representative government. A form of government including an assembly elected by the citizens but not necessarily incorporating the principle of responsible government. (11)

Residual powers. Those powers not given to the provinces in the Constitution Act, 1867, that were assigned to the federal government under the POGG clause in section 91. (12)

Responsible government. A form of government in which the political executive must retain the confidence of the elected legislature and resign or call an election if and when it is defeated on a vote of non-confidence. (1, 11, 15)

Returning officer. The official in charge of running the election in each electoral district. (8)

Right. That part of the ideological spectrum that cherishes individualism and believes in leaving the private sector to operate with minimal government intervention. (9)

Royal Proclamation of 1763. The British policy enunciated after conquering Quebec that in a large area called Indian Territory forbade the purchase or settlement of land without a treaty between the Crown and the Indian peoples concerned. (4, 11)

Rule of law. The constitutional principle that all government action must be based on law and that governments and government officials must obey the law. (11)

Safe seat. A constituency that a single party can be assured of winning, election after election. (15)

Sexual orientation. One's sexual preference, usually either heterosexual or homosexual. It now constitutes a ground on which discrimination is prohibited. (4)

Shared-cost programs. Government programs whose cost is shared by the federal and provincial governments. (12)

Social democracy. A moderate leftist ideology that emphasizes the principle of equality and that usually prescribes a large role for government to intervene in society and the economy. (9)

Social movement. An informal network of organizations and individuals who, on the basis of a collective identity and shared values, engage in political struggle intended to expand the boundaries of the existing system, such as the women's and environmental movements. (1, 10)

Social Union Framework Agreement. An overall framework of federal–provincial relations agreed to in 1999 by all governments except Quebec that sought to end long-standing irritants on both sides. (12)

Sovereignty. Ultimate control or independence, such as Canadian national sovereignty vis-à-vis that of other countries. (1, 5)

Sovereignty-association. The Parti Québécois proposal in which Quebec would be sovereign while maintaining an economic association with the rest of Canada. (3)

Speaker. The presiding officer of the House of Commons. (15)

Speech from the Throne. The document prepared by the prime minister and Cabinet and read by the governor general at the opening of each session of Parliament that outlines the government's legislative proposals for the session. (13, 15)

Spending power. The unofficial power of the federal government to spend money in any field, including those within provincial jurisdiction. (12)

Spin doctors. Party officials and ministerial aides who talk to the media and try to influence media coverage by putting the best face on an event from their party's point of view. (7, 8)

Standing committees. Those committees of the House of Commons that are set up semipermanently and that parallel government departments. (15)

Standing Orders. The written rules of the House of Commons. (15)

Staples theory. The notion that Canadian economic development has gone through a series of stages based on the exploitation of one natural resource or another and the export of such resources, without the development of a secondary or manufacturing sector. (2)

Stare decisis. The legal principle that precedents are binding on similar subsequent cases, which forms the basis of the common law system. (16)

Statute of Westminster. The 1931 British law that declared Canada and the other Dominions to be fully independent. (5, 11)

Supremacy of Parliament. The principle that no other organ of government can overrule Parliament or its laws. (15)

Supreme Court of Canada. The highest court in Canada and the final court of appeal since 1949. (16)

Terrorism. An act intended to cause death or serious bodily harm to civilians with the purpose of intimidating a population or compelling a government to do or abstain from doing any act. (5)

Third-party advertising. Advertising by advocacy groups, as opposed to political parties, during an election campaign. (8, 10)

Transnational corporations. Corporations operating simultaneously in many countries throughout the world that often take orders from company headquarters and that individual states find difficult to control. (5)

Treasury Board. A Cabinet committee whose primary responsibility is to restrain government spending. (13)

Treasury Board Secretariat. The government department that advises the Treasury Board in its deliberations and that functions as a restraining influence on departmental spending. (13, 14)

Treaty rights. Aboriginal rights based on treaties signed with the Crown. (4)

Triple-E Senate. A proposal for Senate reform in which each province would have an equal number of senators who would be elected and who would be given effective powers. (15)

Two-party system. A type of party system in which two main parties are of approximately equal strength and alternate in office. (9)

Two-plus party system. A type of party system in which two main parties are of approximately equal strength and alternate in office but are accompanied by one or more minor parties of significant strength. (9)

Visible minorities. Members of ethnic groups, other than Aboriginal peoples, whose skin colour is not white. (4)

Voluntary sector. That part of the economy operated on a not-for-profit basis by non-governmental groups. (1)

War Measures Act. The law invoked in both World Wars and during the 1970 FLQ crisis under which the federal cabinet was given emergency powers to deal with the crisis. (3)

Welfare state. The characterization of most Western democracies from about 1950 to 1985 in which governments functioned as provider and protector of individual security and well-being through the implementation of a wide array of social programs and income transfers to individuals. (12)

Western alienation. The feeling shared by many Western Canadians that their interests are not taken seriously in the national policy-making process. (2)

Westminster model. The model of government developed in Britain in which the political executive is given extensive power to provide effective leadership. (1, 15)

White Paper on Indians. The 1969 Trudeau–Chrétien policy proposal to do away with the Indian Act and treaties and to fully integrate Aboriginal peoples into Canadian society. (4)

Women's movement. The collection of women's groups that mushroomed across the country, starting around 1970, demanding complete equality for women. (4)

World Trade Organization (WTO). An international organization to which Canada and most other countries belong that has the power to disallow national policies and practices it deems discriminatory against companies from other states. (5)

Notes

Chapter 2

1. See, for example, Pierre Berton, *The National Dream* and *The Last Spike* (Toronto: McClelland and Stewart, 1970 and 1971, respectively); Robert Chodos, *The CPR: A Century of Corporate Welfare* (Toronto: Lorimer, 1973).
2. Task Force on Canadian Unity, *A Future Together* (Ottawa: Supply and Services, 1979), pp. 26–27.
3. Wallace Clement and Daniel Drache, *A Practical Guide to Canadian Political Economy* (Toronto: Lorimer, 1978), pp. 9–14.
4. David Kilgour, *Uneasy Patriots: Western Canadians in Confederation* (Edmonton: Lone Pine Publishers, 1988) and *Inside Outer Canada* (Edmonton: Lone Pine Publishers, 1990); Don Braid and Sydney Sharpe, *Breakup: Why the West Feels Left Out of Canada* (Toronto: Key Porter Books, 1990); Roger Gibbins and Loleen Berdahl, *Western Visions, Western Futures* (Peterborough: Broadview Press, 2003).
5. Donald Smiley, *The Federal Condition in Canada* (Toronto: McGraw-Hill Ryerson, 1987), p. 159.
6. Roger Gibbins, *Prairie Politics and Society* (Toronto: Butterworths, 1980), p. 191.
7. "The Rich 100," *Canadian Business* (November 2009).
8. Hugh Mackenzie, *Banner Year for CEOs* (Ottawa: Canadian Centre for Policy Alternatives, 2009).
9. Linda McQuaig, *Behind Closed Doors* (Toronto: Penguin, 1987).
10. *Exposing the Facts of Corporate Rule: A Handbook on How to Challenge the Big Business Agenda* (Toronto: Centre for Social Justice, 1998).
11. Irving Abella, ed., *On Strike* (Toronto: James Lewis & Samuel, 1974); Walter Stewart, *Strike!* (Toronto: McClelland and Stewart, 1977), ch. 4.
12. Statistics Canada, "Unionization," *Perspectives on Labour and Income*, Cat. No. 75-001-XPE (July 2009).
13. Human Resources and Skills Development Canada, "Union Membership in Canada—2008," at http://www.hrsdc.gc.ca/eng/labour/labour_relations/info_analysis/union_membership/index.shtml.
14. Gad Horowitz, *Canadian Labour in Politics* (Toronto: University of Toronto Press, 1968).
15. Lars Osberg, *A Quarter Century of Economic Inequality in Canada: 1981–2006* (Ottawa: Canadian Centre for Policy Alternatives, April 2008).
16. *The Canadian Fact Book on Poverty—2000* (Ottawa: Canadian Council on Social Development, 2000), p. 2.
17. Armine Yalnizyan, *Canada's Great Divide: The Politics of the Growing Gap Between Rich and Poor in the 1990s* (Toronto: Centre for Social Justice, 2000).
18. Campaign 2000, *Pathways to Progress: Structural Solutions to Address Child Poverty* (Toronto, May 2004).

Chapter 3

1. Dale Thomson, *Jean Lesage and the Quiet Revolution* (Toronto: Macmillan, 1984).
2. Kenneth McRoberts, *Misconceiving Canada: The Struggle for National Unity* (Toronto: Oxford University Press, 1997).
3. Graham Fraser, *René Lévesque and the Parti Québécois in Power* (Toronto: Macmillan, 1984).
4. Roy Romanow, J. Whyte, and H. Leeson, *Canada… Notwithstanding: The Making of the Constitution, 1976–1982* (Toronto: Methuen, 1984); Edward McWhinney, *Canada and the Constitution, 1979–82: Patriation and the Charter of Rights* (Toronto: University of Toronto Press, 1982).
5. Patrick J. Monahan, *Meech Lake: The Inside Story* (Toronto: University of Toronto Press, 1991).
6. Alan C. Cairns, *Constitution, Government, and Society in Canada* (Toronto: McClelland and Stewart, 1988); *Disruptions: Constitutional Struggles, from the Charter to Meech Lake* (Toronto: McClelland and Stewart, 1991).

7. Kenneth McRoberts and Patrick Monahan, eds., *The Charlottetown Accord, the Referendum and the Future of Canada* (Toronto: University of Toronto Press, 1993); Peter Russell, *Constitutional Odyssey: Can Canadians Become a Sovereign People?*, 3rd ed. (Toronto: University of Toronto Press, 2004).

8. Richard Johnston, *The Challenge of Direct Democracy: The 1992 Canadian Referendum* (Kingston: McGill-Queen's University Press, 1996).

9. *Reference re Secession of Quebec*, [1998] 2 S.C.R. 217.

10. Thomas Courchene, "Market Nationalism," *Policy Options*, October 1968.

11. Kenneth McRoberts, "Quebec: Province, Nation, or Distinct Society?" In Michael S. Whittington and Glen Williams, eds., *Canadian Politics in the 20th Century*, 6th ed. (Toronto: Nelson, 2004), p. 399.

12. Chantal Hébert, *French Kiss: Stephen Harper's Blind Date with Quebec* (Toronto: Knopf Canada, 2007).

Chapter 4

1. Statistics Canada, Ethnocultural Portrait of Canada Highlight Tables, 2006 Census, available at http://www12.statcan.ca/census-recensement/2006/dp-pd/hlt/97-562/pages/page.cfm?Lang=E&Geo= PR&Code=01&Data=Count&Table=2&StartRec=1&Sort=3&Display=All&CSDFilter=5000 and http://www12.statcan.ca/census-recensement/2006/dp-pd/hlt/97-558/pages/page.cfm?Lang=E&Geo= PR&Code=01&Table=1&Data=Count&Sex=1&Age=1&StartRec=1&Sort=2&Display=Page.

2. Indian Affairs and Northern Development *Canada, Basic Departmental Data, 2004* (December 2005); Geoffrey York, *The Dispossessed: Life and Death in Native Canada* (Toronto: Lester & Orpen Dennys, 1989).

3. Geoffrey York and Loreen Pindera, *People of the Pines: The Warriors and the Legacy of Oka* (Toronto: Little Brown, 1991); Craig MacLaine and Michael Baxendale, *This Land Is Our Land* (Toronto: Optimum, 1990).

4. It is virtually impossible to keep pace with the many Supreme Court decisions related to Aboriginal issues, but several are listed on the book's website. In 2010, the Government introduced a bill in response to the McIvor decision of the B.C. Court of Appeal to ensure that grandchildren of women who lost status as a result of marrying non-Indian men will become entitled to Indian status.

5. *Nisga'a Final Agreement*, http://www.ainc-inac.gc.ca/pr/agr/nsga/nisdex12_e.pdf, retrieved November 15, 2004.

6. Alan C. Cairns, *Aboriginal Peoples and the Canadian State* (Vancouver: UBC Press, 2000); Cairns, *First Nations and the Canadian State: In Search of Coexistence* (Montreal: McGill-Queen's University Press, 2005); Michael S. Whittington, "Aboriginal Self-Government," in Michael Whittington and Glen Williams, eds., *Canadian Politics in the 21st Century*, 6th ed. (Toronto: Nelson, 2004).

7. Yasmeen Abu-Laban and Christina Gabriel, *Selling Diversity: Immigration, Multiculturalism, Employment Equity, and Globalization* (Peterborough: Broadview Press, 2002); Will Kymlicka, *Finding Our Way: Rethinking Ethnocultural Relations in Canada* (Toronto: Oxford University Press, 1998).

8. Neil Bissoondath, *Selling Illusions: The Cult of Multiculturalism in Canada* (Toronto: Penguin, 1994), but see also Phil Ryan, *Multicultiphobia* (Toronto: University of Toronto Press, 2010).

9. Penney Kome, *Women of Influence* (Toronto: University of Toronto Press, 1985), p. 86; Sylvia Bashevkin, *Women, Power, Politics: The Hidden Story of Canada's Unfinished Democracy* (Toronto: University of Toronto Press, 2009).

10. Statistics Canada, *Women in Canada: Work Chapter Updates*, available at http://www.statcan.gc.ca/ bsolc/olc-cel/olc-cel?land=eng&catno=89F0133X; Statistics Canada, *Women in Canada: A Gender-Based Statistical Report* (Catalogue No. 89-503-XPE, March 2006), p. 14; Melissa Cooke-Reynolds and Nancy Zukewich, "The Feminization of Work," *Canadian Social Trends* (Statistics Canada, Catalogue No. 11-008, Spring 2004).

11. Statistics Canada, *The General Social Survey, Matter of Fact, No. 9*, Catalogue no. 89-630-X, "Are women spending more time on unpaid domestic work than men in Canada?", available at http://www. statcan.gc.ca/pub/89-630-X/2008001/article/10705-eng.htm.

12. Penney Kome, *The Taking of Twenty-Eight* (Toronto: Women's Educational Press, 1983); *Women of Influence*, ch. 10.

13. Janine Brodie et al., *The Politics of Abortion* (Toronto: Oxford University Press, 1992).

14. David P. Ross, Katherine J. Scott, and Peter J. Smith, *The Canadian Fact Book on Poverty, 2000* (Ottawa: Canadian Council on Social Development, 2000).

15. Miriam Smith, *Political Institutions and Lesbian and Gay Rights in the United States and Canada* (New York: Routledge, 2008).

Chapter 5

1. R. McGregor Dawson, *The Government of Canada*, 5th ed., rev. Norman Ward (Toronto: University of Toronto Press, 1970), p. 54.

2. Donald Creighton, *Canada's First Century* (Toronto: Macmillan, 1970); George Grant, *Lament for a Nation: The Defeat of Canadian Nationalism* (Toronto: McClelland and Stewart, 1965); J.L. Granatstein, *How Britain's Weakness Forced Canada into the Arms of the United States* (Toronto: University of Toronto Press, 1989).

3. Lloyd Axworthy, *Navigating a New World: Canada's Global Future* (Toronto: Knopf Canada, 2004); Steven Holloway, *Canadian Foreign Policy: Defining the Canadian National Interest* (Peterborough: Broadview Press, 2006).

4. Canada, *Foreign Direct Investment in Canada* (Ottawa: Supply and Services, 1972), p. 14; John McDougall, *Drifting Together: The Political Economy of Canada–US Integration* (Peterborough: Broadview Press, 2006).

5. Human Resources and Social Development Canada, "Union Membership in Canada—2007, available at http://www.hrsdc.gc.ca/eng/lp/wid/union_membership.shtml.

6. Statistics Canada, "Television Viewing," March 2006, Cat. No. 87F0006XIE, http://www.statcan.gc.ca/pub/87f0006x/87f0006x2006001-eng.htm.

7. Solid statistics are hard to come by, but see Victor Rabinovitch, "The Social and Economic Rationales for Canada's Domestic Cultural Policies," in Dennis Browne, ed., *The Culture/Trade Quandary: Canada's Policy Options* (Ottawa: Centre for Trade Policy and Law, 1998), p. 30.

8. G. Bruce Doern and Brian Tomlin, *Faith and Fear: The Free Trade Story* (Toronto: Stoddart, 1991).

9. Duncan Cameron and Mel Watkins, *Canada Under Free Trade* (Toronto: Lorimer, 1993); John Warnock, *Free Trade and the New Right Agenda* (Vancouver: New Star Books, 1988).

10. Government of Canada, "The North American Free Trade Agreement at a Glance," Cat. No. E75-56/1-1993E; Jeffrey M. Ayres, *Defying Conventional Wisdom: Political Movements and Popular Contention Against North American Free Trade* (Toronto: University of Toronto Press, 1998).

11. Stephen Clarkson, *Uncle Sam and Us: Globalization, Neoconservatism, and the Canadian State* (Toronto: University of Toronto Press, 2002).

12. Stephen Clarkson, *Does North American Exist? Governing the Continent after NAFTA and 9/11* (Toronto: University of Toronto Press, 2008).

13. Linda McQuaig, *The Cult of Impotence: Selling the Myth of Powerlessness in the Global Economy* (Toronto: Viking, 1998); Maude Barlow and Tony Clarke, *Global Showdown: How the New Activists Are Fighting Global Corporate Rule* (Toronto: Stoddart Publishing, 2000); Brian Bow, *The Politics of Linkage: Power, Interdependence, and Ideas in Canada–US Relations* (Vancouver: UBC Press, 2009).

14. Foreign Affairs and International Trade Canada, "International Crime and Terrorism," available at http://www.international.gc.ca/crime/terrorism-terrorisme.aspx?lang=en.

Chapter 6

1. Henry B. Mayo, *An Introduction to Democratic Theory* (New York: Oxford University Press, 1960), ch. 4.

2. Seymour Martin Lipset, *Continental Divide* (New York: Routledge, 1990), p. 8.

3. Pierre Berton, *Why We Act Like Canadians* (Toronto: McClelland and Stewart, 1982).

4. *Maclean's*, July 1, 1995, p. 15.

5. Will Kymlicka, *Finding Our Way: Rethinking Ethnocultural Relations in Canada* (Don Mills: Oxford University Press, 1998). See also Michael Adams, *Unlikely Utopia: The Surprising Triumph of Canadian Pluralism* (Toronto: Penguin Canada, 2007).

6. Matthew Mendelsohn and J. Scott Matthews, "The New Ontario: The Shifting Attitudes of Ontarians toward the Federation," Mowat Centre for Policy Innovation, University of Toronto, February 2010.

7. Canadian Information Office, *Government Communications Survey—Wave IV: Final Survey Findings* (Fall 1999); Shawn McCarthy, "Albertans Embrace Federation," *The Globe and Mail* (February 14, 2001). See also Statistics Canada, "2003 General Social Survey on Social Engagement, Cycle 17: An Overview of Findings," Cat. No. 89-598-XWE (July 2004).

8. W. Wolfson and B. Murphy, "Income Inequality in North America: Does the 49th Parallel Still Matter?" *Canadian Economic Observer*, Cat. No. 11-010-XPB (August 2000); Miles Corak, "Equality of Opportunity and Inequality Across the Generations: Challenges Ahead," *Policy Options*, March/April 2005.

9. Neil Nevitte, *The Decline of Deference* (Peterborough: Broadview Press, 1996).

10. Michael Adams, *Fire and Ice: The United States, Canada and the Myth of Converging Values* (Toronto: Penguin, 2003).

11. Environics Research Group, Environics/CBC 2006 Election Survey, January 2006 at http://erg.environics.net/news/default.asp?aID=598.

12. Marcel Trudel and Genevieve Jain, *Canadian History Textbooks: A Comparative Study* (Ottawa: Royal Commission on Bilingualism and Biculturalism, 1970).

13. Ronald Landes, "Political Education and Political Socialization," in Jon Pammett and Jean-Luc Pépin, eds., *Political Education in Canada* (Halifax: Institute for Research on Public Policy, 1988), p. 17.

14. Frederick Fletcher, "The Mass Media and Political Education," in Pammett and Pépin, p. 92; Leslie-Anne Keown, "Keeping Up with the Times: Canadians and Their News Media Diet," *Canadian Social Trends* (Statistics Canada, Cat. No. 11-008-XWE, March 2007).

15. Alan Frizzell et al., *The Canadian General Election of 1988* (Ottawa: Carleton University Press), p. 69.

16. William Mishler and Harold D. Clarke, "Political Participation in Canada," in Michael Whittington and Glen Williams, eds., *Canadian Politics in the 1990s*, 4th ed. (Scarborough: Nelson Canada, 1995), p. 130.

17. Jon H. Pammett and Lawrence LeDuc, "Explaining the Turnout Decline in Canadian Federal Elections: A New Survey of Non-Voters," March 2003, http://www.elections.ca/loi/tur/tud/TurnoutDecline.pdf, retrieved November 22, 2004.

18. Ibid.; Anne Milan, "Willing to Participate: Political Engagement of Young Adults," *Canadian Social Trends* (Statistics Canada, Cat. No. 11-008, Winter 2005); Elections Canada, "Estimation of Voter Turnout by Age Group at the 38th Federal General Election" (June 28, 2004), Final Report, December 2005, http://www.elections.ca/loi/report_e.pdf; Paul Howe, *Citizens Adrift: The Democratic Disengagement of Young Canadians* (Vancouver: UBC Press, 2010).

19. Elisabeth Gidengil et al., *Citizens* (Vancouver: UBC Press, 2004), p. 69.

20. R. Kenneth Carty, William Cross, and Lisa Young, *Rebuilding Canadian Party Politics* (Vancouver: UBC Press, 2000).

21. Judy Torrance, *Public Violence in Canada* (Montreal: McGill-Queen's University Press, 1986).

Chapter 7

1. Paul Nesbitt-Larking, *Politics, Society, and the Media: Canadian Perspectives* (Peterborough: Broadview Press, 2001); David Taras, *Power and Betrayal in the Canadian Media* (Peterborough: Broadview Press, 1999); James Winter, *Democracy's Oxygen: How Corporations Control the News in Canada* (Toronto: McClelland and Stewart, 1980); John Miller, *Yesterday's News: How Canada's Daily Newspapers Are Failing Us* (Halifax: Fernwood Publishing, 1998).

2. Frederick J. Fletcher and Daphne Gottlieb Taras, "Images and Issues: The Mass Media and Politics in Canada," in Michael Whittington and Glen Williams, eds., *Canadian Politics in the 1990s*, 3rd ed. (Scarborough: Nelson Canada, 1990), p. 229.

3. Edwin R. Black, *Politics and the News: The Political Functions of the Mass Media* (Toronto: Butterworths, 1982), p. 80.

4. Peter Trueman, *Smoke and Mirrors: The Inside Story of Television News in Canada* (Toronto: McClelland and Stewart, 1980), p. 161.

5. Statistics Canada, "Television Viewing: Data Tables," March 2006, Cat. No. 87F0006XIE, accessed at http://www.statcan.gc.ca/pub/87f0006x/87f0006x2006001-eng.htm.

6. Taras, *Power and Betrayal*, ch. 3; Russell Mills, "Reflections on the State of Canadian Media," *Canadian Parliamentary Review*, Winter 2003–04; Catherine McLean, "Television's Penetration May Force Policy Review," *The Globe and Mail*, January 18, 2006.

7. Wayne Chu, "Of Blogs and Broadcasters: The Influence of Web Logs in Electoral Campaigns," paper presented at the Canadian Political Science Association, June 2007; Gareth Lewis, "Blogging Democracy: The Contribution of Political Blogs to Democracy," Friends of Canadian Broadcasting site, 2007 Winners of the Dalton Camp Award, http://www.friendscb.org/DCA/2007_winners/garethlewis.asp, accessed October 24, 2007.

8. The general thrust of David Taras in *The Newsmakers* (Scarborough: Nelson Canada, 1990).

9. Ibid., 30–31; Fletcher, *The Newspaper and Public Affairs* (Ottawa: Royal Commission on Newspapers, 1981), p. 16; Fletcher and Taras, "Images and Issues," p. 222; Black, *Politics and the News*, p. 183; Peter Desbarats, *Guide to Canadian News Media*, 2nd ed. (Toronto: Harcourt Brace Jovanovich, 1990), p. 149; Arthur Siegel, *Politics and the Media in Canada* (Toronto: McGraw-Hill Ryerson, 1983), p. 14. Of course, other players also have their agendas, especially the prime minister and the bureaucracy.

10. Taras, *The Newsmakers*, ch. 3; Allan Levine, *Scrum Wars: The Prime Ministers and the Media* (Toronto: Dundurn Press, 1993).

11. Environics Media Study (Environics Research Group, December 1986), cited by Desbarats, *Guide to Canadian News Media*, p. 28, and its *1991 Media Study*.

12. Taras, *The Newsmakers*, p. 102.

13. Taras, *The Newsmakers*, ch. 4; Knowlton Nash, *Trivia Pursuit: How Showbiz Values Are Corrupting the News* (Toronto: McClelland and Stewart, 1998).

14. Henry Milner, "Civic Literacy in Comparative Context," *Policy Matters* 2, no. 2 (2001); Leslie-Anne Keown, "Keeping Up with the Times: Canadians and Their News Media Diet," *Canadian Social Trends*, Statistics Canada, 11–008-XWE; Elisabeth Gidengil et al., *Citizens* (Vancouver: UBC Press, 2004), pp. 25–35.

15. Allan Fotheringham, *Birds of a Feather: The Press and the Politicians* (Toronto: Key Porter Books, 1989), p. 139.

16. Frederick J. Fletcher and Robert Everett, "The Media and Canadian Politics in an Era of Globalization," in Michael Whittington and Glen Williams, eds., *Canadian Politics in the 21st Century*, 6th ed. (Toronto: Thomson Nelson, 2004), p. 428.

17. Black, *Politics and the News*, p. 12; Taras, *The Newsmakers*, p. 234.

18. Black, *Politics and the News*, p. 168.

19. Frizzell, *1988*, p. 91.

20. Taras, *The Newsmakers*, 187, 192–94; Desbarats, *Guide to Canadian News Media*, p. 138.

21. Christopher Page, *The Roles of Public Opinion Research in Canadian Government* (Toronto: University of Toronto Press, 2006).

22. Ibid., p. 184.

23. Ibid., Conclusion.

Chapter 8

1. Elections Canada. "Representation 2004. Representation Formula: Detailed Calculations for 2001 Census," http://www.elections.ca/scripts/fedrep/federal_e/repform_e.htm.

2. "Canada's Government Restores Fair Representation in the House of Commons," April 1, 2010, http://www.democraticreform.gc.ca/index.asp?lang=eng&page=news-comm&doc=news-comm/2010040/.

3. Alan Frizzell and Jon Pammett, eds., *The Canadian General Election of 1997* (Toronto: Dundurn Press, 1997); Jon H. Pammett and Christopher Dornan, eds., *The Canadian General Election of 2000* (Toronto: Dundurn Press, 2001).

4. Stephen Clarkson, "Yesterday's Man and His Blue Grits: Backward into the Future," in Alan Frizzell, *The Canadian General Election of 1993* (Ottawa: Carleton University Press, 1994), p. 33.

5. Lawrence LeDuc and Richard Price, "Great Debates: The Televised Leadership Debates of 1979," *Canadian Journal of Political Science*, March 1985.

6. William Cross, *Political Parties* (Vancouver: UBC Press, 2004), ch. 4; William Cross, "Candidate Nomination in Canada's Political Parties," in Jon H. Pammett and Christopher Dornan, eds., *The Canadian General Election of 2006* (Toronto: Dundurn Press, 2006), ch. 7.

7. Peter H. Russell, *Two Cheers for Minority Government: The Evolution of Canadian Parliamentary Democracy* (Toronto: Emond Montgomery, 2008).

8. Alan C. Cairns, "The Electoral System and the Party System in Canada," *Canadian Journal of Political Science*, March 1968: 55–80.

9. Henry Milner, ed., *Making Every Vote Count: Reassessing Canada's Electoral System* (Peterborough: Broadview Press, 1999); Law Commission of Canada, *Voting Counts: Electoral Reform for Canada* (Ottawa, 2004).

10. *Harper v. Canada* (Attorney General), [2004] 1 S.C.R. 827.

11. Jon H. Pammett, "Elections," in M. Whittington and G. Williams, eds., *Canadian Politics in the 1990s*, 4th ed. (Scarborough: Nelson Canada, 1995), p. 242.

12. Elisabeth Gidengil, Joanna Everitt, Patrick Fournier, and Neil Nevitte, "Anatomy of a Liberal Defeat," paper presented at the 2009 Canadian Political Science Association; Cameron D. Anderson and Laura B. Stephenson, eds., *Voting Behaviour in Canada* (Vancouver: UBC Press, 2010).

13. Jon Pammett, "Class Voting and Class Consciousness in Canada," *Canadian Review of Sociology and Anthropology* 24, no. 2 (1987): 269–90; Keith Archer, "The Failure of the New Democratic Party: Unions, Unionists, and Politics in Canada," *Canadian Journal of Political Science*, June 1985: 353–66.

14. See the section on class-based parties in Chapter 9 of this book; Janine Brodie and Jane Jenson, *Crisis, Challenge and Change: Party and Class in Canada Revisited* (Ottawa: Carleton University Press, 1988); Pammett, "Class Voting"; and Archer, "The Failure."

15. André Blais et al., *Anatomy of a Liberal Victory: Making Sense of the Vote in the 2000 Canadian Election* (Peterborough: Broadview Press, 2002), ch. 7.

16. Harold D. Clarke et al., *Absent Mandate: Canadian Electoral Politics in an Era of Restructuring*, 3rd ed. (Toronto: Gage, 1996).

17. Jon H. Pammett and Christopher Dornan, eds., *The Canadian General Election of 2004* (Toronto: Dundurn Press, 2004).

18. Pammett and Dornan, *The Canadian General Election of 2006*.

19. Jon H. Pammett and Christopher Dornan, eds., *The Canadian General Election of 2008* (Toronto: Dundurn Press, 2009); Elisabeth Gidengil, Joanna Everitt, Patrick Fournier, and Neil Nevitte, "Anatomy of a Liberal Defeat," paper presented at the 2009 Canadian Political Science Association.

Chapter 9

1. In traditional European terms, a multiparty system implies that no party has a majority, leading to coalition governments. That was not the case in Canada between 1993 and 2004.

2. H.G. Thorburn, "Interpretations of the Canadian Party System," in H.G. Thorburn, ed., *Party Politics in Canada*, 6th ed. (Scarborough: Prentice-Hall Canada, 1991).

3. Janine Brodie and Jane Jenson, *Crisis, Challenge and Change: Party and Class in Canada Revisited* (Ottawa: Carleton University Press, 1988); Charles Taylor, *The Pattern of Politics* (Toronto: McClelland and Stewart, 1970); Gad Horowitz, "Toward the Democratic Class Struggle," in Trevor Lloyd and Jack McLeod, eds., *Agenda 1970* (Toronto: University of Toronto Press, 1968).

4. Jon Pammett, "Class Voting and Class Consciousness in Canada," *Canadian Review of Sociology and Anthropology* 24, no. 2 (1987), pp. 269–90; Keith Archer, "The Failure of the New Democratic Party: Unions, Unionists, and Politics in Canada," *Canadian Journal of Political Science* (June 1985),

pp. 353–66; André Blais et al., *Anatomy of a Liberal Victory: Making Sense of the Vote in the 2000 Canadian Election* (Peterborough: Broadview Press, 2002), p. 94.

5. Horowitz, "Toward the Democratic Class Struggle," p. 254.

6. Thorburn, "Interpretations of the Canadian Party System"; Reginald Whitaker, *The Government Party: Organizing and Financing the Liberal Party of Canada, 1930–58* (Toronto: University of Toronto Press, 1977); Stephen Clarkson, *The Big Red Machine: How the Liberal Party Dominates Canadian Politics* (Vancouver: UBC Press, 2005); George Perlin, *The Tory Syndrome: Leadership Politics in the Progressive Conservative Party* (Montreal: McGill-Queen's University Press, 1980).

7. John Meisel, "Decline of Party in Canada," in Thorburn, *Party Politics*; John Meisel, "The Dysfunctions of Canadian Parties: An Exploratory Mapping," in Thorburn, *Party Politics*; John Meisel and Matthew Mendelsohn, "Meteor? Phoenix? Chameleon? The Decline and Transformation of Party in Canada," in H.G. Thorburn and Alan Whitehorn, eds., *Party Politics in Canada*, 8th ed. (Toronto: Prentice-Hall, 2001).

8. Paul Howe and David Northrup, "Strengthening Canadian Democracy: The Views of Canadians," *Policy Matters* 1, no. 5 (July 2000).

9. Louis Hartz, *The Founding of New Societies* (New York: Harcourt, Brace and World, 1964); Gad Horowitz, "Conservatism, Liberalism and Socialism in Canada: An Interpretation," *Canadian Journal of Economics and Political Science*, May 1966, pp. 143–71; Colin Campbell and William Christian, *Parties, Leaders, and Ideologies in Canada* (Toronto: McGraw-Hill Ryerson, 1996).

10. For a good comparison of party policies in the 2006 election campaign, see the CBC—Canada Votes 2006 website at http://www.cbc.ca/canadavotes/leadersparties/issues.html.

11. Alexandra Dobrowolsky, "Political Parties: Teletubby Politics, The Third Way, and Democratic Challenge(r)s," in Michael Whittington and Glen Williams, eds., *Canadian Politics in the 21st Century*, 6th ed. (Toronto: Thomson Nelson, 2004).

12. William Cross, *Political Parties* (Vancouver: UBC Press, 2004), ch. 2.

13. John C. Courtney, *Do Conventions Matter? Choosing National Party Leaders in Canada* (Montreal: McGill-Queen's University Press, 1995); Maureen Mancuso et al., eds., *Leaders and Leadership in Canada* (Toronto: Oxford University Press, 1994).

14. Cross, *Political Parties*, p. 46.

Chapter 10

1. Paul Pross, *Group Politics and Public Policy* (Toronto: Oxford University Press, 1986); Lisa Young and Joanna Everitt, *Advocacy Groups* (Vancouver: UBC Press, 2004); Miriam Smith, "Interest Groups and Social Movements," in Michael Whittington and Glen Williams, eds., *Canadian Politics in the 21st Century*, 6th ed. (Toronto: Thomson Nelson, 2004).

2. Pross, *Group Politics and Public Policy*, esp. ch. 11.

3. William D. Coleman, *Business and Politics: A Study of Collective Action* (Montreal: McGill-Queen's University Press, 1988); Stephen Brooks and Andrew Stritch, *Business and Government in Canada* (Scarborough: Prentice-Hall Canada, 1991), ch. 7; Geoffrey Hale, *The Uneasy Partnership: Politics of Business and Government in Canada* (Peterborough: Broadview Press, 2006).

4. William D. Coleman, "One Step Ahead: Business in the Policy Process in Canada," in Mark Charlton and Paul Barker, eds., *Crosscurrents: Contemporary Political Issues*, 2nd ed. (Scarborough: Nelson Canada, 1994).

5. Pross, *Group Politics*, ch. 5.

6. Susan Phillips, "Interest Groups, Social Movements, and the Voluntary Sector: En Route to Reducing the Democratic Deficit," in James Bickerton and Alain-G. Gagnon, eds., *Canadian Politics*, 4th ed. (Peterborough: Broadview Press, 2004).

7. Jeffrey M. Ayers, *Defying Conventional Wisdom: Political Movements and Popular Contention Against North American Free Trade* (Toronto: University of Toronto Press, 1998).

8. Leslie Pal, *Interests of State: The Politics of Language, Multiculturalism, and Feminism in Canada* (Montreal: McGill-Queen's University Press, 1993).

9. William Coleman and Grace Skogstad, eds., *Policy Communities and Public Policy in Canada* (Mississauga: Copp Clark Pitman, 1990); Young and Everitt, *Advocacy Groups*, pp. 76–82.

10. Pross, *Group Politics*, ch. 6; Coleman and Skogstad, *Policy Communities and Public Policy in Canada*; Leslie Pal, *Beyond Policy Analysis: Public Issue Management in Turbulent Times*, 3rd ed. (Toronto: Thomson Nelson, 2006), ch. 6; Young and Everitt, *Advocacy Groups*, p. 7.

11. Robert Presthus, *Elite Accommodation in Canada* (Toronto: Macmillan, 1973). Presthus calls this phenomenon "elite accommodation."

12. Young and Everitt, *Advocacy Groups*, pp. 115–121; Smith, "Interest Groups," p. 220.

13. Young and Everitt, *Advocacy Groups*, pp. 131–32.

14. Ibid., pp. 133–34.

15. Ibid., p. 134.

16. Ibid., pp. 47–51.

17. Malcolm Taylor, "The Role of the Medical Profession in the Formulation of Public Policy," *Canadian Journal of Economics and Political Science*, February 1960, pp. 108–27.

18. Ian Greene, "Conflict of Interest and the Canadian Constitution: An Analysis of Conflict of Interest Rules for Canadian Cabinet Ministers," *Canadian Journal of Political Science*, June 1990, pp. 233–56.

19. John Sawatsky, *The Insiders: Government, Business, and the Lobbyists* (Toronto: McClelland and Stewart, 1987), pp. 315–16.

20. John A. Chenier, ed., *The Federal Lobbyists, 1995* (Ottawa: ARC Publications, 1995), p. ii.

21. Young and Everitt, *Advocacy Groups*, pp. 82–86; Democracy Watch website, http://www.dwatch.ca.

Chapter 11

1. Bayard Reesor, *The Canadian Constitution in Historical Perspective* (Scarborough: Prentice-Hall Canada, 1992).

2. Lord Durham, *Report of the Affairs of British North America*, ed. Gerald M. Craig (Toronto: McClelland and Stewart, 1963).

3. P.B. Waite, *The Confederation Debates in the Province of Canada, 1865* (Toronto: McClelland and Stewart, 1963); Donald Creighton, *The Road to Confederation* (Toronto: Macmillan, 1964).

4. Alan C. Cairns, *Constitution, Government, and Society in Canada* (Toronto: McClelland and Stewart, 1988), p. 31.

5. Andrew Heard, *Canadian Constitutional Conventions: The Marriage of Law and Politics* (Toronto: Oxford University Press, 1991). The author's definition is an amalgam of those Heard cites.

6. Reesor, *The Canadian Constitution*, ch. 4. In the Quebec Secession Reference case, the Supreme Court enunciated the following Canadian constitutional principles: federalism, democracy, constitutionalism and rule of law, and respect for minorities.

7. Rather than footnote the cases referred to, I refer the reader to this book's website, which has a catalogue of such decisions. But see Heather MacIvor, *Canadian Politics and Government in the Charter Era* (Toronto: Thomson Nelson, 2006), and Thomas M.J. Bateman, et al., *The Court and the Charter: Leading Cases* (Toronto: Emond Montgomery, 2008).

8. Ian Greene, *The Charter of Rights* (Toronto: Lorimer, 1989), p. 172.

9. F.L. Morton and Rainer Knopff, *The Charter Revolution and the Court Party* (Peterborough: Broadview Press, 2000).

10. Peter Russell, "The Political Purposes of the Canadian Charter of Rights and Freedoms," *Canadian Bar Review*, March 1983.

11. Paul Howe and David Northrup, "Strengthening Canadian Democracy: The Views of Canadians," *Policy Matters* 1, no. 5 (July 2000), p. 100.

12. Michael Mandel, *The Charter of Rights and the Legalization of Politics in Canada*, rev. ed. (Toronto: Wall and Thompson, 1994). Along similar lines, see Andrew Petter, *The Politics of the Charter: The Illusive Promise of Constitutional Rights* (Toronto: University of Toronto Press, 2010).

13. Morton and Knopff, *The Charter Revolution*. (Peterborough: Broadview Press, 2000).

14. Seymour Martin Lipset, *Continental Divide* (New York: Routledge, 1990).

15. Greg Hein, "Interest Group Litigation and Canadian Democracy," *Choices* 6, no. 2 (March 2000).

16. Janet Hiebert, *Charter Conflicts: What Is Parliament's Role?* (Montreal: McGill-Queen's University Press, 2002); *Kent Roach, The Supreme Court on Trial: Judicial Activism or Democratic Dialogue* (Toronto: Irwin Law, 2001).

Chapter 12

1. Donald Smiley, *The Canadian Political Nationality* (Toronto: Methuen, 1967).

2. Provincial representation within the institutions of the national government is sometimes called "intrastate federalism," as opposed to relations between federal and provincial governments, or "interstate federalism."

3. Peter Russell et al., *Federalism and the Charter* (Ottawa: Carleton University Press, 1989); Peter Hogg, *Constitutional Law of Canada* (Toronto: Carswell, Student edition, annual).

4. V.C. MacDonald, "Judicial Interpretation of the Canadian Constitution," *University of Toronto Law Journal* 1 (1935–36), pp. 260–85; Senate of Canada, *O'Connor Report* (1939); John T. Saywell, *The Lawmakers: Judicial Power and the Shaping of Canadian Federalism* (Toronto: University of Toronto Press, 2003). It is ironic that judicial interpretation contributed to decentralizing a centralized Canadian federation but centralized a decentralized federation in the United States. See Roger Gibbins, *Regionalism* (Toronto: Butterworths, 1982), ch. 4.

5. Alan C. Cairns, "The Governments and Societies of Canadian Federalism," *Canadian Journal of Political Science*, December 1977, pp. 695–725; Cairns, "The Judicial Committee and Its Critics," *Canadian Journal of Political Science*, September 1971, pp. 301–45.

6. Direct taxes are derived from the very people who are intended to pay them, while indirect taxes are extracted from one person with the expectation that they will be passed on to someone else.

7. Donald Smiley, *Canada in Question: Federalism in the Seventies* (Toronto: McGraw-Hill Ryerson, 1972), p. 56.

8. Ibid.

9. Herman Bakvis and Grace Skogstad, eds., *Canadian Federalism: Performance, Effectiveness, and Legitimacy* (Toronto: Oxford University Press, 2002), p. 11; Jennifer Smith, *Federalism* (Vancouver: UBC Press, 2004).

10. J. Peter Meekison, Hamish Telford, and Harvey Lazar, eds., *Canada: The State of the Federation, 2002: Reconsidering the Institutions of Canadian Federalism* (Kingston: Institute of Intergovernmental Relations, 2002); Garth Stevenson, "Federalism and Intergovernmental Relations," in Michael Whittington and Glen Williams, eds., *Canadian Politics in the 21st Century*, 7th ed. (Toronto: Thomson Nelson, 2008).

11. Gérard Boismenu and Peter Graefe, "The New Federal Toolbelt: Attempts to Rebuild Social Policy Leadership," *Canadian Public Policy* 30, no. 1 (2004); Bakvis and Skogstad, 2nd ed., 2008; Bakvis, Gerald Baier and Douglas Brown, *Contested Federalism: Certainty and Ambiguity in the Canadian Federation* (Toronto: University of Toronto Press, 2009).

Chapter 13

1. Leslie A. Pal, *Public Policy Analysis: An Introduction* (Toronto: Methuen, 1987), p. 4.

2. Samuel A. Bottomley, "Locked and Loaded: Gun Control Policy in Canada," in Robert M. Campbell et al., eds., *Real Worlds of Canadian Politics: Cases in Process and Policy*, 4th ed. (Peterborough: Broadview Press, 2004).

3. David E. Smith, *The Invisible Crown* (Toronto: University of Toronto Press, 1996).

4. Frank McKinnon, *The Crown in Canada* (Calgary: McClelland and Stewart West, 1976), p. 124; Edward McWhinney, *The Governor General and the Prime Ministers: The Making and Unmaking of Governments* (Vancouver: Ronsdale Press, 2005).

5. Andrew Heard, *Canadian Constitutional Conventions: The Marriage of Law and Politics* (Toronto: Oxford University Press, 1991), pp. 47, 123.

6. Peter H. Russell and Lorne Sossin, eds. *Parliamentary Democracy in Crisis* (Toronto: University of Toronto Press, 2009).

7. In the case where no party wins a majority of seats, the convention is that the incumbent prime minister has a right to stay in office until defeated in a non-confidence vote in the House of Commons.

8. Kenneth Kernaghan and David Siegel, *Public Administration in Canada: A Text*, 2nd ed. (Scarborough: Nelson Canada, 1991), pp. 379–85.

9. Donald J. Savoie, *Governing from the Centre: The Concentration of Power in Canada* (Toronto: University of Toronto Press, 1999); Donald J. Savoie, *Court Government and the Collapse of Accountability in Canada and the United Kingdom* (Toronto: University of Toronto Press, 2008); Jeffrey Simpson, *The Friendly Dictatorship* (Toronto: McClelland and Stewart, 2001).

10. Leslie Pal and David Taras, eds., *Prime Ministers and Premiers: Political Leadership and Public Policy in Canada* (Scarborough: Prentice-Hall Canada, 1988); Peter Aucoin, "Prime Ministerial Leadership: Position, Power, and Politics," in Maureen Mancuso et al., *Leaders and Leadership in Canada* (Toronto: Oxford University Press, 1994).

11. Savoie, *Governing from the Centre*, pp. 137–39, 343.

12. Leslie Pal, "Hands at the Helm? Leadership and Public Policy," in Pal and Taras, *Prime Ministers and Premiers*, p. 25.

13. Frederick Fletcher, "The Prime Minister as Public Persuader," in Thomas A. Hockin, ed., *Apex of Power*, 2nd ed. (Scarborough: Prentice-Hall Canada, 1977).

14. David Taras, "Prime Ministers and the Media," in Pal and Taras, *Prime Ministers and Premiers*.

15. Denis Smith, "President and Parliament: The Transformation of Parliamentary Government in Canada," in Hockin, *Apex of Power*, 315.

16. Graham White, *Cabinets and First Ministers* (Vancouver: UBC Press, 2004), p. 83.

17. Herman Bakvis, *Regional Ministers* (Toronto: University of Toronto Press, 1991); "Cabinet Ministers: Leaders or Followers," in Mancuso, *Leaders and Leadership*.

18. W.A. Matheson, *The Prime Minister and the Cabinet* (Toronto: Methuen, 1976), pp. ix, 22–23.

19. S.L. Sutherland, "Responsible Government and Ministerial Responsibility: Every Reform Is Its Own Problem," *Canadian Journal of Political Science*, March 1991, p. 101. Both the Martin and Harper cabinets suffered from policy-oriented Cabinet resignations.

20. Donald Smiley, *The Federal Condition in Canada* (Toronto: McGraw-Hill Ryerson, 1987), p. 88.

21. Bruce Doern and Peter Aucoin, eds., *Public Policy in Canada* (Toronto: Macmillan, 1979).

22. Christopher Dunn suggests the best label would be "prime minister-centred cabinet" in Dunn, ed., *The Handbook of Canadian Public Administration* (Toronto: Oxford University Press, 2002).

23. Privy Council Office, *Decision-Making Processes and Central Agencies in Canada: Federal, Provincial and Territorial Practices* (Ottawa: PCO, 1998), and other PCO documents.

24. Commission of Inquiry into the Sponsorship Program and Advertising Activities, *Restoring Accountability* (Ottawa: Minister of Public Works and Government Services, 2006), p. 147.

25. Donald J. Savoie, *Court Government and the Collapse of Accountability in Canada and the United Kingdom* (Toronto: University of Toronto Press, 2008), p. 16.

Chapter 14

1. Glen Milne, *Making Policy: A Guide to the Federal Government's Policy Process* (Ottawa: Glen Milne, 2000), p. 4.

2. Kenneth Kernaghan and David Siegel, *Public Administration in Canada: A Text*, 2nd ed. (Scarborough: Nelson Canada, 1991), p. 137.

3. S.L. Sutherland, "Responsible Government and Ministerial Responsibility: Every Reform Is Its Own Problem," *Canadian Journal of Political Science*, March 1991, pp. 91–120.

4. Kernaghan and Siegel, *Public Administration in Canada*, pp. 379–85; S.L. Sutherland, "The Al-Mashat Affair: Administrative Responsibility in Parliamentary Institutions," *Canadian Public Administration*, Winter 1991, pp. 573–603.

5. Auditor General, Reflections on a Decade of Serving Parliament, Report of the Auditor General of Canada, February 2001, http://www.oag-bvg.gc.ca/domino/reports.nsf/html/01cap_e.html, retrieved December 6, 2004.

6. Donald J. Savoie, *Breaking the Bargain: Public Servants, Ministers, and Parliament* (Toronto: University of Toronto Press, 2003); Donald J. Savoie, *Court Government and the Collapse of Accountability in Canada and the United Kingdom* (Toronto: University of Toronto Press, 2008).

7. Gordon Osbaldeston, *Keeping Deputy Ministers Accountable* (Toronto: McGraw-Hill Ryerson, 1990); Savoie, *Breaking the Bargain and Court* Government.

8. Linda McQuaig, *The Cult of Impotence* (Toronto: Penguin, 1998).

9. Milne, *Making Policy*, 43.

10. J.L. Granatstein, *The Ottawa Men: The Civil Service Mandarins, 1935–1957* (Toronto: Oxford University Press, 1982).

11. Privy Council Office, Sixteenth Annual Report to the Prime Minister on the Public Service of Canada (March 2009), available at http://www.pco-bcp.gc.ca/index.asp?lang=eng&Page=information&Sub=publications&Doc=ar-ra/16-2009/table-eng.htm, accessed cited on April 25, 2009.

12. Kathleen Archibald, *Sex and the Public Service* (Ottawa: Queen's Printer, 1970); *Task Force on Barriers to Women in the Public Service, Beneath the Veneer 1* (Ottawa: Supply and Services, 1990).

13. S.L. Sutherland, "On the Audit Trail of the Auditor General: Parliament's Servant, 1973–80," *Canadian Public Administration*, Winter 1980, pp. 616–44; S.L. Sutherland, "The Politics of Audit: The Federal Office of the Auditor General in Comparative Perspective," *Canadian Public Administration*, Spring 1986, pp. 118–48.

14. Kernaghan and Siegel, *Public Administration in Canada*, pp. 498–502.

15. Leslie A. Pal, *Beyond Policy Analysis: Public Issue Management in Turbulent Times*, 4th ed. (Toronto: Nelson Education, 2010); Guy B. Peters and Donald Savoie, *Taking Stock* (Montreal: McGill-Queen's University Press, 1998).

16. Jocelyn Bourgon, *Third Annual Report to the Prime Minister of Canada* (1995), http://www.pco-bcp.gc.ca/default.asp?Page=Publications&Language=E&doc=3rept95/cover_e.htm, retrieved December 6, 2004; Treasury Board, Getting Government Right: Governing for Canadians (February 1997), http://www.tbs-sct.gc.ca/report/govrev/Gfce.asp, retrieved December 6, 2004.

17. Jeffrey Roy, *E-Government in Canada: Transformation for the Digital Age* (Ottawa: University of Ottawa Press, 2006).

Chapter 15

1. C.E.S. Franks, *The Parliament of Canada* (Toronto: University of Toronto Press, 1987); David C. Docherty, *Legislatures* (Vancouver: UBC Press, 2005).

2. John Bejermi, *Canadian Parliamentary Handbook* (Ottawa: Borealis Press, annual); Caroline Andrew, John Biles, Myer Siemiatycki, and Eric Tolly, eds. *Electing a Diverse Canada: The Representation of Immigrants, Minorities, and Women* (Vancouver: UBC Press, 2008).

3. This and much more interesting and useful information about the House of Commons can be found on the Parliament's website at http://www.parl.gc.ca; click on "About Parliament" and go to the "A to Z Index."

4. Franks, *The Parliament of Canada*, p. 142.

5. Ibid., pp. 6, 29, 96, 268.

6. Paul Thomas, "The Role of National Party Caucuses," in Peter Aucoin, ed., *Party Government and Regional Representation in Canada* (Toronto: University of Toronto Press, 1985).

7. *Standing Orders of the House of Commons* (2010), http://www.parl.gc.ca/information/about/process/house/standingorders/toc-e.htm; *Compendium of Procedure* (2008), http://www.parl.gc.ca/compendium/web-content/c_a_index-e.htm?Language=E; *Glossary of Parliamentary Procedure* (2009), http://www.parl.gc.ca/information/about/process/house/glossary/Gloss-e.htm?Language=E.

8. Martin Westmacott, "Whips and Party Cohesion," *Canadian Parliamentary Review* 6, no. 3 (Autumn 1983).

9. Docherty, *Legislatures*, p. 25.

10. Gomery Report, *Restoring Accountability*, ch. 4, pp. 75–80 and ch. 6, pp. 117–19.

11. The Library of Parliament regularly publishes excellent summaries of political issues for the benefit of MPs and senators. These research publications can be accessed online at http://www2.parl.gc.ca/Sites/LOP/VirtualLibrary/ResearchPublications-e.asp.

12. Docherty, *Legislatures*, p. 32.

13. Russell, Peter H. *Two Cheers for Minority Government: The Evolution of Canadian Parliamentary Democracy* (Toronto: Emond Montgomery, 2008).

14. Other defeats that did not cause much fanfare are noted in Franks, *The Parliament of Canada*, p. 139.

15. Russell, Peter H., and Lorne Sossin. *Parliamentary Democracy in Crisis* (Toronto: University of Toronto Press, 2009).

16. R.A. MacKay, *The Unreformed Senate of Canada*, rev. ed. (Toronto: McClelland and Stewart, 1967).

17. MacKay, *The Unreformed Senate*, 91–95; F.A. Kunz, *The Modern Senate of Canada, 1925–1963: A Re-Appraisal* (Toronto: University of Toronto Press, 1965), pp. 337–47. Andrew Heard argues that a constitutional convention is emerging that the Senate may not insist on altering the financial provisions of money bills. See *Canadian Constitutional Conventions*, p. 94.

18. Kunz, *The Modern Senate*, pp. 53–56. The case was officially referred to as *Edwards v. Att. Gen. of Can.*, [1930] A.C. 124.

19. MacKay, *The Unreformed Senate*, p. 110; Kunz, *The Modern Senate*, p. 186.

20. Colin Campbell, *The Canadian Senate: A Lobby from Within* (Toronto: Macmillan, 1978), pp. 12–19, 147.

21. MacKay, *The Unreformed Senate*, pp. 96–112.

22. In 1873, Alexander Mackenzie had asked the British government to summon additional senators but was refused on the grounds that this was not necessary at the time.

23. Peter McCormick, "Canada Needs a Triple E Senate," in Paul Fox and Graham White, eds., *Politics: Canada*, 7th ed. (Toronto: McGraw-Hill Ryerson, 1991), pp. 435–39; H. McConnell, "The Case for a 'Triple E' Senate," *Queen's Quarterly*, Autumn 1988, pp. 683–98.

24. Serge Joyal, *Protecting Democracy: The Senate You Never Knew* (Montreal: McGill-Queen's University Press, 2003).

Chapter 16

1. Peter Russell, *The Judiciary in Canada: The Third Branch of Government* (Toronto: McGraw-Hill Ryerson, 1987), p. 5.

2. Ibid., p. 14.

3. Peter Russell, "The Effect of a Charter of Rights on the Policy-Making Role of the Canadian Courts," *Canadian Public Administration*, Spring 1982, p. 2.

4. Peter McCormick, *Canada's Courts* (Toronto: Lorimer, 1994), p. 3.

5. Ian Green, *The Courts* (Vancouver: UBC Press, 2006), p. 72.

6. Russell, *The Judiciary in Canada*, p. 6.

7. Gerald L. Gall, *The Canadian Legal System*, 3rd ed. (Toronto: Carswell, 1990), pp. 23–28.

8. Ibid., p. 30.

9. McCormick, *Canada's Courts*, p. 56.

10. Russell, *The Judiciary in Canada*, p. 290.

11. Ibid., pp. 313, 319–27; Peter Hogg, *Constitutional Law of Canada*, 2nd ed. (Toronto: Carswell, 1985), pp. 142–48.

12. James G. Snell and Frederick Vaughan, *The Supreme Court of Canada: History of the Institution* (Toronto: The Osgoode Society, 1985); Russell, *The Judiciary in Canada*, p. 337.

13. Recent insights about its operation can be gleaned from biographies of two key players in Robert J. Sharpe and Kent Roach's *Brian Dickson: A Judge's Journey* (Toronto: University of Toronto Press, 2003) and Ellen Anderson's *Judging Bertha Wilson: Law as Large as Life* (Toronto: University of Toronto Press, 2002).

14. Carl Baar quotes an oft-repeated maxim that "to become a judge in the United States, you must be elected; to become a judge in Canada, you must be defeated," in "The Structure and Personnel of the Canadian Judiciary," in Paul Fox and Graham White, eds., *Politics: Canada*, 7th ed. (Toronto: McGraw-Hill Ryerson, 1991), p. 513.

15. Andrew Heard, *Canadian Constitutional Conventions: The Marriage of Law and Politics* (Toronto: Oxford University Press, 1991), p. 135.

16. During the Mulroney government's first term, 48 percent of all judges appointed were known Conservative supporters, as against seven percent who supported opposition parties. Peter Russell and Jacob Ziegel, "Federal Judicial Appointments: An Appraisal of the First Mulroney Government's Appointments and the New Judiciary Advisory Committees," *University of Toronto Law Journal* 41 (1991), pp. 4–37.
17. McCormick, *Canada's Courts*, p. 112.
18. Jacob S. Ziegel, *Merit Selection and Democratization of Appointments to the Supreme Court of Canada* (Montreal: Institute for Research on Public Policy, 1999); Standing Committee on Justice, Human Rights, Public Safety and Emergency Preparedness, "Improving the Supreme Court of Canada Appointments Process" (May 2004), http://www.parl.gc.ca/committee/CommitteePublication.aspx? SourceId=84157, retrieved December 6, 2004.
19. Dennis Olsen, *The State Elite* (Toronto: McClelland and Stewart, 1980), ch. 3; Russell, *The Judiciary in Canada*, pp. 164–65.
20. Ian Green estimates that one-quarter of all judges are now women, *The Courts*, p. 60.
21. Heard, *Canadian Constitutional Conventions*, p. 124; Russell, *The Judiciary in Canada*, p. 176; Gall, *The Canadian Legal System*, pp. 227–39.
22. Canadian Judicial Council website; Heather MacIvor, *Parameters of Power: Canada's Political Institutions* (Toronto: Nelson Education, 2010), p. 358.
23. *Valente v. the Queen*, [1985] 2 S.C.R. 673; Green, *The Courts*, pp. 88–93; Perry S. Millar and Carl Baar, *Judicial Administration in Canada* (Montreal: McGill-Queen's University Press, 1981).
24. *Provincial Court Judges' Assn. of New Brunswick v. New Brunswick (Minister of Justice)*, [2005] 2 S.C.R. 286; MacIvor, *Parameters of Power*, pp. 347–49.
25. Heard, *Canadian Constitutional Conventions*, p. 131; Russell, *The Judiciary in Canada*, pp. 85–89; Gall, *The Canadian Legal System*, pp. 236–38; McCormick, *Canada's Courts*, pp. 130–31; Green, *The Courts*, pp. 95–96. As a member of the Supreme Court, Mr. Justice Bastarache was criticized by the Judicial Council as follows: "it is clearly preferable for judges to exercise restraint when speaking publicly."

Index

Note: Figures are indicated by an "f" following the page number. Tables are indicated by a "t" following the page number. Illustrations are indicated by page numbers in italic type.